WORLD PEACE

VOLUME EIGHT

ENVIRONMENT AND PEACE

Suresh Chandra Mallick
Pritam Mallick

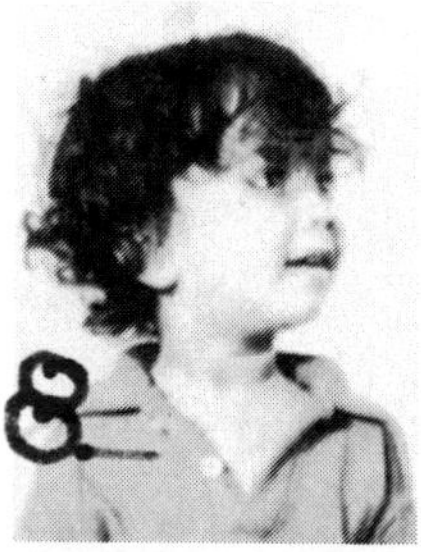

ENVIRONMENT AND PEACE

Institute of Development Studies and Policy Research, Pritam Bhawan, 93, Dharma Vihar, Khandagiri, Bhubaneswar - 751030 (Orissa), INDIA

Publisher and International Distributer:
The AMAZON, PO – Box No. 80683, Seattle,
WA 98108 – 0683, USA

ISBN: 978-81-924851-7-1

First Edition

2013

E- Publication Price: US $ 4

Dedicated to

Mr. Mikhail S. Gorbachev
Nobel Laureate in Peace and
Former President, USSR (Russia)

PROLOGUE

Man needs clean air, drinking water, hygienic food, good environment, and faithful friends to lead a happier life. The scientists, philosophers, epics and religious books have shown us the ways to live in peace. The writers, poets and saints have identified how this life could be connected to Him, the Omnipotent, Omniscient and Almighty God. But we, the most advanced people of this planet take all steps to challenge the very existence of the Almighty and His creation. We move towards self-destruction, environmental pollution, global warming, climate change, green house emission, air pollution, rise of sea level, loss of bio-diversity and ultimately for a dark future. Today, people encounter with health hazards, natural disasters, crop failure, poverty, mass suicides and uprisings. Moreover, 3 billion of people spend less than $ 2 a day.

If manmade disasters cannot be checked now, it would become the greatest blunder of all governments and the world organizations as these institutions cannot protect all living beings of the world from disaster. We therefore give more emphasis to check the climate change. Most of the activities of civilized people would follow mass suicides.

A small example may be cited to show how our technology takes us to diseases including deaths. There are approximately a million known dyes and dye intermediaries out of which, 5,000 are produced commercially. The colored products contain hazardous metals like lead, mercury, nickel, cobalt and chromium. The colour is not harmful to the environment but the process of colorization causes solid wastes, sludge and pigments that are hazardous wastes. The sewage of dying process damages river water; kills aquatic flora and fauna and can contaminate ground water. Women who use permanent hair dyes have twice the risk of bladder cancer than non-users. Germany produces dyes to the extent of 22 percent of world production of dye followed by United States at 18 percent.

In this manuscript, the possibility of a friendly environment has been discussed for strengthening WORLD PEACE. Without a favourable climate, temperature and a pollution free environment, it would not be possible to protect the life of living beings including people. We have suggested a number of policy options for a better environment for all countries. We have quoted 'A decade of Climatic Change' and the 'Earth that witnesses Apocalypse now' to emphasize on Environment and Peace.

In the first chapter, it is predicted that the world is advancing towards catastrophe, but it could be checked through strict environment laws and implementation of the laws. Environment is continuously depleted in both the developed and developing countries; hence, environmental policy must be drawn up for the whole world. Chapter II highlights environmental pollution such as air pollution, water pollution, ground water pollution, mining pollution, E–waste pollution, greenhouse pollution, pesticide pollution, and plastic pollution must be checked to the minimum. Pollution was more prevalent in developed countries and now pollution is increasing in a galloping manner in the developing countries. Unregulated industrial policy and practice, massive deforestation through mining, sharp increase of vehicular traffic, water pollution through municipal solid wastes and industrial wastes cause to air, water and soil pollution excessively. Moreover, agricultural pesticides, fertilizers and use of plastic have increased pollution to unbearable situations.

The Chapter III clearly explains that global warming and climate change have challenged the very existence of living beings on earth. Hence, strict international policy should be adopted to stop further deterioration of environment. Chapter IV describes the problems and conflicts caused by environmental pollution harm the people and living beings. The most polluters are peopling themselves, who suffer. The poachers and mafias must be punished legally within a month or so. Chapter V highlights the internal conventions on Environment. But till date, powerful countries are avoiding environmental laws and the world is not yet free from wars. The United Nations must give top priority to bring all countries together to adopt the Kyoto proposal for the greater interest of achieving WORLD PEACE. Every person can live in peace in amicable environment.

The Chapter VI explains that deforestation must be checked at any cost. The tribal people must be protected and allowed forest rights to safeguard the forest and earn an income from forest produce. They have to stop forest fire, which they create. Governments of most of the countries neglect forests and grant leases of forest areas at pleasure. The international law should include warnings and punishments to these erring governments, if possible. The Environmental Laws must be carefully chalked out, so that mining hazards would be checked. (Chapter VII).

Each government should take effective measures to protect forestland. It is the government, which can protect the environment through effective control measures through research, planning, watching and management practices. The factors of dangers to environment must be studied but it could be practiced through watch and ward of effective machinery. The press and publicity department should focus on the utilities of clean environment. Government should award prizes to people and officials to induce the people for clean environment. (Chapter VIII)

The Chapter IX focuses on fixing accountability on the culprits and the governments, which cannot protect forests. A corrupt government is an enemy to the people because it sells the forests for increasing its own purse. The forests should not be leased to private parties or foreign countries. If the government cannot manage the forests, it should be forced to step down morally and by Law of the land. Mis-management of forests would invite Terrorists, Maoists and Naxalites and it would result in misrule and anarchy in the state. Chapter X illustrates how environment can be utilized for world peace and prosperity. We have to make our cities carbon neutral and we should co-operate each other for a peaceful world. And it is possible.

We are grateful to Wikipedia, Google in search and a number of Newspapers for collection of facts on environment and government policies. We acknowledge the contribution of authors, the national, international and world organizations which fight against environmental pollution, climate change and undertake tasks in protecting environment. We will appreciate for constructive criticism aiming at improvement of the subsequent editions of the book. We will be happy, if a small step towards world peace is contemplated through this Endeavour.

December 12, 2012 Suresh Chandra Mallick

A Decade of Climatic Changes

The Chile earthquake of February 2010 was so powerful that it likely shifted an Earth axis and shortened the length of a day. By speeding up Earth's rotation, should have shortened an Earth day by 1, 26 millionths of a second, according to NASA

The World Meteorological Organization reports that 2000 - 2010 has been the warmest decade on record, and 2010 is likely to be among the warmest three years since 1850.

This decade (2000-2010), global temperatures averaged 0.46 0C above the 1961-1990 average, 0.03 0C above the 2000-2009 average and the highest value ever recorded for a 10-year period.

The Arctic ice cap reached an all-time low in 2007. Climate scientists predict the region will be ice-free during the summer within the next decade.

Climate change in this decade has emerged in powerful ways: Drought, earlier springs, disappearing polar bears and frog extinctions are signs that global warming is already having an effect on the planet. The limits of fresh water for consumption, irrigation and manufacturing bored into public consciousness this decade. The demand for water is putting many of our water systems at stress and it tends to be a critical issue not only for human well-being but also environmental sustainability.

Ground water used for crop irrigation is being depleted in India, china, USA and Pakistan – the top four irrigators of the world.

Many rivers around the world fail to reach the sea during parts of each year due to drought and groundwater used for crop irrigation is being depleted in India, China, the USA and Pakistan.

Sixth strongest hurricane in Atlantic history, Katrina claimed 1,836 lives, with 705 people missing, causing economic losses of $125 billion. Only $66 billion of this was insured

The US contributes 25 percent emissions into the atmosphere even though it only makes up 5 percent of the world's population. Canada protected more than 125 million acres, area bigger than California. In US, 2 million acres of new wilderness have been designated

A global push away from Greenhouse Gas-emitting fossil fuels such as oil and coal spurred increased research & investment in renewable energy sources ranging from wind turbines to dog poop. According to a 2009 UN report, $155 billion invested globally in renewable energy

The Earth That Witnesses Apocalypse Now

The 2001 Gujarat earthquake was a flattener. With a magnitude of 8.1 on the Richter scale, the quake killed 20, 000 people, injured 167,000 and destroyed 400,000 homes. The shock waves spread 700 km. 21 districts were affected and 600,000 people left homeless.

The 2004 tsunami killed over 230,000 people in 14 countries, inundating coastal communities with waves up to 100 feet high. One of the deadliest natural disasters in recorded history; the tsunami hit Indonesia the hardest, followed by Sri Lanka, India and Thailand. With a magnitude of between 9.1 and 9.2 on the Richter scale, it is the third largest ocean earthquake ever recorded. This earthquake had the longest duration of faulting ever observed, between 8.3 and 10 minutes. It caused the entire planet to vibrate as much as 1c m and triggered other earthquakes as far as Alaska.

On October 2005, a magnitude of 7.6 earthquake damaged northern Pakistan and border areas of India. Over 7,000 people died. The earthquake of 2005 in Kashmir (India) caused 75, 000 deaths. The world philanthropy institutions donated US $ 5.4 billion in aid for the victims. The September 2007 Sumatra earthquakes were series of mega thrusts that struck the Java Trench off Sumatra, Indonesia. The quake crippled communications. The toll was 21 with 88 people injured. The 2010 Haiti earthquake was a catastrophic magnitude 7.0 on the Ritcher. An estimated three million people were hit: 230,000 people died, 300,000 people were injured. 250,000 houses and 30,000 commercial buildings collapsed, including royal palace.

An enormous ash cloud from an Icelandic volcano caused the biggest flight disruption over Europe and stranded travelers on six continents in April 2010. The cloud, floating miles above earth and capable of knocking out jet engines, wrecked travel plans for hundreds of thousands of people from tourists and business travelers to politicians and royals. Britain, Ireland, Denmark, Norway, Sweden, Finland and Belgium closed their air space, as did France. Ash led to the cancellation of 4000 flights within Europe.

The Deep Water Horizon oil spill in the Gulf of Mexico is the largest accidental marine spill in the history of petroleum industry. The spill stemmed from a sea - floor oil gusher that resulted from April 20, 2010 Deep-water Horizon drilling rig explosion. On July 15, after it had released about 4.9 million barrels of crude oil, the leak was stopped. The capping the gushing wellhead stopped the oil leak. The escape of oil spill was to the extent of 53, 000 barrels per day. The spill continues to cause extensive damage to marine and wildlife habitats as well as fishing and tourism industry in the gulf.

Forest Fact File

Forests cover 31 percent of total land area in the world. Forests are home to 80 percent of terrestrial biodiversity. Forests provide a home to more than 300 million people worldwide. Forests play a key role in our battle against climate change – storing carbon and sucking in carbon dioxide from the atmosphere and locking it into their biomass. More than three-quarters of the world's accessible fresh water comes from forested catchments. Water quality declines with decrease in forest condition and cover.

Forest flora and fauna constitute the most biologically diverse ecosystems on land. Some of the world's most threatened and endangered species, crucial to sustaining the ecosystem, live in these forests. Forests provide homes, security and livelihoods for 60 million indigenous people, whilst contributing to the livelihoods of 1.6 billion people worldwide. In many developing countries, more than 80 percent of total energy consumed by people and industry is derived from forests, such as fuel wood and charcoal. Trade in timber and other forest product is estimated at about US $ 330 billion per year.[1]

---

[1] United Nations Environment program (UNEP)

ACRONYMS

AFP	Agency France Press
AR 4	Fourth Assessment Report
BOD	Biochemical Oxygen Demand
CA	Compensatory Afforestation
CAMPA	Compensatory Afforestation Fund Management and Planning Authority
CCEA	Cabinet Committee on Economic affairs
CEC	Certified Emission Credits
CENC	Center for Environment and Nature Conservation
CITES	Convention on International Trade in Endangered Species of Wild Fauna & Flora
CFCs	Chlorofluorocarbons
CFUGs	Community Forest Users' Group
C L E A R	Carbon Limits and Energy for America's Renewal Act
C L I	Crop Life International
C O P A S	Canopy Operation Permanent Access System
C O P D	Chronic Obstructive Pulmonary Disease
C O	Carbon Monoxide
C O2	Carbon Dioxide
C R F	Chest Research Foundation
C S E	Center for Science an Environment
C S Os	Combined Sewer Overflows

D F O	Divisional Forest Officer
D U	Depleted Uranium
D R R	Disaster Risk Reduction
E I A	Environmental Investigation Agency
E I A	Environmental Impact assessment
E I S	Environmental Impact statements
E N V S E C	Environment and Security Initiative
E P A	Environmental Protection Agency
E P S	Energy Performance Score
E Q A	Environmental Quality Authority
E R	Elephant Reserve
E S A	Ecological Sensitive Area /Eco Sensitive Area
E S I	Environmental Sustainable Index
F A O	Food and Agriculture Organization
F C C C	Framework Convention on Climate Change
F R A	Forest Rights Act
E U	European Union
G C P	Global Canopy Program
G H G	Green House Gases
G T Z	German Technical Cooperation Agency
G O M E	Global Ozone Monitoring Experiment
H F A	Hyogo Framework for Action
H I P C	Heavily Indebted Poor Countries
I A E A	International Atomic Energy Agency
I C A	International Consultation Analysis
I C A N	International Canopy Network
I C E S C R	Internal Convenient on Economic, Social and Cultural Rights
I C Z M	Integrated Coastal Zone Management
I D S P	Integrated Disease Surveillance Project
I I T M	Indian Institute of Tropical Meteorology
I L O	International Labour Organization
I O C	International Olympic Committee
I P C C	Intergovernmental Panel on Climate Change
I U C N	The World Conservation Union / International union for Conservation of Nature and Natural Resources
I S R O	Indian Space Research Organization

J C E R D C	Joint Clear Energy Research & Development Center
K S O P	Nature Conservation Complex Scheme of Leningrad Region
L R A	Large-scale Biosphere Atmospheric Experiment
R E D D	Reduced Emissions from Deforestation in Developing Countries
R S P M	Respirable Suspended Particulate Matter
M E A	Multilateral environmental Agreements
M I T	Massachusetts Institute of Technology
M D G	Millennium Development Goals
M E N A	Middle East and North America
MIC	Methyl I-so Cyan-ate
M o E F	Ministry of Environment and Forest
M O U	Memorandum of Understanding
M P C As	Medicinal Plants Conservation Areas
M S W	Municipal Solid Waste
N A A Q S	National Ambient Air Quality Standard
N B W L	National Board of Wild Life
N E P A	National Environmental Policy Act / National Environmental Protection Agency
N P D E S	National Pollution discharge Elimination System
O C H A:	The United Nations Office for the Coordination of Humanitarian Affairs
O D S	Ozone Depleting Substances
O S C E	Organization for Security and Cooperation in Europe
P A C E	Partnership to Advance Clean Energy
P. P. P.	Public Private and Partnership
P R T R	Pollutant Release & Transfer Register Law
P W A	Palestinian Water Authority
R R N	Rural Reconstruction Nepal (An NGO)
S F G	Strategic Foresight Group
SLOE	Sustainable Living Ottawa East
S O2	Sulphur Dioxide
S P C B	State Pollution Control Board

S P N A	Specially Protected Natural Areas
S T R	Simlipal Tiger Reserve
S P C B	State Pollution Control Board
S W O T	Strength Weakness Opportunity and Threats
T D S	Total Dissolved Solids
T E R I	The Energy Research Institute
T S P	Total Suspended Particles
U D H R	Universal Declaration of Human Rights
U ME F	Union Ministry of Environment and Forests
U N D P	United Nations Development Program
U N E P	United Nations Environment Program
U N F CCC	U.N. Framework Convention on Climate Change
U P A	United Political Alliance
W B CSD	World Business Council for sustainable Development
W F D	Water Framework Directive
W H O	World Health Organization
W S O	Wildlife Society of Orissa
W. W. II	World War II
Z S I	Zoological Survey of India

+++++

CONTENTS

INTRODUCTION

Clean environment promotes peace. It is possible if some people desire to do justice to people around them. Human power can make an impossible task a reality. Three components are necessary to create an environment for peace building in a specific area, such as: trust, a rehabilitation program and grassroots initiative. Political people create problems but true friends solve problems. Each person involved in a peace program should live in the area, believe in a leader and allow the work to move ahead. The involvement of children, youths, employees and senior citizens would strengthen a peace movement.

The United Nations Human Rights Council recognized that climate poses an immediate and far-reaching threat to people and communities around the word. The global climate system is warming and doing so mainly because of man-made greenhouse gas emissions. The global warming will affect, and already is affecting, the basic elements of life of millions of people around the world. Effects include an increasing frequency of extreme weather events, rising sea levels, droughts, increasing water shortages, and the spread of tropical and vector borne diseases.

It is clear that projected climate change-related effects threaten the effective enjoyment of a range of human rights, such as the right to safe and adequate water, food, healthcare and adequate housing facility. Equally, the human rights perspective brings into focus that climate change is set to hit the poorest countries and communities the hardest.

The international human rights standards serve as a guide to tackle climate change, underscoring the fundamental moral and legal obligations to protect and promote full enjoyment of the rights enshrined in the Universal Declaration of Human Rights and in the core universal human rights treaties.

The challenges are:

(a) How to build a green economy to lift people out of poverty without destroying the environment;
(b) How to improve international coordination for sustainable development.
(c) How to ensure full coherence between efforts to advance the green economy, on the one hand, and their human rights obligations on the other and
(d) How to complement and strengthen the UN Millennium Development Goals.

The climate change-related issue poses problems, such as:

(a) The effective enjoyment of human rights;
(b) Population who are already in a vulnerable situation;
(c) Effective international cooperation;
(d) National efforts for the realization of human rights implicated by climate change-related impacts; and

(e) Strengthen international and national policy-making.
(f) Identify best practices to address the adverse effects of climate change; and
(g) Enhance cooperation between human rights and climate change-awareness advocates.

A Sustainable Living Ottawa East (SLOE) program made a renaissance in climate change. Their suggestions are:

(a) Expand the market share of sustainably-produced food (locally-grown, organic, fairly traded)
(b) Increase food-growing within the community
(c) Reduce consumption of non-renewable, G H G emitting energy
(d) Increase transportation alternatives (e.g., pedestrian, cycling), including recreational options
(e) Minimize car use
(f) Enhance the ecological health of existing public, institutional and residential green space
(g) Promote and create green spaces that residents will enjoy

So there could be peace organizations in every hamlets, districts, states or countries to protect environment. The peace workers should not blame others but they should mobilize others to be part of good environment programs. People have the power to change politics and environment for the benefits of all. We can avoid catastrophe; we can promote environment; we can achieve peace through better environment and it is possible.

Effective environmental program should maintain the quality, quantity and diversity of natural endowments; undertake a high level of environmental protection and set out sustainability objectives for agriculture, energy, industry, tourism and marine so as to encourage long-term growth and competitiveness within a quality environment. The program must look into strategies to address climate change, and waste management. Environment program must adopt to improve water, air and soil quality. The government should not allow industries, which pollute air, water and soil. Even scientific agricultural practices, such as fertilizers and pesticides, cause harm to air, soil and water.

The urban growth in all the countries poses an extra burden to the governments. This is because cities need huge resources – natural, human and budgetary – to sustain themselves. Both industrialization and urbanization could do more harm to people residing throughout the countries. These steps would cause pollution of air, River water, drinking water, plastic pollution, E-waste pollution and cause Vector-borne diseases.

The World should once again try to find a balance between environment protection and industrialization.

War and natural calamities cause environmental pollution and cause mass causalities'.

+++++

Chapter I

A MARCH TOWARDS CATASTROPHE

Sustainable Development has been defined as development that meets the needs of the present without compromising the ability of future generations to meet their own needs.

The World Commission on Environment and Development, 1987

Environment includes natural conditions of resources such as land, forest, natural heritage, eco-system, atmosphere and water. The close link between environment and sustainable development regulates the life and behavior of people around the globe. People in forest area enjoy the forest resources such as fuel, fruits, edible roots, leaf and the twigs or logs of wood. The tribal people practice hunting and kill animals for food purposes. In many cases inhabitants set fire in the forests for the purpose of having an easy prey and for acquiring land to grow cassava, millets, or maize or simply to enjoy the flames of burning of forest. The Department of Environment is responsible for land planning, preservation of public utilities, and pollution control in air, water and soil.

The governments cause serious threats to the eco-systems by construction of National Highways, dams and capital-intensive industries. Prawn farming, excavations of large - scale mines, construction of railways and roads, rapid growth of urbanization, hospital wastes, use of chemicals, fertilizers and pesticides, increase of vehicular traffic, use of polythene, and greenhouse effect cause harm to environment. The rich become richer by exploitation of natural resources but the poor become nomads. The natural calamities like flood, cyclone, drought, and hailstorms cause imbalances in flora-fauna systems. The world now faces strong challenges in climatic changes, air pollution, water pollution, sound pollution, depletion of forest, increase in birth-death ratio, soil erosion, increase of HIV/AID victims, and nuclear weapons along with a load of 1.2 billion poor people.

The climatic change causes more droughts and floods, terrible storms, hot days and diseases. The Carbon Dioxide emissions by an American = 19 Indians = 49 Sri Lankans = 107 Bangladeshis = 134 Bhutanese =269 Nepalese (1996 report). If the average temperature of the earth is not checked by reducing emissions by 50-70 percent below 1990 levels, a 15-95 cm rise in sea level could drown the island nations within a couple of years. Hence, the rich nations should implement the 1997 Kyoto protocol for the ultimate aim of world peace (Down to Earth, Nov. 30, 2002).

In this chapter, global warming, polluted countries, climate change and man versus nature have been discussed.

Global Warming

A glance at the damage already done from pole to pole—and what scientists say is still to come.

Poison in the Air: Greenhouse gases—caused by burning fossil fuels such as oil, coal, and gas — can stay in the atmosphere for centuries, trapping heat from the Earth's surface and warming the planet. Greenhouse gas emissions jumped 70 percent between 1970 and 2004. Ice cores suggest that the current atmospheric concentration of carbon dioxide—the greenhouse gas most produced by humans—far exceeds the natural range of the past 650,000 years.

Warm Water: Oceans have absorbed 80 percent of the heat we've added to the climate, increasing average water temperatures even at depths of almost 10,000 feet.

On Thin Ice: The Arctic warmed twice as fast as the rest of the planet over the past 100 years. Its cap of sea ice has shrunk by an average of 8.4 percent each decade since the 1970s, and this year reached a record low. Less Arctic ice is there to reflect sunlight, but more the heat the sea absorbs.

Rising Tide: For the past two millennia, the sea level has risen between 0.1 and 0.2 millimeters per year. Rates have averaged 10 times that in the past century, and 30 times that since 1993.

Oh-No-Zone: First observed in the early 1980s, the hole in the Antarctic ozone—the stratospheric gas that protects Earth from ultraviolet light—now grows to an area larger than Antarctica most years. At the South Pole itself, ozone depletion reached 99 percent in early October 2006.

Perfect Storms: Tropical sea surface temperatures during the hurricane season have increased 1°F since 1970, possibly boosting the intensity of North Atlantic storms. The number of category four and five hurricanes—registering winds of more than 131 mph—has nearly doubled worldwide since then.

Acres Ablaze: Significant drought affected 52 percent of the United States in 2006 and contributed to a record wildfire season in which almost 10 million acres burned.

Not So Permanent: The top layer of permafrost has increased in temperature by 5.4°F since the 1980s, causing some to thaw for the first time in more than 125,000 years. As it melts, permafrost releases concentrated volumes of the greenhouse gas methane.

Goodbye, Glaciers: The 11,000-year-old ice caps of Mount Kilimanjaro in Tanzania have melted by about 82 percent over the past century—and could be gone altogether by 2020.

Shrinking Antarctica: In the space of 35 days in 2002, about 1,255 square miles of Antarctica's Larsen B ice shelf disintegrated into the ocean. Until this event, scientists estimate the sheet measured more than 700 feet in thickness and had likely existed for 12,000 years. It is now 40 percent of its previous size.

Forecasts

Submerge: Current-warming trends could raise sea levels as much as 3.5 inches by 2100. However, the real danger would occur when Greenland's ice sheet begins to melt rapidly. Even if only part of it slides into the Atlantic, this would cause flooding along the Gulf Coast and the eastern seaboard from Boston to Miami, while places such as Bangladesh would become uninhabitable. If the ice sheet melts completely, as some scientists predict, it could raise sea levels by 23 feet, it could submerge much of Florida and threaten London and Los Angeles.

Carbon Overload: Experts predict global emissions of carbon dioxide will jump an additional 75 percent by 2030.

Loss of Life: By 2050, more than a million species of plants and animals may be on the road to extinction as a result of global warming. Nearly 30 U.S. states could lose their official state trees or flowers, and seven may lose their state birds, as changing climates make those locations less habitable. If summer ocean temperatures increase by just 1.8°F, the world's coral reefs—considered the "rain forests of the ocean" for their rich, delicate ecosystem—could cause them to die en masse. During one of the warmest periods on record in the late 1990s, about 16 percent of reefs worldwide were severely damaged.

Unquenchable Thirst: By 2050, nearly one-sixth of the world's population—including some in the western United States would face water shortages as they receive 10 to 30 percent less snow pack runoff than today. [2]

Agriculture: More frequent floods and droughts will decrease crop production, especially in low-altitude, subsistence regions.

Top Ten Polluted Countries in the World

Pollution is a silent killer that endangers not just a person's health, but also his or her environment. Here are the top 10 most polluted countries in the world along with the reasons for why you should be more concerned about your environment.

Peru: The environmental problems in Peru include deforestation, soil erosion, soil pollution, water pollution and air pollution. Water pollution in Peru is caused by oil-related waste, sewage waste and

---

[2]NYU Alumni Magazine Issue: Fall 2007

industrial waste. Peru has 1,746 cubic kilometers of renewable water resources. Seven percent is for industrial activity and 86 percent is used for farming. In Lima, vehicular and industrial emissions bring air pollution, which has always been a serious problem in the country's capital city.

Pakistan: There is hardly any attention paid to the environmental issues in Pakistan. Potable water and sanitation are the main problems in this country. Almost 80 percent of the total population in Pakistan does not have flush toilets. Research conducted by the Pakistan Medical Research Council show that a large number of people with diseases in Pakistan suffer specific health problem because of the consumption of polluted water. A whopping 38 percent of the entire population of Pakistan receives water that run through dirty pipelines, which, in turn, may lead to the consumption of seriously contaminated water.

Kuwait: The oil fires have already been put out and a large part of the oil spills are now cleaned up. However, Kuwait is still suffering from the health and environmental costs brought about by the Gulf War and Iraq's occupation.

Oil pollutes a large part of the deserts of Kuwait. Oil covers a larqe patch of Kuwait's seabed off the coast. The coral reefs in Kuwait need to undergo a serious recovery. The ruptured tanks from the war left debris all over Kuwait that still pollute and destroy Kuwait's environment after 10 years. Since 1991, children in Kuwait have been acquiring leukemia caused by residues from DU or depleted uranium.

Saudi Arabia: Dead dolphins on the beach of the Persian Gulf have become an environmental concern to the country.

The pollution in Saudi Arabia is caused by other factors outside the country. For example, in the Persian Gulf War in 1991, 910 million liters of oil was released into the gulf. This caused severe pollution in the different bodies of water in Saudi Arabia. The country is also currently dealing with rapid population growth because sewage systems are now being out spaced. Underground water is also contaminated and unfit for human use. The oil wells in Kuwait also caused air pollution in Saudi Arabia. A number of species have also become endangered because of constant hunting and depletion of natural resources. Saudi Arabia is currently working on ozone layer protection, proper management of hazardous wastes and climate change.

Ethiopia: Air pollution is evident in Ethiopia. Soil pollution is among the many environmental problems in Ethiopia. Since this country needs to boost its economy, its people have thought of capitalizing on its agricultural assets. Chemical inputs have risen and spread like fire. A lot of farmers were not educated or even oriented on the use and management of fertilizers and pesticides. Agricultural workers did not understand the proper handling of chemicals. Chemical input on the soil became out of control, later polluting the environment and affecting human health. The severe case of land pollution in Ethiopia has caused famine and worsened the case of AIDS.

Russia: Air pollution in Russia is increasing continuously. The ecological collapse and massive pollution in Russia is caused by the secret industrial and military development in the country. These developments did not consider health and environmental consequences. Russia is a major contributor to the depletion of the ozone layer since it is the largest consumer and producer of ozone depleting substances in the world. The big cities in Russia are so used to pollution that infants grow to be accustomed to it. The health of millions of Russians and the condition of forestry and agriculture are threatened by pollution.

Indonesia: Indonesian rivers are infected with garbage. Water pollution is also a serious problem because of the lack of sewage systems and unsuitable fishing practices. The rapid population growth in Indonesia is responsible for many of its environmental concerns. From 1980 to 2001, six million people were added to the total population of Indonesia. Industrialization process became as rapid as its population growth. The environment is being destroyed every day because of trade-led industrialization in Indonesia, which later captured the attention of the government. Environmental and natural resource laws were authored by the Senate but were not well implemented. In the 1980s and 1990s, environmental degradation became a major problem in Indonesia. The annual air pollution damage was to the extent of $ 400 million per year.

India: Tons and tons of trash in the rivers of India cause serious water pollution. Three billion liters of waste is no laughing matter. Three billion liters of waste thrown into the river every single day is as serious as killing the inhabitants occupying a whole country. An unimaginable case of pollution such as this one is exactly what the residents around Yamuna River in Delhi deal with every day.

The problem in Yamuna River is minute compared to the prevailing case of pollution in the whole country. Out of the total urban waste in India, 80 percent of it goes straight to rivers and other bodies of water. Almost all bodies of water in India are now unsafe for human use. But people use this polluted water for drinking and cooking purposes.

China: Water pollution in China causes numerous dead fishes. China is known as one of the biggest industrial powers in the world. It is also a country that demonstrates a direct link between industrial power and environmental damage. Today, public health is at great risk because of the pollution caused by industrial emissions. Safe drinking water is also scarce in China. In fact, a gray shroud now wraps the skies of China. There are around 500 million people who suffer from drinking unsafe water. The current Chinese government is indeed having difficulty in fighting this problem; authorities know that it will take decades before the damage caused by pollution will be undone.

United States of America: American factories cause massive air pollution. The United States of America is the biggest polluter in the world. A report from BBC reveals that in 1990, the US was accountable for worldwide greenhouse emissions that totaled to 36.1 percent. The people living in America represent only 4 percent of the world's population, but this country contributes about 25 percent of the total emissions of carbon dioxide in the world. To see how much the United States is contributing to world pollution, a comparison can be made. In Britain, 3 percent of greenhouse emissions are released to the atmosphere. India contributes to pollution as much as Britain does, but the population of India is 15 times larger than that of Britain's. With these figures, America can only be said to provide greener pastures that are paved with pollutants. Depletion of the ozone layer and the environment in general means the depletion of human health and life. What good is a life full of wealth if you breathe air that is killing you?[3]

Polluted countries

It is reported that Qatar is the most polluted country in the world. The average carbon per person is 20.05 tons in 2010. It is followed by United Arab Emirates (10.36 Tons of Carbon per

---

[3]Sohttp://crunkish.com / top-10-pollution-causes/source, Posted on January 5th, 2008

person), Kuwait (8.69), Guam (7.76), Bahrain (7.66), Singapore (7.04), United States (6.04), Luxembourg (5. 69), Brunei 5.28 and Australia 5.29 tons of carbon per person.[4]

Countries like Peru, Pakistan, Kuwait, South Arabia, Ethiopia, Russia, Indonesia, India, China, and United States of America were most polluted countries in 2012.

In other words, all countries are infected with pollution because of inefficiency or corruption of regulatory authorities in checking pollution.

Polluted Cities in USA

Pittsburgh and Los Angeles are the most polluted US cities in the World. Six out of ten Americans live in urban areas where air pollution can cause major health problems. While a new report for the American Lung Association acknowledges substantial progress against air pollution in many areas of the USA, it finds nearly every major city was still burdened by air pollution. Despite America's growing "green" movement, the air in many cities became dirtier during the past 12 months. The research names Pittsburgh, Los Angeles and Bakersfield as the most polluted US cities.

The report finds that air pollution hovers at unhealthy levels in almost every major city, threatening people's ability to breathe and placing lives at risk. Some of the biggest sources of air pollution, including dirty power plants, dirty diesel engines and ocean-going vessels, also worsen global warming.

Many cities, like Los Angeles, New York, Atlanta, Charlotte, Philadelphia, Washington, DC and

---

[4] Residents of Baltic Coast Countries Fear Pollution, The Independent Environment, October 17, 2010

Baltimore have made considerable improvements in their air quality over the past decade. People living in some of these cities however, are breathing even dirtier air than what was reported in the Lung Association's previous report. Only one city, Fargo of North Dakota, ranked among the cleanest in all three air pollution categories covered by the research.

Sixteen cities making this year's 25 most ozone-polluted list experienced worsened ozone (smog) problems than last year. Some 58 per cent of people in the United States live in counties with recorded unhealthy levels of ozone air pollution, measured against the tighter standard in effect since March 2008.

The new standard showed that unhealthy ozone levels are more widespread and more severe than previously recognized. The report's review of the past 10 years identified consistent improvements in ozone in some cities, most notably in Los Angeles, which has long been recognized for its serious ozone problem. By contrast, two cities, Dallas-Ft. Worth and Las Vegas, have higher ozone levels than 10 years ago.

Ozone is the most widespread form of air pollution. When inhaled, ozone irritates the lungs, resulting in something like bad sunburn. The health effects of breathing ozone pollution can be immediate. Ozone can cause wheezing, coughing and asthma attacks. Breathing ozone pollution can even shorten lives.

Emerging research has redefined the severity and immediate health impacts of particle pollution and ozone, as well as an expanded definition of specific groups at great risk. New data show that women in their 50's may be particularly threatened by air pollution and that diesel truck drivers and dockworkers who are forced to breathe exhaust on the job may face a greater risk of developing lung cancer or chronic obstructive pulmonary disease. California researchers have tripled their estimate of the number of people that particle pollution kills each year in their state.

Low-income people and some racial and ethnic groups often face greater risk from pollutants. Pollution sources like factories and power plants may be closer to their homes. Many live near areas with heavy highway traffic or have poor access to health care, which makes them even more vulnerable. Some racial and ethnic groups have a higher prevalence of diseases like asthma or diabetes, which compounds the ill effects of air pollution for these groups. [5]

Civilian Disaster and National Security

Hurricane Katrina[6] underscored how extreme weather events—which are expected to become more severe and more numerous with climate change—can overwhelm civilian disaster response capabilities and become national security issues. As climate negotiators gather in Bali, Indonesia, a new Council Special Report argues that new policies are needed at home and abroad in order to strengthen national security and reduce vulnerabilities to climate disasters. "Domestically, extreme weather events made more likely by climate change could endanger large numbers of people, damage critical infrastructure (including military installations), and require mobilization and diversion of military assets," says report author Joshua W. Busby of the LBJ School of Public Affairs at the University of Texas-Austin.

He argues that internationally, climate change could also lead to large-scale refugee and humanitarian

---

[5]A report by the American Lung Association, May 17, 2009

[6] Hurrican Katrina, United Nations, Council Special Report, Maxims News Network, publication / 14862, December 2, 2007,

crises and thus contribute to instability in other countries and regions. In order to minimize the worst possible security consequences of climate change, the report – Climate Change and National Security: An Agenda for Action – says that there is several policies the United States should support:

No Regrets: "The United States should prioritize so-called 'no regrets' policies, those that it would not regret having pursued even if the consequences of climate change prove less severe than feared," Busby says. They include establishing comprehensive evacuation and relocation plans in response to natural disasters, particularly hurricanes; improving building codes for low-lying and coastal populations; and increasing water conservation efforts for agriculture and human consumption.

Invest in Infrastructure: Minimize security risks by improving domestic infrastructure, which will not only improve disaster responses, but will have a spillover benefit to the overall economy. "The United States should support this infrastructure investment program and dedicate a healthy portion to 'climate proof' vulnerable infrastructure, particularly in coastal areas," says the report.

Risk Reduction: The United States and the international community will be called upon to intervene when natural disasters strike. It will be much more cost effective to support risk reduction and adaptation than it will be to respond when disasters happen. "The government effort should begin by providing incentives for individuals and firms to reduce risk, particularly through building codes and ensuring that federally funded disaster insurance discourages dangerous coastal settlements," Busby says.

Climate Change Diplomacy: Engage countries such as China and India to encourage a reduction in greenhouse gases. Climate damages are likely to exceed most governments' adaptive capacities unless a major reduction in greenhouse gases takes place before the mid-twenty-first century. "While advanced industrialized countries bear historic responsibility for existing concentrations of greenhouse gases, China will be increasingly fingered as a climate culprit in the future," Busby says. "This will create a common interest between the United States and China in avoiding world condemnation for being 'climate villains.' Enlightened climate diplomacy could build on that common interest to improve U.S.-China relations."

Institutional Reform: Integrate climate security into the National Security Strategy; create a deputy undersecretary of defense position for environmental security at the Department of Defense; and create new positions in the National Security Council and the office of the president so climate security concerns get the attention they deserve. "The importance of climate policy to national security demands that it receive much greater prioritization across the U.S. federal government," Busby says. "Other players in the federal government have largely been sidelined. There are few efforts to integrate climate concerns into top-level decision-making."

"The policy proposals presented here...have the potential to strengthen national security by reducing U.S. vulnerabilities to climate change at home and abroad, securing and stabilizing important partners, and contributing to other goals such as energy security and industrial revitalization. In a world of new security challenges, forging a climate policy along these lines must be a national priority," the report concludes.

The Earth Went Wild in 2010

This was the year the Earth struck back. Earthquakes, heat waves, floods, volcanoes, super typhoons, blizzards, landslides and droughts killed at least a quarter million people in 2010; the deadliest year in more than a generation. More people were killed worldwide by natural disasters this year than have been killed in terrorists in the past 40 years combined.

Craig Fugate, who heads the US Federal Emergency Management Agency said, "It just seemed like it was back-to-back, and it came in waves. It handled a record number of disasters in 2010. The term '100-year event' really lost its meaning this year. And we have ourselves to blame most of the time, scientists and disaster experts say. Even though many catastrophes have the ring of random chance, the hand of man made this a particularly deadly, costly, extreme and weird year for everything from wild weather to earthquakes. Poor construction and development practices conspire to make earthquakes more deadly than they need be. More people live in poverty in vulnerable buildings in crowded cities. That means that when the ground shakes, the river breaches, or the tropical cyclone hits, more people die. All the change that's made is man-made.

The January earthquake that killed well more than 220,000 people in Haiti is a perfect example. Port-au-Prince has nearly three times as many people, many of them living in poverty, and more poorly built shanties than it did 25 years ago. So had the same quake hit in 1985 instead of 2010, total deaths probably would have been in the 80,000 range.

In February, an earthquake that was more than 500 times stronger than the one that struck Haiti hit an area of Chile that was less populated, better constructed, and not so poor. Chile's bigger quake caused fewer than 1,000 deaths.

Climate scientists say Earth's climate also is changing thanks to man-made global warming, bringing extreme weather, such as heat waves and flooding.
In the summer, one weather system caused oppressive heat in Russia, while farther south it caused flooding in Pakistan that inundated 62,000 square miles (160,580 sq. kilometers), about the size of Bangladesh. That single heat-and-storm system killed almost 17,000 people, more than the entire worldwide airplane crashes in the past 15 years combined.

It's a form of suicide, isn't it? We build houses that kill ourselves (in earthquakes). We build houses in flood zones that drown ourselves. It's our fault for not anticipating these things. You know, this is the Earth doing its thing. I think it is the end of the world. Our planet warns us against what would happen if we don't care about nature.

The excessive amount of extreme weather that dominated 2010 is a classic sign of man-made global warming that climate scientists have long warned about. They calculate that the killer Russian heat wave, which set a national record of 111 degrees (44 Celsius), would happen once every 100,000 years without global warming.

Preliminary data show that 18 countries broke their records for the hottest day on record. These (weather) events would not have happened without global warming. That is why the people who study disasters for a living say it would be wrong to chalk 2010 up to just another bad year. The Earth strikes back in cahoots with bad human decision-making. It's almost as if the policies, the government policies and development policies are helping the Earth strike back instead of protecting from it. We've created conditions where the slightest thing the Earth does is really going to have a disproportionate impact.

How Deadly:

While the Haitian earthquake, Russian heat wave, and Pakistani flooding were the biggest killers, deadly quakes also struck Chile, Turkey, China and Indonesia in one of the most active seismic years in decades. Through mid-December there have been 20 earthquakes of magnitude 7.0 or higher, compared with the normal 16.

This year is tied for the biggest quakes since 1970, but it is not a record. Nor is it a significantly above average year for the number of strong earthquakes, US earthquake officials say.

Flooding alone this year killed more than 6,300 people in 59 nations through September, according to the World Health Organization. In the United States, 30 people died in floods in the Nashville, Tennessee region. Inundated countries include China, Italy, India, Colombia and Chad. Super Typhoon Megi, with winds of more than 200 mph devastated the Philippines and parts of China. The charity Oxfam says 21,000 of this year's disaster deaths are weather related.

The Associated Press reports that through Nov. 30, nearly 260,000 people died in natural disasters in 2010 according to Swiss Re. The World Health Organization figures past Sept. 30, are just shy of250,000. By comparison, deaths from terrorism from 1968 to 2009 were less than 115,000, according to reports by the US State Department and the Lawrence Livermore National Laboratory.

How Extreme:

A strong early year blizzards paralyzed the US mid-Atlantic and record snowfalls hit Russia and China, the temperature turned to broil.

The year may go down as the hottest on record worldwide or at the very least in the top three, according to the World Meteorological Organization. The average global temperature through the end of October was 58.53 degrees (14.74 Celsius), a shade over the previous record of 2005, according to the National Climatic Data Center.

Los Angeles, California, had its hottest day in recorded history on Sept. 27: 113 degrees. In May, 129 degrees (54 Celsius) set a record for Pakistan and may have been the hottest temperature recorded in an inhabited location. In the Southeastern United States, the year began with freezes in Florida that had cold-blooded iguanas becoming comatose and falling off trees. Then it became the hottest summer on record for the region. As the year ended, unusually cold weather was back in force.

Northern Australia had the wettest May-October on record, while the southwestern part of that country had its driest spell on record. And parts of the Amazon River basin struck by drought hit their lowest water levels in recorded history.

How Costly:

Disasters caused $222 billion in economic losses in 2010, more than Hong Kong's economy, according to Swiss Re. That is more than usual, but not a record. That is because this year's disasters often struck poor areas without heavy insurance, such as Haiti.

A volcano in Iceland paralyzed air traffic for days in Europe, disrupting travel for more than 7 million people. Other volcanoes in the Congo, Guatemala, Ecuador, the Philippines and Indonesia sent people scurrying for safety. New York City had a rare tornado.

A nearly 2-pound (0.9-kilogram) hailstone that was 8 inches (20.3 centimeters) in diameter fell in South Dakota in July to set a U.S. record. The storm that produced it was one of seven declared disasters for that state this year.

There was not much snow to start the Winter Olympics in a relatively balmy Vancouver, British Columbia, while the US East Coast was snowbound.

In a 24-hour period in October, Indonesia got the trifecta of terra terror: a deadly magnitude 7.7 earthquake, a tsunami that killed more than 500 people and a volcano that caused more than 390,000 people to flee. That is after flooding, landslides and more quakes killed hundreds earlier in the year.

Even the extremes were extreme. This year started with a good sized El Nino, a recurring Pacific Ocean weather oscillation, which causes all sorts of extremes worldwide. Then later in the year, the world got the mirror image Pacific weather system with a strong La Nina, which causes a different set of extremes. Having a year with both a strong El Nino and La Nina is unusual. The Federal Emergency Management Agency declared that there were 79 major disasters as against the average year has only 34 major disasters.

A list of day-by-day disasters in 2010 compiled by The Associated Press runs 64 printed pages long.

Greg Holland says, "The extremes are changed in an extreme fashion. For example, even though it sounds counter intuitive, global warming likely played a bit of a role in US "Snow mage don" early this year. That is because with a warmer climate, there is more moisture in the air, which makes storms including blizzards, more intense.

John Holdren says, "people should become acclimated used to climate disasters or do something about global warming. The science is clear that we can expect more and more of these kinds of damaging events unless and until society's emissions of heat-trapping gases and particles are sharply reduced. And that is just the "natural disasters." It was also a year of man-made technological catastrophes. BP's broken oil well caused 172 million gallons to gush into the Gulf of Mexico. Mining disasters, men trapped deep in the Earth, caused dozens of deaths in tragic collapses in West Virginia, China and New Zealand. The fortunate miners in Chile who survived 69 days underground provided the feel good story of the year.

In both technological and natural disasters, there runs a common theme of 'pushing the envelope'. The world's population is moving into riskier mega cities on fault zones and flood-prone areas. He figures that 400 million to 500 million people in the world live in large cities prone to major earthquakes. A Haitian disaster will happen again - It could be Algiers - It could be Tehran - It could be any one of a dozen cities.[7]

Human Rights and Climate Change

The first principle of the first major international commitment linking human rights and environmental protection highlighted the connections between international human rights and environmental law:

Man has the fundamental right to freedom, equality and adequate conditions of life in an environment of quality that permits a life of dignity and well-being, and he bears solemn responsibility to protect and improve the environment for present and future generations.

---

[7]Julie Reed Bell and Seth Borenstein, "When the Earth Went Wild", The Irrawaddy, February 2, 2011

Why there has been, to date, so little uptake on the human rights implications of climate changes? International environmental law and international human rights law are at the same time similar in their purpose and different in their nature. It could be argued that they have the same purpose: to put human beings at the center of concerns of the international community. But at the same time, their nature is fundamentally different. While the purpose of international environmental law is to regulate relations between States, international human rights law sets limits and guarantees entitlements in the relations between individuals and States. Environmental law can also be described as a law of co-operation, in which States undertake commitments to support each other's to address global concerns, while human rights law aims to empower people and make States accountable in a more directly answerable manner. Moreover, the complex and transnational bas is of climate change poses a significant challenge to international human right law's dominant structures.

A second possible obstacle to action might be the fact that, much as the effects are increasingly being experienced today, climate change harms are generally located in the future; they remain a matter of prediction and probability and they are, by their nature, unprecedented. Human rights, on the other hand, are generally viewed in a factual light, as either fulfilled or violated, protected or unprotected, in the present. As a matter of priority then, human rights groups must seek a credible language to express expected and unprecedented rights infringements and to address them through policy measures rather than with legal tools alone.
It has become widely accepted nowadays that the international community must take into account international human rights obligations in the course of negotiations addressing climate change. The outcome of the UNFCCC negotiation process should

ensure that fundamental human rights would not be violated by climate change impacts. It would seem valuable to recognize and reference human rights principles within the post-Kyoto regime. Agreements under the UNFCCC umbrella could usefully note that actions taken in the context of mitigation and adaptation should respect human rights 16. In response to climate change, the human rights approach would require a triple task to be performed by the governments:

(1) To avoid harmful emissions nationally in order to respect the right to live in freedom from human induced climate perturbations;
(2) To protect human rights against third-party emissions of countries or corporations through international co-operation; and
(3) To fulfill human rights obligations by upgrading people's capability to cope with climate change through adaptation measures.

Further, States must give due attention to threatened economic, social and cultural rights in the course of the negotiations of international climate change agreements. This attention is not only a moral obligation, but also a legal duty resulting from the ICESCR and other human rights treaties.

In the climate change context, mitigation and adaptation measures are considered as policies that can help s slowing down or even stopping the negative effects of climate degradation. Mitigation measures seek to reduce the anthropogenic causes of dangerous climate change, especially by reducing greenhouse gas emissions. On the other hand, adaptation measures include policies and actions that seek to adjust to new environmental conditions and reduce the harmful impacts caused by climate change. However, while many mitigation and adaptation measures can ensure human rights, such measures can also have the opposite effect, undermining the rights of individuals. Most recently, the effects of bio-fuel policies in the EU and the USA have raised questions about the impacts of these policies on food security, particularly in vulnerable food-importing countries.

Similarly, adaptation policies to move populations from areas threatened by climate change may have the intention of protecting the life, security and health of individuals. However, if these policies are implemented in ways that unfairly discriminate, or are carried out without ensuring procedural protections (access to information, community participation, etc.) the result can be that human rights are undermined. The cases of poorly planned migration of threatened populations to new areas would lack adequate infrastructure and facilities.[8]

Humanity Demands 1.4 Earths

It would now take nearly one and a half Earths to generate all the resources humanity consumes and absorb all our CO2 emissions, according to the latest Ecological Footprint and bio-capacity calculations. These figures are based upon source data from 2006, the most recent year for which such data are available, and are released on the eve of the Copenhagen climate conference by the Global Footprint Network.

The data show that humanity's demand on the biosphere for providing natural resources and absorbing carbon dioxide emissions is 44 per cent more than what nature can provide. This ecological overshoot means it now takes approximately 18 months for the Earth to regenerate what we use in one year. The urgent threats we are facing today – most notably climate change, but also biodiversity

[8]United Nations Human Rights , Office of the High Commissioner for Human Rights, Ohchr Org

loss, shrinking forests, declining fisheries and freshwater stress – are symptoms of this trend.

Global Footprint Network President Mathis Wackernagel opined that the future would be shaped by these resource limitations, so, it's clearly in the self-interest of every country to transition quickly from carbon and resource-intensive economies to the economies of the future. While international agreements are critical, many nations are not taking a 'wait-and-see' approach; rather they are investing now to take advantage of the world's demand for renewable energy and clean technology.

Who uses what?

Every year, Global Footprint Network calculates the Ecological Footprint of the world's nations and humanity as a whole, and compares that with bio-capacity, the amount of resources nature is able to produce. The data show that in 2006, the most recent year for which data are available, humanity's Ecological Footprint grew almost 2 percent from the year before, and 22 per cent from a decade before, due to both rising population and per capita consumption. At the same time, bio-capacity has not increased, and may even have fallen slightly.

The average Ecological Footprint per person worldwide is 2.6 global hectares (6.5 global acres), while the average bio-capacity available per person is 1.8 global hectares (4.5 global acres.) But some countries' level of ecological demand per person is much higher than world average, and some is much lower.

The United Arab Emirates has the highest Ecological Footprint per capita, 10.3 global hectares (26 global acres). The Emirates adopted a national Ecological Footprint Initiative in 2007 and has been working to reduce its Footprint. Along with investing billions in renewable energy and other sustainability initiatives, UAE researchers and government agencies are working with Global Footprint Network to identify policies that could significantly cut the country's per capita Footprint.

The average American has an Ecological Footprint of 9.0 global hectares (23 acres) – the size of 17½ American football fields. The average European has a Footprint of 4.5 global hectares, half that of the average American, but still well above both the world average and what is available per person.

On the other end of the scale are Malawi, Haiti, Nepal, and Bangladesh, with Footprints of about half a global hectare (1.25 acres), in most cases too small to provide for basic food, shelter and sanitation.

Population growth

Population is another critical factor driving overshoot. The productivity of our ecosystems has not kept pace with increases in population. The result is that as our numbers expand, the amount of bio-capacity available per person shrinks.

The US now requires 23 per cent of world bio-capacity, while China – which has a much lower per capita Footprint but over four times greater total population – requires 21 per cent. Together, China and the US require almost half of all human demand on nature's services. China's resource use is rising at a much faster rate due to population growth, suggesting it will soon surpass the US in total consumption, although the US remains much higher per person.

If everyone lived like a resident of United States of America, the global requirement would be 5 planets; as a UK resident, the global requirement would be 3.4 planets; as a resident of Argentina, it would require 1.7 planet; as a resident of South Africa, it would require 1.5 planet; as a resident of China, it would cover the entire planet (1 planet) and as a resident of India, it would cover only 0.4 planet and as on today, the global requirement would require 1.4 planet.

Changing the curve

Global Footprint Network President Mathis Wackernagel says: Despite these sobering findings, there are key opportunities to change our trajectory. Even as world leaders have acknowledged that an agreement at Copenhagen is out of reach, governments we work with from Ecuador to the United Arab Emirates and we see the importance of taking bold unilateral action. Once city, country and business leaders realize that the best way to remain competitive and prepared for the future is to make the policy decisions and drive the technological innovations we need to live within nature's means, we will begin to change these trends. The good news is that, many governments we work with are moving forward to reduce their Ecological Footprint, no matter what happens next month in Copenhagen. These leaders realize the longer they wait, the greater the risks to their economies and their citizen's well-being.[9]

Ethiopia Faces Climate Change

Climate change is hitting the world's poorest countries, the people least able to cope, according to a new case study on Ethiopia[10]. Researchers looked at which groups in the country are most vulnerable, what community members say they need to adapt, and the role of family planning and reproductive health in increasing resilience to climate change impacts.

---

[9]People and Planet Net

[10] People and Planet Net, December 3, 2009

The Ethiopia example shows that we must fulfill the global demand for contraception to improve the lives of women and communities. Leaders in Copenhagen should integrate family planning into global efforts to mitigate and adapt to climate change. Ethiopia is expected to more than double its population by 2050. The report highlights how rapid increase in the population is likely to exacerbate the effects of climate change. In the study, women and men from two areas of Ethiopia speak about the increasing challenges they face in adapting to climate change. They recount how rising temperatures, more frequent droughts, increased flooding, receding grazing land and diminishing forests are making it more difficult for their families and communities to cope.

Nothing seems... like in the past. On the contrary, the problems are getting worse. The temperature, shortage of food and rainfall situation is worsening. If a family has limited children, it will have enough land for its kids and hence we can protect the forests. Limiting the number of children will help us to cope with the change in climate. We're helping to fulfill the needs of women while addressing climate change. In contrast, so much of the dialogue leading up to Copenhagen focuses on taking away people's rights to use energy or consume natural resources.

Nepal Signs Climate Pledge at Everest

The Government of Nepal[11] signed a 10-point Everest Declaration, at Mount Everest today. This includes a commitment by the government to help communities cope with the impacts of climate change and to work alongside other countries to mitigate the impact of global warming.

Prime Minister Madhav Kumar Nepal, along with 23 ministers, officials, and international journalists, some

[11] People and Planet Net, December 3, 2009

of them with oxygen masks, held the historic 'cabinet meeting' at the Kala Patthar plateau, in the foothills of Mt. Everest to draw attention to the impact of climate change in the Himalayas.

The declaration supported developed countries' plans to contribute 1.5 per cent of GDP to a climate fund for developing countries and bring down greenhouse gases to pre-industrial levels. It will be presented at the Copenhagen Climate Change Summit next week.

One of the most immediate threats arising from increased temperatures in the Himalayan region is the 'glacial lake outburst floods' or GLOF. These occur when a melting glacier, which then bursts, creates a glacial lake. Around 25 glacial lakes in the Himalayas are dangerously full and at risk of flooding populated areas, potentially risking not only homes and lives, but also the devastation of Nepal's tourism industry.

Nepal mountaineer and climate campaigner Dawa Steven Sherpa has said that his country is the 'canary in the mine shaft' of climate change, with the effects of global warming such as melting glaciers and changing weather patterns being felt faster and quicker there than elsewhere. The Everest meeting also announced three new conservation areas that will increase the number of national parks in Nepal and help secure the future of the Eastern Himalayan landscape.

"The importance of these newly protected areas is that they start to fill in the gaps on the conservation map. Plants and animals do not recognize national or political boundaries and are often restricted to smaller areas than is ideal. This announcement is a really positive step in linking up these separate areas to a size that makes sense for wildlife.

Saving a Bhutan lake

The first phase of an international project to reduce the risk to a Bhutan valley from the threatening bursting of a growing and increasingly unstable glacial lake emphasis sing the huge costs of climate change adaptation in the Himalayas.

Thorthormi Tsho is a glacial lake perched precariously at 4428 meters above sea level in the remote Lunana area of northern Bhutan Rated as one of Bhutan's likeliest future catastrophes, a breach and flood through Thorthormi Tsho's unstable moraine walls would almost certainly spill into the also vulnerable Raphsthreng Tsho 80 meters below, with the combined flood suddenly releasing up to 53 million cubic meters of water and debris into the upper catchments of the Po Chu river.

This could damage crops and livestock over more than half of the fertile and economically critical Punakha and Wangdi valleys destroy a vital bridge and roads, damage to hydropower facilities under construction and threaten 16 historic monuments. A large effort by the government, communities and WWF, supported by the Global Environment Facility (GEF), the United Nations Development Program (UNDP) and the Austrian Coordination Bureau this year succeeded in lowering the lake level by 86 cm, in the first phase of a project intended to artificially lower the water level at Thorthormi Lake by 5 meters in 3 years. 'The Cost of Climate Change: The Story of Thorthormi Glacial Lake in Bhutan' is a WWF report on the project and the growing risk to Himalayan nations by glacial lake outburst events.[12]

Impact of Coastal Area in Ireland

On a global level, coasts comprise 20 percent of the Earth's surface, yet they host a significant portion of the entire human population (approximately 50

---

[12]People and Planet Net, December 4, 2009

percent of human population live within 200 km of the coast (UN, 2002). Coastal ecosystems are highly productive containing high biological diversity, rich fishery resources and significant seabed minerals. Coasts also support a diverse array of related industries (e.g. fisheries and aquaculture, tourism, shipping, oil and gas industries), which provide enormous economic productivity. However, the shared demands placed by densely populated coastal regions impose stresses on finite coastal systems and resources.

For example, at a global level, 48 percent of fish stocks are fully exploited and 28 percent are depleted, overexploited or recovering (FAO, 2001). Water quality is impacted by pollution from ships and pollution from land-based sources (e.g. intensification of agricultural practices contributes to the impact of nutrient loading and eutrophication of estuaries and bays). Fossil fuels continue to exacerbate global climate changes with severe consequences for coastal ecosystems and coastal inhabitants.

Connolly et al., (2001)[13] have studied the impacts of the coastal area as follows:

Coastal Development: Developmental pressure on the coastal area continues as a result of social and economic driving forces such as urban expansion, retirement, second homes and the tourism industry. For example, coastal tourism has led to increases in the numbers of marinas, golf courses and residential buildings near the coast. There is insufficient information by which to judge the current rate and long term environmental implications of coastal development.

---

[13]Connolly N. et al (2001), "Assessment of Human Activity in Coastal Zone", University of Wales under Maritime Ireland

Coastal Agriculture: Agriculture has been identified as the biggest source of pollution in Irish rivers and lakes, which has implications for coastal water quality. Intensive agriculture in Ireland has also led to a reduction in semi-natural habitats and to a decrease in biological diversity.

Coastal Erosion and Flooding: It is now recognized that the regional impacts of climate change are becoming more severe. Climate studies in CMRC and the Department of Geography, University College Cork, indicate that increased impacts from storminess are likely to be significant for Ireland. If sea level rises in tandem with greater and more frequent storms, coastal flooding and erosion problems will become exacerbated in vulnerable coastal areas.

Tourism and Recreational Use: Coastal tourism depends on the quality and diversity of the coastal environment; increases in tourist numbers have been shown to threaten areas of high ecological and resource value in our coastal marine environment. Furthermore, tax relief on property investment schemes aimed at generating economic activity in seaside resorts (Section 48) has resulted in increased ad hoc development without significantly boosting tourism revenues in coastal locations.

Coastal Industry, Ports and Harbours: Many chemical and pharmaceutical industries are based on the coast, particularly in Cork Harbour and the Shannon Estuary. Major ports are located in Dublin, Cork, Shannon-Foynes and Belfast. Demand for port expansion has resulted in loss of various habitats in harbours around the country. There is increased competition between leisure activities and commercial shipping in ports. Maintenance dredging in ports can also lead to disturbance and dispersal of contaminated sediments.

Fishing and Aquaculture Industry: Serious concerns exist regarding the sustainability of our fisheries. Some fish stocks have been seriously over fished including cod and whiting from the Irish Sea. Some coastal communities have diversified by developing aquaculture industries (particularly along the coasts of Donegal, Mayo, Galway, Kerry and Cork). Aquaculture activities are set to increase by 300 percent from 2000 to 2015. Developments in aquaculture need to be balanced with requirements for protecting coastal habitats. Loss of seascape due to the silting of aquaculture installations can cause potential conflict with the tourism industry.

Water Quality: Direct discharges into Irish coastal waters include urban wastewater, domestic sewage and industrial (trade effluent) inputs. Non-source discharges such as agricultural run-off are also known to have a detrimental effect on water quality.

Offshore Resources: If not carefully managed, exploitation of our offshore oil and gas reserves can have negative impacts on the coastal regions where the reserves are brought ashore, through loss of landscape and seascape because of terminal developments, to potential for pollution as a result of accidental spills. Demands for sand and gravel for the construction industry have extended to offshore resources.

The location of wind farm sites is being considered, particularly off the east coast. The potential impacts of such offshore developments may include impacts on herring spawning grounds, salmon migratory routes, migratory birds and cetaceans.

Man versus Nature

No water, no future; no food, no future; no energy, no future; no environment, degraded future. Thus might one with a penchant for the pithy explain the nexus between these essentials and the gravity of the emergent global crisis? The world is indeed entering an era of scarcity. Water, food, energy and the environment have got intertwined in a spiral of decline and degradation. The challenge is to slow the spin and reverse the direction. How and through whom, is the question? The present structures of decision-making and governance do not facilitate strategies that are holistic and which adequately address such interrelationships.

Water faces an endemic global shortage. One report has estimated that people consume 10 percent more water annually than nature can replenish. Moreover, global warming is melting glaciers and receding snowlines. The impact is visible. Seventy rivers have stopped flowing into the sea; aquifers are depleting and there is mounting concern that water will be a flash point for political, social and economic turmoil.

Food security has also reappeared on the international agenda. Inflation is currently more of a worry than physical availability. There is no one explanation but a contributor has certainly been the 'fuel for food' policies pursued by some governments. In the US for instance, the price of corn has surged because of the incentives provided to farmers to shift to ethanol. Similarly, in parts of Europe and South-East Asia, the quest for bio-fuels has taken land out of the agricultural cycle and altered cropping patterns. Water shortage and salinity has also impacted productivity.

The energy question has seldom been out of the news. But today with North Africa in turmoil and oil prices crossing into triple digits, it is on the front pages. The problem is familiar. Demand is surging, supply is not keeping pace and the environment is under stress. Demand is growing because of increasing population and rising prosperity. China, India and (to a lesser extent) the Middle East are the drivers of this demand growth. Supply, on the other hand, is under pressure. Coal is an abundant resource but it is a dirty fuel; it faces infrastructure bottlenecks and is not a substitute for gasoline and diesel – the transportation fuels that account for 60% of total energy consumption. Oil is also not in short supply but it is no longer easily accessible. The 'era of easy oil' has in effect ended. This means that whilst new large accumulations are available they are mostly in harsh and logistically complex regions (viz deep offshore, Siberia, the Arctic) and as such difficult to locate, and once located, problematic to develop on a commercial basis. Renewable energy – nuclear, solar, wind and bio – has undoubted potential but it faces (currently) the hurdle of competitiveness and infrastructure. Renewable cannot be scaled up unless and until the existing distribution and transmission infrastructure is radically overhauled ('smart' grids, redesigned retail pumps etc). Renewable also do not offer a credible and competitive transportation fuel.

The fourth leg of this quadrilateral conundrum is environment. It is impacted by everything that happens in the other three sectors and they in turn impact it. There is an inextricable linkage. The gravity of the crisis stems from the fact that the natural balance between them has been disrupted. Copenhagen and Cancun notwithstanding, most people now accept that unless and until this balance is restored, the reality of sustainable development will remain a chimera.

The question is how. Where in the interstices of public governance are matters like the compounded impact of such an imbalance addressed? Where are questions such as 'What is the full cost-benefit of producing diesel or bio-fuels?' debated? (it takes 9,200 liters of water to produce one liter of diesel; 4,200 liters for one liter of bio-fuels). Where do issues of water and land rights get coalesced? Who in government has accountability for optimizing water and energy usage?

The answer appears to be nowhere and no one. There is no institutional framework that facilitates a coordinated approach. Most governments tend to look at these issues through a narrow compartmentalized eyeglass. In India, for instance, there are separate ministries for food, water, environment and energy. In fact, four ministries (coal, petroleum & natural gas, non-conventional and atomic) handle the energy sector. But the ministries are responsible for major energy consumers: power, steel and fertilizers. Each of these ministries has a political boss; each a phalanx of civil servants, each a set of public sector entities and each a complex of vested interests. Their objective is understandably to protect turf and not to pull together the threads that bind one ministry to another.

The situation clearly demands that strategy be framed within a holistic framework. It requires that institutions be created to enable the execution of such strategy. The problem is that such demands push against conventional wisdom and vested interests. They are therefore difficult to meet. Nature will not, however, wait on man's inertia. The crisis will deepen over time, and unless action is taken, the risks of a 'no-future' future will become alarmingly real.[14]

Conclusion

The industrialized nations emit more CO2 per capita than the developing countries. These developed

---

[14]Vikram Singh Mehta (2011), " Man Versus Nature", The Times of India, February 14, 2011

countries must follow Kyoto protocol first and force the developing countries to follow later. World peace is possible if people live in peace everywhere. The scientific achievements are mis-utilized by the governments and industrialists. The industrialization process has resulted in poisoning air, rising tides, thinning ice, poisoning water, unavailability of drinking water and wide spread of contagious diseases. The rich countries are acting as 'climate villains'. Climate change would result in more human deaths by sunstroke, flood, cyclone, earthquakes, and hail storms. A number of plant and animal species have disappeared from earth and others would follow, if nature were not protected. There should be strict international law and monitoring mechanism to safeguard the environment.

The per capita emission of CO_2 is only 1.75 tons in India as compared to 4 tons (world average) or 10 + developed country average.

Water, food, energy and the environment have got intertwined in a spiral of decline and degradation. The challenge is to slow the spin and reverse the direction. Forest fire or drinking water cannot wait government sanction. Environmental deterioration has to be checked at the earliest period for survival of human beings, other living beings and plant kingdom.

The world organization on **'Saving Earth'** should be the apex organization to safeguard environment. The United States of America, China and India must follow environmental laws.

+++++

Chapter II

ENVIRONMENTAL POLLUTION

Mahatma M K Gandhi had said that nature has enough to satisfy everyone's need but has not enough to satisfy an individual man's greed. Sadly our ever-expanding greed has put us in a precarious situation. In all developing countries, governments have adopted the policy for industrialization, national highways, metal-led village roads, welfare schemes, free gifts, Foreign Direct Investments, and World Bank loan for gaining popularity. Industrialization is not without a price. The policy of industrialization has helped the rich to become richer and the poor become poorer. The disparity has further widened in the Twenty-first century. All these have a direct bearing on environmental pollution leading to climatic change. We, all witness the deleterious effects of climate change. The whole world is now anxious to repair the damage. But what can be done?

The politicians, bureaucrats, industrialists, and contactors are enjoying royal life by maintaining double standards in action and speech. They are neither worried for the hungry people nor the environment.

Unless we check depletion of environment, save forest coverage, allow free air, abundant rainfall, and more area for cultivation, land for construction of houses for expanding population, we cannot achieve a peaceful world. The good environment is the life line of people.

In this chapter, environmental pollution in Baltic Coast, China, India and other countries have been explained. It includes air pollution, river water pollution, ground-water pollution, plastic pollution, environmental pollution, greenhouse gas emission, pesticide as killer and impact of war on environment.

Residents of Baltic Coast Countries fear Pollution

Heini Ahtiainen – a researcher of Greenpeace explains that many residents of the nine countries surrounding the Baltic Sea have concerns about its environment and pollution levels, but deny responsibility.

The Baltic Survey, for which 9,000 residents of Poland, Germany, Lithuania, Denmark, Latvia, Sweden, Estonia, Russia and Finland were interviewed, showed that up to 50 percent of Finns and more than a quarter of Swedes, Latvians and Estonians thought the environment of the Baltic Sea is "very bad" or "rather bad."

The interviewed people expressed concern on issues such as litter, heavy metals and hazardous substances, everyday oil leakages and risk for major oil spill, damage to flora and fauna and algal blooms.

A majority of residents in all countries except Poland and Sweden tended to disagree that they personally affected the condition of the sea.

The residents of countries around the Baltic – 80 percent of who spend leisure time at its shores – believed that increasing charges on emissions was the best way to fund actions to improve the environment.

Increasing pollution fees received more than 50 percent of support in all nine countries.

Over-fished, polluted by agricultural nutrient discharge and uncared for, the Baltic is so toxic that pregnant women should not eat its fish.

Leaders from countries in its vicinity pledged urgent action to generate the "miracle" needed to save the almost landlocked and brackish sea at a summit held in Helsinki earlier this year.[15]

Poor ambient air quality prevails in China

Zhao Weijun (1997), deputy director of the air pollution department of NEPA, expressed that the residents of many of China's largest cities are living under long-term, harmful air quality conditions. China has long recognized air pollution as a critical problem. Ambient concentrations of total suspended particulates (TSP) and sulfur dioxide (SO2) are among the world's highest. In 1995, more than one half of the 88 cities monitored for SO2 were above the World Health Organization (WHO) guideline. All but two of the 87 cities monitored for TSP far exceeded the WHO guideline. Some cities such as Taiyuan and Lanzhou had SO2 levels almost 10 times the WHO guideline.

---

[15]The Independent Environment, China Environment News, October 17, 2010

Largely because of controls at power plants and within households, particulate emissions have not risen as much as might have been expected with the doubling of coal consumption. Overall, particulate emissions in China have remained relatively level since the early 1980s. In fact, in some large cities, ambient particulate concentrations have decreased markedly since the 1980s. In contrast, SO2 emissions have roughly paralleled the increase in coal consumption, reflecting heavy coal burning and inadequate sulfur control measures.

Coal burning - the primary source of China's high SO2 emissions, accounts for more than three quarters of the country's commercial energy needs, compared with 17 percent in Japan and a world average of 27 percent. China's consumption of raw coal has increased annually by 2 percent between 1989 and 1993. Meanwhile, SO2 emissions increased by more than 20 percent and TSP increased by approximately 10 percent. The country is expected to burn 1.5 billion metric tons of coal annually by the year 2000, up from 0.99 billion metric tons in 1990. Without even more dramatic measures to control emissions than are currently in place, the deterioration of air quality seems inevitable.[16]

Pollution in India

India may let power companies start trading renewable-energy credits in May in a push to create a multibillion-dollar market to encourage reductions in greenhouse-gas emissions. The estimates trade in renewable energy credits could rise to as much as $10 billion by 2020. India is pressing ahead with its own efforts to fight climate change after last month's Copenhagen talks failed to reach a new global climate treaty. The move puts the world's fourth-largest

[16]China's Health and Environment: Air pollution and health effects, World Resources Institute

emitter ahead of China and other developing nations in creating a domestic emissions-trading market to boost investment in solar, wind and other clean-energy projects.

India is the second-largest generator of carbon credits in the United Nations Clean Development Mechanism, the world's second-biggest greenhouse-gas trading market. Certified Emissions Credits, or CERs, issued for pollution- cutting projects in India are sold to businesses in Europe and elsewhere seeking to meet either mandatory or voluntary limits.

Mr. Birabhadra Singh, Union Minister of Industries, Government of India is more worried for POSCO and Vedant industries and Orissa Chief Minister Mr. Navin Patnaik has allowed the government machinery to fight on behalf of Vendant industries in the Supreme Court for establishment of mega industries. Why the government pleads for an unknown industrialist at the cost of poor farmers and tribal people, who would be displaced and become nomads? In Orissa, 130 **farmers have committed suicides** for crop failure because of sporadic rain during crop-harvest period in 2010. Climate change has caused heavy loss to the peasants. Farmers' suicides continue in 2011 too because of crop failure and high crop loan outstanding. Most of these deceased farmers had borrowed credit more than 20 thousands of Indian rupees.

Air Pollution

The World Health Organization estimates that about two million people die prematurely every year as a result of air pollution, while many more suffer from breathing ailments, heart disease, lung infections and even cancer. Fine particles or microscopic dust from coal or wood fires and unfiltered diesel engines are rated as one of the most lethal forms or air pollution caused by industry, transport, household heating, cooking and ageing coal or oil-fired power stations.

India is now world's third biggest carbon dioxide emitting nation after China and the US. The new emission data from the United Nations published in early October 2010 is a probable cause of worry for India's climate negotiators at the next round of talks that started in Tianjin in China on October 11, where rich countries are expected to ask India and China to take legally binding emission cuts after 2012, when present global climate treaty expires. Environment Minister Jairam Ramesh said the country could not have high economic growth and a rapid rise in carbon emissions now that the nation was third after China and US.

India and US clean energy pact: India and the U.S. on November 8, 2010 inked an agreement to establish a bilateral energy cooperation programme to promote clean and energy-efficient businesses, Indian and U.S. companies inked joint venture deals worth $175 million in the renewable energy sector.

The US President Barack Obama and Prime Minister Manmohan Singh announced the setting up of Joint Clean Energy Research and Development Centre. The proposed center is part of the Partnership to Advance Clean Energy (PACE), which forms the core of the "green partnership". Funding for the center is expected from national budgets and the private sector. Each government proposes to commit $25 million over the next five years.

A Comprehensive environmental assessment of industrial clusters, undertaken by IIT Delhi and the CPCB, found that the environmental pollution levels in 10 major industrial hubs had reached a "very alarmingly high" level. The World Bank Group has sanctioned two loans worth around 11, 850 million INR environment management projects in India on

July 22, 2010. Of this, 8970 million INR go for the Integrated Coastal Zone Management (ICZM) project and the remaining for Capacity Building for Industrial Pollution Management project.

There are four reasons of air pollution are - emissions from vehicles, thermal power plants, industries and refineries. The problem of indoor air pollution in rural areas and urban slums has increased.

A latest example industrial pollution is the leak of chlorine gas in Mumbai. On July 14, 2010 nearly 76 people were treated in hospital on after chlorine gas leak from an industrial area in Mumbai. The land owned the Mumbai Port Trust mainly uses an industrial area for storage and delivery of cargo and containers.

India's environmental problems are exacerbated by its heavy reliance on coal for power generation. Bikash Sinha professor of the department of atomic energy, on October 6, 2010 said, "More than 80 per cent of energy is produced from coal, a fuel that emits a high amount of carbon and greenhouse gases.

Coal pollution kills more than 300, 000 people every year in India.

Yet the Government of Orissa is continuing with its policy of roping in private players to set up coal-fired power plants in the state. It has signed 30 MOUs with Independent Power Producers (IPPs) to generate electricity in the state. The last three memorandums were signed on January 4, 2011. The state does not bother for air pollution and would like additions of further steel industries and coal-fired industries in future because it has created good understanding with the government of India. What the Environment Department is doing?

Dr. R C Sinha in a five-day workshop on air pollution organized by Patna University's Centre for Environment and Nature Conservation (CENC) on November 28, 2010 pointed out that as many as **800,000 people in Asia** were dying every year due to air pollution. Unprecedented increase in the number of motor vehicles with inferior technology, poor maintenance and inferior quality of fuel has aggravated the problem of air pollution.

T V Jayan says that mosquito coils used in Asia emit carcinogenic chemicals, which is dangerous for human health. It contains cancer-causing substance. A single coil releases particulate matter equal to 75 to 137 cigarettes, which has been published in 'Environmental Health Perspectives' (September 2003 issue). Moreover, windows are closed during sleeping hours. These factors make people (especially children) more vulnerable to the harmful chemicals. Most coils used in the developing world have parathyroid insecticides, particularly dallethrine, as the active ingredient. A chemical compound used as the synergist (called s-2 or octacholorodipropyl) is quite dangerous. Hence, the consumers should switch over to herbal products, which are available in plenty. The neem (Melia Azadirachta) made herbal product is more efficient and good for health and easier on pocket.

Aircraft pollutants

According to a study published in the journal Environmental Science and Technology (EST) in the first week of October 2010, almost 8,000 people will die due to aircraft pollutants this year, and 3,500 of them would be from India and China. Experts say this means people exposed to such pollutants will also suffer from respiratory diseases.

A recent report by Massachusetts Institute of Technology (MIT) researchers says that the harmful pollutants emitted by an aircraft at an altitude of 35,000 ft are fatal for people. The report says that nitrogen and sulphur oxides emitted by aircraft at approximately 35,000 ft combine with other gases in the atmosphere to create noxious particulate matter.

Vehicle emissions are responsible for 70 percent of the country's air pollution. The major problem with government efforts to safeguard the environment has been enforcement at the local level, not with a lack of laws. Air pollution from vehicle exhaust and industry is a worsening problem for India. Exhaust from vehicles has increased eight-fold over levels of twenty years ago; industrial pollution has risen four times over the same period. The economy has grown two and a half times over the past two decades but pollution control and civil services have not kept pace. Air quality is worst in big cities like Kolkata, Delhi, Mumbai, Chennai etc.

According to the Society of Indian Automobile Manufacturers, India's auto production has doubled from 7 million units in fiscal year 2004 to over 14 million units in fiscal year 2010 largely on the back of a buoyant domestic market.

Bangalore: holds the title of being the asthma capital of the country. Studies estimate that 10 per cent of Bangalore's 600 hundred thousand population and over 50 per cent of its children below 18 years suffer from air pollution- related ailments.

Chennai: Exhaust from vehicles, dust from construction debris, industrial waste, burning of municipal and garden waste are all on the rise in the city. So are respiratory diseases, including asthma. At least six of the 10 top causes of death are related to respiratory disease, says Dr. D Ranganathan, director (in-charge), Institute of Thoracic Medicine.

Mumbai: Not only are levels of Suspended Particulate Matter above permissible limits in Mumbai, but the worst pollutant after vehicular emissions has grown at an alarming rate. The levels of Irrespirable Suspended Particulate Matter (RSPM), or dust, in Mumbai's air have continued to increase over the past three years.

The air pollution in Mumbai is so high that Mumbai authorities have purchased 42,000 liters of perfume to spray on the city's enormous waste dumps at Deonar and Mulund landfill sites after people living near the landfill sites complained of the stench. The British first used the Deonar landfill site; one of India's largest, in 1927. Today, the festering pile covers more than 120 hectares and is eight stories high.

Bhopal: Bhopal Gas Tragedy was the greatest industrial disaster in the world that took place at a Union Carbide pesticide plant in the Indian city of Bhopal, Madhya Pradesh. At midnight on 3 December 1984, the plant accidentally released Methyl Iso Cyan-ate (MIC) gas, exposing more than 500,000 people to MIC and other chemicals. The first official immediate death toll was 2,259. The government of Madhya Pradesh has confirmed a total of 3,787 deaths related to the gas release. Others estimate 8,000-10,000 died within 72 hours and 25,000 have since died from gas-related diseases, making it the deadliest man-made environmental disaster in history.

On July 14, 2010 Chlorine gas leaked from the Sewri industrial area on land owned by the Mumbai Port Trust and nearly 76 people were treated in hospital.

The effects of air pollution are obvious: rice crop yields in southern India are falling as brown clouds block out more and more sunlight. And the brilliant white of the famous Taj Mahal is slowly fading to a sickly yellow. In the "Tajmahal Case" a very strong step was taken by Supreme Court to save the Tajmahal being polluted by fumes and more than 200 factories were closed down.

Birds and species affected: Studies conducted by the high altitude zoology field station of the Zoological Survey of India (ZSI) based in Solan town of Himachal Pradesh have recorded a drastic fall in butterfly numbers in the western Himalayas, famous for their biodiversity.

The population of 50 percent of the 288 species recorded in the western Himalayas, comprising areas of Himachal Pradesh and Jammu and Kashmir, have declined more than half in just 10 years,' Avtar Kaur Sidhu, a scientist with the field station, told IANS on World Environment Day 2010. We noticed a large number of dead butterflies on the Khardung La (the world's highest motorable road in Ladakh) during one of our visits. It was primarily due to a rise in vehicular traffic by the tourists,' she said.

Indoor air pollution: Indoor air pollution is the most important cause of chronic obstructive pulmonary disease (COPD) in India, says a prevalence study conducted by Pune-based Chest Research Foundation (CRF) and the Imperial College, London in November 2010. Over 700 million people in India suffer from high levels of indoor air pollution affecting women and young children as 75 per cent homes use biomass fuel like wood, crop residue and dung cakes.

River water Pollution

Contaminated and polluted water now kills more people than all forms of violence including wars, according to a United Nations report released on March 22, 2010 on World Water Day that calls for turning unsanitary wastewater into an environmentally safe economic resource. According to the report titled "Sick Water?" – 90 percent of wastewater-discharged daily in developing countries is untreated, contributing to the deaths of some 2.2 million people a year from diarrhea diseases caused by unsafe drinking water and poor hygiene. It is estimated that at least 1.8 million children die every year from water-related diseases, which are less than 5 years of age.

Fully 80 percent of urban waste in India ends up in the country's rivers, and unchecked urban growth across the country combined with poor government oversight means the problem is only getting worse. A growing number of bodies of water in India are unfit for human use, and in the River Ganges, holy to the 82 percent Hindu majority in India, is dying slowly due to unchecked pollution.

New Delhi's body of water is little more than a flowing garbage dump; with fully 57 percent of the waste finding its way to the River Yamuna. It is that three billion liters of waste are pumped into Delhi's Yamuna River) each day. Only 55 percent of the 15 million Delhi residents are connected to the city's sewage system. The remainder flushes their bath water, wastewater and just about everything else down pipes and into drains, most of them empty into the polluted Yamuna.

According to the Centre for Science and Environment, between 75 and 80 percent of the river's pollution is the result of raw sewage. Combined with industrial runoff, the garbage thrown into the river and it totals over 3 billion liters of waste per day. Nearly 20 billion INR, or almost US $500 million, has been spent on various cleanup efforts.

The frothy brew is so glaring that it can be viewed on Google Earth. Much of the river pollution problem in India comes from untreated sewage. Samples taken recently from the Ganges River near Varanasi show that levels of fecal coli form, a dangerous bacterium that comes from untreated sewage, were some 3,000 percent higher than what is considered safe for bathing.

Groundwater exploitation

Groundwater exploitation is a serious matter of concern today because of legislations and policy measures taken till date by the state governments. Water is a state subject and has not had the desired effect on the situation.

Groundwater Quality and Exploitation is most alarming pollution hazards in India. On April 01, 2010 at least 18 babies in several hamlets of Bihar's Bhojpur district have been born blind in the past three months because their families consume groundwater containing alarming levels of arsenic. The Health Minister of Bihar, Nand Kishore Yadav confirmed the cases of blindness of the newborns in arsenic- affected blocks of the district on Wednesday, 31st March 2010.

'Kids in Punjab villages are losing sights because of polluted drinking water in Fazilka (Punjab)' was published in India Today on August 16, 2010. At Dona Nanka, a village on the Indo-Pak border where children are going blind apparently after drinking contaminated water. At least a dozen children were either born blind or have been gradually losing sight within a few years of birth. It's the same story in several villages nearby. These villages drink groundwater hoisted to the surface by several hand-driven pumps.

The villagers say: **This is what we have been drinking for years. There is no other source from which we can draw clean drinking water. The government, on its part, has simply painted**

warnings on the walls of houses that the groundwater is unfit for human consumption.

Plastic Pollution

Plastic bags, plastic thin sheets and plastic waste are also major sources of pollution. A division bench of Allahabad High Court, comprising Justice Ashok Bhushan and Justice Arun Tandon, in May 03, 2010 had directed the Ganges Basin Authority and the state government to take appropriate action to ban the use of polythene in the vicinity of Ganges in the entire state. Also Plastic Bag Pollution in the country is the biggest hazards. On August 2, 2010, seeking to know whether a fine should be imposed on paan masala or gutkha packet manufacturers for polluting and choking the drainage systems, the Supreme Court has directed the Union government to file its reply in six weeks.

Municipal solid waste

India's urban population slated to increase from the current 330 million to about 600 million by 2030, the challenge of managing municipal solid waste (MSW) in an environmentally and economically sustainable manner is bound to assume gigantic proportions. The country has over 5,000 cities and towns, which generate about 40 million tonnes of MSW per year today. Going by estimates of The Energy Research Institute (TERI), this could well touch 260 million tonnes per year by 2047.

Municipal solid waste is solid waste generated by households, commercial establishments and offices and does not include the industrial or agricultural waste. Municipal solid waste management is more of an administrative and institutional mechanism failure problem rather than a technological one. Until now, MSW management has been considered to be almost the sole responsibility of urban governments, without the participation of citizens and other stakeholders.

The Centre and the Supreme Court, however, have urged that this issue be addressed with multiple stakeholder participation. Cities in India spend approximately 20 percent of the city budget on solid waste services.

Pollution due to Mining

New Delhi-based Center for Science and Environment (CSE) on December 29, 2007 said mining was causing displacement, pollution, forest degradation and social unrest. According to the Centre for Science and Environment (CSE) report the top 50 mineral producing districts, as many as 34 fall under the 150 most backward districts identified in the country.

The CSE report has made extensive analysis of environment degradation and pollution due to mining, wherein it has said, in 2005-06 alone 1.6 billion tonnes of waste and overburden from coal, iron ore, limestone and bauxite have added to environment pollution. With the annual growth of mining at 10.7 per cent and 500-odd mines awaiting approval of the Centre, the pollution would increase manifold in the coming years.

The mines of Mahanadi Coal Fields and NTPC draw about 250 million liters of water per day from the River Brahmani and in return they release thousands of gallons of wastewater, which contains obnoxious substances like Ash, Oil, Heavy Metals, Grease, Fluorides, Phosphorus, Ammonia, Urea and Sulphuric Acid into the River Nandira (A tributary of River Brahmani). The effluents from chlorine plant cause chloride and sodium toxicity to the river Rushikulya – the lifeline of southern Orissa. The Phosphoric Fertilizer Industry discharges effluents containing Nitric acid, Sulphuric acid and Phosphoric acids into the river Mahanadi.

Death has lost its sting in parts of Rajasthan. In neighbouring Shriji Ka Kheda, which falls in Bhilwara district, **more than 70 people from 60 families** have died in the past decade of silicosis caused by inhalation of dust containing free crystalline silica due to stone mining. The stone mining causes several occupational diseases such as pneumoconiosis, silicosis, tuberculosis, asbestosis and asthma but poor people come for engagement in stone – mining projects for a living. Their abject poverty keeps driving villagers for illegal mining. Rajasthan is the largest producer of dimensional stones in the country. The state produces 50 million tonnes of stones a year.

An aluminum refinery in Orissa blithely continues to pollute the surrounding villages, despite the recommendations of the Supreme Court's Central Empowered Committee that it be closed since it poses environmental and health hazards. Rengopalli, Red Mud pond, and the refinery's alkaline waste disposal have created havoc in all bauxite plants.

Red Mud is the final waste product from bauxite. A ton of toxic waste is dumped for every ton of alumna produced in the refinery. The Red Mud pond is built for the refinery's alkaline waste disposal.

In Jharkhand there are abundant coalmines; most of the coalmines are situated in Hazaribag, Chatra, Palamau, Rajmahal, Dhanbad and Ranchi district. Mighty Damodar River and its tributaries flow through these coalmines. Due to extensive coal mining, coal deposits in open field and vigorous growth of industries in these districts have contaminated all water resources.

Due to large scale illegal mining in Orissa, Jharkhand, Bihar, Chhatisgarh and in the Aravalli hills Range in Rajasthan and Haryana state, the forest cover has been depleted 90 percent and drying up wells and affecting agriculture. The governments remain silent in these years. Due to media and public protest the Supreme Court on February 20, 2010 directed cancellation of 157 mining leases operating in Rajasthan's eco-sensitive Aravalli Hills.

On August 24, 2010 the Ministry of Environment and Forest (MoEF) **has rejected permission for the Anil Agarwal promoted Vedanta mining project in Orissa. In a statement, the Ministry has said, "the forest clearance for Vedanta stands rejected".**

But Anil Agrawal is making vigorous attempt to acquire 8,000 acres of seacoast land on the Bay of Bengal to start a Vendant University. The Government of Orissa has shown excess interest in the matter and has appealed the Supreme Court of India against the Orissa High Court judgement. But two Supreme Court Justices have opted out of Vendant Varsity case. They are Justice A K Ganguly and Justice A. K. Patnaik.

(a) Justice A K Ganguly recused from hearing the appeal when it came up for hearing before a bench headed by Justice G S Singhvi on January 21, 2011.
(b) On January 5, 2011, Justice A K Patnaik' recusal led to the hearing being deferred by a fortnight
(c) On November 16, 2010, Orissa High Court set aside acquisition of nearly 8000 acres on the Puri- Konark stretch on the seacoast of Bay of Bengal.

Why the industrialists are so much worried to start mega industries and mega universities in a state, where the number of Maoists, Naxalites and Terrorists is increasing each day? Where farmers are committing suicides for crop loss owing to unpredicted climate? Each day the newspapers cover mass rally, farmer's suicides, corruption news and road closed by Naxalites. Why the elected governments at New Delhi and Bhubaneswar are forcing the peasants to surrender land to industrial houses? The climate is changed and the state marches towards desertification and diseases.

On January 22, 2011, the Government of Orissa shut down 23 mines in Joda area in Keonjar district (Orissa) because the companies could not produce required information, such as environment and forest clearance. Unauthorized mining in Orissa is possible through kickbacks with government knowledge. So pollution, corruption, smuggling and theft of minerals are the root causes of forest devastations and climate change.

The Saxena committee accused the Vedanta smelters in Orissa. It has found fault of the government of Orissa for the POSCO Integrated Steel project in Orissa, a mega project of 560 billion INR that is the single-largest foreign direct investment in India. Similarly, the Jindal thermal power plant in Chhattisgarh (100 billion INR), hydroelectric projects on Bhagirathi in Uttarakhand and the Navi Mumbai airport in Maharashtra (79.72 billion INR) have been protested by tribal people of the area. The governments invited all these projects from international industrial houses just after the general elections and were cleared by single window system without consent of people. The POSCO (company) of South Korea faces strong opposition by the farmers of the state. The Vedanta chapter is almost closed for industry and University. The governments are not free from public doubts.

On January 31, 2011, the Ministry of environment and Forest, Government of India again permitted the POSCO to start mega steel industry on the coastal area of the Bay of Bengal that too on low-lying rice fields of poverty stricken peasants with 28 conditionality's and a port with 32 conditionality's within the limits of Paradip port. Who would protect the seacoast, rice fields and poor peasants? Agitations have already started in the area.

Pollution due to biomedical waste is likely to spread disease dangerous to life and making atmosphere noxious to health. In early April 2010 a machine from Delhi University containing cobalt-60, a radioactive metal used for radiotherapy in hospitals, ended up in a scrap yard in the city. The death from radiation poisoning of a scrap yard worker in Delhi has highlighted the lax enforcement of waste disposal laws in India. The International Atomic Energy Agency said it was the worst radiation incident worldwide in four years.

India is being used as a dumping ground for hazardous waste from foreign countries.

The officials of Special Intelligence and Investigation Branch attached to the Customs Department recently detained twenty containers with goods. Packs of broken toys, used diapers, empty perfume bottles, used battery cells, thermocol used aluminum foil packing materials and colored surgical gloves were found in the containers. It could also lead to contamination and spread of communicable diseases.

E-Waste Pollution

The UNEP report "Recycling – from E-Waste to Resources" was released on the Indonesian island of Bali on February 22, 2010. The authors highlighted that by 2020 e-waste in South Africa and China will have jumped by 200-400 per cent from 2007 levels and by 500 per cent in India.

India produces about 3, 80,000 tonnes of e-Waste per annum, which includes only the waste generated out of television sets, mobile phones and PCs, a major chunk of which comes from organizations. E-waste produced in India includes over 100,000 tonnes from refrigerators, 275,000 tonnes from TVs, 56,300 tonnes from personal computers, 4,700 tonnes from printers and 1,700 tonnes from mobile phones. The un- organized recycling sector, which fails to practice eco-friendly e-Waste recycling methods release large amount of toxic chemicals. The toxic gases and the large volume of Electronic Waste add environmental pollution in India.

India imports almost 50,000 tonnes of e-waste yearly. It generated 330,000 tonnes of e-waste in 2007 and the number is expected to touch 470,000 tonnes by 2011, according to a study on e-waste assessment conducted jointly by MAIT and the German government's sustainable development body GTZ in April 2010. Till date, there were no definite e-Waste rules in India to regulate the management of e-waste. In September 2009, MAIT, GTZ (German Technical Cooperation Agency), Green peace and Toxics Link, in consultation with all stakeholders, submitted a set of draft rules for e-Waste management to Government of India.

Delhi's air is choking with pollutant PM 2.5 The CSE report claimed that 2010 winter pollution levels are not only high but also different — along with high levels of tiny particles, more pollutants have added to the toxic cocktail. The official air quality index shows several locations in Delhi are reeling under concoction of pollutants like nitrogen and carbon monoxide (CO).Patients complaining of chest and throat infections have shot up in the past two weeks. Experts have blamed high pollution levels in the Capital for this.

Delhi's air is choking with pollutant PM 2.5 that is only 2.5 microns in diameter and is extremely very small particle. Being so small, it escapes emission apparatus prescribed by Euro II and III. Any kind of combustion, especially of vehicular origin, contains this particle. If PM 2.5 is not regulated it will ensure major health hazards. The number of Asthma patients will rise and in future there may huge rise of lung cancer cases also. The toxic value of PM 2.5 is such that metals like lead present in the PM 2.5 get inhaled deeper into lungs, which deposits there. The children are most affected by depositing lead due to inhaling the poisonous air. The increasing amount of PM 2.5 is like a poison in the air we breathe.

Toxic smog is set to engulf Delhi once again this winter after a six-year respite because of the huge number of new cars clogging the roads. New Delhi adds nearly 1,000 new cars a day to the existing four million registered in the city, almost twice as many as before 2000. Pollution levels are up to 350 micrograms per cubic meter in 2006-2007 and the levels of nitrogen oxides have been increasing in the city to dangerous levels, which is a clear sign of pollution from vehicles. Of these it is the diesel cars that are responsible for the pollution. Diesel emissions can trigger asthma and in the long run even cause lung cancer.

A survey by the Central Pollution Control Board and the All India Institute of Medical Sciences survey showed that a majority of people living in Delhi suffered from eye irritation, cough, sore throat, shortness of breath and poor lung functioning. One in 10 people have asthma in Delhi. Worse, the winter months bring respiratory attacks and wheezing to many non-asthmatics who are old, who smoke, have respiratory infections or chronic bronchitis.

Across the national capital and its suburbs, polluted air is killing people, bringing down the quality of life, and leaving people feeling ill and tired.

Greenhouse Gas Emission

India emits the fifth most carbon of any country in the world. At 253 million metric tons, only the U.S., China, Russia, and Japan surpassed its level of carbon emissions in 1998. Carbon emissions have grown nine-fold over the past forty years. In this Industrial Age, with the ever-expanding consumption of hydrocarbon fuels and the resultant increase in carbon dioxide emissions, that greenhouse gas concentration have reached levels causing climate change. Going forward, carbon emissions are forecast to grow 3.2 percent per annum until 2020. To put this in perspective, carbon emissions levels are estimated to increase by 3.9 percent for China and by 1.3 percent for the United States. India is a non-Annex I country under the United Nations Framework Convention on Greenhouse gases and climate change, and as such, is not required to reduce its carbon emissions. An historical summary of carbon dioxide (CO_2) emissions from fossil fuel use in India is increasing rapidly and causes global warming.

All inhabitants of our planet have an equal right to the atmosphere, but the industrialized countries have greatly exceeded their fair, per-capita share of the planet's atmospheric resources and have induced climate change. The most developed countries possess the capital, technological and human resources required for successful adaptation, while in the developing countries, a large proportion of the population is engaged in traditional farming that is particularly vulnerable to the changes in temperature, rainfall and extreme weather events associated with climate change.

According to the UN Framework Convention on Climate Change and the Kyoto Protocol, the most industrialized countries are mainly responsible for causing climate change. Thus equity requires that they should sharply reduce their emissions in order to arrest further climate change and allow other countries access to their fair share of atmospheric resources in order to develop. It is also observed that all countries are rushing for environmental pollution.

Pollution of Indian Seas

Two merchant vessels – MSC Chitra and Khalijia-III collided off the Mumbai coast on August 7, 2010 causing an oil spill. Several containers from one of the vessels fell into the sea. Nearly 100 containers that fell into the waters following the collision between two merchant vessels off the Mumbai coast are still missing and two of them are carrying hazardous chemicals reported on August 17, 2010. Describing the ship collision off the coast of Mumbai as a "freak accident", environment minister Jairam Ramesh said that India has never seen an oil spill like the one resulting from the incident.

A first-ever exercise on March 25, 2010, the country's 7500-km-long coastline will be surveyed to demarcate areas vulnerable to sea erosion, high tide and waves in order to help government take measures in protecting community living in such pockets. The Cabinet Committee of Economic Affairs (CCEA) approved an 11,560 million INR Integrated Coastal Zone Management (ICZM) project, which among other things cover coastline survey, capacity building of the people living near to coast, and demarcation of sensitive and hazardous zones.

The ship Platinum-II arrived in Indian waters on 8 October 2009. The ministry of environment and forests said it inspected Platinum-II and found the ship contained toxic material. The Platinum-II – formerly known as SS Oceanic or the SS Independence – was destined for the Alang ship-breaking yard. It is Asia's largest ship-breaking yard and known as the "graveyard of ships". It said many of the workers tested showed early signs of asbestosis – an incurable disease of the lungs. An unknown ship dumped tons of waste oil into the sea off Goa, creating tar balls that were heaping on Goa's famed beaches September 1, 2010, officials said.

Union Minister for Environment and Forests Jairam Ramesh said on March 13, 2010 at IIT- Powai:

A dedicated satellite would be launched with the support of Indian Space Research Organisation (ISRO) by 2012 to monitor India's greenhouse gas emission. The objective is to study the impact of climate change, fallout of greenhouse gas emissions on the environment by monitoring it through satellite technology. Another satellite for protection and development of the forest cover in India would be ready by 2013. As the forests are getting depleted at a rapid pace elsewhere in the world, there seems to be a need for a satellite.

Environmental Pollution and chronic diseases

In an Indo-US joint workshop, on September 05, 2008 at Chandigarh, Prof S K Jindal said it has been globally recognized that environmental factors have important links with infectious as well as non-infectious diseases of both acute and chronic nature.

The WHO estimates that 24 per cent of global disease burden and 23 per cent of all deaths can be attributed to environmental factors. The burden is more on the developing than the developed countries. In developing countries, an estimated 42 per cent of acute lower respiratory infections are caused by environmental factors. The major burden of these hazards is borne by the lungs. Bronchial Asthma and other allergies; chronic obstructive lung disease, respiratory infections including tuberculosis and occupational lung diseases are some of the common problems with a strong environmental risk which, account for a large disease burden all over the world, including in India. There is a need for extensive studies to gauge the effects of environmental factors on the human health.

According to New England Journal of Medicine, 2007, even a short exposure to traffic fumes can increase your chances of Heart Disease, including heart attack. People who exercise in areas where there is heavy traffic may be especially at risk. Lifestyle, environmental changes, and growing pollution are the major causes for the incidence of rising strokes among the youngsters.

This gaseous air-pollutant along with other noxious gases emitted from the burning of firecrackers on the eve of Diwali or Holi festival aggravates the risk of triggering an attack in 30-minute asthmatics in India and also has the potential to cause new cases of asthma.[17]

Vector-borne Diseases on the Rise in India

As clean water continues to remain out of the reach of villagers in remote areas in the country, it was not surprising that four outbreaks of acute diarrhoea or gastroenteritis were reported from villages of States like Orissa, Bihar and Gujarat during the past 30 days. Spread by drinking focally contaminated water, cholera is an acute diarrhoea illness caused by the bacterium Vibrio cholera infecting the intestine. Rapid dehydration and shock in severe cases can lead to death within hours. Even as three deaths due to Congo fever in Gujarat brought to the fore new lethal virus waiting to attack human beings, the country dealt with at least 13 outbreak of vector borne diseases such as measles, malaria and viral Hepatitis across the States in the past 30 days alone that struck 639 persons and claimed seven lives.

---

[17] News papers published in India

Much to the concern of the health authorities, it was for the first time that air respiratory illness was reported among children in Dharachula block of Dehradun in Uttarakhand. According to the Integrated Disease Surveillance Project (IDSP) of the Union Health Ministry two kids have died while five are under surveillance. In Barnala district of Punjab alone maximum number of 247 patients got affected following the outbreak of deadly Hepatitis A & E in four villages namely Kalalan, Chananwal, Chiniwal and Sahjera reported early December last year.

Cholera outbreak was declared in Orissa on January 2 when at least 20 people from village Chandanpuri in Puri district were admitted in hospital for its treatment after they fell ill due to consumption of contaminated water. The situation is stated to be under control.

Similarly in Sandhidhar in Junagadh, Gujarat, 97 people fell ill due to suffering from diarrhoea disease reported on 29 December 2010 and 16 persons in village Navapara of Namarda in Bihar. In Jorhat in Assam, one person died due to cholera while five were declared ill during the period from December 2010 to January 9 this year, according to the IDSP which has noted that Hepatitis-C cases were already prevalent in these villages.

Most of these cases were in the age group of 15-60 years. In Araria in Bihar, deadly chickenpox reared its ugly head with 32 persons hospitalized for the viral disease, but much to the relief of authorities no deaths were reported due to the disease that was reported on December 30, 2010.

In Gujarat's Patan, food poisoning cases were reported, affecting 60 persons. They had reportedly consumed contaminated seeds of Jatropa (Ratanjyot) tree. In the Nawarangpur district of the State too, food poisoning claimed three lives while 16 were given medical treatment.

During the period, Assam and West Bengal battled against deadly measles, which is among the world's most contagious diseases and one of the leading causes of death among children in India.

A total 26 persons were inflicted with measles in Amreli (9 children) and Darjeeling (17) districts respectively in Assam and West Bengal. Like in Punjab, in Kerala's Palakkad district too, Viral Hepatitis-A made its presence felt, though it was not as serious -with 21 people falling ill to the disease. The situation is stated to be under control.

A gas-poisoning outbreak was reported from Barrackpore in the North 24 Parganas district in West Bengal which killed one and 70 people taken seriously ill after inhaling toxic ammonia gas that leaked following a cylinder burst in an ice-making factory.[18]

Pesticides as Killers

The fact is that 18, 000 workers in agriculture die every year from pesticide poisoning.

Many workers exposed to pesticides, put themselves at risk of cancers and neurological problems. Pesticides can harm those who work with or around chemicals. Now days, peasants commit suicides in India through pesticides, when they are over-burdened with bank loans or crop failure.

Organo-phosphates and other pesticides affect most children causing birth defects, cognitive impairment and behavioral problems and possibly leukemia. Pesticides may contribute to higher rates of autism in

---

[18]Archana Jyoti, "Vector-borne Diseases on the Rise in India", The Pioneer January 24, 2011

recent years. Human exposure to pesticides can also cause liver damage, Parkinson's, prostate cancer, breast cancer, infertility, immune deficiency, and more.

Exposure to harmful pesticides is also harmful and causes greater risk through inhaling. The pesticides sprayed from planes will be able to travel easily through the air and the district. The chemicals can also pollute both water and land outside the business. This is one of many reasons that the use of pesticides should be prohibited. In occasional cases farmers should be permitted to use insecticides with the knowledge of the farm scientists. Insecticides and pesticides cause leukemia. The risks of exposure to pesticides must be advertised and people need to stop when it comes to the rationalization of public safety. There is a clear choice.

Those of us see if we need to be exposed to pesticides to make responsible decisions for our safety and health of our children. And 'our conscious decision here in our responsibility and take care of us. Suddenly, it was purchased strawberries at the supermarket does not seem so attractive. The next time you know to buy the Organic and subsequent island. Yes, they are not for sale, and yes, do something more than the average costs for the federal government, but you will be surprised if you eat some really tired and feel. They are what they tasted a real strawberry makes you remember when you were a child. Will it be fully satisfied and much healthier?

A global ban was proposed in October at the Stockholm Convention on Persistent Organic Pollutants, held at Geneva. Over 68 countries have already prohibited the use of this insecticide. But our Government seems reluctant to clamp down on its production and use, apparently under pressure from manufacturers since India is one of the world's biggest producers and consumers of Endo-sulfan. Use of the chemical, sprayed mainly on grains, fruits, vegetables, and tea, coffee, tobacco and cotton plants is prohibited in Kerala but the campaign for a nation-wide ban is mounting. Environmentalists, who blame the alarming decline in the number of vultures, to ingestion of this pesticide by the carrion birds, also support the campaign.

Organic farming is a viable, healthy option, as it was in the past, when natural fertilizers and insecticides, derived from cow dung, urine, neem oil, neem cake and diverse non-toxic sources were used, as they still are by those who cannot afford agrochemicals and prefer traditional methods and knowledge. The Bhopal gas leak disaster could have been pre-empted had the Union Carbide pesticides factory not been built. However, with cash-rich transnational agrochemicals and seeds corporations shaping agricultural policies, the cry to go organic is unlikely to be heard by pliable policy-makers. Now, agricultural exports strictly encourage fruits produced through non-use of pesticides and insecticides. Organic food is free of pesticides. Food-Bio is the only way to the vitamins and minerals that occur naturally in foods preserved. The governments all over world should popularize organic food.

Invasive alien species

Invasive alien species are species whose introduction and/or spread outside their natural habitats threaten biological diversity. They occur in all groups, including animals; plants, fungi, bacteria and viruses, and can affect all types of ecosystems. They can directly affect human health. Infectious diseases are often traced to invasive alien species. It can be imported by travelers or vectored by exotic species of birds, rodents and insects. It also has indirect health effects on humans as a result of the use of pesticides and herbicides, which pollute water and soil. The biggest casualty of such species has been our rich biodiversity, and threats to food security.

Mikania Micrantha is of the most prominent invasive aliens in India. It is a major threat in many parts of the country, it grows 8 to 9 cm a day and muzzles small plants and chokes larger trees such as coconut and oil palm.

Parthenium is a poisonous plant. It now occupies 10 million hectares of land in the country and has become a major health hazard for people and animals.

Prosopis Juliflora was introduced in India in last century as a very promising species for the forestation of dry and degraded land. But now it has emerged as a noxious invader that can grow in diverse ecosystems, enable it to wipe out other plant species in its surroundings.

Allegations against Bt. Brinjal (A vegetable)

The latest scientific analysis on the bio-safety of Bt Brinjal conducted by toxicology and epidemic expert Dr Lou Gallagher shows that the food safety studies were not conducted in accordance with the published standards and ignored toxic end points for rats fed Bt Brinjal.

The report also viewed that the rats' experienced organ and system damage including ovaries, spleen and white blood cells and even toxic effect to the liver.

The scientists and regulators who are taking decision on behalf of the consumers of India do not have long-term vision for substantial development. The scientific study is biased because the genetically modified (GM) crop investors fund the scheme. Hence, the State Government should enact bio-safety legislation at the

State level so that its Constitutional right and responsibility in the matter is upheld.

Soil Pollution: Causes and Effects

Soil pollution is one of the gravest problems existing on the earth. The earth itself is getting contaminated and polluted. The conquest of utilizing land and soil resources and conducting experiments on it is for our benefits. But it certainly is not, at the cost of its health and wellness. Mankind has been trying out several different things and has made several arrangements in the soil, to make life happy and comfortable. However, how often have we thought of contamination of soil?

Soil pollution is defined or can be described as the contamination of soil of a particular region. Soil pollution mainly is a result of penetration of harmful pesticides and insecticides, which on one hand serve whatever their main purpose is, but on the other hand, bring about deterioration in the soil quality, thus making it contaminated and unfit for use. Insecticides and pesticides are not to be blamed alone for soil pollution, but there are many other leading causes of soil pollution too.

What Causes Soil Pollution?

Soil pollution is a result of many activities and experiments done by mankind and some of the leading soil pollution causes are discussed below.

(a) Industrial wastes, such as harmful gases and chemicals, agricultural pesticides, fertilizers and insecticides are the most important causes of soil pollution.
(b) Ignorance towards soil management and related systems.
(c) Unfavorable and harmful irrigation practices.

(d) Improper septic system and management and maintenance of the same.
(e) Leakages from sanitary sewage.
(f) Acid rains, when fumes released from industries get mixed with rains.
(g) Fuel leakages from automobiles, that gets washed away due to rain and seep into the nearby soil.
(h) Unhealthy waste management techniques, which are characterized by release of sewage into the large dumping grounds and nearby streams or rivers.

The intensity of all these causes on a local or regional level might appear very small and you may argue that soil is not harmed by above activities if done on a small scale! However, thinking globally, it is not your region or my place that will be the only sufferer of soil pollution.

In fact, it is the entire planet and mankind that will encounter serious problems, as these practices are evident almost everywhere in the world. Want to know what are those problems, which can turn more serious in the near future?

What are the Effects of Soil Pollution?

The effects of pollution on soil are quite alarming and can cause huge disturbances in the ecological balance and health of living creatures on earth. Some of the most serious soil pollution effects are mentioned below.

(a) Decrease in soil fertility and therefore decrease in the soil yield. Definitely, how can one expect a contaminated soil to produce healthy crops?
(b) Loss of soil and natural nutrients present in it. Plants also would not thrive in such a soil, which would further result in soil erosion.

(c) Disturbance in the balance of flora and fauna residing in the soil.
(d) Increase in salinity of the soil, which therefore makes it unfit for vegetation, thus making it useless and barren.
(e) Generally crops cannot grow and flourish in a polluted soil. Yet if some crops manage to grow, then those would be poisonous enough to cause serious health problems in people consuming them.
(f) Creation of toxic dust leading is another potential effect of soil pollution.
(g) Foul smell due to industrial chemicals and gases might result in headaches, fatigue, nausea, etc. in many people.
(h) Soil pollutants would bring in alteration in the soil structure, which would lead to death of many essential organisms in it. This would also affect the larger predators and compel them to move to other places, once they lose their food supply.[19]

Impact of War on Environment

Dead and wounded soldiers and citizens have always been the true currency of war. But another of war's consequences -- and sometimes its cause -- is the destruction of natural resources; the two go hand in hand. In 2001, the United Nations declared November 6 "International Day for Preventing the Exploitation of the Environment in War and Armed Conflict." It is a day to reflect on the massive damage done to ecosystems during war -- damage that can last well beyond the duration of the conflict itself.[20]

Through our work in the Horn of Africa and elsewhere, the Women's Refugee Commission is all

---

[19]Buzzle. Com

[20]Erin Patrick, "When War stops, the impact on the environment live on", Huffington Post, November 4, 2011

too familiar with the serious, negative impacts of conflict and displacement on the environment. Conflict produces refugees, and when gathered together in large numbers they put extra strain on already stressed resources. The marginal, semi-arid lands where so many displaced persons' camps are located may have been able to effectively support their small dispersed resident populations in the past. However, sudden large concentrations of people living in the crowded camps that emerge during conflict or after natural disasters can rapidly deplete the land's carrying capacity and make it difficult for the environment to recover.

Safe, sustainable access to cooking fuel is of particular concern. Cooking fuel is not provided on any measurable scale in most humanitarian emergencies, and thus women and children are forced to forage for firewood on their own, which can have a devastating impact on the environment. For example, refugees fleeing the Rwandan genocide in the 1990's collected an estimated 1,200 tons of firewood each day, causing permanent deforestation in Tanzania and other host countries. Years of collecting firewood and shelter material (timber and thatch as well as fired mud bricks) by both displaced and host communities in Darfur has also taken a visible toll on the environment, with few or no trees remaining in vast swaths of the region. To find firewood, women and children are forced to travel ever-greater distances -- as far as 10 miles outside of their camps -- which puts them at high risk of attack.

It is so dire in Darfur that in many cases women have resorted to digging holes in areas where trees used to be, in the hope of being able to pull up a root they can burn for fuel. In addition to the physical toll of such hard labor, this complete stripping of natural resources hinders the possibility for reforestation in the long run.

In Kenya, where forest cover has been reduced from 12 percent 50 years ago to 1.7 percent today, we've interviewed women who have lived in the Dadaab refugee camps for over 20 years and have watched trees disappear in an ever-widening circle. They are forced to travel farther and farther every year to find any wood. The massive influx of new refugees from the famine in Somalia is only exacerbating the problem.

Clearly a new approach is needed to protect the environment and the women and children at risk. The first step should be to support the direct provision of cooking fuel in emergencies -- including sustainably harvested firewood where necessary -- to help decrease the unsustainable and often unsafe collection of firewood. Non-wood shelter construction materials, such as unfired soil blocks, should also be promoted whenever feasible.

In the longer term, the environmental field should play a lead role in developing and promoting both fuel-saving devices, such as cook stoves, and alternatives to firewood, such as briquettes or gas-based fuels. When firewood must be collected because alternatives do not exist or are not feasible, local environmental workers should ensure that it is done in the most sustainable way possible, by teaching sustainable harvesting techniques and introducing controls on the frequency or location of firewood collection. They should also develop and promote environmental protection and conservation activities, such as planting woodlots and undertaking reforestation programs in tandem with local governments and environmental authorities. Taking these actions can play an important role in protecting women and children -- and the environment in which they live.

Reduce pollution

(a) **Green Court launched**: India launched a **"green" court** on October 19, 2010 to make polluters pay damages as it steps up its policing of the country's environmental laws. Environment Minister said: India was only the third country in the world after Australia and New Zealand to set up such a tribunal. This is the first body of its kind (in India) to apply the polluter pays principle and the principle of sustainable development. Anybody and everybody can approach the tribunal to claim civil damages arising out of inadequate implementation of environment laws, who has been carving out a reputation as a green crusader. He further insisted that India's desire for fast economic growth must not come at the expense of the environment.

(b) **National Action Plan on Climate Change:** The Centre has made a provision of **250 trillion INR** to mitigate the effects of climate change, a serious problem that India will face in the coming decades. The Minister of State for Environment and Forests told the Upper House in Parliament on August 21, 2010 that the Finance Ministry has also sanctioned **50 trillion INR** as recommended by the 13th Finance Commission to tackle this serious problem. About 220 scientists from 120 research institutions were working on assessing the impact of climate change on agriculture, water, health and forests. The research covered the impact on the Himalayan glaciers, the northeast, the Western Ghats and coastal areas. The increased pollution levels associated with industrialization and urbanization, a number of proactive steps have been proposed in the Union Budget (2010/11).[21]

Gits 4 U COM / Environmental Pollution in India / Ministry of Environment and Forests / United Nations Environment Program / Asian Brown Cloud / Pollution and Society / Carbon dioxide Charts[21]

The major steps include: National Clean Energy Fund (NCEF) for funding research and innovative projects in clean energy technology. Allocation for National Ganga (Ganges) River Basin Authority has been doubled in 2010-11 to 5 billion INR (Indian Rupees). The "Mission Clean Ganga 2020" under the National Ganga River Basin Authority (NGRBA) with the objective that no untreated municipal sewage or industrial influent will be discharged into the national river has already been initiated.

Relaxation of sitting criteria will legalize the illegal actions of stone crushers and will invite air pollution closer to habitation. In most of the states the sitting criteria remains still harder and because the units are not complying to the sitting criteria, change in sitting criteria to suit the units will not yield in betterment of environment. Also the previous action of OSPCB in issuing closure notice and sealing of the unit was upheld by Orissa High Court in its order dated 27th January 2009, hence the Pollution Control Board should not make its stand weaker by further diluting the sitting criteria.[22]

Conclusion

The government must be determined to curb pollution, climate change, air pollution and water pollution by legislation and action. For example, the Delhi state government allows encroachment of Yamuna riverbed and flood plains in violation of all green laws and court directives. The location of Asian Games village, Delhi Transport Corporation bus depot, residential buildings and Metro mall are recently created in ecologically sensitive area. The Delhi government did it in spite of objections raised by irrigation specialists and citizens. The myopic and

[22] Shankar Pani, "Pollution by Stone Crushing", Meria News, March 9, 2010

irresponsible policy makers are responsible for continuing devastation of the Yamuna environment. In heavy rains, the river water would enter to low-lying areas and pollute the river water.

The Ministry of Environment and Forest should not allow industry or township or permanent structures that create environmental hazards. The Ministry should examine the proposal thoroughly before it finally allows. In no case temporary permission for construction or temporary permits for mining should be awarded. It causes resentments, uprisings, and loss of peace and causes heavy kickbacks in the project. It was thought that individuals hide mistakes and the governments are as clean as sunlight; but the elected governments in all developing countries are more corrupt, partisan and wicked than an average citizen.

It is because corruption rules the state, government and people. There should not be any mining leases. It controls politics, elections and governments. The government should undertake mining by creating a number of Mining Corporations and sell minerals at market prices on weight-basis and all payments must be accepted through bank transactions. It cannot abandon corruption totally but can certainly check corruption.

The polluting industries must be denied permission to operate. Forests should not be privatized. The villagers in the forest areas should be shareholders in forest management. The villagers would watch the forests and they would receive 25 percent of sale price of log of woods sold in open auction.

+++++

Chapter – III

CLIMATE CHANGE

The earth, the air, the land and the water are not an inheritance from our forefathers but on loan from our children. So we have to hand over to them at least it was handed over to us.

Mahatma M. K. Gandhi

Climate change is already affecting the world's poorest countries – from increased frequency and severity of flooding in Bangladesh to changing rainfall patterns across Africa, bringing drought and crop failures to countries like Ethiopia, Kenya and Sudan. As well as being hit first, the poorest are also hit hardest because they are less equipped to cope with the effects of climate change. With a 2 degree increase in temperature we could see: Increased weather variability, more frequent and intense extreme events, and greater exposure to coastal storm surges would lead to a much higher risk of catastrophic and irreversible impacts.

Climate change impacts individual species as well as the entire food chain. Since different species react to climate change in different ways, the natural cycles of interdependent creatures - such as birds, and the insects they feed on - may fall out of sync, causing population declines. Climate change could drive more than a quarter of land, animals and plants to extinction. Climate change projected to happen between now and 2050 will place 15 to 37 percent of all species in several biodiversity-rich regions at risk of extinction.

A DFID report predicts that between 100 million and 400 million more people could be at risk of hunger; 1-2 billion more people facing water shortages; a permanent loss of 4-5 percent GDP in Africa and South Asia. That's why international support is needed to help communities adapt to the impacts of climate change and to help countries develop infrastructure that supports growth and withstands future climate instability.

In this chapter, global climate change has been discussed to save the earth from destruction. It includes global warming, climate change, human rights, human rights affected by climate change, the role of United Nations and DFID in mitigating climate change and the necessity of climate policy to safeguard the animal and plant kingdom.

Earth is Getting Warmer

Global warming is a serious problem, but to put all our eggs in the carbon bucket would be foolhardy, especially after two decades of all talk and little action. Mr. Utpal Kumar says that we must protect the earth form destruction,[23]

---

[23] Utpal Kumar (2010), ""Earth is getting warmer but don't just blame CO 2", The Sunday Magazine, Pioneer, Bhubaneswar, August 29, 2010,

More than 1,600 people die in Pakistan's catastrophic floods, which have already affected as many as 12 million people and damaged over 600,000 homes — ironically, the monsoon season is only halfway through. Flood-related incidents in China this year claim nearly 4,000 lives, even as Beijing continues to struggle with rising waters along the Korean borders. Russia witnesses an unbearable temperature of 38 degree Celsius — the highest since records began 130 years ago — leading to scores of summer deaths and, of course, deadly wildfires. New York bakes in a thick tropical heat and humidity, as people line up to buy Air Conditioners and coolers. Back home, cataclysmic mudflow strikes Leh, killing more than 160 people.

Seemingly disconnected, most environmentalists attribute these events to global warming, caused mostly by human excesses. They say the earth has begun to sizzle as rising levels of greenhouse gases trap more and more of the sun's heat in the lower atmosphere. Their contention seemed to have been vindicated recently when sensors from across the world showed that 2010 could end up becoming the hottest year on record.

The global warming phenomenon, according to them, leads to increase in average air and ocean temperatures, melting of snow and ice, and rising sea levels. They also cite a large body of evidence to suggest that climate change increases the number of heat waves and make them longer. Since 1880, for instance, heat waves across Europe have doubled, and are expected to increase five-fold by 2100. Temperatures have also risen by 0.74 degree Celsius in the last century. Though the increase may seem insignificant, it needs to be understood that the difference in temperature between the Ice Age and today is a mere five degree Celsius.

For these environmentalists, the problem began with the Industrial Revolution, which enabled us to use in a big way what energy expert Rochelle Lefkowitz calls "fuels from hell" — coal, oil and natural gas. These fuels come from underground, are exhaustible, emit carbon dioxide (CO2) and other pollutants, and are in sharp contrast to what Lefkowitz calls "fuels from heaven" — wind, hydroelectric, tidal, biomass, and solar power. The latter come from above ground, are renewable, and produce no harmful emissions.

The Industrial Revolution led to urbanization, which in turn paved the way for mindless consumption of energy. From four cities with a population of over a million in 1850 to more than 300 now, the human civilization has come a long way. And, with this has increased our insatiable appetite for energy. If legendary Indian nuclear scientist Homi J. Bhabha is to be believed, half of all the energy consumed in the past 2,000 years has been used in the past 100 years. So, it all turned into a vicious cycle of more people, more development, more buildings and more cars, and thus the need for more coal, oil, and gas to build and power them.

There are, however, others who blame the sun, and not CO2, for global warming. They say that the 4.5 billion-year-old earths has gone through a succession of ice ages and warming periods, and that the medieval world was warm by up to three degree Celsius. Then, there were no glaciers in the tropical Andes, today, they are there. There were Viking farms in Greenland; now, they are under permafrost. There was little ice at the North Pole, so much so that a Chinese naval squadron could sail right rounds the Arctic in 1421; today, it is all frozen. Sami Solanki, a solar physicist, supports their claims when he says that in the past 50 years the sun has been warmer, for longer, than at any time in the past 11,400 years.

There is no doubt that the amount of CO2 in the atmosphere has increased substantially over the past 100 years — from about 280 parts per million to 380.

The critics, however, say that the CO_2 level some 80 million years ago was at least 1,000 parts per million. So, the changes don't necessarily mirror human activity.

They also believe that any overemphasis on CO_2 is misplaced. "CO_2 is not the major greenhouse gas. The major greenhouse gas is water vapour," says Nathan Myhrvold, the former chief technology officer at Microsoft. Incidentally, current climate models don't know how to handle water vapour.

Citing the Pakistan floods, these critics say, they are less the work of climate change, and more due to the fact that forests cover only 5.2 per cent of land in that country. Sarhad Awami Forestry Ittehad, a local NGO, has claimed that in parts of Malakand Agency, Khyber-Pakhtunkhwa, "more than 70 per cent of forests were illegally cut down between 2007 and 2009, when Pakistani Taliban controlled the region". The situation is worse is Sindh province where forests cover only 2.3 per cent of the total land area. Another report in *The Guardian* claims that the flooding has been intense in areas where the timber mafia is active. It states that the force of water dislodged the felled trees stacked in ravines for the purpose of smuggling, thus sweeping away bridges, people and weakening the dam walls along its way.

While taking on the 'traditionalists', these critics look at geophysical phenomenon — volcanoes, sunspots, etc — for understanding the intricacies of climate change. In fact, the connection between volcanoes and climate is hardly a new idea. Anthropologist Stanley Ambrose has argued that about 70,000 years ago a super-volcanic explosion took place at Sumatra's Lake Toba which completely blocked the sun, triggering an Ice Age. In 1784, Benjamin Franklin wrote about volcanic eruptions in Iceland that had caused a particularly harsh winter and cool summer with "constant fog over all Europe and (a) greater part of North America". Also, the massive eruption of Mount Tambora in Indonesia produced 'The Year without a summer' in 1815.

What distinguish a "big-ass volcano" — a term given by Myhrvold — isn't just how much stuff it throws out, but where the matter goes. A typical volcano ejaculates sulfur dioxide into the troposphere, the atmospheric layer closest to the earth's surface, which soon falls back to the surface as acid rain. But big volcanoes throw sulfur dioxide higher into the stratosphere which, rather than quickly returning to the earth's surface, absorbs stratospheric water vapour and forms an aerosol cloud that blankets most of the planet, thereby cooling the atmosphere.

Even Paul Crutzen, a Dutch scientist who won a Nobel Prize for his research on atmospheric ozone depletion, in his essay in journal *Climate Change* in 2006, acknowledged that an injection of sulfur in the stratosphere "is the only option available to rapidly reduce temperature rises and counteract other climatic effects". He said so while lamenting our "grossly unsuccessful" efforts to emit fewer greenhouse gases.

So, the 'heretics' have a solution: Put sulfur dioxide in the stratosphere, and the world will be a cooler place to live in, though how to do so remains debatable. Their primary contention is that as we have miserably failed to control the release of greenhouse gases in the atmosphere, we need to have an alternative plan in place.

The climate science establishment, dominated by traditionalists, however, refused to accommodate dissent. Even Michael Crichton's novel, State of Fear, based on the story of a high-profile NGO hyping the science of global warming to further the ends of evil eco-terrorists, failed to provide any academic foothold to their theories. But then, in 2009, 'climate gate' broke out, and people started questioning the very 'prophets of doom', turning *State of Fear* into the gospel of truth. People found similarity between the fictional National Environmental Resource Fund and the real Intergovernmental Panel on Climate Change (IPCC), charged with cornering millions of dollars in the name of climate research.

'Climate gate' not only boosted the prospect of these critics, but also, ironically, discredited the global warming issue. A Pew survey said that the number of Americans who regarded global warming as "a very serious problem" had declined from 44 per cent in April 2008 to 35 percent last October. A recent *BBC* study, too, found a similar trend in Britain, where the support for the issue plummeted from 41 per cent in November 2009 to 26 per cent. And in Germany, *Der Spiegel* magazine reported that only 42 per cent feared global warming, compared with 62 per cent in 2006.

A fatalistic trend it might seem, but it was expected after 20 years of all talk and little action on global warming. How can this be reversed? For this, we need to adopt a two-pronged approach. First, the climate change establishment must get rid of people like Al Gore who have made a lucrative business out of scare stories. No doubt, a startling statistic makes us sit down and listen, but it also turns us thick-skinned, thus requiring ever more outrageous scenarios to move us. Also, such stories are more likely to fall flat for their exaggerated, outlandish claims.

This was recently seen in the IPCC's audacious prediction that by 2035 all the Himalayan glaciers would vanish!

Once the systemic rot is cleaned the focus must shift to the real problem — global warming. Herein we must first analyze why the greenhouse formula has over the years turned into a 'Clean Ganges' project — the more you clean, the dirtier it becomes. Thereafter, we should look for an alternative mode of curbing global warming: If the carbon formula doesn't work, give sulfur a chance! At least we should see whether it's a feasible idea or not. Also, we must adopt green lifestyle, technology and policies. Warming or no warming, there's no alternative to trees, as has recently been seen in Pakistan.

Global warming has, of late, become an easy excuse for a wrong happening in the world. Let's take an example. If we face water scarcity in some parts of the country, we instantly blame climate change for it.

Such things used to happen in the past as well, but then we had a rich tradition of water harvesting. We knew water needed to be preserved for hard times. But when the British came, they told us it was the work of the mother-father Government, and not society, to preserve and provide water. We, therefore, abdicated our responsibility— first reluctantly, then happily.

The professional mourners need to understand that of all the countries in the world, India gets the most rainfall per square unit of land area. And, if the country is walled and no rainwater is allowed to escape into the sea, we would have water one meter deep on the ground every year!

This, however, doesn't mean global warming isn't a serious issue. The basic premise of this writer is that we should stop being alarmist. At the same time, we need to go green, turn traditional in water harvesting and, of course, look for an alternative mode of curbing global warming. For me, if carbon can't do the tricks, let sulfur do it.

Global Climate Warming

There is a question: Which consequences can entail of a global climate warming in the forestry of northwest region of Russia?

It is doubtless, that the local populations of trees have adapted during evolutionary development under rather stable climatic conditions and corresponded to local conditions. At slow enough change of climatic conditions there will be evolutionary changes in a population of wood plants; therefore the population will again correspond to new environmental conditions. If there is no time for evolutionary processes, in this case the local population will be replaced with other population, which is more adapted to new conditions. Thus the changes should occur not only at a population level, but also at a species level. The motley picture will be observed. One species will be oppressed; the development of the others will be stimulated.

The increase of temperature occurs so quickly, that, the last scenario is more possible. It is clear, that the climate warming will not have a negative effect on plants growth but rather positive. Increase of temperature occurs on a background of increase of CO_2 concentration. This leads to increase of diseases and pest's populations. They sensitively will react by their number to slightest changes in balance of a tree and environment. Thus, at fast global climate warming would increase the number and scale of outbreaks of insects and diseases. It would cause mass decline of forests in a century. The prompt ruin of pine forests in the south Pskovskaja region in Russia and ruin of coniferous forests in Byelorussia connected with root rot and insects are the consequences of a climate warming. If the assumption about stimulation of pest and disease activity by a climate warming is correct, the forestry enters into a condition of instability.

The geographical variability of hereditary properties of forest species, efficiency and stability of forests, and improvement of the seed district division are the prime needs of Russia. The Government has undertaken a lot of forest plantations schemes to test the seeds of main forest species from various geographical areas. The study of an opportunity of pine and spruce seeds moving from other geographical areas for use in the Leningradskaja region has shown that usually the best is possible in warmer areas. It is observed that southern climatic types have surpassed local species in height and diameter. There is no problem of shortage of the local seeds in the Leningradskaja region.

Therefore it is suggested that study of geographical cultures, forests monitoring, insect surveillance, climate warming, establishment and improvement of forests are necessary stability in northwest region of Russia.[24]

Climate change has begun to tamper with ecosystems the world over. But some scientists refute that climate change is not human-induced but a result of cosmic influences. Scientists like S. Fred Singer, Richard Lindzen, Robert C Balling jr, Sallie Baliunas, and Parick Michaels have opined that moderate global warming is natural.

Climate talks at new crossroads

The global climate change negotiations are at a new crossroads, as evident after the latest round of meetings that ended in Bangkok on 7 September, 2012.

"Crossroads" because the talks and the emerging climate change regime may go into one of various

[24] Chabounine D.A., Pelevina N.N, Nikolaeva M.A., Saint-Petersburg Forestry Research Institute, Saint-Petersburg

directions, or else become stuck in an impasse. "New" because the climate talks had faced crossroads before over the past five years.

The Bangkok negotiations of the UN Climate Change Convention, held over 10 days, revealed a major split between developed and developing countries over many issues that the latter wanted to continue discussing because they had not been resolved.

Most developed countries, led by the USA, believe there is no need for further discussion because they had been closed off by a decision taken at the last Conference of Parties in Durban last December. The wrangling over a seemingly procedural issue of what remains on the agenda and what should be removed is a sign of a far larger question ~ what the respective responsibilities of developed versus developing countries are in the years ahead. As evidence on the ground and in the science mounts over the devastating effects of climate change, it seems that the international community increasingly has become less able to address the crisis.

At the heart of the problem is the continuing attempt by several developed nations' governments to run away from their previously agreed dual obligations ~ to lead in sharp emissions reductions in their own countries, and to provide finance and technology to developing countries for them to take their own climate actions.

It was this columnist who broke the news during an earlier Bangkok session in 2009 that the rich nations were plotting to kill the Kyoto Protocol (KP). Under the legally binding KP, all developed countries (except the US, which is not a member) agreed to cut their emissions by specified rates; the overall average rate was 5 per cent by 2012 compared to 1990.

Cuts for a second period starting 2013 have been negotiated in a KP working group since 2005. The new cuts are supposed to be at least 25-40 per cent for all developed countries; the developing countries have demanded 40 per cent or more.

Another working group on long-term action (AWG-LCA) was created in 2007 in Bali that mandated those developed countries that were not in the KP (only the USA at that time) to undertake a mitigation commitment comparable to countries in the KP. For the past three years there has been a see-saw battle to save the Kyoto Protocol, as one country after another indicated it was jumping ship to join the US in the relatively safe haven of the AWG-LCA. At the 2011 Durban conference, it was clear that Canada, Japan and Russia would not take part in a second KP period, and Australia and New Zealand adopted a wait-and-see attitude.

Thus only the European countries are left in the KP's active roll call for post-2012 cuts. Up to now, well past the deadline, even they have not stated what cuts they are willing to commit to. With the virtual abandonment of the KP, the developed countries have now plotted to kill the AWG-LCA.

The USA dislikes the group and its Bali Action Plan for at least three reasons: it obliges all developed countries to make a comparable mitigation effort (the US is not willing to do as much as the European Union); it treats developing countries more leniently; and it links the developing countries' actions to the funds and technology transferred to them from the developed countries.

At Durban, a draft decision was put forward to end the life of the AWG-LCA by December 2012. This draft had not even been seen, let alone discussed, by developing countries, but was put on the floor in the last hours of the conference and adopted together with all other decisions on a take-it-or-leave-it basis. In Bangkok earlier this month, many developing countries put forward proposals on several issues not yet resolved in the AWG-LCA, including financing of their actions, technology transfer, adaptation, mitigation, trade and other measures against their capacity building.

AWG-LCA chair Mr. Aysar Tayeb prepared a compilation of issues drawn from countries' submissions that had to be resolved or transferred to other bodies, so that the working group could successfully conclude its work and close by December.

However, the developed countries led by the USA and the "Umbrella Group" vehemently opposed further discussion on most of the issues, and claimed the chair's paper had no status and was wrongly raising expectations. It is evident that the USA and its allies want to kill the AWG-LCA and its associated Bali Action Plan and get rid of their three inconvenient elements ~ comparability of efforts, different treatment of developed and developing countries, and the link between developing countries' actions and finance and technology.

A new group on the Durban Platform was formed in Durban to negotiate a new agreement. The US is insisting that the Platform will not have these three elements of the Bali Action Plan. But to many developing countries, that is wishful thinking. For them, the principles of equity and common and differentiated responsibilities are key in the Convention and in the new Platform.

If the LCA group is to expire, all its issues and principles have to be transferred to other bodies in the Convention, including the Platform. At stake is whether globally agreed actions to address the climate crisis are fair, or whether the powerful countries will continue to abandon their obligations and shift the burden to the developing world. Meanwhile, Nature continues to ignore the slow progress or reversal of commitments in human affairs. As emissions continue to increase and the average global temperature rises, a series of extreme weather events are wreaking havoc all over the world. [25]

Rights affected by Climate Change

Clearly, climate change[26] has had and will continue to have adverse impacts on fundamental human rights:

1. **Right to life:** The quality of the environment affects the ability of people to enjoy the universally held right to life. Direct impacts include the increased incidents of natural disasters, while indirect impacts include poorer standards of health, nutrition, access to clean drinking water and susceptibility to disease. The immediacy of these threats indicates that positive action must be taken to ensure the full enjoyment of the right to life. Given the fact that mitigation remains the only known means to fully prevent the catastrophic impacts of climatic change and that the critical decisions do not lie within the control of each state itself, the full protection of the right to life from climate change mostly depends upon the actions of the international community.

2. **Right to development:** The attainment of the right to development by developing countries will be severely impaired by impacts on food and water

---

[25] Martin Khor (2012), "Climate talks at new crossroads", Statesman, 18 September 2012

[26] Convention on the Conservation of European Wild life and Natural Habitats, 4th Meeting of the Group of Experts on Biodiversity and Climate Change, Human Rights and Climate Change, Document prepared by Ms Maria Blazogiannaki, Trainee at the Council of Europe, March 2009

security, decreases in the earth's landmass, drastic weather patterns and the destruction of ecosystems.

3. **Right to property:** Climate change may result in the deprivation of property without compensation, particularly in coastal areas, and may also have an effect on land uses as a result of changing weather patterns.

4. **Right to self-determination:** The right of all peoples to self-determination is recognized in Artic le 1 of both the ICCPR and the ICESCR, as well as in Articles 1 and 55 of the UN Charter. If climate change continues unmitigated, sea-level rise is expected to result in the total inundation of small island states. It may thus destroy one of the hallmarks of statehood: the country's territory. Additionally, the combination of sea- level rise, rising temperatures and extreme weather events threatens to render the islands inhabitable. Therefore, climate change impacts constitute a threat to the enjoyment of the right of certain people to self-determination. The loss of land and State renders all other rights, political and civil as well as economic, cultural and social rights unattainable. Without international cooperation, Small Island developing states, which as a whole emit however less than 1% of global GHG emissions, have little capacity to reverse the impacts of climate change in extinguishing their territory.

5. **Right to health:** The right to health includes a range of factors necessary to lead a healthy life, such as food, nutrition, housing, access to safe water and a healthy environment. Climate change is likely to increase deaths from malnutrition, heat stress and infectious diseases worldwide. It will also alter traditional sources of, and access to, clean water.

6. **Right to food:** The right to food is addressed in several international human rights conventions and has been further recognized in subsequent

declarations made by the international community. Climate change will have an impact on food security by reducing the availability of food, changing access to food, worsening the stability of food supply and affecting the utilization of food. People of outer islands in particular are in danger of suffering from hunger and chronic malnutrition. Moreover, the effects on agricultural production will be visible at the global level. Diverting agricultural lands and food crops toward the production of bio-fuels may indirectly result in rising food prices, food shortage affecting especially the poor, and a threat to the basic right to food in affected populations.

7. Right to water: Climate change will result in changes to components of the hydrological cycle and hydrological systems such as changing rainfall patterns, intensity and extremes. Recently, the 2007 OHCHR Report, issued pursuant to Decision 2/204 of the Human Rights Council, addressed the scope and content of human rights obligations related to safe drinking water and sanitation. Under ICCPR and ICESCR, the right to water provides for "equal and non-discriminatory access to a sufficient amount of safe drinking water for personal and domestic issues...to sustain life and health". State Parties have a duty to take measures to fulfill the right to water, including the obligations to facilitate and promote universal access to water, as well as to provide water for individuals who lack access for reasons beyond their control.

8. Rights of the Indigenous Peoples: According to the IPCC AR4, the communities who live in marginal lands and whose livelihoods are highly dependent on natural resources are among the most vulnerable to climate change. Biodiversity loss as a result of adverse impacts of climate change will affect indigenous peoples in many different ways, such as depriving them of important food sources and reducing their ability to cope with pests and diseases with the help of medicinal plants.

Indigenous peoples still have limited or in many cases no participation in the decision-making processes of the UNFCCC (the REDD –Reduced Emissions from Deforestation in Developing countries- mechanism for instance), despite the fact that their rights and their experience in sustainable forest management make their participation in these flora imperative. Moreover, the implementation of the three flexible mechanisms of the Kyoto Protocol, often without their prior and informed consent also causes human rights violations, like forced relocations or introduction of environmental contaminants, etc.

Climate change will also have impacts on emergency response and disaster recovery, particularly for vulnerable developing countries. It also threatens to drive millions of people around the globe to migrate within and across State borders. Finally, international and national decision-makers need to be open and welcome a thought-provoking debate on climate change issues in order to make better-informed decisions on how to tackle this global phenomenon.

Climate Change vs. Human Rights

In the two decades since it first appeared on the international agenda, climate change has moved from the sidelines to the center-stage of international discourse. The global average temperature has increased by 0.74 centigrade in the last century, the largest and fastest warming trend in the history of the Earth. It is predicted to increase by between 1.8 and 6.4°C by the end of the 21st Century.

Rajamani analyzes the effects of climate change on human rights. Climate change is predicted to increase the severity of droughts, land degradation and desertification, the intensity of floods and tropical cyclones, the incidence of malaria and heat-related mortality, and decrease crop yield and food security. The wave of weather-related disasters the world has witnessed this summer, and the human costs of these, is sadly merely a precursor to what is to come.

Notwithstanding the magnitude of the problem and the years that the international community has spent engaging on this issue, an effective and universal solution to address it has thus far proved elusive. The United Nations Framework Convention on Climate Change (FCCC), 1992, and its Kyoto Protocol, 1997, contains emissions reduction commitments that are both inadequate and inadequately implemented. Negotiations scheduled to arrive at an "agreed outcome" at Copenhagen in December 2009 are still ongoing, and the light at the end of the tunnel is far from visible. The non-binding Copenhagen Accord arrived at in December 2009 among heads of states of 28 parties to the FCCC, takes but a limited step forward. The Accord agreed to limit temperature increase to 2°C, but did not prescribe what states would need to do to achieve this goal, or how the burden of achieving this goal is to be shared between states. It allowed states, developed and developing alike, to record their self-selected targets and actions in appendices to the Accord. At least 138 states have since associated with the Accord and inscribed their targets and actions in its appendices. Early analyses suggest, however, that the pledges countries have inscribed set the world on a 3°C or more warming trend.[27]

Meanwhile the impacts of climate change continue to prejudicially affect the poor, dis-empowered, culturally distinct, and geographically disadvantaged across the globe. It is axiomatic that the documented impacts of climate change are likely to undermine the

---

[27] Lavanya Rajamani (2010), "Climate Change Vs. Human Rights" Sunday Pioneer August 29, 2010

realization of a range of protected human rights. Among them, the right to life, right to health, right to adequate food, right to water, right to an adequate standard of living and to the extent is it recognized the right to development. Yet it is only in the recent past that an explicit human rights approach has been brought to bear on the climate change problem.

The primary defining feature of a human rights approach is its normative focus on individual welfare — that is, "in the dignity and worth of the human person" (UN Charter). A focus on the dignity and worth of every individual renders efforts to deal-seek for the majority problematic. And it is this that states in the climate negotiations are engaged in, deal-seeking for perceived aggregate welfare which may well be incompatible with individual rights for particular people or groups of people. The principal objective of the climate regime is the "stabilization of greenhouse gas concentrations in the atmosphere at a level that would prevent dangerous anthropogenic interference with the climate system". (FCCC Article 2)

But, what constitutes "dangerous" anthropogenic interference with the climate system? And, how is it to be determined? The Intergovernmental Panel on Climate Change (IPCC) notes that this is a value judgement determined through socio-political processes, taking into account considerations such as development, equity and sustainability, as well as uncertainties and risk. This involves a judgement about the kind of danger that is acceptable, and to whom. Even the 2°C limit arrived at in the Copenhagen Accord will have significant impacts on the inhabitants of small island states and the Arctic Inuit. In India, it will impact the Sundarbans and on our island territories. It appears then that the costs (to the global community) of limiting climate change to 2°C must have been deemed to outweigh the benefits it will bring to a small (in proportion) number of people. A focus on individual rights would make such determinations of aggregate welfare questionable, for the "language of rights strengthens the power of the marginalized".

This is not to suggest that human rights of particular individuals are determinative in such an instance, and that the regime should be structured around a negligible temperature increase. It is conceivable that the costs, economic and opportunity, and the corresponding rights implications, may be prohibitive for the rest.

And, human rights are not absolute — as evidenced by the fact that economic and social rights are to be "progressively realized" and even some civil and political rights can be derogated from in emergencies. Human rights approaches in such situations would merely shift focus to the right to restitution, compensation and rehabilitation for the affected individuals. It is worth noting that small island states have proposed temperature increase be limited to well below 1.5ºC, and reduction of CO2 emissions by greater than 85 per cent by 2050.

The focus on individual rights, however, offers little guidance in situations where rights seemingly conflict, as they often do. To take a paradigmatic case, in India where 44 per cent of its population does not have access to electricity, provision of universal access to energy will result in rapid increases in greenhouse gases (GHGs). Such increases could result, directly or indirectly, in the loss of the island of Tuvalu. The question is can we protect the rights of 500 million Indians to an adequate standard of living or the rights of 12,000 Tuvaluans to their culture, property and territorial integrity. On what principle, we have to award justice to both.

Political philosopher Caney argues that since both sets of rights relate to vital interests, it should be possible to satisfy both. There are many fossil fuel-intensive climate endangering activities in other (primarily industrialized) parts of the world that relate to relatively trivial interests, and these must be reduced so as to create space for increased greenhouse gases emissions for individuals without access to electricity, as well as to protect the territorial integrity, and cultural rights of the small islanders. Two aspects of this argument are interesting:

(a) First, this argument finds resonance in the climate regime, which is premised on a redistribution of the ecological space.
(b) And, second, this argument distinguishes between trivial and non-trivial interests that may be served by climate endangering activities.

This distinction has a long history in the climate negotiations where India and China have consistently argued that developing country emissions are "survival emissions" while industrialized country emissions are "lifestyle" or "luxury" emissions. Human rights protect the former, not the latter. They provide benchmarks against which actions can be evaluated.

Another defining feature of human rights approaches is its power to hold authorities to account. It is the enforcement potential of human rights approaches, given the glacial pace and distant promise of the climate negotiations, that first captured the legal imagination. A series of cases have been filed in national and international forums seeking recompense for climate damage. Few of these cases have resulted in clear victories. In their 2005 petition before the Inter-American Commission on Human Rights, the Arctic Inuit claimed that the impacts of climate change, caused by acts and omissions of the United States, violated their fundamental human rights — in particular the rights to the benefits of culture, to property, to the preservation of health, life, physical integrity, security, residence and a means of subsistence. The Inuit case was held inadmissible.

Although the Commission did not offer detailed reasons for its decision, these are not hard to fathom. There are serious hurdles in terms of establishing clear and binding obligations (given the contextual and soft language used in the climate treaties), jurisdiction (since states seldom recognize the jurisdiction of various international dispute settlement forum), standing (as every state both contributes to and suffers the impacts of climate change), causation (between the GHG emissions of the defendant state and impacts suffered by the plaintiff state / individuals), and damage (as much of it may be in the future). Indeed, the climate change problematic exposes the fault lines and limits of international law.

National-level human rights climate change litigation has fared better. In the Nigerian Gas Flaring Case, the Federal High Court of Nigeria held that the practice of gas flaring by Nigeria in the Niger Delta, a practice which contributed more to climate change than all other sources in Sub-Saharan Africa, violated guaranteed constitutional rights to life and dignity. It is worth noting that whatever the outcome, the act of filing of these cases itself has considerable rhetorical and practical impact. The focus on specific injuries builds political support, and the "story-telling quality" of the cases makes climate change tangible. And, even if individual cases fail they build pressure for policy and legislative action.

A host of internationally protected rights and progressive realization towards them will be at risk from climate impact. The vast majority of states have signed the core human rights treaties, including in particular the International Covenant on Civil and Political Rights and the International Covenant on

Economic, Social and Cultural Rights. State parties have obligations to respect, protect and fulfill the rights contained in these treaties. These obligations are binding on every state party, and must be given effect to in good faith. The extent of application and enforcement of protected human rights will, of necessity, differ from state to state depending on national circumstances, constitutional culture, legislative proclivity, judicial creativity, and governance mechanisms, but at a minimum, the core human rights treaties set standards and benchmarks in place, and impose process obligations — obligations to integrate human rights concerns into policy planning.

Most of the parties to the core human rights treaties are also the members to the FCCC and the Kyoto Protocol. States, at least those, that are party to both the climate treaties and the human rights treaties, are obliged to approach the climate change problematic not just as a global environmental problem, but also as a human rights issue. States are obliged to identify and explore the human rights that might be placed at risk by climate impacts, and take pre-emptive action in that regard. They are also obliged to design policies and measures to mitigate and adapt to climate change sensitive to the impacts that these could have on the progressive realization of protected human rights.

States may have perfected the art of dragging their feet in designing an effective regime to address climate regime, but can they afford the human and political costs of ignoring their obligations under existing human rights instruments?

How Climate Change undermines Human Rights

The OXFAM International Briefing Paper clearly explains that climate change influences both the current and future human rights as per International Law.

These are as follows:

(1) The Right to Life and Security: Everyone has the right to life, liberty and security of person. (UDHR, Article 3)

There will be more deaths, disease, and injury due to the increasing frequency and intensity of heat waves, floods, storms, fires, and droughts.

Rising sea levels will increase the risk of death and injury by drowning. Up to 20 percent of the world's population lives in river basins that are likely to be affected by increased flood hazard by the 2080s.

Heat waves are likely to increase deaths among elderly or chronically sick people, young children, and the socially isolated. Europe's 2003 heat wave – induced by climate change – resulted in 27,000 extra deaths.

2. The Right to Food: The State Parties to the present Covenant recognize the fundamental right of everyone to be free from hunger... (ICESCR, Article 11)

Future climate change is expected to put close to 50 million more people at risk of hunger by 2020, and an additional 132 million people by 2050.

In Africa, shrinking arable land, shorter growing seasons, and lower crop yields will exacerbate malnutrition. In some countries, yields from rain-fed agriculture could fall by 50 per cent as soon as 2020.
In parts of Asia, food security will be threatened due to water shortages and rising temperatures. Crop yields could fall by up to 30 per cent in Central and South Asia by 2050.

3. The Right to Subsistence: Everyone has the right to a standard of living adequate for the health and well-being of himself and of his family, including food, clothing, housing' (UDHR, Article 25). In no case may a people be deprived of its own means of subsistence. (ICCPR, Article 1.2 and ICESCR, Article 1.2)

Water: By 2020, between 75 million and 250 million people in Africa are likely to face greater water stress due to climate change. Reduced water flow from mountain glaciers could affect up t o one billion people in Asia by the 2050s.

Natural resources: Approximately 20–30 per cent of plant and animal species assessed so far are likely to be at increased risk of extinction if average global temperatures rise more than 1.5–2.50C. Coral bleaching and coastal erosion will affect fish stocks – currently the primary source of animal protein for one billion people.

Property and shelter: Millions more people risk facing annual floods due to sea level rise by t he 2080s, mostly in the mega-deltas of Asia and Africa. On small islands, too, sea-level rise is expected to exacerbate inundation, storm surge, and erosion, threatening vital infrastructure, settlements, and facilities that support the livelihoods of island communities.

4. The Right to Health: The State Parties to the present Covenant recognize the right of everyone to the enjoyment of the highest attainable standard of physical and mental health. (ICESCR, Article 12)

Child malnutrition will increase, damaging growth and development prospects for millions of children.

Increasing floods and droughts will lead to more cases of diarrhea and cholera. Over 150,000 people are currently estimated to die each year from diarrhoea, malaria, and malnutrition caused by climate change.

Changing temperatures will cause some infectious diseases to spread into new areas. It is estimated that 220–400 million more people will be at risk of malaria. The risk of dengue fever is estimated to reach 3.5 billion people by 2085 due to climate change.[28]

International Climate Policy

U.S. climate policy is essential to halting global climate change. To succeed in reducing emissions, climate policy must be rigorous and based on sound economic principles. To successfully make its way through Congress, it must address its disproportionate effects on lower-income groups and on the states with the most greenhouse gas emissions per person today. Stanton and Ackerman (2010) have appreciated the US climate policy. They have presented a new model of the economic impacts of carbon prices, rebates, and green investments by state and by income group, as well as an overview of the recent economic literature on climate policy. Our most important finding was a pair of rules for the design of climate policy:[29]

The price of carbon (whether it is a tax, fee, or permit price) determines how much the policy reduces greenhouse gas emissions. As long as a large share of carbon revenues is returned to households, the price of carbon has little effect on equity among states or among income groups.

---

[28]Oxfam International Briefing Paper, Climate Wrongs and Human Rights: Putting People at the Heart of Climate Change Policy P6.

[29]Elizabeth A. Stanton and Frank Ackerman (2010), "No State Left Behind: A Better Approach to Climate Policy, An E3-SEI Climate Policy White Paper" August 2010

In contrast, rebates to households primarily determine how equitable the policy is among states and among income groups. The share of revenues returned to households has little impact on the extent of emission reductions.

In this white paper we discuss our findings in the context of three climate bills recently considered by Congress — the American Clean Energy and Security Act of 2009 (Waxman-Markey), passed by the House in June 2009, and the Carbon Limits and Energy for America's Renewal (CLEAR) Act (Cantwell-Collins) and American Power Act (Kerry-Lieberman), both introduced in the Senate — and set out seven key questions that we, and our elected representatives, should be asking about any climate policy proposal.

Seven Questions for a Good Climate Policy

Our analysis identified several policy measures that are essential to making climate bills successful. That analysis leads to seven questions to ask about any proposed climate legislation.

1. Are the emissions targets low enough to do the job?

Legislation before Congress in 2010 calls for emission reductions below 2005 levels on the order of 17 to 20 percent by 2020, 42 percent by 2030, and 83 percent by 2050. While reaching these targets would represent a big improvement over current practice, there are at least two problems. First, the targets allow a comparatively slow start, assuming that the pace of emission reduction will accelerate sharply after 2030. Second, even an 83-percent U.S. reduction by mid-century may not be enough to achieve the global emission reductions that are needed. It is at the looser end of IPCC recommendations[30], and current climate science suggests that tighter standards may be needed.

In a previous study, we found that lowering carbon dioxide (CO2) concentrations in the atmosphere from today's 385 parts per million (ppm) to the recommended "safe" level of 350 ppm by 2200 would require reduction in emissions to 98 percent below 2005 by 2050, or massive use of carbon sequestration (primarily reforestation) to remove CO2 from the atmosphere (Ackerman et al. 2009).

Faster reductions will require tighter emission limits and, consequently, higher carbon taxes or prices, than the current legislative targets. This need not mean greater economic burdens: If household rebates are a large share of revenues, a high carbon price can still lead to net benefits for most households (Stanton and Ackerman 2010).

2. Will price ceilings interfere with emission reductions?

All the recent legislative proposals include low price ceilings, $32 to $41 per metric ton of CO2 in 2020. Staying below these ceilings will make it impossible to meet even the modest proposed emission reduction targets, unless large-scale non-price efficiency and clean energy measures are also undertaken. We found that achieving a 17-percent emission reduction below 2005 levels by 2020 would require a $75 per metric ton CO2 carbon price *and* a vigorous program of investment in energy efficiency (Stanton and

---

[30]To stabilize atmospheric concentrations at 450 ppm of CO2-equivalent (roughly comparable to 350 ppm of CO2 alone), the IPCC's 2007 report projected a need for 80- to 95-percent reductions from 1990 in developed countries (Working Group III 2007, p. 776). For the United States, this is equivalent to an 83- to 96-percent reduction from 2005 levels, because emissions grew by 19 percent from 1990 to 2005 (EPA 2010).

Ackerman 2010). All three current bills, however, treat their low price ceilings as absolute limits, and would release additional permits when the ceiling is reached; more permits in the system would allow higher emissions, ensuring a failure to hit the reduction goal.

Enforcing a strict emissions cap under a market-based climate policy requires either that the carbon price can vary freely (i.e., without a ceiling) in response to the supply and demand for permits; or that non-price measures such as government regulation and green investments be used to reduce demand if the market hits the price ceiling.

The insistence on price ceilings is based on the mistaken notion that a higher carbon price has to mean a greater economic burden on consumers. Our model shows that even with very high carbon prices, equal per capita rebates of most of the revenue can ensure that there are net benefits to all but the richest households (Stanton and Ackerman 2010). With that in mind, it is worth considering a much broader range of carbon prices. In much of Western Europe, gasoline prices are $4 a gallon higher than in the United States. We would reach that level if we had a carbon price of $400 per metric ton of CO2 that was passed on in higher prices at the gas pump. European countries with high-priced gasoline have a quality of life much like ours — but they have lower carbon emissions per capita, and use energy much more efficiently than we do.

3. Will a significant share of revenues be rebated to households?

If businesses pass on the costs to their customers, a carbon tax or a system of carbon permits will mean "carbon costs" for every household. At a $75 per metric ton CO2 carbon price in 2020, we estimate these costs would range from an average of 6.3

percent of income for the poorest tenth of U.S. households, to 2.4 percent of income for the richest tenth. This would be an important increase to many families' budgets, and the impact would be felt most strongly by those with lower incomes and by residents of states that rely primarily on coal for their electricity generation.

To assure that half of all households receive a net benefit from carbon policy, at least 65 percent of all carbon revenues must be returned to households. If 85 percent of the revenues were returned to households, 80 percent of all U.S. households would receive a net dividend, i.e. a rebate greater than their carbon costs (Stanton and Ackerman 2010). Alternatively, part or all of revenues could be returned to households as a reduction to payroll taxes or an increase to the Earned Income Tax Credit or Social Security payments, while still giving a net gain to all working- and middle-class households (Burtraw et al. 2009).

4. Are emission permits given away?

Under a cap-and-trade policy, funds are available for significant rebates to households only if permits are sold rather than given away. This choice — whether to sell permits or give them away — makes little or no difference in how effective legislation is at reducing emissions, but it makes all the difference to whose pocket the carbon revenues end up in. Carbon prices work by increasing prices on carbon-intensive goods. So the customers would buy something where there is less or no carbon. When carbon permits are given away, businesses will "pass along" the cost of the permits — even though they didn't pay for them! If permits are sold (or a carbon tax is adopted) and the revenues are rebated to households, the money ends up with households. If the revenues are collected and used for green investments, the money ends up creating new green jobs. But if permits are given away, the revenue goes to private companies in the form of higher profits: Prices paid by customers go up, while costs of production are unchanged.

5. Are large-scale investments made in energy efficiency?

One area in which states with the highest per capita greenhouse gas emissions today may have an advantage is in implementing low- and even no-cost energy efficiency measures. States that have little in the way of an existing green economy — with a long way to go in terms of assisting households and businesses to conserve energy — may find energy efficiency options that are "low hanging fruit." States that have made the most progress in building a green economy may have already exhausted some of their lowest-cost options. Based on research showing that an investment of 4.5 cents in efficiency measures can reduce energy use by 1 kWh, we model a 15-percent reduction in electricity emissions from energy efficiency by 2020, with investments targeted to the most coal-intensive states. To achieve a 17-percent reduction in total emissions by 2020 while staying below existing bills' carbon price ceilings, our projected level of energy efficiency savings would have to be tripled (Stanton and Ackerman 2010).

6. Is there a strategy for retiring coal plants?

Rebating climate policy revenues back to households is not the only way to protect states and households from high carbon costs. Plowing climate policy revenues into building natural gas and renewable power plants in order to retire coal generation would greatly reduce carbon costs, in exactly the places where it is most needed: the states with the most coal-dependent electricity systems, and therefore the highest per capita emissions. These are the states whose residents will face the highest costs from climate policy, and the smallest net gains (or in some scenarios, net losses) even after receiving their per capita dividends.

Although many activities affect carbon emissions, the use of coal is, not surprisingly, the key to interstate variation in per capita emissions. Electricity generated from coal results in twice the emissions of natural gas generation. Looking at the full life-cycle emissions — from mining materials and building facilities to generating electricity and disposing of wastes — coal is 2.4 times more carbon-intensive than natural gas, 33 times more intensive than photo-voltaic, and 105 times more intensive than wind or hydroelectric power.

Nuclear power, sometimes touted as the solution to retiring coal and reducing electricity emissions, is a more problematic alternative. It remains quite expensive, in no small part due to the high cost of numerous essential safety precautions. It requires substantial amounts of cooling water, which will be a scarce resource in a climate-constrained future. And the long-term problem of nuclear waste disposal has not yet been solved (Stanton and Ackerman 2010).

Replacing coal does not have to pose a large economic burden: A detailed scenario for phasing out all coal generation by 2050, while also reducing the use of nuclear power, has been projected to cost just $9.6 billion in 2020 — less than the energy efficiency investment assumed in our model — and would start to save money, on balance, before 2040 (Keith et al. 2010). It is difficult to see how the United States could meet its emission reduction targets without a strategy for replacing coal.

7. Is green investment directed toward the states most affected by climate policy?

Climate policy will not affect all states equally; states differ widely in carbon-intensity of electricity generation, heating and cooling requirements, and transportation needs. Rebating funds to households or states in proportion to their carbon costs would undermine the market incentive for emission reduction — and that incentive effect is the central purpose of a carbon price. A better way to address inequitable impacts is to target green investment, in such areas as energy efficiency and retirement of coal plants, to the states with highest costs from climate policy, simultaneously creating green jobs and lowering their greenhouse gas emissions.

The employment impacts of retiring all coal plants would be negligible — in 2007, coal miners represented 0.05 percent (i.e., 5 /100thof 1 percent) of the U.S. labor force. Even in Wyoming, with the nation's largest share of employment in coal mining, they were only 2.2 percent of the workforce. This means that providing job retraining or other supports for them would be relatively inexpensive; it can be built into plans for green jobs and energy efficiency projects (Stanton and Ackerman 2010).

UN Climate Change Conference

Cancun, 11 December 2010

The UN Climate Change Conference in Cancun, Mexico, ended on Saturday with the adoption of a balanced package of decisions that set all governments more firmly on the path towards a low-emissions future and support enhanced action on climate change in the developing world.

UN Climate Change Conference in Cancun delivers balanced package of decisions, restores faith in multilateral process. UNFCCC Executive Secretary Christiana Figurers expressed that Cancun has done its job. The beacon of hope has been re-ignited and faith in the multilateral climate change process to deliver results has been restored. Nations have shown they can work together under a common roof, to reach consensus on a common cause. They have shown that consensus in a transparent and inclusive process can create opportunity for all. Governments have given a clear signal that they are headed towards a low-emissions future together, they have agreed to be accountable to each other for the actions they take to get there, and they have set it out in a way which encourages countries to be more ambitious over time. This is not the end, but it is a new beginning. It is not what is ultimately required but it is the essential foundation on which to build greater, collective ambition. .

Nations launched a set of initiatives and institutions to protect the poor and the vulnerable from climate change and to deploy the money and technology that developing countries need to plan and build their own sustainable futures. And they agreed to launch concrete action to preserve forests in developing nations, which will increase going forward.

They also agreed that countries need to work to stay below a two-degree temperature rise and they set a clear timetable for review, to ensure that global action is adequate to meet the emerging reality of climate change.

Elements of the Cancun Agreements include:

1. Industrialized country targets are officially recognized under the multilateral process and these countries are to develop low-carbon development plans and strategies and assess how best to meet them, including through market mechanisms, and to report their inventories annually.

2. Developing country actions to reduce emissions are officially recognized under the multilateral process. A registry is to be set up to record and match developing country mitigation actions to finance and technology support from by industrialized countries.

Developing countries are to publish progress reports every two years.

3. Parties meeting under the Kyoto Protocol agree to continue negotiations with the aim of completing their work and ensuring there is no gap between the first and second commitment periods of the treaty.

4. The Kyoto Protocol's Clean Development Mechanisms has been strengthened to drive more major investments and technology into environmentally sound and sustainable emission reduction projects in the developing world.

5. Parties launched a set of initiatives and institutions to protect the vulnerable from climate change and to deploy the money and technology that developing countries need to plan and build their own sustainable futures.

6. A total of US $30 billion in fast start finance from industrialized countries to support climate action in the developing world up to 2012 and the intention to raise US $100 billion in long-term funds by 2020 is included in the decisions.

7. In the field of climate finance, a process to design a Green Climate Fund under the Conference of the Parties, with a board with equal representation from developed and developing countries, is established.

8. A new "Cancun Adaptation Framework" is established to allow better planning and implementation of adaptation projects in developing countries through increased financial and technical support, including a clear process for continuing work on loss and damage.

9. Governments agree to boost action to curb emissions from deforestation and forest degradation

in developing countries with technological and financial support.

10. Parties have established a technology mechanism with a Technology Executive Committee and Climate Technology Centre and Network to increase technology cooperation to support action on adaptation and mitigation.[31]

U N Framework Convention on Climate Change,

Christiana Figueres said the following facts in the UN Framework Convention on Climate Change (UNFCCC). These are:

Cancún must be followed by higher global emission cuts and rapid launch of new climate bodies and funds. Nations must follow up their successful UN Climate Change Conference in Cancún with higher global emission cuts and the rapid launch of new institutions and funds to show the world that a new era of international cooperation on climate change is an established fact.

Cancún was a big step, bigger than many imagined might be possible. But the time has come for all of us to exceed our own expectations because nothing less will do. The Cancún Agreements, reached on 11 December 2010 in Cancún, Mexico, call for countries to list under the UNFCCC the emission reduction targets and actions which they announced in 2010, forming the collective basis for the largest mitigation effort the world has ever seen. They also agreed to build a comprehensive system of mutual accountability towards these goals.

[31]United Nations Environment Program, Bonn, December 20, 2010

It needs to be implemented as fast as possible, and it needs to be accompanied by credible accountability systems that will help in measuring real progress. If all these targets and actions are fully implemented, UN estimates show they could deliver only 60 percent of the emission reductions that science says will be needed to stay below the agreed two degree rise in average temperatures, and two degrees does not guarantee the survival of the most vulnerable peoples. All countries, but particularly industrialized nations, need to deepen their emission reduction efforts and to do so quickly. Building up agreed support to the developing world the Cancún Agreements also include the most comprehensive package ever agreed by governments to help developing nations deal with climate change, including new institutions, funding channels and a technology transfer mechanism to help the developing world build its own sustainable, low-emissions future, adapt more effectively to climate change, and preserve and protect its forests for the good of all nations. In Cancún, governments renewed their trust in each other, but to succeed fully they need to press boldly ahead with what they have agreed. Implementation is the most effective avenue to harness the support of business and civil society, both of which are critical.

These institutions must be rapidly launched with expert and active management, and then capitalized. Many millions of the poor and vulnerable people of the world have been waiting years to get the full level of assistance they need. Industrialized nations will soon have a clear, comprehensive structure into which they can direct the funding they have promised.

The UNFCCC secretariat will work intensively to support all governments in this new work. I sincerely hope that when governments meet in South Africa in a year time they can point to new and concrete examples of success that are benefitting people and having impacts on the ground. I expect in particular to see rapid decisions on appointing the board of the new Green Fund and the Committee of the Technology Mechanism. I also look forward to receiving the details of fast-start financing from industrialized countries so the secretariat can compile the information that shows clearly the amounts that have been raised and are being disbursed.

The Cancún Agreements asked developed nations to send the UNFCCC secretariat details of their part in the US $ 30 billion of fast-start finance, which they promised to deliver between 2010 and 2012 to support developing countries, ahead of an agreed long-term finance programme, which will raise at least US $ 100 billion a year by 2020. The first fast-start finance reports to the UNFCCC secretariat are due in May next year. The Green Fund establishes a long-term climate finance institution for the first time under the oversight of the Parties to the climate change Convention and with a 24-member board that balances representation between developed and developing nations.

The Cancún has significantly expanded the menu of climate implementation and resources available to countries under the United Nations, and the UN system together is ready to respond rapidly in line with country's needs. The imperative to act is now. About the UNFCCC with 194 Parties, the United Nations Framework Convention on Climate Change (UNFCCC) has near universal membership and is the parent treaty of the 1997 Kyoto Protocol.

The Kyoto Protocol has been ratified by 192 of the UNFCCC Parties. Under the Protocol, 37 States, consisting of highly industrialized countries and countries undergoing the process of transition to a market economy, have legally binding emission limitation and reduction commitments. The ultimate objective of both treaties is to stabilize greenhouse gas concentrations in the atmosphere at a level that will prevent dangerous human interference with the climate system.[32]

Role of DFID in Climate Change

DFID is working to ensure that aid addresses both the causes and likely effects of climate change so that current and future progress in tackling poverty continues.

(a) We are climate-proofing all our aid programmes.
(b) We are supporting developing countries to adapt to climate change – for example, through practical on-the-ground support, by building climate knowledge and capacity in vulnerable countries and by helping to ensure countries get access to sufficient finance.
(c) We are also supporting the development of low carbon technology and the increased use of renewable energy to ensure that developing countries can move to a low carbon future that supports economic growth.

Climate change has the potential to undermine efforts to tackle poverty which is why the UK has confirmed its commitment to 1.5 billion pounds in Fast Start finance over three years (2010 – 2012).[33]

Reality and the law:

Environmental Variations Can Remake Geography

ENVIRONMENTAL impact assessment (EIA) is a scientific technique to ensure that environmental

---

[32]Press Release, UNFCCC, Bonn, Germany, December 20, 2010

[33]United Nations Climate Change Conference ,Cancun, Mexico, 28 Nov - 10 Dec 2010

concerns are properly addressed before decisions are taken on the implementation of projects. Nations have formulated their own principles of impact assessment. The European Economic Commission's standards are known to be the most scientific. Considerable care is taken in the selection of sites and public opinion is accorded a very high priority. China, on the other hand, being a one-party state, does not care for public opinion.

When planners conduct an EIA, they almost invariably assess how constructions will affect the existing environment, not how a changing environment might affect the construction. While it is essential to ensure that capital intensive projects do not result in major and unnecessary environmental damage, there seems to be an assumption that the installations themselves would not suffer any damage as the environment changes. It is taken for granted that water levels will remain constant, the sea level will remain the same and precipitation levels will follow historical patterns. This makes it difficult to estimate either the lifespan of a site or the potential impact of environmental change over the next 50 years. This is a very conservative time-span for nuclear and hydel power plants.

To grasp the two sides of EIA, it would be useful to recall the Hoover Dam story. The dam was completed in 1935 ~ at the peak of the Great Depression ~ across the Colorado River on the Arizona-Nevada border by impounding Lake Mead. Electricity generated from Hoover Dam has paid back the full cost of the project, with interest, to the federal government. This has been made possible through efficient use of technology. Indeed, technology was tailored to take care of environmental variations.

The Gorges Dam, that spans the Yangtze River in China, will push the Itaipu Dam in Brazil to the second rung in terms of power generation. The sale of electricity from the dam will cover the construction cost after 10 years of full generation. The dam has caused significant ecological change, flooding archaeological and cultural sites. It has displaced nearly 1.4 million people. China did not care for international condemnation. The dam has affected ecology but the government claims that variation in ecology will not affect the dam.

The story is not the same for hydro-electric power utilities in India. Damodar Valley Corporation started functioning in 1948. The other utilities came in later. Hydel-power production in India has remained behind target. The reasons are: increase in temperature, lower water flow and alterations in the pattern of rainfall. In 2008-09, the generation of hydro-electricity in India declined by about 8.5 per cent relative to the previous year. By the summer of 2009, the shortfall was 12 per cent. The loss was attributed to inadequate rainfall.

The impact of the environment was not taken into consideration while drawing up the energy production targets. The cost-benefit ratio was calculated on the assumption that the environment would remain the same.

Fukushima Daiichi was commissioned in 1971 by the Tokyo Electric Power Company (TEPCO). This was the first nuclear power plant constructed and run entirely by TEPCO. Hence the name Daiichi which means "number one". Reports reveal that the plant was located on a cliff which was originally 35 metres above sea level. TEPCO lowered the height of the cliff primarily to minimize the cost of running the sea water pump low. The reduced height resulted in the plant being extremely vulnerable to tsunami.

India's ambitious nuclear power generation program has met with stiff resistance. As regards Koodankulam, the Centre is yet to declare that the project is absolutely safe in terms of environment, ecology, the lives and livelihood of the people. The impact needs incisively to be assessed. The government has not clarified whether this requirement has been met, let alone the potential impact of environment change over the next 50 years. The confidence gap has been increasing by the day and that too when 140 billion INR has already been invested in Koodankulam. The Fukushima disaster has further intensified the opposition of the people. In India, much of the information about the nuclear industry is not in the public domain. It ought to have been sufficiently transparent. This is an area where decisions should be open, transparent and accountable. Koodankulam is only the beginning. Twenty reactors are functioning in the country. Unless the government takes the people into confidence, resistance movements are inevitable. The uncertainty over the country's nuclear energy program will deepen.

While the effects of the new variables on physical infrastructure are relatively easy to ascertain, the possible impact on the legal infrastructure is still rather obscure. In some cases, the outcome can be equally disruptive. A case in point is the UN Convention on the Law of the Sea. In many ways this is an excellent document, setting out as it does the much-needed global norms for resolving disputes in international maritime law. The drawback of the Convention is that it stipulates that a country's maritime Exclusive Economic Zone (EEZ) extends 200 miles off its coastline, unless it comes up against another maritime zone or has a continental shelf, in which case the seabed claim can be extended up to 350 miles from the coastline. This presupposes that the coastline upon which all the measurements are made will not change substantially.

In Bangladesh, for example, a relatively limited rise in the sea-level floods the coastline for hundreds of miles inland. According to the Convention, that might mean that Bangladesh's EEZ would also retreat dramatically, putting its offshore fossil fuel resources in international waters, or allowing them to be claimed by India or Myanmar. To get around this, a special one-off deal was made with Bangladesh to fix its coastline. However, as more and more coastlines change with inundation, tailoring the law may not be feasible. The law was simply not designed to take care of environmental changes.

Offshore islands can also be used to anchor claims. In South China Sea, tiny coral outcrops, barely above sea level at high tide, are being claimed as national territory so that the claimant nation can exploit the vast hydrocarbon reserves in its EEZ.

It is uncertain what will happen legally to those claims as the sea level rises and those outcrops get inundated. Regardless of the cause, it is an indicator of problems to come. The Convention is just one example of the dangers of the law ignoring physical realities.[34]

It is imperative that existing laws, treaties, subsidies, regulations, and other instruments are re-examined to see if they resolve problems or accentuate them in the event of environmental change. These instruments should also be assessed to ascertain their ability to adapt to the new variables. Mankind built societies; infrastructure and economies to fit a certain set of physical and environmental conditions that it thought were constants. It now turns out they are not. These new variables may trigger economic, political, social and security changes. It has often been remarked that geography makes history. Now, environmental change is remaking geography.

---

[34]H Khasnobis (2011), "Reality and the law: Environmental Variations Can Remake Geography", The Statesman. December 3, 2011

A sea of scandal

It has now become traditional for climate change summits to open with a new, dazzling prediction of impending catastrophe. The UN Climate Conference under way in the South African coastal town of Durban is no exception. This year's focus is on a familiar and certainly arresting argument: sea levels are rising at a catastrophic and unprecedented rate mainly due to man-made global warming. No one makes this point with quite so much panache as Mohamed Nasheed, President of the Maldives. In the run-up to the summit, he declared that he leads "an island nation that may slip beneath the waves if all this talk on climate does not lead to action soon".

Since chairing a meeting of his Cabinet underwater, Nasheed has been busy rallying other low-lying countries to make similar points. He chaired a summit of them in Bangladesh, to compare notes ahead of the Durban summit, and they agree to limit their own carbon emissions. Ban Ki-moon, the head of the United Nations, was delighted — saying that it was unfair to ask "the poorest and most vulnerable to bear the brunt of the impact of climate change alone" and called for them to be given subsidies by richer countries to adapt. Such funds do not seem to be forthcoming. It seems the summit in Durban will, like so many climate summits, be disappointing.

I may be able to help. As someone with some expertise in the field, I can assure the low-lying countries that this is a false alarm. The sea is not rising precipitously. I have studied many of the low-lying regions in my 45-year career, recording and interpreting sea level data. I have conducted six field trips to the Maldives; I have been to Bangladesh, whose environment minister was claiming that flooding due to climate change threatened to create in her country 20 million "ecological refugees". I have carefully examined the data of "drowning" Tuvalu.

And I can report that, while such regions do have problems, they need not fear rising sea levels.

My latest project was a field expedition to India, to the coast of Goa, combining observations with archeological information. Our findings are straightforward: there is no ongoing sea level rise. The sea level there has been stable for the last 50 years or so, after falling some 20cm in around 1960; it was well below the present level in the 18th century and some 50 to 60cm above the present in the 17th century. So it is clear that sea levels rise and fall entirely independently of so-called "climate change".

Explaining this to the public can be very hard. There are so many misconceptions about sea levels, not least that they are constant throughout the world. In fact, there are big variations — by as much as two meters. You need to think not of a constant, level surface, but of an agitated bath where the water is slipping back and forth. This is a dynamic process. In 900 AD, for example, the high level was in Tanzania and the low was in Peru; a century later this had reversed. It is also often forgotten that while sea levels may rise and fall ("eustasy"), so too may the land mass itself ("isostasy").

Today, all people talk about is the sea level — because it coincides with the Intergovernmental Panel on Climate Change's (IPCC) narrative about melting ice sheets, diminishing glaciers and man-made global warming. This leads to confusion over cases such as Bangladesh, whose plight is the exact opposite of the one claimed by environmental lobbyists and the IPCC.

Bangladesh is cursed because of rain over the Himalayas. This has nothing to do with the sea. It is also cursed because of the cyclones which push water inland. Again, this has nothing to do with the sea. Bangladesh is cursed because about half of its land mass lies less than eight meters above sea level — making it highly vulnerable to coastal flooding. But this has always been the fate of delta regions: it has little if anything to do with "climate change". Two years ago, I visited the Sundarban delta area in Bangladesh and was able to observe clear evidence of coastal erosion, but no rise in sea level. In fact it has been stable there for 40 to 50 years. One way to tell this is by examining the mangrove trees, whose horizontal root systems now hang some 80cm above the mudflats as a result of erosion. But the IPCC's Fourth Assessment Report (2007) tells a different story: "Even under the most conservative scenario, sea level will be about 40cm higher than today by the end of 21st century and this is projected to increase the annual number of people flooded in coastal populations from 13 million to 94 million. Almost 60 per cent of this increase will occur in South Asia."

This is nonsense. The world's true experts on sea level are to be found at the International Union for Quaternary Research (INQUA) commission on Sea Level Changes and Coastal Evolution, not at the IPCC. Our research is what the climate lobby might call an "inconvenient truth": it shows that sea levels have been oscillating close to the present level for the last three centuries. This is not due to melting glaciers: sea levels are affected by a great many factors, such as the speed at which the earth rotates. They rose in the order of 10 to 11cm between 1850 and 1940, stopped rising or maybe even fell a little until 1970, and have remained roughly flat ever since. So any of the troubles attributed to "rising sea levels" must instead be the result of other, local factors and basic misinterpretation. In Bangladesh, for example, increased salinity in the rivers has in fact been caused by dams in the Ganges, which have decreased the outflow of fresh water.

The IPCC's Fourth Assessment claimed that "there is strong evidence" of sea level rising over the last few decades. It goes as far as to claim: "Satellite observations available since the early 1990s provide more accurate sea level data... This decade-long satellite altimetry data set shows that since 1993, sea level has been rising at a rate of around 3mm yr−1, significantly higher than the average during the previous half century."Almost every word of this is untrue. Satellite altimetry is a wonderful and vital new technique that offers the reconstruction of sea level changes all over the ocean surface. But it has been hijacked and distorted by the IPCC for political ends. In 2003 the satellite altimetry record was mysteriously tilted upwards to imply a sudden sea level rise rate of 2.3mm per year. When I criticized this dishonest adjustment at a global warming conference in Moscow, a British member of the IPCC delegation admitted in public the reason for this new calibration: "We had to do so; otherwise there would be no trend."This is a scandal that should be called Sea-level-gate.[35]

Conclusion

The greatest challenge to the world civilization and people is that we are unsafe because of pollution, global warming and increasing trend of CO2 in air. Climate change challenges agricultural production, causes flood and drought, causes destruction of our property through cyclone, hailstorm and coastal storms. This is caused by industrial revolution, higher energy consumption, urbanization and vehicular traffic and deforestation in large scale. The water scarcity has posed problems in agricultural crops and clean drinking water is unavailable in all developing countries. Perhaps the Sun is warmer than yester years or the ozone layer is depleted by our faults. The volcanic eruption in Iceland, hot wind waves in Russia

---

[35] Nils-Axel Mörner (2011), " A Sea off Scandal", Deccan Chronicle, Friday, December 2, 2011

and massive eruption in Mount Tumbora in Indonesia are caused by nature.

The world organizations need to be alert on the 'Safeguarding the Nature' for our future generations. We have to make international climate policy and it must be implemented strictly. The United Nations must see that the planet is safe to accommodate all living beings.

But we feel that the United Nations is acting as voluntary organization, which is financially weak and has not yet treated all countries as equal partners. So how could this organization treat each individual person as equal? But we are confident that it is possible to achieve the WORLD PEACE through the UN. The international policy for 'Safeguarding the Nature' must be unbiased for particular country or countries.

Hence, one-third of geographical area should be under forest cover.

Let the world organization make thorough studies on climate, geographical hurdles, forest monitoring, insect surveillance, and propose improvement of the forests all over the globe. Let it devise plans and decide geographical area and forest area proportions, forest area per capita, ownership of forests, and policy for CO_2 reduction, policy for human rights to life, development, property, health and drinking water. The rights of indigenous people should be properly worked out to award justice to all. If the International Climate Policy is accepted and implemented by all countries, WORLD PEACE would be possible in all countries.

+++++

Chapter - IV

ENVIRONMENTAL PROBLEMS, CONFLICTS AND SECURITY

The most environmental problems are: nuclear war, exponential growth of population, waste of natural resources, inadequacies in urban design and organization, poverty and pollution.

Merril Eisenbud (An Environmental Odyssey, 1990)

The Mount Everest is losing its natural beauty. In 1953, snow and ice reached up to the base camp, but now it ends more than eight kilometers above. The year 2010 would be remembered as the world watched in horror as a high quantity of oil gushed from a broken BP oil well in the Gulf of Mexico. It occurred with Deep-water Horizon rig, operated by BP, sank on April 22 following an explosion that killed 11 workers. Almost five million barrels of oil were spilled into the Gulf of Mexico, putting it in the top oil spills of all times. The rescue of the Chilean miners turned out to be one of the most uplifting stories of the year, as more than one billion viewers around the globe watched as each miner emerged safely from over two months of captivity underground. The story was set on motion on August 5 when a cave-in occurred at the San Jose copper-gold mine in the Atacama Desert near Copiapo, Chile. The accident left 33 men trapped 700 meters below ground. The miners survived underground for a record 69 days.

It is also reported that about 25 million people were killed through natural calamities in 2010 alone.

So the people living today around the globe must plan for a future not only for them but also for their progenies. We have to hand over the nature and natural resources what we have received from our forefathers to the future human population for whom we are responsible. Those who would come to this world in future must feel that their parents and grandparents have saved nature, natural resources and peace for their peaceful living. So the Environmental problems and environmental conflicts must be solved and environmental security must be awarded to all living beings. A favourable environment would result in joy, happiness, food security, good health and WORLD PEACE.

In this chapter, environmental problems and environmental conflicts are discussed with facts and figures. Moreover the role of environmental security towards world peace is discussed. Three countries namely India, Nepal and Slovakia are discussed to highlight the present scenario as on today.

This would pave further analysis to bring suitable international policies for saving the environment, and the living world. Unless we study the real facts that cause immense harm to the poor, tribal and nomads, possibly we cannot derive a solution of our problems.

NEPAL Glacier lakes: **Growing danger zones in the Himalayas**

Fears rise of huge outburst flooding in the Himalayas as glaciers melt due to climate change. It's strangely calming to watch the Imja glacier lake grow, as chunks of ice part from black cliffs and fall into the grey-green lake below.

But the lake is a high-altitude disaster in the making – one of dozens of new danger zones emerging across the Himalayas because of glacier melt caused by climate change.

If the lake, situated at 5,100m in Nepal's Everest region, breaks through its walls of glacial debris, known as moraine, it could release a deluge of water, mud and rock up to 60 miles away. This would swamp homes and fields with a layer of rubble up to 15m thick, leading to the loss of the land for a generation. But the question is when, rather than if.

Mountain regions from the Andes to the Himalayas are warming faster than the global average under climate change. Ice turns to water; glaciers are slowly reduced to lakes.

When Sir Edmund Hillary made his successful expedition to the top of Everest in 1953, Imja did not exist. But it is now the fastest –growing of some 1600 glacier lakes in Nepal, stretching down from the glacier for 1.5 miles and spawning three small ponds.

At its centre, the lake is about 600m wide, and according to government studies, up to 96.5m deep in some places. It is growing by 47m a year, nearly three times as fast as other glacier lake in Nepal.

"The expansion of Imja Lake is not a casual one," said Pravin Raj Maskey, a hydrologist with Nepal's ministry of irrigation.

The extent of recent changes to Imja has taken glacier experts by surprise, including Teiji Watanabe, a geographer at Hokkaido University in Japan, who has carried out field research at the lake since the 1990s.

Watanabe returned to Imja in September, making the nine-day trek with 30 other scientists and engineers on a US-funded expedition led by the Mountain Institute. He said he did not expect such rapid changes to the moraine which is holding back the lake.

Watanabe says: We need action, and hopefully within five years. I feel our time is shorter than what I thought before. Ten years might be too late. Unlike ordinary flash floods, a glacier lake outburst is a continuing catastrophe.

Sharad Joshi, a glaciologist at Kathmandu's Tribhuvan University, who has worked on Imja says: It's not just the one-time devastating effect. It would be a common event each year for the coming years. It triggers landslides and reminds villagers that there could be a devastating impact every year. Some of the Tibetan lakes that have had outburst floods have flooded more than three times.

But mobilizing engineering equipment and expertise to a lake 5,100m up and several days' hard walking away from the nearest transport hub is challenging in Nepal, one of the poorest countries in the world. People living in the small village of Dingboche below the lake say scientists and government officials have been talking about the dangers of Imja for years.

Some years ago one of the visiting experts was so convincing about the dangers of an imminent flood that the villagers packed up all their animals and valuables and moved to the next valley. They came back after a week when the disaster did not materialize, but say it's hard to dismiss the idea that there could be a flood one day.

Angnima Sherpa, who heads a local conservation group in Dingboche explains: When I was 21 I went to the lake and it was black and really small. Two years ago I went there and it was really big. I couldn't believe it could get so big. It was really scary. But scientists and engineers still cannot agree on whether to rate Imja as the most dangerous glacier lake in the Himalayas, or a more distant threat.

Mobilizing international assistance for large-scale engineering projects during a global recession is also difficult. The Mountain Institute's initiative was to call in experts from the Andes, where Peruvians have developed systems for containing glacier floods since a disaster in the 1940s killed nearly 10,000 people.

Cesar Portocarrero, who heads the department of glaciology at Peru's national water agency, has overseen engineering works to drain more than 30 glacier lakes, building tunnels or channels to drain the water and reduce the risk of flooding. But he conceded it would be an enormous challenge to apply these methods at Imja.

"It's not easy to say 'we are going to siphon the water out of the lake'," Portocarrero said. "Where do you find the people who can work at high altitudes? How do you move in the equipment? What do you do in bad weather? You have to have exhaustive planning." There are also other contenders for immediate action, with some 20,000 glacier lakes across the Himalayas, although many are concentrated in the Everest region. Bhutan alone has nearly 2,700.

Three of those, known as the Lunana complex, are practically touching, increasing the possibility of cascading floods far more devastating than any rupture at Imja.

"If the barrier fails between them we are going to have a massive glacier lake outburst flood," said Sonam Lhamo, a geologist for the Bhutanese government.

The United Nations Development Program and other agencies have supported a project to drain the lakes but those funds are running out.

John Reynolds, a British engineer and expert on glacier lakes who has worked in Nepal, argues that the international community has focused on Imja because of its proximity to Everest and trekking routes popular with western tourists. He says there are other, more hazardous lakes elsewhere.

The Nepali government ranks Imja among the six most dangerous glacier lakes in the country largely because it is growing so quickly. More than 12 other such lakes are also seen as high risk.

But Reynolds argued: "Just because a lake is getting bigger doesn't necessarily mean that it is getting more hazardous. As the climate is changing, generally speaking more glacial lake systems are forming.

"The question is how to decide which ones are hazardous now and which ones have the propensity to become hazardous in the future."

Imja, though fast-growing, is held in by a relatively wide moraine, which makes it secure in comparison to some others.

Most glacial lake floods begin as high-altitude tsunamis. A large block of ice falling from a glacier at great height sets off a series of giant waves that wash over the moraine.

That's not such a risk for Imja. The glaciers feeding the lake are gradual in slope, which reduces the risk of a large chunk of ice falling from a great height and setting off large waves.

Watanabe concedes the geography of the lake could keep disaster at bay, at least in the next year or two. But, he says, there are signs that an outlet channel at the bottom of the lake may be widening dangerously.

Reynolds said Nepal and the international community need to think of a Himalaya-wide action plan.

"As the climate is changing more glacial lake systems are forming," he said. "The question is how to decide which are hazardous now and which are going to become hazardous in the future."[36]

INDIA

Wildlife activists flay Government for dropping elephant reserve projects

Wildlife activists blamed the State Government for falling prey to a plot by the industries lobby and withdrawing two elephant reserve proposals. The secretary of the Wildlife Society of Orissa said the Center had already approved of the proposals for

---

[36]Suzanne Goldenberg (2011), "Growing danger zones in the Himalayas", at Imja lake, Nepal guardian. Co UK. Monday, October 10, 2011

South Orissa elephant reserve (ER) and the Baitarani elephant reserve (ER) but now the State Government has asked the Center to drop the proposal. According the wildlife activists, Orissa has more than 90 per cent of eastern India's elephant population, including a good proportion of breeding adult tuskers. The State's elephant population of 1,862 shall be seriously threatened by this disastrous move as mega bauxite and iron ore mines proposed to come up in these areas will find it easy to obtain clearance without an assessment of their impact on wild elephants, they argued.

The south Orissa ER was proposed over an area of 4,216 sq. km. in Rayagada, Kandhamal and Kalahandi and the Baitarani ER comprising Keonjhar and Sundargarh spread over 10,516 sq km. Meanwhile, according to the Wildlife Conservation Strategy, 2002, lands falling within 10 km within the boundaries of national parks and sanctuaries should be notified as ecologically sensitive areas but in Orissa there is a move to reduce them to five km from the borders of Karlapat Wildlife Sanctuary. Similarly, an irrational limit of only 2 km has been proposed as ESA around the southern, eastern and western fringes of the Hadgarh Wildlife Sanctuary in Keonjhar district in order to enable the operation of chromites' mines. There is another move to limit this area to only 1 km within the borders of the Balukhand-Konark Wildlife Sanctuary.[37]

Kandhamal (Orissa) poachers operate with Arunachal Tribal's

The wild animal skin mafia operating in Kandhamal district has spread its network up to Arunachal Pradesh. This is evident after the Kandhamal district police nabbed two poachers near Baliguda and seized two panther skins, a leopard skin and a trophy made

---

[37]The Pioneer, Bhubaneswar

from a barking deer skull recently. Moreover, the interrogations revealed that the poachers have a direct link with the hunting Lushiya tribal's of Arunachal Pradesh. Lushiya tribal's are also coming to Kandhamal forests for poaching of elephants, leopards, panthers, bear and deer.[38]

Forest tree felling should be stopped to save Similipal tigers:

While the entire country, including the Prime Minister is concerned over plummeting population of tigers; the Orissa forest department has officially undertaken a disastrous exercise to destroy valuable forests adjacent to Simlipal Tiger Reserve (STR).

The Wildlife Society of Orissa (WSO) in a letter to the National Tiger Conservation Authority and the State Chief Minister has demanded an immediate stop to all forest working operations in the areas within a 10 km radius of the Simlipal Tiger Reserve. The chief wildlife warden of the State has also been urged to stop forest working in these areas. The State should forthwith demarcate and notify such areas as "ecologically sensitive areas" (ESA) under Section 3 of the Environment Protection Act, 1986. The forest department has started cutting timber trees according to the approved working plans in the Baripada and Karanjia forest divisions. Many of these forests border the STR and are used by tigers for movement and hunting. Under this plan, green felling has commenced at Noto Reserve Forests. This reserve forests are an important animal corridor adjacent to the core area of STR. The area is strategically located and serves as a corridor for movement of wildlife, including tigers and elephants, to the forests of Keonjhar and Balasore districts. It is

---

[38] The Pioneer, Bhubaneswar March 8, 2007

the only bridge between the STR and Kuldiha Wildlife Sanctuary for Simlipal tigers.[39]

The Simlipal has become a poachers' paradise. Everyday hundreds of people enter the forest with guns, bows and arrows and go on killing the animals. On Monday i.e. February 14, 2011 (Valentine day) about 400 poachers assembled at Kulipal near Jenabil in Mayurbhanj district. On this day three jumbos were poisoned and killed. In April 2010, 10 elephants were found dead. There is no protection worth the name put in place. If the present trend continues, Simlipal forest could completely lose its animal population. The Orissa State (India) faces the gravest danger to forest animals because of devastation of forests through mining operations in hundreds, drying of ponds, forest mis-management and lack of governance.

Chilika Lake

The wildlife society of Orissa has urged upon the ministry of tourism to conduct a thorough and independent environment impact assessment for the proposed tourism development plans regarding Chilika Lake and to protect the lake's fragile eco-system and wildlife. Chilika is a Ramsar site and habitats several endangered species including the Irrawady dolphins, migratory birds and Barkudia skink and limbless lizard. The OTDC plans to make Chilika Lake a popular tourist destination with a grant of 55.6 million (INR).

Noting that the OTDC has yet to carry out an impact assessment study to gauge the likely adverse effects of the proposed activities, plans to buy fan driven airboats for dolphin tours would be disturbing the dolphins. Dolphin watching should be only allowed in country boats without any power. There are plans to stop the feeding of dolphins by the visitors since it is

---

[39]Pioneer News Service, Cuttack, March 13, 2007

wrong and amounts to the "baiting of wildlife". This will endanger them since they will not leave the feeding area, which shall affect their ecology and breeding habits. There is a move to set up steel watchtowers inside the water around the Nalabana bird sanctuary. The watchtowers will get corroded in a couple of years due to the saline water. The impact of the proposed activities like water skiing and the use of motorized boats need to be studied. A recent study says that there were 804 thousands and 438 visiting birds in the Chilika Lake in 2010.[40]

Man Eating Leopards

The leopard is the most secretive and elusive of the large carnivores. It is also the shrewdest. It is known to be the strongest climber among large cats and capable of killing prey larger than itself. The Cheetah has a speed of 114 KM/hour, leopard has a speed of 80 KM/hour, lion has 65 KM/hour, tiger has 65 KM/hour and USAIN BOLT has speed of 37.5 KM/hour.

Leopards are known for their ability to go undetected. Many live on the fringes of human habitation. Are agile climbers and can descend from a tree a headfirst. Leopards are strong swimmers but not as fond of water as tigers. Mainly nocturnal but can at any time of day and hunt at daytime. These cats are solitary and avoid one another. Hearing and eyesight are their bigger strength. Although smaller than other big cats, leopard can still take large prey using its large skull and powerful jaws. Males are larger than females. Leopards can leap over 20 feet horizontally and jump up to 9.8 feet vertically. The leopard has been at the receiving end for straying into towns and villages from its shrinking habitats across the country.

---

[40] The Statesman News Service, Bhubaneswar, February 8, 2007

But in 2010, 24 leopards killed in conflicts with villagers; 22 died in road accidents; 8 were shot dead by the forest department, 7 died in rescue operations; 2 were killed by other cats; 2 leopards were electrocuted; 78 more were found dead and 180 were killed by poachers. In total, there were 328 leopards' deaths in 2010 in India. Similarly, poachers kill the elephants in India very often. The forestland is reducing each day because of mining, high ways, roads, industries, railways, school and colleges and government offices and through unauthorized occupations. The elephants come to the villages and towns in search of food and are killed.

The Environmental Investigation agency (EIA) believes that at least one tiger is killed daily for its use in traditional Chinese medicines and the black market value of a tiger today is estimated around 50, 000 INR, which is a good 20 million of INR plus once it is used for medicinal purpose. A corporate NGO barked that only 1,411 tigers are left in India till 2010 although the Government of India released 2015 million of INR during 2009-2010 for 'Tiger Projects'. Poaching and poisoning of tigers are the gravest threats followed by habitat loss. The forest department has become a toy by the state administrations.

Unless there is national and international laws for specifying the minimum requirement of forestland, all forestland would be converted to buildings and industries and all forest animals would be killed by the people. Will the tigers survive? What about green canopy? [41]

Turtles in Trouble in India

The Orissa (India) coast is once again dotted with carcasses of the endangered Olive Ridley sea turtles, thousands of which have been washed ashore after

[41]The Times of India, Bhubaneswar, February 2, 2011

allegedly being killed by mechanized fishing boats. Dead Olive Rid-leys have been spotted in large numbers at Gahirmatha, the Devi and Jatadhar river mouths, Harishpur, Chilika coast and Puri. In the past 14 years, more than 1, 30,000 turtles have been found dead on the Orissa coast. Last season, 9,000 turtles were killed while the figure till December 2006 was 5,753.

Hundreds of fishing boats from Kharnasi, Jamboo, Talchua, Dhamra and Kasaphal operate daily inside the marine sanctuary "without any restrictions". The turtle congregation is now breaking up and there is little chance of mass nesting. Kendrapara district reported that the situation had worsened at Gahirmatha after the forest guards refused to go on patrolling duty following the arrest of a colleague who accidentally killed a fisherman last month.

Just seven species make up the known diversity of the world's sea turtles today, but these evolutionary marvels are encountering a growing number of threats. The marine reptiles, all of them endangered, have persisted for millions of years, moving from the sea to land for nesting, and traversing the great tropical and sub-tropical ocean basins as part of their life cycles. Yet, as the 30th Annual Symposium on Sea Turtle Biology and Conservation held recently in Goa (Kerala State) has highlighted, the modern human-dominated era poses grave challenges for their survival. With each passing year, nesting habitat is degraded or lost, feeding grounds are polluted, and more turtle's die in mechanized Fisheries and the threat of mindless port development looms large. Two environmental crises in the past few weeks highlight the dangers. The large oil spill in the Gulf of Mexico has turned the major feeding grounds of the rare Kemp's Ridley turtle into a veritable death zone. In South Asia, which hosts five species, thousands of Olive Rid-leys making their annual journey to Orissa's Rushikulya rookery for nesting had to suffer the effects of a massive oil leak from a ship in the Ganjam port. If a healthy population of turtles must survive into the future, there is a need for a new conservation paradigm.

The first-order priority is to identify and protect the nesting habitat of sea turtles on the Indian coastline. This can be achieved through a full environmental audit of all port projects. If the proposals discussed at the Goa symposium are accurate, no fewer than 331 ports are planned, and notifications have been issued for over 200. The scale of coastal development warrants an aggressive conservationist stance on the part of the Ministry of Environment and Forests. To its credit, the MoEF has supported the International Sea Turtle Society in organizing the global symposium, for the first time in the country. It must now strike a blow for protection by enforcing environmental norms. For a start, it can declare the 'no development zone' of 10 kilometers around turtle nesting beaches, and the 25-km buffer zone that conservation biologists suggest. This needs to cover all new port projects and the expansion of existing ones. A second priority relates to fisheries. While artisan low-intensity fishing in sensitive zones does not appear to be unsustainable, the catchall ferocity of mechanized boats is killing vast numbers of turtles. A regime of restrictions is, therefore, justified. This should set seasonal curbs for intensive commercial fishing, enforce regulations on turtle excluder devices, and control trawler density. Only determined measures can save these wonderful creatures.

Wildlife is dying by thousands outside of the Gulf of Mexico because of oil, but unfortunately it has not made headline news. This week, the confirmed death of thousands of endangered Olive Ridley sea turtles comes from India. Rabindranath Sahu, secretary of the Rushikulya Sea Turtle Protection Committee, stated that thousands of eggs on the Rushikulya beach in Ganjam district have failed to hatch this year because of the large spill of furnace oil in Gopalpur on April 12th, 2010. The slick has spread over a 7 km area. Unfortunately the tides pushed the oil onshore, right where the turtle nests were located. We have found that the hatching of the eggs, which ended last week, have gone down by 40 to 50 percent this year as the eggs, numbering thousands, got spoiled after the leaked oil soaked the nesting site on the beach.

The authorities cleaned only 2-3 km stretch of the beach. The rest of the 5-km nesting site remained contaminated for days as a layer of oil was found on the beach. Many eggs were damaged due to the toxic effect of oil deposits. Moreover, many baby turtles failed to move out of the nest as the soil also got harder."And it is not just the hatchling turtles that have been killed.

Villagers have even reported seeing carcasses of adult turtles along the coast since the spill. It was believed that roughly 155,000 Olive Rid-leys had been nesting on the beach since March. The overall mortality of the hatchling sea turtles is naturally high, with approximately only 75 percent actually hatching and only one in a thousand living to adulthood. Yet the state government in Orissa plans to continue to expand these ports in these marine turtle habitats. The location of the ports near ecologically sensitive areas is a long term risk being taken by the government. As long as we will have ports near ecologically critical areas, they will adversely impact marine biodiversity. Now with the Deep-water Horizon oil spill in the Gulf of Mexico, which is getting all the media attention, we wait and see what the impact will be on the local wildlife, including several different species of endangered sea turtles.[42]

---

[42]Candace M. Hansen, "How Does a Single Oil Spill Kill Thousands of Sea Turtle? The Hindu May 21, 2010

Why so many Ports?

A port being built on India's eastern coast is a "killing field" of rare Olive Ridley turtles and other marine life, and should be shut down. The Green Peace says the Dhamra port in Orissa state, being built by Indian conglomerate Tata group, is close to the beaches of Gahirmatha, one of the few remaining mass nesting sites of the Olive Rid-leys in the world. The group recently conducted a 40-day study of the ecology around the port site and came across more than 2,000 turtles, rare horseshoe crabs, crab-eating frogs, dolphins and snakes, killed by mechanized fishing boats.

The port site is not a turtle nesting ground, but is part of the breeding and feeding ground for many species and is intrinsically rich in bio-diversity. The Tata's, who claim to be a socially responsible company, now have to decide if they want to place profits above environment. We have an incontrovertible scientific critique of their project and we have sent a report to them as well. The Tata's had earlier said the port would not harm the turtles and if it did they would not build the project. The port's draught is 18 meters, which would make it India's deepest port. Its 13 berths can handle more than 80 million tonnes of cargo per year. Hundreds of thousands of Olive Ridleys swim up to Orissa beaches every year to nest, but their numbers are falling drastically, victims of government neglect and rapid industrialization.[43]

The Government of Orissa has planned and **started 14 new ports in the state to cover 483 Kilo Meters** of Orissa Coast to assist the movement of cargo ships. So all olive riddles that come for nesting to Orissa would be simply killed by the cargo ships.

---

[43] Krittivas Mukherjee, "Port threatens Olive Rid leys in Orissa" Reuters Net Alert, June 8, 2007

The National High Ways are overburdened with 25, 000 trucks; the railways utilize dozens of goods-trains and the Paradeep port is over-burdened with cargo ships for transport of iron ores, coal and other minerals. In January 2011, Government of India has allowed for expansion of Paradeep port and the POSCO steel company is interested to start a port very nearer to Paradeep port at Jatadhari confluence and has got government clearance on January 31, 2011 with 32 conditions to fulfill.

Now, it is also necessary to undertake a reality check. Only the BJD party and the BJD Government are more worried for industrialization of the state, when each day a peasant commits suicide in the state. The question is who is benefited through industrialization? Who is displaced? Why the Government is more interested for inviting foreign industrialists? Are there kickbacks in the deals? Why the Central Bureau of Investigation (India) is completely silent? Why the government of India digests all allegations of a state party, which has received less than even 2 percent of popular votes in the 2009 General Election in India.

Each government must at least think and analyze the difference between development, sustainable development and whims of the government. How can the state bear the loss of forests, minerals and tribal people for the benefits of politicians and industrialists? During the first decade of twenty-first century, all rivers are polluted in Orissa state; actual forest area has come down to only 17 percent from 37 percent. Elephants are poached; water borne diseases are increasing and hundreds of people are dying. Unauthorized mines are operated without any checks. If this action continues, the state would be a desert within a decade.

During 2000–2010, there is rapid growth of Maoists, Naxalites and Terrorists in the state. These warring boys and girls have challenged both the government of India and the state government in Orissa. Lawlessness, lacks of governance and corruption have created fear psychosis in the minds of majority of people. The cities are even permeable to these Naxalites.

Green Agenda in a Green Zone

It's good that the Environment Ministry has scrapped Vedanta's mining project at Niyamgiri hills in Orissa, but tribal people cannot be confined to 'reservations' forever.

"The age-old issue of environment versus development returned forcefully to the nation's agenda recently with the cancellation of Vedanta's mega mining project in Orissa by the Government of India. Although the timing and carefully calibrated triumphal displayed by Nehru-Gandhi scion Rahul in the aftermath of the Environment Ministry's decision reeks of politics, the cancellation of the project was widely applauded by most. It is a rare instance of the 'system' refusing to succumb to corporate pressure and bureaucratic manipulation. In the past flagrant violations of environmental and relief and rehabilitation norms by powerful corporate houses have merely been winked at. If a significant number of tribal people have swelled Maoist ranks it is very largely in protest against unfair treatment at the hands of land-grabbing industrialists, rapacious traders, exploitative administration and high-handed law-enforcement machinery.

Chandan Mitra[44] analyzes how Niyamgiri forest was saved in Orissa state. The plan to mine bauxite, found in abundance in the Niyamgiri hills of southern Orissa, would have entailed not only large-scale displacement of tribal people from their traditional homeland but also massive deforestation, disruption

---

[44]Chandan Mitra (2010), " Green Agenda in a Green Zone", The Pioneer Sunday Magazine, August 29, 2010

of wildlife habitats and violation of sacred sites. For once, the Ministry of Environment took into account the costs involved in the permanent loss to ecology and cultural traditions in estimating the damage that would result from the mining operations instead of focussing only on potential material gains.

At the same time, a developing country like ours, where more than 70 per cent of the population is estimated to earn less than 20 INR per day, also needs to progress materially. Industrialization is a necessary engine of economic growth whose requirements too cannot be ignored. So, how do we strike a balance between the conflicting demands of preservation of traditional lifestyles and the environment on the one hand and industry's need to harness natural resources?

When it comes to minerals in particular, the fact is that the bulk of this resource is located in forested areas inhabited by tribal people. That the Orissa Government is now scouting for new sites to relocate the mining project away from tribal areas suggests that such options do exist. Why, then, were they not explored at the outset? Is it only because it's easier to displace tribal people and wantonly destroy forests compared to more expensive alternatives? This is the mindset that needs to change.

I recall the isolation of Chipko movement leader Sunderlal Bahuguna when he attempted to stop the Tehri Dam in Uttarakhand. Mr. Bahuguna not only lost his iconic status among local people but also was jeered at by hostile crowds who wanted the dam built quickly so they could get jobs while electricity reached their homes. It is quite possible that resounding applause for Mr. Rahul Gandhi's much-hyped 'victory' rallies in the foothills of Niyamgiri will remain confined to his own peer group, dominated by NGO-types. When local people realize that job prospects and other benefits of industrialization have shifted elsewhere, the initial euphoria at having wrested backs their traditional habitat from greedy tycoons and land sharks may just vanish.

This is not to justify the Vedanta project. It should never have been cleared in the first place. The controversial company, which has seen a mercurial rise in its fortunes since it took over BALCO, has a reputation for persuading the Orissa Government in particular to give away vast tracts of land at throwaway prices. Last year, I visited the site of their proposed University on the Konark- Puri Marine Drive where they sought to acquire 6,000 acres of triple-cropped rice-growing land.

Vedanta's MoU (Memorandum of Understanding) with the Orissa Government underlined that the university project would also include construction of an international airport, multi-storied apartment blocks, sea-facing chalets and an entertainment park! Understandably, farmers were in a state of extreme agitation there. A movement led by farmers determined to resist land acquisition. Thanks to the decree of Honourable Orissa high court and Rahul Gandhi's open support to the tribal people have awarded justice to the hungry people. Given its track record, it is most gratifying that Vedanta's foray into Niyamgiri has been firmly halted.

It is this rapacious intent, brazenly displayed by promoters of industry, mining barons, and increasingly the education mafia that has resulted in widespread protests against any kind of land acquisition. Singur and Nandigram are important milestones in the growing folklore of peasant resistance in contemporary India. These two agitations not only succeeded in thwarting the designs of corporate houses and insensitive CPI (M) apparatchiks, they are on the verge of changing West Bengal's political complexion, perhaps irrevocably.

However, it cannot be anybody's case that no land must be acquired, irrespective of the need for industrialization. Factories producing industrial and consumer products and concomitantly generating employment are essential for the economy to prosper and alleviate poverty. But the issue of land has become almost as sensitive as family planning was in the late-1970s. The overzealous, often brutal methods used to coerce people into sterilization produced a political backlash that derailed India's pursuit of population stabilization, perhaps forever.

Land acquisition too is fast becoming a political hot potato, which could stymie industrial progress in the long run. Instead of the haphazard and case-by-case approach being adopted by the Union and State Governments at present, it is essential to develop a uniform, fair and humane methodology for procurement of land from farmers, that too only when a project is deemed absolutely essential and not aimed primarily at fattening private pockets.

With mounting popular unrest over land acquisition, be it for industrial or infrastructure purposes — as witnessed recently in Aligarh and Agra over the Yamuna Expressway — it is important that the Government evolve an appropriate mechanism to conduct a social and environment audit for every mega project in which all stakeholders must be given appropriate say. Indian industry, riding piggyback on an effete political leadership and a malleable bureaucracy has had it very easy so far. They have caused enormous damage to the fragile ecology in many parts of India.

The country cannot afford to replicate the European or American experience of industrialization, which ended up destroying forests, snuffing out wildlife and also decimated indigenous people along with their traditions and cultures.

Our generation has to leave behind an ecological legacy that is at least as good as what we inherited, if not better, even as we build a prosperous India.

Treasure trove turns into Deathtrap

Recently, Orissa hit the headlines for its environment. The news originated in New Delhi and its tremors were felt in Kalahandi. Though belated, the Union Ministry of Environment and Forests (UMEF) took up the issue on a priority basis and put a big question mark on the future of the Vedanta at Lanjigarh. Similar seems the fate of the proposed mega steel project of Posco – India Ltd.

While environmentally conscious people across the State and nation have commended the UMEF, the people of mineral-rich Keonjhar view the UMEF's role differently. For them, the UMEF is yet to play a pivotal role to redress their untold suffering and plight as far as Keonjhar's acute environmental pollution is concerned.

For the last ten years, Keonjhar has been made to suffer from air pollution. Rampant mining activities together with mushrooming of iron ore crushers, coming up of steel projects and sponge iron units, bad roads, plying of 30,000 iron ore carrying trucks and thousands of private vehicles have been pumping out pollutants into the ambient air of Barbil, Joda, Bolani, Thakurani, Bhadrasahi, Bamebari and Banspani.There is a constant rise in air pollutants like sulphur dioxide, nitrogen oxide, carbon monoxide, carbon dioxide, ammonia, Particulate Matters (PM), Respirable Suspended Particulate Matters (RSPM) in the ambient air causing harm to humans and other living organisms.

For the control of air pollution and protection of public health, the Union Government has put in place a revised National Ambient Air Quality Standards

(NAAQS) in November 2009 removing the earlier distinction between residential and industrial areas, which is said to be more stringent for industrial areas. The standards are considered almost at par with the European Union and US levels.

It prescribes that an ideal air of one cubic meter of volume must not contain more than 60 microgram of sulphur dioxide (S O2), 60 microgram of nitrogen oxide (NO2), 140 microgram of PM (2.5) and 60 microgram of RSPM.

Though a year has elapsed, it has brought no relief to Keonjhar. Critical levels of PM and RSPM are observed at Joda-Barbil. Annual average concentration of PM is 600-800 microgram per cubic meter of air and that of RSPM is 250-320 microgram as against the NAAQS's 140 microgram and 60 microgram, respectively.

This is even worse in summer and winter. In 2008, while presence of PM varied from 900-2900 microgram per cubic meter of air, RSPM varied from 300-700 microgram throughout the year during 6 am to 10 pm except on rainy days (June-September).

As reported by the State Pollution Control Board (SPCB), the Joda-Barbil area is having the most polluted air as far as the presence of PM and RSPM is concerned. Thanks to the Union Government and pollution control boards sitting cross-fingered, simply formulating policies and setting up different authorities and agencies to ensure effective enforcement of the standards. Several studies have brought out gory statistics on large-scale human sufferings due to air pollution. Air pollution has caused around 2.4 million human deaths every year, as per the World Health Organisation (WHO) report.

A startling study reveals: around 3,000-4,000 people are affected by TB, jaundice and respiratory complications every year and 300-400 patients succumb to them in the mining region of Keonjhar.

Since 2001, air pollution has claimed 3,000 lives in Keonjhar district.

The situation in Keonjhar is more disastrous than the Bhopal Gas Tragedy of 1984 that killed 2,000 people outright and injured hundreds of thousands. But, no Anderson is here to be blamed for. Besides, a number of people are suffering from chest diseases while TB; jaundice and liver infections are on a constant rise. People, who can afford, are going in for treatment out of the district while the majority of poor tribal, in the absence of adequate medical hands and infrastructure, are suffering and dying a premature death for no fault of theirs.

The SPCB(2008-09- Annual Report) has identified Joda, Barbil and Bhadrasahi as critical zone with regards to presence of PM and RSPM in the ambient air, it has not yet initiated any corrective measures to curb the air pollution for giving respite to those suffering. They have neither the plan of shifting the affected people to safer or neither cleans areas nor any proposal to provide free or affordable medical help at the doorsteps with the assistance of corporate houses that gain from mining activities and are indirectly responsible for the unhealthy atmosphere. Hundreds of thousands of people are living in a region that is not worthwhile to live in. While the mining-money influx to the State capital city reportedly makes it clean and beautiful, it leaves Keonjhar to rot. Both the State Government and the SPCB are far from their primary job — the welfare of people.

In a memorandum to the Chief Minister, Keonjar Development Council (Keonjhar Vikash Parishad), a voluntary organization, had warned the administration one-and-a-half years back that if the air quality persisted, there would be no man free from TB, jaundice, asthma or other chest complications, but to no avail. It all seems that the Government has turned a blind eye towards Keonjhar district that contributes a lion share to the State exchequer.[45]

Pollution trading

India may let power companies start trading renewable-energy credits in May in a push to create a multibillion-dollar market to encourage reductions in greenhouse-gas emissions. The estimates trade in renewable energy credits could rise to as much as $10 billion by 2020. India is pressing ahead with its own efforts to fight climate change after last month's Copenhagen talks failed to reach a new global climate treaty. The move puts the world's fourth-largest emitter ahead of China and other developing nations in creating a domestic emissions-trading market to boost investment in solar, wind and other clean-energy projects. India is the second-largest generator of carbon credits in the United Nations Clean Development Mechanism, the world's second-biggest greenhouse-gas trading market. Certified Emissions Credits, or CERs, issued for pollution- cutting projects in India are sold to businesses in Europe and elsewhere seeking to meet either mandatory or voluntary limits.

Emissions of gaseous pollutants

Scientists and researchers from around the world gathered at ESRIN, ESA's Earth Observation Centre in Frascati, Italy, recently to discuss the contribution of satellite data in monitoring nitrogen dioxide in the atmosphere. Using nitrogen dioxide (NO2) data acquired from 1996 to 2006 by the Global Ozone Monitoring Experiment (GOME) instrument aboard ESA's ERS-2 satellite, Nitrous oxide emissions over

---

[45]Dambaru Dhar Ghana, "Keonjhar 's Treasure trove turns into Deathtrap", The Pioneer, October 28, 2010

India is growing at an annual rate of 5.5 percent /year. The location of emission hot spots correlates well with the location of mega thermal power plants, mega cities, and urban and industrial regions. Emissions of gaseous pollutants have increased in India over the past two decades. According to Dr. Sachin Ghude of the Indian Institute of Tropical Meteorology (IITM), rapid industrialization, urbanization and traffic growth are most likely responsible for the increase. Because of varying consumption patterns and growth rates, the distributions of emissions vary widely across India.

Pollution due to Distilleries

The distillery sector is one of the seventeen categories of major polluting industries in India. These units generate large volume of dark brown coloured wastewater, which is known as spent wash? Spent wash contains high organic pollutants such as Total Dissolved Solids (TDS) - 85000 to 95,000 mg/l, Biochemical Oxygen Demand (BOD) - 45,000 to 60,000 mg/l and Chemical Oxygen Demand 80,000 to 1,20,000 mg/l. Thus, the distillery wastewater causes serious pollution problems in the recipient water bodies when discharged, resulting in depletion of dissolved oxygen in water and adverse effect on aquatic life, fish, phytoplankton etc. Also, it pollutes groundwater and drinking water when discharged on land. Application of distillery wastewater for irrigation of crops causes soil pollution i.e. salinity. The Government has notified environmental standards for the distillery sector under the Environment (Protection) act, 1986. The Government is also encouraging the distilleries to achieve zero discharge of effluent. (Lok Sabha on August 4, 2010)

Government puts forest-dwellers on a tight tether

Having pushed the cause of restoring rights to forest-dwellers, the government has now dealt a double whammy to those who live in and around national parks and sanctuaries. The ministry of environment and forests has devised regulations to quickly and smoothly evict people from wildlife sanctuaries and national parks, and, check all activities in the periphery of these protected wildlife areas. The first set of rules falls foul of the Forest Rights Act (FRA); the others are set to fail due to sheer political naiveté.

Summary evictions and destruction of forest villages led to violence, which, in turn, gave rise to a national movement for the FRA. Thousands living in the forests - predominantly tribal people - were being evicted or threatened in their traditional lands because the forest department decided to summarily turn these pockets into no-man lands for greater common good. The groundswell of anger ensured Congress passed the FRA, meant to set right the historical injustice done to the people.

The Act requires that each national park and sanctuary be reviewed. The government has to prove there is scientific justification for having it -- there are sanctuaries that are more like sugarcane fields than forests -- and for not having people in it. And before that, consider and prove that it is really not possible for people and the wildlife to cohabit. Put the proof before the people who own the lands and get their consent. Convince them; get them on your side and save wildlife. The foresters disliked and fought against such provisions. The supreme cause of greater good and control was more important than the rights of thousands. But now, the law had been passed.

For three years, there has been little implementation. Now, the foresters have come up with a short cut. Doing away with the need for scientific evidence and consent, the environment ministry's new guidelines asks foresters and their designated experts to re-forge the boundaries of these national parks and sanctuaries, even expand them further. The authorities are to collect data on how these poor people eat into the forests and then go to the affected tribal people with a compensation of one million Indian rupees (INR), in cash or kind.

At the same time the ministry has decided to protect the periphery of these lands too. The logic goes: the national parks and sanctuaries are like islands today in a vast matrix of agricultural fields, industries, cities, mining zones, a maze of roads high tension wires, canals and railway lines. The pace of change and development around the forests are turning them into more disconnected moth-eaten patches.

In 2002, the government decided to give a protective cover along the periphery of these wildlife zones. The activities and development in lands falling within 10 kilometers of each park and sanctuary should be restricted and land use controlled, the National Wildlife policy recommended.

The government decided it would declare these areas as ESA under the Environment Protection Act. This would empower the state governments and forest departments to control activities on the periphery of a park. The powers under the act would make people living in the fringes of these wildlife zones go to the administration, foresters or revenue officials, each time they wanted to change a bit of their land – construct a building, change the crop, build a road, dig a well, build a factory or mine an ore.

Generally speaking, one can categorize the area around a typical national park and sanctuary dominated by three or four classes – poor farmers and poorer tribal people, rich miners and hoteliers.

There are enough not-so-poor and not-so-powerless local interests for sure.

Naturally, the state governments refused to create these ESA. The Supreme Court stepped in and ordered that ESA be created. States still did not budge. Now, the Centre has stepped up pressure and demanded that ESA be created soon. It has accommodated the need to not be strict about the 10 km limit but it has given states the guidelines to impose the Eco-sensitive Area (ESA).

Imagine an army of administrators and foresters descending on hundreds of villages around these national parks and sanctuaries checking for infringement of a "master plan" made to preserve status quo on land demarcated without consultation, let alone consent, of the people it will affect. From building houses to changing crop to digging wells for irrigation to cutting a tree, all activities will be questioned and verified on the basis of a "master plan". Any sub-divisional magistrate will agree, it's an impossible job and a recipe for petty corruption - some will be part of it. It is the license administration (raj) that PM Manmohan Singh refers to very often being imposed in the name of environmentalism. Except this one will work against the poor but not the rich and powerful.

There is enough scientific proof wildlife biologists can proffer for some patches of forests to be kept inviolate. But it is politically naïve to believe that one can actually keep these patches inviolate and safe with a million or more people living around them in poverty and anger. Park after park, the country has witnessed wildlife zones turn into battlegrounds between the dispossessed tribal people and the foresters ordered to "protect the land against them". These battle zones gave fuel to Naxalism and also gave rise to the FRA. It also helped organized poachers find the poor but expert tribal who will kill a tiger for a few hundred rupees.

These two guidelines promise to turn the clock to the 70s and 80s when experts went around demarcating no-go forestlands and summarily evicting people. Environment minister, GOI has protested he won't let that happen. But he and his army of foresters and bureaucrats should have first proven they have the political will to stop powerful miners, hoteliers and industrialists from grabbing forestlands before they went after the easy prey.[46]

They know that the industrialists and miners control the government in India.

Is nuclear energy a solution of global warming?

India a country of 1.1 billion people currently gets only a fraction of its electricity from nuclear power. Now the US atomic trade pact with India and an atomic energy pact with France, India can fight global warming with clean nuclear energy. Nuclear energy has been recognized as a clean as CO_2 to the atmosphere after its reaction that could damage our environment. It's also known that nuclear energy has reduced the amount of greenhouse gas emission, reducing emissions of CO_2 for about 500 million metric tons of carbon. India's Civil Liability for Nuclear Damage Bill, 2010 is meant to pave the way for India to sign International Atomic Energy Agency (IAEA)'s Convention on Supplementary Compensation (CSC) for Nuclear Damage, 1997.

The question that stares citizens in the face is: whether or not the proposed liability Bill and the pre-existing IAEA's compensation treaty in the supreme

---

[46]Nitin Sethi, (2011), "Government puts forest-dwellers on a tight tether"' The Times of India, New Delhi, February 18, 2011

interest of present and future generation of Indians? As on August 23, 2010 among the 18 amendments suggested to the Nuclear Liabilities Bill is one that leaves a window open for private operators of nuclear plants. The standing committees had expressed its opinion against private operators.

Most polluted places in India

The United States, with fewer than 5 percent of the world's population, accounts for more than 20percent of total carbon emissions. India, with more than 17 percent of the global population, accounts for just 5.3 percent of emissions. The most polluted places in India are:

Vapi in Gujarat and **Sukinda** in Orissa (India) is among the world's top 10 most polluted places, according to the Blacksmith Institute, a New York-based nonprofit group.

(a) In Vapi, about 71, 000 people are affected. Pollutants: Chemicals and heavy metals due to its Industrial estates.

(b) In Sukinda, 2, 6000, 000 people are affected. Pollutants: Hexavalent chromium due to its Chromites mines.

As many as 51 Indian cities have extremely high air pollution and among these cities, Patna, Lucknow, Raipur, Faridabad and Ahmedabad top the list. An environment and forest ministry report, released on September 14, 2007 has identified 51 cities that do not meet the prescribed Respirable Suspended Particulate Matter (RSPM) levels, specified under the National Ambient Air Quality Standards (NAAQS). In 2005, an Environmental Sustainability Index (ESI) placed India at 101st position among 146 countries.

Taking a cue from the finding, the Central Pollution Control Board (CPCB) formulated NAAQS and checked the air quality, which led to the revelation about air quality in leading cities.

According to the report, Gobindgarh in Punjab is the most polluted city, and Ludhiana, Raipur and Lucknow hold the next three positions. Faridabad on the outskirt of Delhi is the 10th most polluted city, followed by Agra, the city of Taj Mahal. Ahmedabad is placed 12th, Indore 16th, Delhi 22nd, Kolkata 25th, Mumbai 40th, Hyderabad 44th and Bangalore stands at 46th in the list. The Orissa town of Angul, home to National Aluminum Company (NALCO), is the 50th polluted city of the country.

NEPAL

Projects for the poor excluded in Nepal

Nepal, one of the poorest countries in the world, recently witnessed a decade-long Maoist insurgency. Public service delivery became irregular, infrastructure fell into disarray and poor people's livelihoods were disrupted. With the support of DFID, the NGO Rural Reconstruction Nepal (RRN) implemented a wide-ranging rural community development project in 16 conflict-affected districts from 2003 to 2008. Its experiences, now compiled in the form of a briefing note, provide insights into the feasibility of poverty reduction activities in conflict-affected environments.

Designed in a participatory way, the project covered a range of activities including irrigation and hydropower, school building and furniture support in addition to micro-enterprise and institutional development. In consultation with local government institutions and development actors, project activities were targeted particularly at conflict-affected areas where trust building also formed a core part of the intervention.

The program was designed to deliver both immediate as well as medium-term benefits for target communities. While irrigation support helped improve food security, livelihood support activities allowed communities to generate income through self-employment activities in livestock, candle making and beekeeping, amongst others. Women were also enabled to engage in income-generating activities by making safe drinking water more readily available thereby reducing their workloads. Communities were trained in problem-solving strategies in resources management and in social organization and mobilization by forming water user groups and saving and credit associations, for instance.

Since communities were encouraged and enabled to identify their development needs, take initiatives and contribute resources to the program from the start, project activities have been sustained. In line with its exit strategy, the user groups formed by RRN were converted into Operation and Maintenance Committees, which were provided with administrative and financial training. Since the end of the project, these committees have raised local funds to continue development interventions in project areas. The brief points out that the program was designed and implemented in a cost-effective way, utilizing local skills and resources to the extent possible and since benefits were shared equitably among the target communities, RRN's efforts are likely to bear fruit for some time to come.[47]

Addressing the underlying risk factors

There is a growing trend towards greater and more catastrophic natural disasters. Of the ten disasters

---

[47]Joshi, N. N and K. Dahal (2008), "Project for the Poor", Rural Reconstruction Nepal (2009), Conflicts and Disaster, Eldis Organization, Lessons from Community Development Programme in Nepal

with the highest death tolls since 1975, half have occurred in the five-year period between 2003 and 2008 with the developing world witnessing nine of the ten worst. A range of factors such as compounds such terrible natural events:

(a) Climate change and the decline of ecosystems;
(b) Increasing urbanization and poor urban governance; and
(c) Low incomes and fragile rural livelihoods.

This first edition of the biennial Global Assessment Report on Disaster Risk Reduction (DRR) aims to review and analyze the natural hazards threatening humanity and seeks to provide new evidence on how, where and why disaster risk is increasing globally. The report focuses on: (a) Global disaster risk: patterns, trends and drivers and (b) Deconstructing disaster: risk patterns and poverty trends at the local level.

The recommendations include:

(a) Economic development increases a country's exposure at the same time as it decreases its vulnerability. However, in low- and middle-income countries with rapidly growing economies, exposure increases at a far faster rate than vulnerability decreases, leading to increased risk overall.
(b) Risk drivers: economic and social development plays a crucial role. These include income and economic strength; and governance factors such as the quality of institutions, openness and government accountability;
(c) Climate change: more than two thirds of the mortality and economic losses from internationally reported disasters is associated

with meteorological, climatologically and hydrological hazard;

(d) Poverty and poor governance: the translation of poverty into risk is conditioned by the capacity of urban and local governments to plan and regulate urban development, enable access to safe land and provide hazard mitigating infrastructure and protection for poor households;

(e) Areas of HFA progress reported: progress has been made in strengthening capacities, institutional systems and legislation to address deficiencies in disaster preparedness and response. However, little progress is being made in the mainstreaming of DRR into economic, social, urban, rural, and environmental and infrastructure planning

(f) Community and local level approaches, particularly when supported by effective decentralization processes and government-civil society partnerships can increase the relevance, effectiveness and sustainability of DRR across all practice areas, reduce costs and build social capital. [48]

SLOVAKIA

Forests, their status and their socio-economic importance in Slovakia

Institutional and socio-economic aspects:

Slovakia occupies the western part of the Carpathian Mountains. About 65 percent of the territory and thus a large proportion of forests have a mountainous character. The area of forests in Slovakia is 19,990

---

[48]2009 Global assessment report on disaster risk reduction: risk and poverty in a changing climate Prevention Web (2009), Eldis Organization, Note; Progress in the implementation of the Hyogo Framework for Action(HFA: a ten-year framework adopted by 168 countries in order to mitigate the effect of natural disasters)

sq. km what equals 41 percent of the total country's territory (49,036 sq. km). Another 1, 775 km 2 of forests are found on abandoned farmlands (Forest Information Center, 2001).

The Ministry of Land Management administers the forestry sector. The nature and environmental conservation comes under the Ministry of Environment. Categories of utilization of forest stands are: 73 percent forests with predominating production function, 15 percent protective forests, and 17 percent forests with special functions (watershed areas, nature conservation, recreation forests).

Restitution of ownership has resulted in a broad variety of ownership types, increased number of owners and users. Approximately 44 percent of forests are owned by non-state bodies or private persons. Restitution of another 8 percent is in progress. The state-owned forests represent 42 percent. Approximately 6 percent of forests remain un-reclaimed, with unknown owner or non-reclaimable upon valid legislation. Medium-size estates with average size 100- 700 hectares predominate in the category of non-state forests. A considerable part of forests (489,000 ha or 24 percent of forest area) is in a shared ownership. Smallholdings up to 5 hectares (average size 1.06 ha) cover only 1.3 percent of forestland.

Contribution of forestry to the gross domestic products decreased from 1.2 percent in the beginning 1990s to 0.66 percent in 2000. Total contribution to the GDP of forestry, wood processing, and pulp and paper industries, is estimated to 8.5 percent, however. Slovakia is a net exporter of nearly all forest and wood-derived products.

Both quantitative and qualitative indicators, except of those related with forest health due to high air pollution of trans-boundary origin, show that the management of forests is done in a relatively sustainable way. In the scores published by the WWF in 2000, the care of forests in Slovakia was ranked at the third to fifth position among the European countries. In spite of this fact, there are several problems, which make promotion of more nature-conforming forestry practices difficult. These are related especially with the high share of incidental felling, which represents more than 50 percent of the total annual cut throughout the 1990s. Their prevalence over planned regeneration felling is an obstacle to regular forest management and systematic forest regeneration.

Forest Vegetation

Large vertical variation and transitional position between the oceanic and continental parts of Europe contribute to the large forest ecosystem diversity. The forest classification which is routinely used in the forest management planning (Zlatnik 1959), recognizes 350 forest types grouped into 55 associations and eight forest vegetation zones. Main forest ecosystems include rive rain forest vegetation, oak and mixed oak beech forest, pure beech woods, mixed fir-beech, spruce-fir-beech and sub alpine spruce forests, and the mountain pine dominated vegetation at the alpine tree limit. The share of broadleaves in the overall species composition is 56.9 percent, with beech dominating (29.6 percent) and oaks second (13.7 percent). The share of Noble Hardwoods (maples, ash, elms, alders, limes, and wild fruit species) is 4.1 percent. Conifers represent of Norway spruce (27.5 percent), silver fir (4.6 percent) and pines (7.7 percent) of the total forest area, 40-45 percent are semi-natural forests originating from natural regeneration and differing only slightly from natural forests in terms of species composition. More than 70 fragments of natural and virgin forests with a total area of 18,000-20,000 ha (1 percent of all forests) are found in Slovakia.

Frames for Forest Biodiversity Conservation

The forestry authorities declared the first nature reserves in the territory of Slovakia at the end of the 19th century. The IUCN nature conservation categories I and II cover only 19 percent of the forest land in the country. **This represents both strict nature reserves and national parks**. There are 561 strict nature reserves of which 93.5 percent (87,623 ha) and 6 national parks of which 80 percent (283,601 hectares) are forests. Another 460 thousand hectares are included in the IUCN categories III-VI represented mainly by the Protected Landscape Areas.

Establishment of the gene reserve forests has a central role among the systematic forestry activities aimed at conservation of forest biodiversity. With the aim to provide condition for long-term conservation of forest genetic resources, 32 thousand hectares of gene reserve forests were declared or proposed for declaration by January 2000. Minimum area of each gene reserve forest is 100 hectares, which provides relatively good basis for sustainable genetic, species and partially also forest ecosystem conservation. Under adequate management, each gene reserve provides an opportunity to demonstrate dynamic conservation of forest biodiversity but also practical applicability of nature-conforming forestry methods.

National system for conservation of forest genetic resources includes in- situ and ex-situ measures: approved stands for seed collection (55,221 hectares), plus trees (3,204 registered plus trees), seed orchards (81 units - 203 ha), two clone archives (comprising approximately 1,000 genotypes) and the Forest seed bank with 350 entries.

In 1998, preparation of a completely new national forestry legislation started. A draft of a new Forest Act was subjected to inter-sectoral discussion in 2001. It includes several new elements, which should help to mitigate discrepancies between the forestry and nature conservation. Promotion of the category of Valuable Woodland Habitats should allow for more efficient biodiversity conservation also in the forests with the priority of wood production function.[49]

Environmental Conflicts and Environmental Security

Michael Renner (2006) has extensively studied environmental security and environmental conflicts. He opines that environmental security would solve environmental conflicts and would strengthen WORLD PEACE.

Since the late 1970s and 1980s, there has been an ongoing discourse with regard to the connections between environment, resources, security, conflict, and peacemaking. These connections gradually became more accepted among academics and NGOs, but were met with greater reservation by policymakers. By the mid-1990s, Robert Kaplan still felt compelled to lament: "Mention 'the environment' or 'diminishing natural resources' in foreign-policy circles and you meet a brick wall of skepticism or boredom."

During the latter years of the 1990s, environmental issues did begin to find a place in the arena of practical foreign and security policy-making. Then, new difficulties arose in the wake of the attacks of 11 September 2001. In the United States, where policy-makers had begun to embrace notions of

---

[49] Roman Longauer and Peter Straka, Forest Biodiversity in Slovakia, Forest Research Institute and Ministry of Environment of the Slovak Republic, Slovakia

environmental security in the 1990s, the "war on terror" has taken center stage, and largely brought these early efforts to a halt.

The study of how environmental issues and peace and security concerns interact is far from a monolithic undertaking. Different writers have focused on different aspects within the spectrum of connections. Some have focused fairly narrowly (i.e., limiting their inquiry to the connections between environment and the incidence of violent conflict); others have drawn far broader boundaries (i.e., adopting a broader environment and security approach). Some of the writing has focused on the impact of environmental change on the national security of a particular state, whereas other efforts have been primarily concerned with the consequences for global security.

Different schools of thought exist side by side, and the disagreements among proponents of different views and interpretations have at times been very pronounced and in a few cases even quite vehement. And at least some analysts question the conceptual merits of notions like "environmental security" and "environmental conflict."This introduction is not intended to engage the different schools of thought. Rather, its purpose is to provide a brief overview of the various dimensions in which environment intersects with conflict and security. In broad terms, these connections can be grouped in four categories:

The impact of environmental change on conflict formation may emerge from situations of resource and environmental scarcity (overuse and depletion of resources), mediated and sometimes exacerbated by the social and economic repercussions of environmental degradation.

On the other hand, tensions and violence can also arise out of a context of contested resource wealth. This is only partially about access to and control over lucrative resources. Resource extraction often leads to severe environmental and other impacts on local communities. If the benefits and burdens of extractive projects such as oil production, mining, logging, and large-scale dam construction are distributed unequally, the result may be protracted conflict.

The environmental impact of armed conflicts, arms production, maintaining military forces, and preparations for warfare are related with environmental considerations in the cleanup of military bases and in the dismantlement of obsolete or surplus weapons.

Opportunities for "environmental peacemaking" that may arise out of common interests among different countries or communities in safeguarding resources and ecosystems, as well as shared vulnerabilities where ecosystems are heavily degraded.

2. Defining Conflict, Redefining Security

Before discussing these connections in some detail, it is useful to consider the broader context— the effort to broaden and redefine the definition of security. Different analysts often use the terms "conflict" and "security" in very different ways.

(a) Conflict

Conflict is the more easily defined of the two terms, though not without its own set of challenges. A basic distinction needs to be made between armed conflict and disputes that are largely carried out by non-violent means. This is not an absolute distinction: non-violent struggles may at some point turn violent, and vice versa. And conflicts often do not have a well-defined start and end point, as formal declarations of war and even formal peace agreements are becoming rare. The Heidelberg Institute for International

Conflict Research in Germany has identified 249 political conflicts around the world that were active in 2005. Of these, 24 involved a high level of armed violence and 74 some occasional violence. The remainder— 86 "manifest conflicts" and 65 "latent conflicts"— were carried out without resort to weapons.

Within the narrower category of armed conflict, peace researchers have developed a range of definitions and methodologies. Put in simple terms, war and armed conflict require the following elements: there has to be use of armed force (and there has to be some continuity of violence rather than sporadic fighting); the fighting has to be between organized groups and at least one of the conflict parties has to be a government; and there have to be battle deaths (with different thresholds established for minor, intermediate, and major conflicts (or equivalent terminologies) in terms of deaths per year or for the duration of the conflict).

While such criteria are necessary for a systematic, scientific assessment of conflict trends and developments, they are increasingly in danger of being too narrowly drawn, with the consequence that certain types of armed violence fail to be captured in data sets. The methodological focus on battlefield deaths, for instance, means that some conflicts are recorded at a lower level of intensity than appears warranted.

In most contemporary armed conflicts, the number of people killed on the battlefield is usually quite small compared with those who perish because fighting and looting shred public infrastructures, displace civilians, disrupt harvests and halt other economic activity, and prevent delivery of vital health and other services. In many cases, there is a severe lack of reliable data. But a recent study found that for every battle-related death in the Democratic Republic of the Congo, there are 62 non-violent deaths related to the conflict in the country, with malnutrition and a variety of diseases the leading causes. An estimated 3.9 million people have died there since 1998, and about 38,000 civilians continue to die every month.

(b) Security

Security is a rather vague term without a generally agreed definition. Traditionally, it is seen as closely related to the threat or use of violence, and military means are regarded as central to the provision of security. This may once have made sense, when conflicts took place predominantly between different countries, when territorial control was a key objective, and when uniformed soldiers were the combatants. But over the last several decades, this type of conflict has become more the exception than the norm.

A number of efforts were launched to challenge this narrow approach in the 1970s and 1980s, but gained momentum after the end of the cold war. Several high-profile international commissions, NGOs, and academics developed a range of innovative concepts refining and redefining security— by including social, economic, and environmental dimensions. These became known under headings such as common security, comprehensive security, and environmental security. Human security, the most encompassing of these concepts, was first spelled out in detail in the 1994 edition of the Human Development Report. The gathering discourse raised a number of critical questions: What is the object of security? Who is to be protected? What are the "threats"? Who is to provide security? And what are the means?

The unfolding discourse challenged orthodox assumptions about national security, deepening it "upwards" (from national to global security) and "downwards" (from territorial security focused on states and governments to people security—individuals and communities), and widening it by arguing that non-military dimensions, such as social well-being and environmental integrity, are important prerequisites for ensuring security. There is now growing recognition of the important inter-connections between environment, development, and security.

The core insights emerging from this discussion can be summarized as follows:

Weapons do not necessarily provide security— and may even heighten insecurity. This is true for adversarial states armed with weapons of such destructive power that no defense is possible. It is true in civil wars, where the easy availability of weapons empowers the ruthless but offers little defense for civilians.

Real security in a globalize world cannot be provided on a purely national basis, or even on basis of limited alliances. A multilateral and even global approach is needed to deal effectively with a multitude of trans-boundary challenges.

The traditional focus on state (or regime) security is inadequate and needs to encompass safety and well-being for the state's population. If individuals and communities are insecure, state security itself can be extremely fragile. Democratic governance and a vibrant civil society may ultimately be more imperative for security than an army.

Non-military dimensions have an important influence on security and stability. Nations around the world, but particularly the weakest ones, confront a multitude of pressures. They face a debilitating combination of rising competition for resources, severe environmental breakdown, the resurgence of infectious diseases, poverty and growing wealth disparities, demographic pressures, and joblessness and livelihood insecurity.

The human security concept has been criticized by a number of analysts as being too sweeping and analytically unfocused. Critics have charged that the inclusion of a wide array of social, economic, and environmental ailments makes it difficult to set priorities and translate the concept into specific policies.

The point, however, is not to draw up a lengthy list of potential security concerns— doing so may simply run the risk of endless debates about the relative merit and importance of multiple factors. Issues such as infectious disease, water scarcity, or climate change may, at first glance, not necessarily constitute security challenges. But beyond certain thresholds of magnitude, and particularly in combination, they may well create conditions that call into question the basic fabric of communities and nations, and hence their security in a very tangible way.

Today, there are essentially two major conceptions of human security. The first approach focuses primarily on protecting people from acts of violence and violent threats to their rights, safety, or lives— "freedom from fear." Emerging from this approach, the Human Security Centre at the University of British Columbia, Canada, launched a new annual Human Security Report in 2005.The second approach stresses far broader issues of human well-being and dignity and might be characterized as "freedom from want." It focuses on protecting people not only from violence but also from a far more expansive array of social, economic, and environmental challenges. The independent Commission on Human Security spells out this approach in detail in a 2003 report.

Sometimes the connections between environment and security lead to violence. But a number of analysts have warned against overdrawn predictions of widespread or massive "environmental wars."In assessing the connections between environment and conflict, it is important to understand that most conflicts in this category are likely to be sporadic, localized, and limited in terms of numbers of people killed or harmed.

It is equally important to stress that insecurity also manifests itself in ways other than violent conflict, and that such non-violent outcomes are nevertheless reason for concern. The livelihood, welfare, and integrity of communities (or entire societies) may be compromised in fundamental ways. The result could be prolonged periods of instability and mass suffering even short of armed violence. The task, then, is to enhance the understanding of the interactions and dynamics among different factors and the combinations that are likely to bring about destabilizing results.

3. Environmental Change and Conflict

Resource scarcity and environmental degradation are increasingly understood to play an important role in generating or exacerbating conflicts. The depletion of water resources, overexploitation of fisheries, degradation of arable land, decimation of forests, and growing interference in ecosystems from forests to wetlands to coral reefs are among the principal processes of human-induced environmental change. Climate change further augments already-observable challenges, by raising sea levels, shifting vegetation zones, dwindling natural habitats, changing precipitation patterns, and generating more frequent and more intense storms, floods, and droughts.

Conflict may arise over access to renewable natural resources such as water, arable land, forests, and fisheries. This may be the result of a tightening of supplies (depletion or degradation of natural resources), an unsustainable increase in demand (due to population pressures or increased per capita consumption, often related to export-led economic models), distributive inequities, or a combination of these factors. Developing countries, particularly those whose economies are heavily geared toward agriculture and other sectors that directly depend on the health of the natural resource base, are most immediately affected by environmental problems. There, the needs and interests of contending groups tied closely to the land— farmers, nomadic pastoralists, ranchers, and resources extractors— are often incompatible.

A range of case studies— both between different countries and within countries— has been generated over the years, including examples of violent and non-violent disputes relating to water diversion (such as India-Bangladesh), dam construction and irrigation (China's Three Gorges project, India's Sardar-Sarovar, and a dam along the Senegal River involving Senegal-Mauritania), land degradation and desertification (Somalia-Ethiopia, Sudan, El Salvador-Honduras), over fishing (Canada-Spain, and others).

The concept of environmental security should not be equated with an argument that environmental change is the sole causative factor in triggering conflicts or other security concerns— nor even that environmental change is necessarily a direct trigger of conflict. There is probably not a single conflict in the world that can properly be understood as mono-causal. Rather, environmental issues are tied up with other factors. Environmental degradation may be mediated and sometimes augmented by social disparities, ethnic and community rivalries, and political dynamics. A multitude of pressures (whose particular makeup varies from case to case) including persistent poverty, wealth disparities, unequal land distribution, unemployment and job insecurity, population growth, health epidemics, and environmental degradation is provoking social stress, discontent and polarization, leading to political strife in many countries and to devastating violence in some.

Cases such as Rwanda and Chiapas underline this complexity. In Rwanda, mass violence in the mid-1990s grew out of a set of circumstances that included explosive population growth, severe land shortages and inequality, land degradation, lack of non-agricultural employment, a crisis in the country's coffee and tea export sector, and pain inflicted by structural adjustment programs. Against this backdrop, opposing elites engaged in savage competition and extremist politics that led to civil war and genocide.

In Chiapas, Mexico's southernmost state, marginalized peasants, predominantly drawn from Mayan indigenous communities, rose up in 1994. The conflict, which took more political than violent forms, was driven by rampant inequality (widespread poverty in the face of natural wealth), demands for land reform, population pressures, inappropriate farming and ranching methods, rapid deforestation, austerity and lack of rural credit, and the domination of the political system by narrowly-based elites.

Energy, water availability, food security, and infectious disease are among the major concerns in the environment-security-conflict nexus. Below is a brief discussion of these factors, along with considerations of livelihood and habitability issues and the impact of disasters increasingly driven or worsened by environmental degradation.

(a) Energy: Energy issues manifest themselves in a number of ways, and are strongly focused on the dominant and most sought-after commercial source, petroleum.

Especially in the mainstream discussion, the connection between energy and security is being discussed as a challenge of supply security. The current discussion is shaped in particular by the rising demand in fast-developing countries such as China and India, which join the United States, Europe, and Japan as voracious consumers and heavily import-dependent nations. Supply security is both a concern about physical supplies (with the rate of new oil discoveries falling since the 1960s) and political developments in oil-rich nations. The economic security of both supplier and buyer nations is potentially compromised by severe price swings.

Major Powers have repeatedly intervened in resource-rich countries, militarily and by other means, in order to directly control, or more broadly secure access to, lucrative resources. The result has often been enduring political instability. Against the backdrop of surging demand for oil, geopolitical rivalries for preferential access are today again intensifying among major importers.

Oil income has led to a massive militarization in some regions (particularly the Middle East). Governments of oil-rich nations have tended to over invest in weapons and armies, and under invest in human needs. And in a number of oil producing countries (such as Angola, Nigeria, Sudan, Iraq, and Colombia), oil resources have either driven internal conflicts or helped finance such struggles, leading to massive human rights violations and an erosion of human security.

Finally, oil (along with natural gas and coal) of course plays a central role with regard to carbon emissions and thus climate stability, an issue that poses grave threats to human safety everywhere on the planet.

(b) Water: Water is the most precious resource. Both the quantity and quality are crucial for meeting fundamental human needs. Worldwide, more than 430 million people currently face water scarcity, and the numbers are set to rise sharply. Given population growth, nearly 3 billion people are expected to live in water-stressed countries by 2015.

Conflicting claims over water resources have been cited as a possible cause of violent clashes between nations that share rivers such as the Nile, Tigris and Euphrates, Ganges, and Brahmaputra. The waters of the Jordan and Litani rivers did indeed play a role in the Middle Eastern conflicts between Israel and its Arab neighbours. For a number of reasons, cooperation, rather than conflict, has so far been the norm among riparian states. One is that a militarily weak downstream country is unlikely to challenge its upstream neighbour's over water allocation issues. And riparian countries often conclude that a diplomatic solution— working out an agreed plan to share available water resources— is far preferable to a violent solution. Still, this may not necessarily hold true in the future.

Meanwhile, water-related conflict is far more likely to occur within, than between, nations. China, India, Mexico, the United States, Spain, the Central Asian republics, and parts of the Middle East and Africa are among the countries and regions in which growing water scarcities have caused considerable internal disputes and, in some cases, violent confrontations.

(c) Food Security: An adequate and reliable supply of food is one of the most basic determinants of how secure or insecure people are. Food security is at the intersection of water availability, poverty, land distribution, and environmental degradation. And among the major food security threats on the horizon are climate change, the loss of biodiversity, and the possible repercussions of monocultures and factory farming.

After a steady decline during the first half of the 1990s, the U.N. Food and Agriculture Organization found that hunger grew again in the latter part of the last decade. Nearly 2 billion people worldwide suffer from hunger and chronic nutrient deficiencies.

Some 1.4 billion people live precariously off marginal lands. Of these, more than 500 million people live in arid regions, more than 400 million people eke out a meager living on soils of very poor quality, some 200 million small-scale and landless farmers are compelled to cultivate steep slopes, and 130 million people live in areas cleared from rainforests and other fragile forest ecosystems. The soil productivity of slopes and formerly forest-covered lands tends to be exhausted relatively swiftly, forcing people to move on to seek opportunity elsewhere, sometimes in distant cities or in competition with other rural dwellers.

Depending on the circumstances, the outcome of food insecurity may in some cases be a violent one. In Africa's Sahel region, there are increasing clashes between herders and farmers competing for scarce productive land, particularly as desertification increases. Examples include conflicts in northern Nigeria, Kenya, and in Sudan's Darfur region. The clashes may be reported as ethnic and religious struggles (or even be perceived as such by the protagonists), but it is clear that resource scarcities play an important role.

(d) Infectious Disease: Although the poor are most vulnerable, societies across the planet are confronting a resurgence of infectious diseases. Some 20 known diseases have re-emerged or spread geographically in recent years, and many new ones, such as SARS and avian flu, have been identified. Pathogens are crossing borders with increasing ease, facilitated by growing international travel, trade, and migration, but also riding the coattails of social upheaval inherent in war and refugee movements.

Environmental factors play an important role in human susceptibility to and transmission of diseases. Logging, road-building, dam construction, and climate change enable diseases like malaria, dengue fever, and schistosomiasis to spread to previously unaffected areas or bring people into closer proximity with new disease vectors.

Disease burdens can in some cases be sufficiently severe to undermine economies and threaten social stability. In the poorest developing countries, infectious diseases are deepening poverty and widening inequality, drastically reducing life expectancy, overwhelming fragile health systems, and severely taxing overall economic health. The HIV/AIDS epidemic in southern Africa, in conjunction with malaria, already has a devastating impact on farm production and food security because it incapacitates and kills primarily young adults during their peak productive years. (AIDS is projected to claim a fifth or more of the agricultural labour force in most southern African countries by 2020.)

Water, food, and health challenges, among others, can undermine livelihoods, overwhelm communities' ability to cope, and unravel the social fabric of fragile societies, particularly when adverse impacts make themselves felt in highly unequal ways. But they can also lead to violent conflict, setting different communities against each other in direct competition over scarce resources, as has been the case, for instance, between farmers and pastoralists in Darfur.

(e) Livelihood and Habitability Challenges:

Environmental degradation may in some cases be sufficiently extreme to undermine the habitability of a given area and to compel affected populations to leave in search of new homes. Growing water scarcity, soil erosion, desertification, deforestation, and other environmental calamities are now contributing to the uprooting of large numbers of people— in effect creating flows of "environmental refugees." Although reliable (or uncontroversial) estimates do not exist, environmental refugees in all likelihood already number in the tens of millions worldwide. An estimated 135 million people— many in sub-Saharan Africa— are at risk of being driven from their lands because of desertification. And climate change may cause as many as 150 million environmental refugees by 2050, according to the Intergovernmental Panel on Climate Change.

Such displaced populations may find it difficult to find new livelihoods in other rural areas (or in already-crowded cities) and may even clash with unwelcoming host communities. The influx of people can impose a considerable burden on the receiving area in terms of increased competition over land, water, jobs, communal facilities, and social services. This is especially the case if the host community's economy is stagnant or in decline, if government is corrupt and indifferent to the needs of its people, or if the influx is sudden and massive. All too often, newcomers are seen as unwelcome competitors and accused of irredeemably altering the local culture and customs. And political leaders or challengers are sometimes eager to capitalize on stirring up resentments.

(f) Disasters: In addition to the gradual undermining of livelihoods, environmental degradation is setting the stage for more frequent and more devastating natural disasters. And the deterioration of forest watersheds, wetlands, coral reefs, and other ecosystems also means that human communities have less protection against extreme weather events and other disasters.

The number of disasters has risen from about 750 in 1980-84 to almost 2,000 in 2000-2004. The number of people affected has risen from about 500 million to 1400 million during the same period of time.And the pace is likely to accelerate in coming years as climate change translates into more intense storms, flooding, heat waves, and droughts.

Disasters often have devastating impacts on the safety and well-being of affected communities in terms of people killed and injured, health epidemics, dwellings destroyed, and damage to industries, fisheries, agriculture, and critical physical infrastructure. Economic and ecological marginalization worsens the impacts on poor people and ethnic minorities.

Disasters may undermine the long-term habitability or economic viability of an affected area. But even where the effects are more temporary, disasters often exact a heavy toll in terms of indebtedness, poverty, and unemployment. Such adverse effects can easily deepen fault lines— between rich and poor, urban and rural communities, and different ethnic groups. In divided societies, conflict may arise if relief and reconstruction aid are wielded as a tool for dispensing favours to one community or group over another or for tightening the government's political control.

It is not a given that competition over scarce resources or the repercussions of environmental degradation will lead to violent conflict. But they often do sharpen hardships and burdens, heighten the desperation of those most affected, and reinforce the perception that disputes are of a "zero-sum" nature. Different social groups and communities experience the effects of resource depletion and environmental degradation unevenly. These divergences can reinforce social and economic inequities or deepen ethnic and political contention.

Because many societies fall short on conflict prevention and mediation capacities, and political leaders (or their challengers) often find that they can gain influence or strengthen their power by fanning the passions, it is likely that environmental factors will play an increasingly important role in triggering or aggravating conflicts. Worst-case outcomes are more likely where political grievances are left to fester, where public institutions are weak or corrupt, and where weapons (particularly small arms) are easily available.

4. The Repercussions of Resource Wealth

Whereas the connection between resource scarcity and conflict is still relatively a new field of study, and struggles over resource wealth are documented. Indeed, throughout human history, big powers have repeatedly intervened in resource-rich countries, militarily and by other means, in order to control lucrative resources. There are indications that a fresh round of jockeying among major powers (and importers) is in the offing.

During the 1990s and the first decade of the new century, resources such as oil, minerals, metals, diamonds, timber, and agricultural commodities have played an important role in a number of civil wars. The money derived from the often illicit resource exploitation in war zones has secured an ample supply of arms for various armed factions and enriched a handful of people— warlords, corrupt government officials, and unscrupulous corporate leaders. But for the vast majority of the local people, these conflicts have brought a torrent of human rights violations, humanitarian disasters, economic calamity, and environmental destruction. Some 5 million people were killed in resource-related conflicts during the 1990s, close to 6 million fled to neighboring countries, and 11–15 million people were displaced inside their own countries.

We can distinguish three different sets of circumstances as follows:

(a) In some places, including Colombia (oil and cocaine), Angola (oil and diamonds), Afghanistan (opium, lapis lazuli), and Cambodia (timber), the pillaging of resources allowed violent conflicts to continue that were initially driven by grievances, or by secessionist and ideological struggles.

(b) Elsewhere, including Sierra Leone (diamonds), Sudan (oil), and to some extent in the Democratic Republic of the Congo (a range of minerals), governments or armed groups initiated violence as a way to seize control of a coveted resource.

(c) Commercial resource extraction and large-scale infrastructure projects (such as dams) can also be a source of conflict where governance is undemocratic and corrupt. The economic benefits typically accrue only to small domestic elite and to multinational companies and their shareholders, while the local population (most often poorer communities, minority groups, and indigenous peoples) shoulders an array of social, health, and environmental burdens. Often, it is indigenous communities that are confronted by the operations of oil, mining, and logging firms. Examples include Nigeria's Niger Delta (oil), Indonesia's Aceh and West Papua provinces (oil, gas, gold, timber), Papua New Guinea's Bougainvillea Island (copper), India (dam-building for irrigation), and Guatemala (dam-building for power generation).

Some analysts have argued that it is either resource wealth or resource scarcity, but not both, that gives rise to conflict. But this is a false dichotomy, hewing more to the purity of academic theory than allowing for the world's many complexities and contradictions. Where resource wealth is a factor in conflicts, it is primarily non-renewable resources such as fuels and minerals that are at issue (though a nominally renewable one, such as timber, is important as well). On the other hand, where resource scarcity is a factor, it concerns principally resources that cannot be looted and traded, such as farmland and water.

Still, conditions of resource wealth often co-exist with conditions of depletion and deprivation. For instance, the operation of a copper mine on the Pacific island of Bougainvillea, Papua New Guinea, in the 1970s and 1980s caused such massive damage (contaminated rivers and decimated crop harvests) while the economic benefits accrued primarily to the central government and foreign investors that the native population decided to launch a sabotage campaign against the mine. This developed into a full-fledged guerrilla war that shut down the mine and lasted for several years. Although secessionist aspirations had existed on Bougainvillea, these only rose to the forefront (the guerrilla front declared independence in 1990) after the environmental devastation had triggered hostilities.

In Nigeria's Niger Delta, rich oil deposits have generated revenues on the order of $300 billion over the last few decades. Yet not only have the Delta communities been bypassed by this wealth generation because of largely unrepresentative and corrupt government (crushing poverty is the defining reality of the region), but they have also actively suffered from rapacious oil extraction. Leaky pipelines and the practice of flaring off natural gas found in conjunction with oil have polluted their fields and fishing grounds, and human health is impaired.

5. Environmental Impacts of War and War Preparation

While much attention has been devoted to the complex relationship between environmental breakdown and conflict dynamics, there are also important connections in the reverse direction: warfare and war preparation impose a range of environmental costs.

(a) Environmental Impacts of War Preparation

The maintenance of military bases and installations, the production, testing, and upkeep of conventional, chemical, and nuclear arms, and the training of armed forces consumes substantial amounts of energy, generates large quantities of toxic and radioactive wastes, contributes to air pollution and global warming, and imposes a heavy toll on often fragile land.

The maintenance of modern weapons systems and military bases entails the use of large quantities of toxic materials and wastes. In the United States, for example, it was estimated that the armed forces generated about half a million tons of toxic wastes (stemming from fuels, paints, solvents, propellants, explosives, etc.) annually during the 1990s. Negligent handling of such dangerous materials during the decades of the Cold War resulted in more than 17,000 contaminated sites on 1,855 U.S. military bases. Producing and maintaining nuclear arsenals also entails tremendous environmental and human health costs. In the United States, more than 3,200 individual sites were identified after the end of the Cold War as having soil and/or groundwater tainted by radioactive contamination. These waste and contamination problems are matched by those found in the former Soviet Union.

The world's armed forces control large expanses of land. While some areas, off limits to the general public, have thrived as wildlife refuges, land used for weapons testing and military man oeuvres suffer tremendous degradation and pollution. Man oeuvres demolish the natural vegetation and compact and erode soil. Bombing and shooting ranges leave behind a wasteland contaminated and littered with unexploded ammunitions. When weapons and ammunitions become obsolete— either because of changed political and military circumstances or due to the passage of time— the surplus stocks need to be decommissioned. Surplus arms were long incinerated, exploded, or simply jettisoned without much thought as to the release of toxic materials. For instance, conventional munitions and chemical weapons were dumped at sea on a massive scale after World War II, a practice that is now outlawed.

In the aftermath of the Cold War, environmental concerns received far greater attention in disarmament efforts, particularly with regard to the (ongoing) task of chemical weapons disarmament in the United States and Russia. The decontamination of military bases and arms production sites and the proper handling and storage of chemical and nuclear weapons-related materials will ultimately cost hundreds of billions of dollars worldwide. (But the most severely polluted sites may simply have to be kept off limits to human use.)

(b) Environmental Impacts of Armed Conflict

Inevitably, armed conflict causes considerable damage to the natural environment. In recent years, the United Nations Environment Program (UNEP) has shed much needed light on the broad array of impacts in a number of conflict areas. UNEP's Post-Conflict Assessment Unit has undertaken both field research and desk studies concerning Afghanistan, Albania, Bosnia-Herzegovina, Kosovo, Serbia and Montenegro, Macedonia, Iraq, Liberia, and the Occupied Palestinian Territories.

Much environmental degradation caused by armed conflict is unintentional, but some of it is deliberate. Armed conflict often involves the intentional destruction of fields or forests to deny enemy forces access to water, food, feed, and construction materials. Denying an adversary cover or sanctuary, forests have been devastated by a variety of means in wars: spraying with herbicides (Vietnam War), use of heavy tractors equipped with special forest-clearing blades, saturation bombing, and setting of self-propagating wild fires. Landmines and unexploded ammunitions have pernicious impacts on the rural human environment.

A number of important rivers flow through more than one sovereign state, providing an opportunity for an upstream belligerent to divert or befoul the waters before they reach a downstream enemy with which it is engaged in armed conflict, a potentially major social and environmental calamity in an arid region. During the 1991 Gulf War, Turkey threatened to cut off the flow of water from the Tigris River into Iraq, but ultimately did not carry out its threat.

Environmental warfare entails the manipulation of the natural or built environment for hostile military purposes. Attacks may be carried out (and in some cases have been carried out) with the intent of releasing dangerous pent-up forces as a de facto weapon against fresh-water impoundments (during the Sino-Japanese War of 1937-1945, World War II, and the Korean War); nuclear power stations (resulting in the release of radioactive elements); and industrial facilities that could release dangerous chemicals.

During the Gulf War of 1991, Iraqi forces set hundreds of oil wells ablaze (some of which burned for as long a eight months) and released huge amounts of oil into the Gulf waters for hostile purposes. During that same war and in the course of other conflicts such as the 1999 Kosovo War, U.S. and NATO forces attacked refineries, petrochemical plants and other industrial facilities, leading to the release of substantial quantities of toxic materials. And the massive movement of troops and equipment in the Gulf War imperiled an already fragile desert environment.

Over time, the environmental impact of warfare has grown, as technology has boosted the firepower and range of weapons. Any use of biological, chemical or nuclear weapons would likely have an extraordinarily severe impact on the environment. But concern is not limited to wars fought with sophisticated weapons. Low-tech "civil" wars can also have devastating impacts. In fact, many recent resource-related conflicts took place in some of the world's biodiversity hotspots and other areas of great environmental value, in the Democratic Republic of the Congo, Indonesia, Colombia, and other countries.

As noted earlier, lucrative natural resources have attracted a range of armed groups, who have engaged in rapacious resource extraction. Because such activities are carried out illegally, and because loggers and miners are intent on extracting resources before they might lose control over a resource -rich area, they have no incentive to conduct their operations in a responsible manner. Their primary interest is in raising funds for weapons purchases or self-enrichment and they try to extract as much, and as fast, as possible. This translates into tremendous environmental devastation.

Forests, jungles, and wetlands are also sometimes the setting for ongoing battles between rival forces. Additional stress is placed on such areas due to the influx of refugees. For example, the Rwandan civil war of 1990–94 spilled over into neighbouring Zaïre (now the Democratic Republic of the Congo), with both sides conducting military operations in the

Virunga National Park area. The military presence in the forest kept growing, landmines were laid, poachers decimated wildlife, and vegetation was cut down.

Following the Rwandan genocide, nearly 2 million people left Rwanda in a sudden, massive outflow in July 1994; half went to eastern Zaïre and settled mostly on the edge of Virunga Park or inside it. The refugees could not get firewood, so they cut and gathered as much as 1,000 tons of wood a day, causing serious deforestation.

Over a period of 27 months, a total of 113 square kilometers of forestland was affected; of that, 75 square kilometers were clear-cut.

The subsequent Congolese civil wars imposed additional burdens on Congo's national parks—Kahuzi-Biega, Salonga, Virunga, Maiko, Garamba—and the Okapi Wildlife Reserve, driving elephant and eastern lowland gorilla populations to near-extinction.

6. Promoting New Ways of Peacemaking

As the discussion so far has suggested, there are multiple negative feedback loops connecting environment and security. However, in principle there is no reason why environment could not be connected with security in a positive manner. On the basis of shared environmental needs and interests, cooperation is possible among different communities and countries that are otherwise locked into relationships marked by suspicion and hostility.

(a)**Promoting Peace through Environmental Cooperation:** Environmental challenges ignore political boundaries, require a long-term perspective, and encourage and necessitate participation by civil society. These are characteristics that lend themselves to transforming conflict and building peace.

Environmental cooperation can enhance mutual trust (by establishing pragmatic, working-level contacts across political divides); establish cooperative habits (among governments as well as at the society-to-society level); create common regional identities around shared resources; and thus over time helping to generate a new dynamic that could sustain broader peacemaking efforts.

There is indeed a growing array of initiatives worldwide that seek to promote what might be called "environmental peacemaking." They include peace parks straddling international borders, shared river basin management plans, regional seas agreements, and joint environmental monitoring programs. Establishing conservation zones along the contested border between Peru and Ecuador was an important ingredient in settling the armed conflict between the two South American nations. In southern Africa, a joint water commission in the Okavango River Basin among Angola, Namibia, and Botswana is helping to manage these countries' incompatible water use plans and thus to reduce the likelihood of conflict. And in the southern Caucasus, environmental issues may provide a way for the states in this conflict-ridden region (Georgia, Armenia, and Azerbaijan) to cooperate. There is thus some evidence that environmental protection and restoration may be one of the few topics around which ongoing dialogue can be maintained among adversaries. But far more study is required to fully understand the opportunities and obstacles for such initiatives. To date, they have received relatively little attention.

(b) **Promoting Peace through Joint Humanitarian Action:** Environmental protection is ultimately in everyone's interest, but this is a realization that is often concealed by short-term interests. As mentioned earlier, environmental degradation is increasingly translating into more frequent and more devastating natural disasters such as storms, floods, and droughts. In other cases, it weakens the integrity of ecosystems that provide protection against the impact of disasters.

Although disaster prevention is of course the preferable course, disasters sometimes do entail a silver lining. A disaster may inflict suffering that cuts across the divides of human conflict, prompting common relief needs and making protagonists realize that reconciliation is essential for reconstruction and recovery. A prominent example is Indonesia's Aceh province after the December 2004 tsunami. It triggered a new mood of reconciliation that allowed the 29-year conflict there to be brought to an end in 2005.

Still, disasters do not automatically translate into cooperation (and, as developments in Sri Lanka— which was also hit hard by the Indian Ocean tsunami— show, post-disaster dynamics could even rekindle a conflict, if the complex issues are not handled well).Smaller-scale disasters or slow-onset disasters may not generate the sudden jolt necessary to transform conflict dynamics. Political leaders may not possess the courage or wisdom to break with deeply ingrained conflict patterns. Quarrels could even sharpen in the wake of disasters, particularly over the distribution of relief aid. Finally, disputes over scare land and water between different communities would gain precedence over common interests. Both environmental and humanitarian peacemaking thus needs active, visionary political leadership in order to be translated from theoretical opportunity to real-world breakthrough.[50]

---

[50]Michael Renner (2006), "Introduction to the Concepts of Environmental Security and Environmental Conflicts", Institute for Environmental Security, The Hague

Conclusion

Natural calamities, oil spill, mining, deforestation, use of pesticides and coal based thermal plants are mostly responsible for unfavourable environment. Moreover, killing of elephants and tigers, felling of forest trees by mafias, killing of endangered species, killing of dolphins and migratory birds cause environmental loss. The disruption of wildlife habitats, permanent loss of ecology, construction of dams, establishment of mega industries by corporate houses, stone crushers, distilleries and excessive vehicular traffic and forest fire cause air pollution by way of excessive release of Sulphur Dioxide (SO2, Carbon Dioxide, Carbon Monoxide, Nitrogenous Oxide, ammonia and Respirable Suspended Particulate Matter (RSPM). Greenhouse gas emission has exceeded in all industrial estates and in cities. Industrialization, urbanization and traffic growth are the major factors of emissions of gaseous pollutants that pollute air. Deforestation causes extensive damage to forest animals. However, nuclear energy can reduce global warming, carbon dioxide, and carbon monoxide. But use of nuclear energy is limited to a small number of countries.

Water-related conflict is far more likely to occur within nations. China, India, Mexico, the United States, Spain, the Central Asian republics, and parts of the Middle East and Africa are among the countries and regions in which growing water scarcities have caused considerable internal disputes and, in some cases, violent confrontations. Change of climate causes harm to crop production. Each year peasants commit suicides because of absence of markets and low price of the produce in the post-harvest season. But this year, in Orissa state (India), more than 150 peasants committed suicides for loss of grains in rice fields because of un-time excessive rainfall during harvest time.

Industrialization, acquiring of cultivated land, water diversion, dam construction, land degradation, over-fishing and desertification cause conflicts in the society. Similarly, poverty, hunger, wealth disparities, unequal land distribution and unemployment cause social stress and discontentment. There should be food security, water availability, energy supply and medical facilities to all. The environmental security–conflicts nexus is caused when people die of hunger, diseases (such as water related diseases like diarrhea or cholera) and natural calamities. In most of the developing countries livelihood and habitability challenges and disasters create conflicts and even wars. The spread of Naxalism, Terrorism and Maoism is caused because of hunger, unemployment, land acquisition and displacement.

Peace could be achieved through environmental cooperation and joint humanitarian action. Damaging nature and environment would bounce back to those who cause it with or without their knowledge. The governments are more responsible in creating problems and conflicts in environment related issues.

The Forest Rights Act seeks to secure the tribal people, but latest guidelines seek outright eviction or regulation of activities. All governments are causing destruction of forests and natural resources without the consent of people. The Tribal Women Committees may be asked to look after the forests. The governments should ban use of insecticides and pesticides in crop production. Use of bio-fertilizers, compost and farmyard manures should be encouraged. In grave situations in crop loss, insecticides and pesticides could be used with strict supervision.

Moreover, Corruption and whims of the political leaders would bring climate changes and dig graveyards for all.

+++++

Chapter – V

REPORTS ON ENVIRONMENT

We now know, too, that great damage is being done to the Ozone Layer by the production of chlorofluorocarbons and other. But at least we have recognized that reducing and eventually stopping the emission of CFCs is one positive thing we can do about the menacing accumulation of greenhouse gases.

- Margaret Thatcher, Former Prime Minister, the UK, November 8, 1989

Climate change is one of the greatest environmental, social and economic threats facing the planet. There is now unequivocal evidence that the build-up of greenhouse gases (GHGs) in the atmosphere is mainly due to large-scale fossil fuel consumption and deforestation over the last century. The trends of higher surface temperatures, shifting climate patterns and an overall destabilization of the global climatic system are all pointing in the direction of a 'tipping point' — a point in the climate graph beyond which entire ecosystems catapult into a different unpredictable state, one which we might not be able to put right.

The Intergovernmental Panel on Climate Change (IPCC) reports that atmospheric greenhouse gas concentrations are higher today than at any point in history and multiple evidences suggest that this is anthropogenic and not a result of natural mechanisms. Historically, the nation's representing just 25 per cent of the global population have emitted 83 per cent of the world's carbon dioxide (CO2) emissions. But today, as developing nations experience increasingly rapid economic and population growth, they are on a track to quickly become the major emitters of the future.

Year 2010 has been a year of warnings, not only from the scientific community but also nature. Heat waves in Russia ravaged lives and economy alike and the worst ever floods in Pakistan decimated hundreds, displaced millions and required war-footing measures to fight back. In the face of a significantly high frequency of these tragic events, nations which fail to take notice will only be seen as increasingly indifferent and rouge in the eyes of the world.

It will not be an exaggeration to say that we are in times where the essential challenge is to find an answer to climate change, an answer that will be the foundation of a sustainable future for the planet and its inhabitants. There is, of course, no silver bullet because the world needs a solution, which combines the goals of social equity, environmental sustainability and financial benefit. Over the past few years, the annual United Nations Climate Change Conference has become the *sanctum sanctorum* to find an answer to the holy grail of climate change.[51]

---

[51]Aarati Khosla, "No Great Expectorations", The Sunday Pioneer, December 5, 2010

The Vienna Convention (1985), the Montreal Protocol on Substances that Deplete the Ozone Layer (1987), Intergovernmental Panel on Climate Change (1988), United Nations Framework Convention on Climate Change (1992), Kyoto Protocol (1998) and Cancun Conference (2010) are some of the important conferences, which exclusively discussed the environmental degradation in the world. All deliberations are excellent but till today, we are unable to check further deterioration of environment. The Kyoto Protocol expires by the end of 2012 and after that the world community would take a legal step to save the environment (Appendix 1).

In this chapter, reports on 'World Commission on Environment and Development, the Stockholm Environment Institute report and Global Water Crisis' have been included to reveal that the world institutions and the United Nations have taken steps to award peace through regulating clean environment. But till date the objectives have not been fulfilled and environment is being polluted further because of absence of regulatory mechanism and carelessness of national governments.

Report of the World Commission on Environment and Development

The United Nations General Assembly,

Concerned about the accelerating deterioration of the human environment and natural resources and the consequences of that deterioration for economic and social development,

Believing that sustainable development, which implies meeting the needs of the present without compromising the ability of future generations to meet their own needs, should become a central guiding principle of the United Nations, Governments and private institutions, organizations and enterprises,

Recognizing, in view of the global character of major environmental problems, the common interest of all countries to pursue policies aimed at sustainable and environmentally sound development,

Convinced of the importance of a reorientation of national and international policies towards sustainable development patterns,

Recalling that, in its resolution 38/161 of 19 December 1983 on the process of preparation of the Environmental Perspective to the Year 2000 and Beyond to be prepared by the Governing Council of the United Nations Environment Program, it welcomed the establishment of a special commission, which later assumed the name World Commission on Environment and Development, to make available a report on environment and the global problems in the year 2000 and beyond, including proposed strategies for sustainable development,

Recognizing the valuable role-played in the preparation of the report of the World Commission by the Intergovernmental Inter-session Preparatory Committee of the Governing Council of the United Nations Environment Program, as envisaged by the General Assembly in its resolution 38/161,

Recalling that in resolution 38/161 it decided that, on matters within the purview of the United Nations Environment Program, the report of the Commission should in the first instance be considered by the Governing Council of the Program, for transmission to the General Assembly together with the comments of the Council and for use as basic material in the preparation, for adoption by the Assembly, of the Environmental Perspective, and that on those matters which were under consideration or review by the Assembly itself, it would consider the relevant aspects of the report of the Commission,

Taking note of Governing Council decision 14/14 of l9 June l987 transmitting the report of the Commission to the General Assembly,

Noting that the Environmental Perspective to the Year 2000 and beyond has taken account of the main recommendations in the Commission's report,

Recognizing the instrumental role of the Commission in revitalizing and reorienting discussions and deliberations on environment and development and in enhancing the understanding of the causes of present environmental and development problems, as well as in demonstrating the ways in which they transcend institutional frontiers and in opening new perspectives on the interrelationship between environment and development as a guide to the future,

Emphasizing the need for a new approach to economic growth, as an essential prerequisite for eradication of poverty and for enhancing the resource base on which present and future generations depend,

The Commission expresses as follows:

1 Welcomes the report of the World Commission on Environment and Development entitled "Our Common Future",

2. Notes with appreciation the important contribution made by the Commission to raising the consciousness of decision-makers in Governments, inter-governmental and non-governmental international organizations, industry and other fields of economic activity, as well as of the general public, in regard to the imperative need for making the transition towards sustainable development, and calls upon all concerned to make full use in this regard of the report of the Commission,

3. Agrees with the Commission that while seeking to remedy existing environmental problems, it is imperative to influence the sources of those problems in human activity, and economic activity in particular, and thus to provide for sustainable development;

4. Agrees further that an equitable sharing of the environmental costs and benefits of economic development between and within countries and between present and future generations is a key to achieving sustainable development,

5. Concurs with the Commission that the critical objectives for environment and development policies which follow from the need for sustainable development must include preserving peace, reviving growth and changing its quality, remedying the problems of poverty and satisfying human needs, addressing the problems of population growth and of conserving and enhancing the resource base, reorienting technology and managing risk, and merging environment and economics in decision-making;

6. Decides to transmit the report of the Commission to all Governments and to the governing bodies of the organs, organizations and programs of the United Nations system, and invites them to take account of the analysis and recommendations contained in the report of the Commission in determining their policies and programs;

7. Calls upon all Governments to ask their central and sectoral economic agencies to ensure that their policies, programs and budgets encourage sustainable development and to strengthen the role of their environmental and natural resource agencies in advising and assisting central and sectoral agencies in that task,

8. Calls upon the governing bodies of the organs, organizations and programs of the United Nations system to review their policies, programs, budgets and activities aimed at contributing to sustainable development;

9. Calls upon the governing bodies of other relevant multilateral development assistance and financial institutions to commit their institutions more fully to pursuing sustainable development in establishing their policies and programs in accordance with the national development plans, priorities and objectives established by the recipient Governments themselves;

10. Requests the Secretary-General, through the appropriate existing mechanisms, including the Administrative Committee on Co-ordination, to review and co-ordinate on a regular basis the efforts of all the organs, organizations and bodies of the United Nations system to pursue sustainable development, and to report thereon to the General Assembly through the Governing Council of the United Nations Environment Program and the Economic and Social Council;

11. Stresses the essential role of the United Nations Environment Program, within its mandate, in catalyzing the sustainable development efforts of the United Nations system, while fully taking into account the co-coordinating responsibilities of the Economic and Social Council, and agrees with the Commission that that role should be strengthened and that the resources of the Environment Fund should be substantially enlarged, with greater participation;

12. Considers that the Governing Council of the United Nations Environment Program, within its mandate and with participation, when appropriate, at the ministerial level, should examine on a periodic basis the long-term strategies for realizing

sustainable development, and should include the results of its examinations in its reports to be submitted to the General Assembly through the Economic and Social Council;

13. Agrees that the catalytic and co-coordinating role of the United Nations Environment Program in the United Nations system should be reinforced in its future work on environmental and natural resource issues,

14. Reaffirms the need for additional financial resources from donor countries and organizations to assist developing countries in identifying, analyzing, monitoring, preventing and managing environmental problems in accordance with their national development plans, priorities and objectives,

15. Reaffirms the need for developed countries and appropriate organs and organizations of the United Nations system to strengthen technical co-operation with the developing countries to enable them to develop and enhance their capacity for identifying, analyzing, monitoring, preventing and managing environmental problems in accordance with their national development plans, priorities and objectives;

16.Invites Governments, in co-operation with the regional commissions and the United Nations Environment Program and, as appropriate, intergovernmental organizations, to support and engage in follow-up activities, such as conferences, at the national, regional, and global levels,

17. Calls upon Governments to involve non-governmental organizations, industry and the scientific community more fully in national and international activities to support efforts towards sustainable development,

18. Invites the governing bodies of the organs, organizations and programs of the United Nations system to report, as appropriate, through the Economic and Social Council, to the General Assembly, not later than at its forty-fourth session, on progress made in their organizations towards sustainable development, and to make such reports available to the Governing Council of the United Nations Environment Program at its next regular session,

19. Also invites the Governing Council of the United Nations Environment Program to provide comments on matters concerning progress on sustainable development that fall within its mandate, on the above-mentioned reports and on other developments, for submission to the Economic and Social Council at its second regular session of 1989 and to the General Assembly at its forty-fourth session,

20. Requests the Secretary-General to submit to the General Assembly at its forty-third session, through the Economic and Social Council, a progress report on the implementation of the present resolution and to the Assembly at its forty-fourth session a consolidated report on the same subject,

21. Decides to include in the provisional agenda of its forty-third session a sub-item entitled "A long-term strategy for sustainable and environmentally sound development" under the agenda item entitled "Development and international economic co-operation".[52]

---

[52]UN General Assembly, 96th Plenary Meeting, 11, December 1987, A/RES/42/187, The World commission on Environment and development

The Stockholm Environment Institute

The objective of this study is to review the evidence from the economics of climate change literature to assess to what extent developing countries can move towards low or lower carbon patterns of growth, without compromising economic growth. In addition, the study explores the impact of climate change on economic growth, and the investment needs for increasing climate resilience to ensure continued economic growth in future years.

The challenge of climate change is significant. In addition to stringent cuts by developed countries, reducing the risks of dangerous climate change also requires near-term action by developing countries. Without action from the developing world, ambitious stabilization targets towards limiting temperature change to 2ºC (400 to 450 ppm CO2e) are impossible to achieve, and even relatively low levels of stabilization (e.g. 550 ppm CO2e) are unlikely. This is because global emissions need to peak around 2020. However, a rapid increase in emissions over the next 10-15 years is projected, driven by growth in energy demand in developing countries. Decoupling emissions increases from ambitious economic growth targets is going to be challenging, and will require significant additional investment.

However, low carbon patterns of growth may also hold opportunities for developing countries such as improving efficiency and lowering energy costs, developing low carbon industries, improving technology, providing opportunities to raise carbon finance through international mechanisms and safeguarding natural resources, such as forests.

Developing countries will also need to invest in adaptation measures to ensure climate resilience against impacts that will inevitably arise. Such investment will need to ensure that the economy is climate resilient enough to withstand impacts and grow. However, the investment needs to ensure greater climate resilience could impact on growth in the nearer term; hence some complex tradeoffs emerge.

The extent of the transition towards low carbon patterns of growth in developing countries will be dependent on the progress of an international agreement, political will and economic self-interest. Differences in the level of ambition will emerge depending on national circumstances. Due to the level of current and projected emissions, Middle Income Countries (such as the G+5) will need to balance the risks of not adopting carbon reduction targets and incurring liabilities under a future global agreement against nearer term economic growth objectives.

Lower income countries, which have significantly, lower emissions (e.g. <1t CO2/cap) and low levels of development could increase emissions in the near term. However, lower carbon patterns of growth may be in their self-interest in helping meet development objectives due to synergies across other policy areas (reflected by co-benefits), indigenous renewable energy resource potential, and opportunities for raising carbon finances. The additional investment costs of low carbon patterns of growth in developing countries may not be prohibitive. The broader literature on the economics of mitigation (as reviewed for example in the IPCC's 4thAssessment Report) suggests that significant levels of mitigation can be achieved whilst not significantly undermining growth objectives. Modelling suggest impacts on GDP to be in the region of 1-2 percent reduction in GDP (per annum) for stabilization targets focused on restricting levels (or reducing the risks) of warming to 2°C.

The evidence base for developing countries is more limited. A range of studies primarily using marginal abatement cost curve approaches suggests that significant potential exists at relatively low cost of <$20/ t CO2. These low abatement costs are driven by large amounts of energy efficiency potential, which is often negative cost i.e. introducing a measures results in cost savings.

In specific countries, such as Brazil and Indonesia, high mitigation potential in low cost sectors e.g. forestry and agriculture also drives down average abatement costs. For China and India the challenge is significantly greater due to the very fast growth of emissions observed in the last 5 years, and projected for the next 20 years and beyond. Consequently, the relative costs of comparable emission reductions are likely to be significantly higher.

For China and India, it is not clear from the literature how ambitious targets can be, and at different ambition levels what the costs will be. Further research is needed to fully understand what is achievable and at what cost, particularly for these countries which are so crucial in limiting greenhouse gas emissions over the next 10-15 years. For all developing countries, additional investment levels are going to be significant and will require international cooperation (including agreement) to ensure long term certainty for investors, and robust mechanisms are in place to enable carbon trade and access to carbon financing. The wider impacts on economic growth are less well understood although evidence that exists points to opportunities as well as challenges for economies in transition.

Few analyses have dynamically assessed the wider impacts of low carbon patterns of growth on the economy, using macroeconomic analysis. However, those that have (e.g. Mexico and South Africa) point to relatively small reductions in growth (<1 percent) and in some cases increased growth due to improved efficiency of the economy, access to carbon financing (subsidizing investment) and new, emerging industries.

These analyses are all premised on significant cuts, back to and below base year levels. Therefore, we could conclude that for specific countries, less ambitious cuts should not undermine growth. However, extrapolating such findings to other countries and regions is problematic due to very different regional circumstances. Hence, the picture is incomplete.

These macroeconomic analyses also indicate that impacts are not uniformly distributed, with specific sectors, such as heavy industry, incurring higher levels of job losses and greater reductions in output. These impacts also filter down to society, with greater impacts on specific groups e.g. higher energy costs impacting on lower income classes. Again, the evidence base is limited on this issue; however the importance of this issue points to the need for significantly more research.

The co-benefits of low carbon patterns of growth are significant, indicating strong synergies with development objectives. Co-benefits associated with low carbon options include reduced reliance on fossil fuels (air pollution and health, energy security, reduced foreign exchange payments), natural resource protection (ensuring sustainable livelihoods), dissemination of improved technologies (meeting energy needs) and improving urban quality of life. Whilst usually recognized, such benefits are rarely quantified, remaining outside the analysis framework. This can result in economic costs being overplayed at the expense of wider policy benefits.

Implementation of policy remains the key challenge, the costs of which are not fully captured. Without effective implementation, the necessary mitigation potential will not be realized and not at the costs highlighted in this research stock take. Opportunities need to be pursued in a phased manner, reflecting their cost, technological maturity and ease of implementation. In addition to timing, having effective policies across all sectors is crucial, as is the capacity to access international financing opportunities (through donor funding, private investment and international carbon mechanisms). It is also important to highlight that the economic assessments rarely capture those costs associated with implementation, often working from a perspective of perfect competition (not reflecting information failures, severe market imperfections e.g. fuel subsidies, behavioural issues) and not fully capturing transaction and policy costs.

Sectors for which significant levels of negative and low cost potential have been estimated are the most challenging from an implementation perspective. By definition, negative cost, energy efficiency opportunities exist because of the many barriers to realizing them. Agriculture and forestry sectors are highly fragmented and involve many stakeholders, meaning that policy costs will be significant. They are also often premised on mechanisms that will provide adequate access to international financing e.g. REDD+ and at levels to provide the necessary Incentives.

There is a need to consider climate resilient patterns of growth, in addition to the current economics of climate change and costs of adaptation. The existing studies show that climate change will have major economic costs in developing countries. They also report potentially large costs of adaptation are needed. However, a new question is emerging on how to achieve climate resilient growth, considering the patterns of development that are likely to help build an economy's resilience in a future changing mate, both against future long-term trends and also changes in extreme events (shocks). The answer to this question is unclear. Such climate resilient patterns of growth are not well defined and there is little understanding of what this might involve in practice.

Some initial findings are presented. It is clear that achieving climate resilient patterns of growth will involve much more than just 'climate proofing' investments. At the macro-economic level, there will be a need to encourage sectoral shifts away from climate sensitive areas (such as agriculture). Such policies are consistent with development, but are challenging to achieve. There is also a need to encourage long-term planning and policy in areas such as spatial planning to reduce vulnerability, which will require strong institutions, good governance and effective policy enforcement.

Alongside this, there is a continued need to increase the capacity of economies to cope with future climate variability (extreme events or shocks), noting that this will also have benefits for reducing current risks. In all these areas, the potential for climate resilient patterns of growth will be strongly determined by future socio-economic development. Given these challenges, it is likely that the availability of international finance for adaptation will not, on its own, deliver climate resilient patterns of growth. A clear immediate focus is to build the evidence base in this area.

Is it not yet clear how low carbon growth and climate resilient growth will fit together, i.e. whether they will naturally align with similar policies and objectives or whether they will involve conflicts or trade-offs. At the project level, there can be potential synergies or conflicts between low carbon objectives and adaptation. These can be partly reconciled by co-ordination between mitigation and adaptation domains. For example, it is possible to screen low carbon development to ensure options do not inadvertently increase vulnerability to climate change – an example being the screening of future hydropower projects against future climate projections of rainfall.

Similarly, it is possible to check adaptation options to make sure they do not conflict with low carbon objectives, for example, implementing options that do not increase energy related emissions such as passive ventilation rather than energy powered air conditioning to cope with future warmer temperatures. While this sounds relatively easy, in practice there are likely to be potential conflicts or trade-offs involved, e.g. when the need to increase water resources to address future aridity leads to increased energy associated with water transfers or even desalinization.

However, at the aggregate and macro-economic level, it is not yet clear whether the combination of low carbon and climate resilient patterns of growth will align. Some macro-economic shifts, which enhance climate resilience, may lead to economic structures with lower carbon intensity, though this will not always be the case. Such effects will also vary on a geographical basis. Similarly major planning changes towards low carbon development may sometimes reduce vulnerability, but in other cases will not (e.g. higher building / population density in major cities to reduce private transport demand will increase heat island effects and increase the health related vulnerability to higher temperature).

The stocktaking has provided some useful insights on the economic impacts of low carbon, climate resilient patterns of growth. However, important further research is required to improve understanding. The priorities for low carbon growth studies include:

(a) Increasing use of macroeconomic models to better understand the dynamics feedbacks in the economy resulting from the radical changes associated with low carbon patterns of growth
(b) More sensitivity analysis on discount rates, particularly use of higher discount rates, to test cost-effectiveness from private sector perspective, and consumer requirements for faster payback on investment.
(c) Longer term analyses. Focusing on 2030 as an end date means that there is no consideration of additional measures after this date, which is potentially more expensive (and less certain e.g. may not be currently commercial)
(d) Uncertainty assessment would be useful in understanding the financial trade-offs between different levels of ambition, and what might be the optimal hedging strategy
(e) Increased quantification of co-benefits to aid policy makers is important, as is the assessment of socio-economic distributional impacts
(f) Synergies and conflicts between adaptation-mitigation strategies need to be better understood for ensuring nearoptimal investment levels and timing

For climate resilient patterns of growth, priorities include:

(a) Future systematic review of emerging evidence- A large number of studies will emerge over the next 12 months that are assessing the economics of climate change and adaptation. This review should be repeated once this information is available.
(b) Building the evidence - There is a generally low level of evidence on the economics of climate change and adaptation and more studies are needed at different scales and

different locations. This includes more studies that consider the effects of both slow onset change and shocks.

(c) Specifically addressing climate resilient patterns of growth - The recent focus of studies on the economics of climate change/adaptation has not addressed the core question of how to achieve climate resilient growth. This is a priority area for future analysis.

(d) Further work is also needed to explore how to take forward low carbon and climate resilient patterns of growth together (synergistically). This is identified as an urgent priority following on from this study.[53]

Climate Change and the Global Water Crisis:

What Businesses Need to Know and Do

May 2009

Virtually every business decision is also a decision about the use of natural resources. In this paper, we describe how global warming is affecting water and energy resources, and the challenges and opportunities this presents globally. We summarize the way in which connections among climate, energy, and water are likely to affect business and offer general guidance on how companies can respond to the challenges in an integrated way. The paper highlights how regions of the world that will experience the worst impacts of climate change are those near the equator and overwhelmingly impoverished. And we conclude by focusing on the UN Millennium Development Goals (MDGs) as they relate to climate change and alleviating the global water crisis, and suggest ways that business can

[53]Steve Pye et al, "The Economics of Low Carbon Climate Resilient Patterns of Growth in Developing Countries: A Review of the Evidence", Final Report Submitted to DFID, the Stockholm Environment Institute, April 16, 2010. The report covers 134 pages.

partner with the UN to work toward their achievement.

(A) Linkages among climate change, energy, and water:

There is overwhelming scientific evidence that burning fossil fuels has altered the chemistry of the atmosphere. The atmospheric CO2 concentrations are reaching levels that are likely higher than in the last 20 million years. Rising CO2 concentrations along with other greenhouse gases (GHG) are changing the planet's climate. Global mean temperatures have increased three-quarters of a degree Celsius since 1900 and 11 of the 12 warmest years since 1850 have occurred since 1996.

These climatic changes are expected to accelerate over the coming decades. In its most recent report, the Intergovernmental Panel on Climate Change (IPCC) concludes, "water and its availability and quality will be the main pressures on, and issues for, societies and the environment under climate change."Climate-related impacts on water resources are already being documented. In all corners of the world, there is growing empirical evidence of increased severe weather events, flooding, and diminished ice cover, all of which can be attributed to climate change. Numerous scientific studies also show increases in the intensity, duration, and spatial extent of droughts, higher atmospheric temperatures, and warmer sea surface temperatures, changes in precipitation patterns, and diminishing glaciers and snow pack. In the future, climate change will affect water supply, quality, and demand in the following ways.

Climate change will affect water scarcity and sustainable supply.

It will cause the following effects:

(a) Increase water shortages due to changes in precipitation patterns and intensity. In particular, the subtropics and mid-latitudes, where much of the world's poorest populations live, are expected to become substantially drier. Reduced precipitation in some arid regions could trigger exponentially larger drops in groundwater tables.

(b) Decrease natural water storage capacity from glacier/snowcap melting, and subsequently reduce long-term water availability for more than one-sixth of the world's population that lives in glacier- or snowmelt-fed river basins, including major regions of China, India, Pakistan and the western U.S.

(c) Increase the vulnerability of ecosystems due to temperature increases, changes in precipitation patterns, frequent severe weather events, and prolonged droughts. These factors, in turn, will further diminish the ability of natural systems to filter water and create buffers to flooding.

(d) Affect the capacity and reliability of water supply infrastructure due to flooding, extreme weather, and sea level rise. Most existing water treatment plants and distribution systems were not built to withstand expected sea level rise and increased frequency of severe weather due to climate change. Furthermore, climate change will concentrate snowmelt and precipitation into shorter time frames, making both water releases more extreme and drought events more sustained. Current infrastructure often does not have the capacity to fully capture this larger volume of water, and therefore will be inadequate to meet water demands in times of sustained drought.

(e) Impair non-consumptive water uses, including transportation on inland waterways such as the Mississippi River in the U.S. and Rhine River in Europe, where freight transport has already been disrupted due to floods and droughts. Tourism sectors that are dependent on the availability of water or snow are also vulnerable to water scarcity due to climate change. Freshwater fisheries, many of which supply food to the world's poorest populations, also depend on abundant, high quality water resources to remain productive.

Climate change will impact water quality. It will:

(a) Increase extreme precipitation and flooding, which will increase erosion rates and wash soil based pollutants and toxins into waterways.
(b) Contaminate coastal surface and groundwater resources due to sea level rise, resulting in saltwater intrusion into rivers, deltas, and aquifers.
(c) Increase water temperatures, leading to more algal and bacterial blooms that further contaminate water supplies.
(d) Contribute to environmental health risks associated with water. For instance, changes in precipitation patterns are likely to increase flooding, and as a result mobilize more pathogens and contaminants. It is estimated that by 2030 the risk of diarrhea will be up to 10 percent higher in some countries due to climate change.

Climate change will increase water demand.

It will:
(a) Increase water demand for agriculture, primarily for irrigation, due to prolonged dry periods and severe drought. Some research estimates an over 40 percent increase in land needing irrigation by 2080.
(b) Increase water demand for hydration needs for billions of farm animals due to higher atmospheric temperatures.

(c) Increase quantities of water needed for industrial cooling due to increased atmospheric and water temperatures.

The impact of climate change on the water cycle varies regionally. While some areas will benefit from having more water, these benefits are "tempered by the negative effects of increased precipitation variability and seasonal runoff shifts on water supply, water quality and flood risks." Overall, the report IPCC concludes, "the negative impacts of climate change on freshwater systems outweigh the benefits."

In addition, hundreds of millions of people who live in the floodplains of rivers and along the coast will face more severe flooding if nothing is done to protect them. Investments to prevent future catastrophes will be made in some regions, but poor countries lack the financial resources for needed infrastructure. These conditions have the potential to create environmental refugees at a massive scale. It is estimated that 60% of the population live below an elevation of 1 meter in Bangladesh alone. Some islands, like the Marshall Islands or Kiribati, will have to be abandoned altogether.

Providing a safe and reliable supply of water already poses a challenge for water managers throughout the world. Almost 900 million people lack access to improved drinking water, and another 2.5 billion lack proper sanitation. Population and economic growth will likely exacerbate these challenges. Furthermore, feeding more people and the rising percentage of meat based diets can increase water demand in agriculture, which already uses about 70 percent of the world's water. In many industrialized nations, the environment has suffered from over-allocation and pollution of water resources, and many citizens are urging that these aquatic systems be restored.

Climatic change will make meeting these existing and future challenges even more difficult.

Water and energy are strongly interconnected:

Another important aspect of the water-climate change linkage is the strong connection of both to energy. Upon hearing the terms water and energy, most people immediately think of hydropower. And while hydroelectric generation is certainly reliant upon large quantities of water, the connections between water and energy run much deeper. Water is used for extracting, refining, processing, and transporting all forms of energy, from coal to solar. Large volumes of water are used as cooling water in conventional thermal generating plants. Energy production can also cause significant water pollution.

A much less recognized connection between water and energy are the vast amounts of energy used to treat, distribute, and use water. Water is heavy (1 liter weighs one kilogram), so moving it requires a lot of energy. Energy needs are particularly high for places where water is pumped from very deep wells, or where it is piped over long distances and steep terrain. Additionally, heating water is energy-intensive. In California, for example, 19 percent of the electricity use, 33% of the non-electricity natural gas, and 33 million gallons of diesel consumption is water - related.

Presently, the risks of managing water and energy/climate change in isolation of one another are woefully under- appreciated by policy-makers. Indeed, water and energy policies often compete with one another, with decision-makers frequently inadvertently valuing energy production over water protection. Further, many current activities to manage and reduce GHG emissions require large amounts of water, often inadvertently increasing water-related risks. For instance, first generation bio-fuel production has an especially large water footprint, and can also compromise water quality through the leaching of pesticides and nutrients. A large-scale replacement of the gasoline-guzzling U.S. vehicle fleet with plug-in electric vehicles – an important potential solution to reducing GHG emissions from tail pipes – would have significant implications for power production, and thus water use. Recent research in the USA has found that generating electricity for plug-in hybrid electric or all-electric vehicles requires as much as three times the water per mile as gasoline production given the country's current power mix.

Similarly, some measures to manage water scarcity or quality issues require significant amounts of energy. For instance, water pipelines that transport water from water rich to water-scarce regions – a popular solution for addressing water scarcity – require considerable amounts of energy. Likewise, seawater desalination, increasingly considered an option to meet growing water demand, is extremely energy intensive. In California, for example, more energy is required to produce water from desalination than from any other water-augmentation or demand-management option. The future cost of desalinated water will be more sensitive to changes in energy prices than will other sources of water, presenting reliability risks. Water recycling and re-use are seen by many as a low-cost, sustainable water supply option, however, treating water to the high standards required for potable re-use consumes significant amounts of energy.

While these links present challenges, they also provide opportunities, particularly as managers seek to develop climate change adaptation and mitigation strategies. An analysis by the California Energy Commission found that water efficiency programs could provide 95 percent of the energy savings of traditional energy efficiency programs at 55 percent of the cost. Thus, saving water is likely to be an important part of reducing energy use and GHG emissions and helping to mitigate climate change. Additionally, water conservation and efficiency reduces vulnerability to climate change by alleviating scarcity and can be an important adaptation strategy.

(B) Business risks of water and climate change:

Climate change will exacerbate many water and energy-related business risks. As discussed, climate change is likely to exacerbate water availability and quality, which will have a wide range of implications for business.

(i) Water scarcity directly affects business operations, raw material supply, intermediate supply chain, and product use in a variety of ways. Declines or disruptions in water supply can undermine industrial and manufacturing operations where water is needed for production, irrigation, and material processing, cooling and/or washing and cleaning. For example, information technology firms require vast amounts of ultra clean.

(ii) Water quality risks are often overlooked but may have significant financial implications. The quality of process water is critical in many industrial production systems, and contaminated water supply may require additional investment and operational costs for pre-treatment.

(iii) Water scarcity, changes in precipitation patterns, and glacier melt caused by climate change directly affect power generation, curtailing hydro-based power production, and also impacting any power plants that run steam turbines. Whether fired by coal, natural gas, or nuclear energy, electricity generation relies on having an adequate supply of cooling water. Businesses that depend on highly reliable energy from these power sources will be at risk.

(iv) Physical water resource constraints make companies more susceptible to reputation risks. Declines in water availability and quality can increase competition for clean water. In water-scarce regions, tensions can arise between businesses and local communities, particularly in developing countries where local populations often lack access to safe and reliable drinking water. Community opposition to industrial water withdrawals and perceived or real inequities in use can emerge quickly and affect businesses profoundly. For instance, in Kerala, India, opposition to beverage company operations developed over concerns about the effects of bottling plants on local groundwater levels and supplies. When villagers' wells ran dry, local government revoked company operating licenses, affecting both revenues and company reputations.

(v) Reputation risks increase as people become more aware of their rights to access water. The concept of "access to clean water as a human right" is gaining more recognition globally, yet the failure of governments to provide 100 percent coverage for water services means that international and local businesses may find themselves using copious amounts of water in regions where people lack sufficient water to meet basic needs.

(vi) Growing awareness around the ecological impacts of water withdrawal and discharge increases both reputation and regulatory risks. Healthy freshwater ecosystems are an essential part of local communities and livelihoods, not only by serving as a source of clean drinking water, but also by providing cultural, social, aesthetic, and economic value. As a result, significant water withdrawal or wastewater discharge regardless of the extent of actual impacts on the neighboring communities or ecosystems, inevitably increase the risk of conflict with local communities. Moreover, the vulnerability of ecosystems is expected to increase due to climate change.

vii) Physical and reputation pressures affecting water availability and wastewater discharge can result in more stringent water policies. Water scarcity, coupled with increased concern among local communities about water withdrawals, will put pressure on local authorities and policymakers to consider water reallocations, regulations, and development of water markets that cap usage, suspend permits to draw water, and lead to stricter water quality standards.

(viii) Water scarcity will increase water prices. Among other factors, water scarcity is driving shifts toward full-cost pricing aimed at providing economic incentives for efficient water use. In many places, artificially low water prices are rising as subsidies are phased out. Utilities in industrial countries are increasingly implementing "block" or "tiered rates," where water users pay more for increased consumption. These tariff structures are specifically designed to encourage commercial and industrial users to use water efficiently.

(ix). Water-intensive products and services face increased socio-political risks. As water scarcity becomes a serious problem in many parts of the world, there may be corollary pressure, both regulatory and reputation, on products that require a significant quantity of water. Products and services that require large amounts of water or energy to produce or to use may be phased out by law, lose market share to less water-intensive products, or cause reputation damage for the company.

Taken together, this means that businesses will face vastly increased uncertainty about the availability and quality of their water supplies. One of the strongest conclusions in the latest IPCC report is that "climate change will challenge the traditional assumption that past hydrological experience provides a good guide to future conditions." Therefore, it will become increasingly crucial for businesses to incorporate climate change factors when assessing and managing their water risks. Indeed, a critical driver of success in the 21st Century economy will be how companies and investors balance the competing demands for water and energy.

(C) What businesses can do to manage water-climate risks strategically?

To evaluate and effectively address water and climate change risks, companies can take the following actions:

1. Measure water and carbon footprint throughout the value chain.

Some of the most significant water and climate-related risks can be embedded in a company's value chain, well outside of its direct operations or control. In many cases, such as in agriculture-based industry sectors, a company's direct water use pales in comparison with water embedded in the supply chain. Even should water use or GHG emissions occur outside of a company's sphere of influence, they can still pose financial or reputation risks to the company. Companies can only mange what they measure, so in order to accurately assess risks and opportunities, a first step for companies is to conduct a comprehensive and integrated water and carbon accounting. By aligning measurement of water and carbon/energy, businesses can identify how the three are interlinked, providing key basic information for developing a holistic management strategy.

2. Assess physical, regulatory and reputation water risks associated with climate change.

Explicit attention should be paid to understanding energy-related risks posed by water (and vice versa), as well as any potential competing demands the company may have for water and energy. Companies should also seek to align, if not integrate, their water and climate risk assessments. Having a detailed understanding of local water conditions, including hydrological, social, economic, and political factors, can give companies room to anticipate and plan for a wide range of climate change scenarios. Companies should be prepared to provide details on the risks they face from water challenges and to be transparent about the energy trade-offs they may need to make to address them.

3. Integrate water and climate issues into strategic business planning and operational activities.

When developing water management plans, companies will need to consider and integrate the potential impacts of climate change on water supplies and water quality. Climate-related impacts on water should also be considered when making a range of business decisions from factory design and sitting to new product development. Companies should also consider potential energy/water synergy (or conflict) in business planning and decision-making. For instance, integrated approaches to reduce water and energy use simultaneously have allowed companies at a single plant to achieve millions of dollars in savings while increasing output. In addition, such efficiency measures can demonstrate a company's commitment to water management, boost public image, and help build positive relations with the communities where it operates.

4. Engage key stakeholders as a part of water and climate risk assessment, long-term planning and implementation activities

When developing a corporate water and climate change management plan, managers can benefit from sharing information with employees, investors, customers, local communities, and other key stakeholders in order to gain valuable feedback.

Through early and continuous engagement with concerned stakeholders, companies can better understand, anticipate, and respond to emerging issues and expectations. Open dialogue with water providers and local communities may also be helpful in preventing and reducing the risk of future water and climate change related disputes or disruptions. Such discussions may also identify pivotal inputs that help prioritize action steps.

5. Disclose and communicate water and carbon performance and associated risks.

Companies should publicly report management activities and key metrics on their water and energy performance. This information can help shareholders and stakeholders assess how companies are addressing their water and climate change risks. Such metrics are also a useful tool for engaging employees across the enterprise.

6. Seek opportunities for collective action.

Because water and energy are connected to social, cultural, and environmental issues, companies can rarely achieve the best management outcomes on their own. Most solutions to water supply, quality and sanitation, and climate change issues require co-management approaches involving sound water governance, collective action, and partnerships. By pooling resources and bringing together a wide range of expertise and knowledge through partnerships for a common goal, companies can respond to water and climate change concerns more efficiently and effectively than through individual actions. Collaborative actions are particularly helpful in assessing and addressing climate change impacts, since there are large gaps in knowledge related to climate change and water, especially data and prediction modeling at the watershed level.

7. Partnering with the United Nations

There are numerous opportunities for companies to partner with the UN to take action on both climate and water. The UN Global Compact - an initiative within the UN system devoted specifically to improving corporate stewardship practices - has worked since its inception in 2000 to facilitate actions and partnerships that help companies become more sustainable and equitable. The UN Global Compact manages two sub-initiatives for business engagement - The CEO Water Mandate and Caring for Climate - focusing on water and climate, respectively. Established in 2007, The CEO Water Mandate is currently one of the most comprehensive and visible cross-sectoral, public-private partnerships on water. It represents both a call-to-action and a strategic framework for responsible water management by business. It is voluntary in nature, but is built around six core areas of responsibility with which its endorsers must commit to and demonstrate improvement: Direct Operations, Supply Chain and Watershed Management, Collective Action, Public Policy, Community Engagement, and Transparency.

Also launched in 2007, Caring for Climate is voluntary global initiatives that seeks to mobilize the business community to develop solutions that reduce climate risk while at the same time create value for the company. The UN Global Compact, the United Nations Environment Programme (UNEP), and the World Business Council for Sustainable Development (WBCSD) jointly developed the initiative. Caring for Climate helps companies to advance practical solutions, share experiences, inform public policy as well as shape public attitudes. When endorsing the initiative, chief executives are prepared to set goals, develop and expand strategies and practices, and to publicly disclose emissions within the framework of the Compact's Communication on Progress policy. The overarching objective of both UN Global Compact initiatives is to support achievement of the Millennium Development Goals.

(D) Linkage between climate and water and the Millennium Development Goals

Industrialized nations, which have produced most of the greenhouse gases that cause global warming, are already spending billions of dollars to adapt to climate change impacts, such as coastal flooding and drought. However, countries near the equator face the greatest vulnerabilities and have the least capacity to deal with the challenges posed by global warming. International aid organizations traditionally focus on social and economic development. In addition to efforts to reduce GHG emissions, decision-makers are targeting some development assistance to create more resiliencies and help countries avoid some of the worst impacts of global warming.

Responsible businesses can play a role in helping avert climate catastrophe among the world's poor. Because water is one of the resources most affected/vulnerable by climate change, companies can work to understand water-related climate risks and help to support resiliency building and adaptation strategies related to water.[54]

Conclusion

The world needs social equity, environmental sustainability and financial benefits.

Year 2010 has exposed the ferocity of heat waves in Russia and flood in Pakistan. These events have put challenges to the scientists and governments to work for a solution for the future. Why the nature becomes ferocious? It is because the people have challenged

[54] 'Climate Change and the Global Water Crisis: What Business Need to Know and Do', Pacific Institute, UN Global Contact, May 2009

the very existence of nature. It is because people are destroying the nature, the forests, the animals, and even changing scenic wonders that nature has provided to us. We have to search for an environment, which would award social justice to all.

Low carbon patterns of growth may also hold opportunities for developing countries such as improving efficiency and lowering energy costs, developing low carbon industries, improving technology, providing opportunities to raise carbon finance through international mechanisms and safeguarding natural resources, such as forests.

In water-scarce regions, tensions can arise between businesses and local communities, particularly in developing countries where local populations often lack access to safe and reliable drinking water.

Caring for Climate helps companies to advance practical solutions, share experiences, inform public policy as well as shape public attitudes.

Climate change will exacerbate many water and energy-related business risks. Climate change is likely to exacerbate water availability and quality, which will have a wide range of implications for business.

The overarching objective of both UN Global Compact initiatives is to support achievement of the Millennium Development Goals.

Reports on Environments clearly explain that the state should give top priority to the people and permit for industrialization with consent of people. Let life of people is safe in each country, locality and settlement. Let them be assured of free air, clean water and clean environment.

The government must also take steps to allot a piece of land to each landless adult and each nomad. An address-less and income-less person becomes an anti-social and creates conflicts in society. A hungry and unemployed youth joins terrorists' camps to destabilize the government, which ignores poor people and their human rights. Food security to all would create an era when people would avoid suicidal forums.

With the average citizen of New Delhi living in conditions unfit for humans, the Central Pollution Control Board of India has its facts wrong or is feeding lies to the media. As a result, the US, Germany and Japan have considered reducing the tenures of diplomats in New Delhi to reduce their exposure to city's polluted air.

We need a world where everyone is safe and is assured of food, shelter, clothing, education and healthcare. And it is possible. Of course, the degree of achievements would differ in different locations or countries.

+++++

Chapter VI

CONSERVATION OF FOREST

Deforestation and degradation of forests, through conversion to pastureland, infrastructure development, destructive logging, fires and agriculture account for nearly 20 per cent of global greenhouse gas emissions, more than the entire global transportation sector and second only to the energy sector.

Recognizing that their emissions were responsible for the lion's share of the greenhouse gases (GHGs) resulting in climate change, the major industrialized nations of the world agreed under the auspices of the UNFCCC to make commitments to reduce emissions before expecting the same from developing countries. This was the Kyoto Protocol — a historic 'first step' that was agreed in 1997 and came into force in 2005. It provided the first legally binding framework to combat climate change.

The Kyoto Protocol hence divided the world between rich industrialized nations that were given emission reduction targets and the rest. The US failed to ratify it, while Canada has said it won't even try to meet its commitments and Japan and Russia have so far not committed to any meaningful emissions reductions post -2012. Throughout much of the 1990s and into this decade, developing countries held fast to this principle of engagement. Many argued that they had no obligation to take action to reduce their emissions until after the US took action.

Meanwhile, despite their responsibility to reduce their high emissions, the US and most other industrialized nations have been dragging their feet, arguing that if they are forced to cut emissions when others aren't, their businesses and industries would be unable to compete in the global marketplace.

As the finger pointing and rhetoric raged for more than a decade, global emissions have been rising. Between 1990 and 2006, CO2 emissions in the US grew by 18.1 per cent, while Japan's emissions rose by 11.3 per cent and Canada's by 22.9 per cent. While China's emissions per capita remain quite low, the total annual CO2 emissions in China and the US are now similar. India is often pitted against China, despite having lower levels of emissions, higher poverty levels and lower economic capacity relative to China. With 17 per cent of the world's population, India contributes only 4.6 per cent of the world's greenhouse gases (GHGs). However, India is the fourth largest GHG emitter in absolute terms.

With the first commitment period of the Kyoto Protocol expiring at the end of 2012, the next steps to develop a legally binding regime have to be decided as a matter of urgency to ensure that the world does not fall out of the line of scientific imperative. This still appears elusive.

So the evils of deforestation need attentions of both the public sector institutions and the end users. The state government must see that forest should cover one-third of geographical area. Who would supply firewood to the poor natives? Who would be responsible for loss of clean environment? The nature can maintain forests and supply us clean air; take care of forest animals and allow better environment.[55]

Deforestation

Deforestation has been described as the cutting down of trees without planting others in their place. It is hard to think that there was a time when 90 percent of the earth was covered by trees, but this was once the case. If so, one asks, naturally, what happened to all these trees? Why do people cut down trees?

The following are probable reasons:

a) **Demand for land for cultivation:** This has been seen both in Kenya and other parts of the world especially countries that have Agriculture as the backbone of their economy. Trees have been cut down to obtain land for cultivation of both subsistence and cash crops, both by governments and individuals.

b) **Need for firewood:** People, especially those who live in rural areas where electricity and gas are unavailable, resort to use of firewood as a source of heat. Here, wood is cut down and burnt.

c) **Need for land to build industries**: Industries require a lot of land and while industrialization is important for every country, it is the bane of large tracts of forest. People need jobs in order to provide for their daily needs.

---

[55]Aarti Khosla, "No great Expectations", The Sunday Pioneer, December 5, 2010

d) **Need for land to build houses:** With the worldwide increase in population, land to build houses for people to live in is very much required.

e) **Need for wood for furniture**, pencils, paper etc: Whereas the above needs are important and have to be satisfied, cutting down trees is not the most probable solution to these problems. Why? This is because; most people who cut down trees do not plant others in their place. Also, if all the above needs are to be met by cutting down of trees, even planting two for every tree cut will not prevent desertification. This is because trees take so long to grow and mature, especially so for hard wood trees.

(f) **The governments** allot forestland for railways, high ways, industries, schools and colleges or for defense establishments in guise of development.

Deforestation has the following dangers:

Destruction of carbon sinks: Carbon sinks are huge stores of carbon, e.g. Swamps and forests

Soil Erosion: Deforestation makes soil prone to erosion by agents such as wind and water. The roots of trees hold the particles of soil together thus, preventing the fertile topsoil from being carried away. Soil erosion leads to loss of productivity of the land due to loss of mineral nutrients and soil microorganisms

Destruction of animal habitats: Apart from domesticated animals and marine and fresh water animals, all other animals need forests as their habitats. These forests do not only provide a place for the animals to roam day but also provide their food and act as a source of protection from predators through camouflage. Destruction of the animals' habitats literally kills the animals.

Medicinal Plants: Some trees are used as herbs. Trees such as the Cinchona have been used as treatment against Malaria since time immemorial. Destruction of these forests leads to destruction of medicinal plants that could be used as treatment for various ailments.

Trees act as windbreakers: Absence of these trees enables strong winds and or storms e.g. Hurricanes and Tornados. I write this in the wake of a Tsunami at the Indonesian coast where about 150 people have just lost their lives. Hurricanes like Katrina are still fresh in our memories. I cannot over emphasize this point.

Greenhouse effect and global warming: Nature balances the flow of energy and nutrients. Forests plan a very vital role in these cycles e.g. the carbon cycle where deforestation causes carbon dioxide to remain in the atmosphere. Accumulation of carbon dioxide in the atmosphere acts as a blanket that traps long wave radiation of heat and prevents it from escaping the surface of the earth back into the atmosphere. This phenomenon is known as the greenhouse effect. The trapped radiation is converted into heat. This heat causes global warming.

Destruction of forests also causes modification of climate of an area mostly leading to desertification and aridity.

Recommendations:

(a) For every tree that is cut, three, not two should be planted in its case. We have reached such a critical point that to prevent the desertification of the world that many more trees need to be planted.

(b) Unless it is necessary, water catchments areas should strictly be left alone. Quick growing varieties of soft wood trees should be grown for commercial uses e.g. making of furniture, pencils and paper.

(c) We should carry out consistent mass education on a worldwide scale, on the importance of reforestation and the dangers of deforestation

(d) We need to enact and enforce strict laws against deforestation, worldwide.

(e) It is high time that we reduced our dependence on charcoal as a source of fuel and make use of wind and solar energy.

(f) Nature works as a whole cycle. This is seen not only in animals where predator and prey work together but also in the different energy and nutrient cycles. As already explained earlier, forests play a crucial role in this equation.

Effects of Deforestation

(a) Deforestation is the process of converting forested lands into non-forest sites that are ideal for crop raising, urbanization and industrialization. Because deforestation is a serious concept, there are also serious effects to the surroundings.

(b) Effects of deforestation can be classified and grouped into effects to biodiversity, environment and social settings. Because deforestation basically involves killing trees in forests, there are so many effects that can be enumerated as results of the activity.

(c) When forests are killed, nature basically requires people to renew the forest. Reforestation is one concept that is in the opposite direction as deforestation, but is proven to be a much harder effort than deforestation.

(d) So the rate of deforestation has not been offset by the rate of reforestation. Thus, the world is now in a troubled state when it comes to issues concerning the environment.

(e) Pollution is rapidly growing along with population. Forests are greatly helping reduce the amount of pollutants in the air. So, the depletion of these groups of trees is greatly increasing the risk that carbon monoxide would reach the atmosphere and result in the depletion of the ozone layer, which in turn results to global warming.

Environment change

One major effect of deforestation is climate change. Deforestation changes temperatures in the nearby areas abruptly. Forests naturally cool down because they help retain moisture in the air.

Deforestation has been found to contribute to global warming as a climate around the world becomes warmer as more harmful rays of the sun come in through the atmosphere.

The ozone layer is a mass of oxygen or O3 atoms that serves as shield in the atmosphere against the harmful ultraviolet rays from the sun. Because ozone is made up of oxygen atoms, oxygen reacts with carbon monoxide. Such reaction would use up oxygen atoms. It follows that when there are more carbon monoxide atoms going to the atmosphere, the volume of oxygen would decline. Such is the case of ozone depletion.

The third effect to the environment would be on the water table underneath the ground. Water table is the common source of natural drinking water by people living around forests. Water table is replenishing. That means, the supply of water underground could also dry up if not replenished regularly. When there is rain, forests hold much of the rainfall to the soil through their roots.

Thus, water sinks in deeper to the ground, and eventually replenishing the supply of water in the water table. Now, imagine what happens when there are not enough forests anymore. Water from rain would simply flow through the soil surface and not be retained by the soil. So the process of evaporation would immediately set in. Thus, the water table is not replenished, leading to drying up of wells.

Effect to biodiversity

(a) Forests are natural habitats to many types of animals and organisms. That is why, when there is deforestation, many animals are left without shelters. The forest animals manage to go to agricultural fields and residential sites. People then kill these animals and they too kill human beings.

(b) Through the years, it is estimated that there are millions of plant and extinct animal species that have been wiped out because they have been deprived of home. Thus, biodiversity is significantly lowered because of the savage deforestation practices of some people.

(c) Wildlife advocates have been constantly reminding that several wild animals left in the world could still be saved if deforested forests would only be reforested and the practice of slash and burn of forests would be totally abandoned.

Social effects of deforestation

Deforestation is hardly hitting the living conditions of indigenous people who consider forests as their primary habitats. Imagine how they are rendered homeless when forests are depleted. These natives would be forced to live elsewhere, and are usually left to becoming mendicants in rural and urban areas.

Overall, effects of deforestation cannot be offset by the contribution of the practice to development. While it is logical that progress is very much needed by mankind, it must also be noted that nature knows no defeat. Destruct it and it would certainly retaliate, one way or another.[56]

The United Nations has launched a program known as Reducing Emissions from Deforestation and Forest Degradation (R. E. D. D.) **as an effort to create a financial value for the carbon stored in forests**, offering incentives for developing countries to reduce emissions from forested lands and invest in low-carbon paths to sustainable development. This program goes beyond deforestation and forest degradation, and includes the role of conservation, sustainable management of forests and enhancement of forest carbon stocks.[57]

Environment and Tiger

In protecting the big cat, we protect the forest and all those that live within it. We protect our rivers and the groundwater. We protect the life-cycle of this planet itself. If we can't do that, we can write off our future, and the future of coming generations.

Forty years after the inception of Project Tiger, the population graph of the big cat looks more like a graph at the daily stock exchange! Somehow, in spite of the best intentions and efforts from the Government, non-Government organizations and even individuals, the tiger's future still remains a question mark, with more than a few opinions out there predicting total extinction within the next 10 to

---

[56] Nathaline fiset, "Effects of Deforestation on Our Environment Today", Ezine Article

[57] REDD is a UN program launched in September 2008 with expertise of UN Food and Agriculture Organisation (UNFAO), UN Development Program (UNDP) and UN Environment Program (UNEP).

20 years. This is of course, after all, only an opinion, but one which could become frighteningly true. It's not really a matter of getting the date right of when the tiger will go extinct, but the fact that it will be wiped out eventually — unless we do something now. With hugely popular campaigns that went viral like Save the Tiger, the word most certainly is 'out' there, but that's just it — word out there. The action is missing still.

Thanks to years of constant broadcasting of the issue, the challenges of tiger conservation are public knowledge. Poaching, habitat destruction, poisoning are what we've all heard quite often. Awareness is at an all-time high and everyone knows the Jungle bachao, sher bachao (save the forest, save the tiger) chant. But there still remains that elusive gap between information and action.

Since the last tiger census in 2011, India has already lost over a 100 tigers to poaching. Maharashtra, which has 169 resident tigers (2011), went on high alert earlier this year when a tip-off of a poaching contract was received. There was literally a price put on the head of 25 tigers and many millions Indian rupees had exchanged hands as advance payment. The scale and the audacity just go to show what the tiger is up against. Just a few months ago, a tigress was poached in the Itanagar zoo.

The poachers tranquilized her and then hacked her to pieces. What is even more shocking is that this not the first incident in the zoo. In 2006, three tigers and a leopard were poisoned. One tiger died, while the other two other animals survived. A special tiger task force, shoot on sight orders and a Schedule I status for the tiger have not been a good enough deterrent.[58]

---

[58]Schedule I is the highest protected status for an animal in India under the Wildlife protection act of 1972

The 'value' of an apex predator like the tiger goes far beyond what is obvious to our eye. Sure, we've all had the life- cycle image from our school textbooks imprinted on our brains, but what is so simply illustrated is multi-layered and complex. The water cycle is at the very centre of all of this. Without it, everything as it is would cease to exist.

As humans, we've taken far beyond our fair share of the planet, and the delicate balance of nature we often speak about won't just tip — it will spiral. We've already witnessed three sub-species of the tiger lost to extinction; others are on the brink.

In 2010, I had the opportunity to attend the Tiger Summit in St Petersburg, and it was really a coming together of all the tiger nations. Ministers, tiger experts, celebrities and individuals who cared or worked for the tiger, were there. Each country made a presentation and announced its commitment to doubling the tiger population by 2020. It was a huge event covered internationally, with celebrities like Leonardo DiCaprio adding glitter to it. It was at this event where I met a local activist who was campaigning to save the forests in Russia that were threatened by logging, mining and oil exploration. She was desperate to get this information to President Vladimir Putin, and kept saying: "It's not only the tiger; we have to save the forest". She is right. We need to save the forest to save the tiger. It's a beautifully simple plan that will take all the positive intention on the planet to execute.

Unfortunately, we already have examples of what happens when the tiger disappears. The island of Bali, which was home to the Balinese Tiger, stands as evidence. Being an island, Bali only had a local population of tigers with no migrating animals coming in or going out. The last recorded tiger was shot in September 1937, and after that Bali lost its forests to agriculture. All that remains now are fields and an economy that is floating on tourism. Fresh water is a huge issue in Bali. Extensive deforestation and over-consumption of water by huge resorts have drained the fresh water resources of the island. With the majority of the forests gone, the rivers and the groundwater are drying up.

This has happened to many small islands and isolated communities in human history and the most well-known example is that of Easter Island in the south-eastern Pacific Ocean.

The forests of Easter Island were almost completely deforested by its people. What followed was complete destruction and degradation of the eco-system over a period of time. Agriculture was reduced because of soil erosion and fishing wasn't possible as there weren't any large trees left to build boats. The lessons of history are quite clear in what we can expect if things continue the way they are. To protect the forests and all those that live within it, it is crucial for a 'happy human buffer' to exist around such forests. Communities that live close to the forests have to be given special benefits and the support to move beyond the basic levels of existence. With a huge tourism industry around the 'tiger', (which we witnessed recently when tourism was banned in all tiger national parks), the benefits of this economy barely trickle down. There are people and NGOs who are doing great work at the ground level and have made a difference. These have been important but small victories, with individuals and groups doing the best they can, and quite often being driven by their own passion and their own resources.

The crisis of the vanishing tigers is far from over, and it will need a change in perspective and the collective will of the entire nation to turn the situation around. That's not impossible by any means, but it's still a task that needs to become our mission. This is an excerpt from the Mahabharata, which was written around 400 BC:

"Do not cut down the forest with its tigers and do not banish the tigers from the forest. The tiger perishes without the forest and the forest perishes without its tigers. Therefore, the tigers should stand guard over the forest and the forest should protect all its tigers." Are we paying any heed to the advice? Unfortunately, the answer is a big "No".[59]

Declaration of the World Rainforest Movement
Penang, Malaysia, 17 April 1989

Forests, both temperate and tropical, are an integral part of the life support systems of the planet, performing numerous ecological and social functions that are essential for the continuation of life, as we know it on earth. Those functions include:

(a) Regulating climate at both the regional and global level;
(b) Providing a habitat for the majority of species on earth;
(c) Providing a homeland and spiritual basis for millions of forest peoples- maintaining and conserving soils
(d) Regulating hydrological cycles and ensuring water supplies.

2. The continuing loss of the world's forests now constitutes a global emergency.

(a) In temperate areas, the bulk of primary forests have been destroyed. What remains is being lost to logging and acid rain and other pollutants

[59]Gautam Pandey (2012), "More at stake than just the tiger", the Pioneer, November 07, 2012

(b) In tropical areas, forests are disappearing at the rate of 100 acres or more a minute.
(c) Moreover, the rates of destruction are increasing and, on current trends, little will be left within a few decades.

3. The immediate and long-term consequences of global deforestation threaten the very survival of life, as we know it on earth. Indeed, the scale of deforestation and its impact now represents one of the gravest emergencies ever to face the human race.

Such consequences include:

(a) The disruption of climatic equilibrium and the acceleration of global warming;
(b) A loss of biological diversity on an unprecedented scale;
(c) The destruction of forest-based societies;
(d) Increasing droughts, floods, soil erosion and desertification;
(e) The dispossession and displacement of peasants and forest peoples through floods and the other ecological impacts of deforestation.

4. The current social and economic policies and practices that lead to deforestation throughout the world in the name of development are directly responsible for the annihilation of the earth's forests, bringing poverty and misery to millions and threatening global ecosystems with collapse.

Such policies and practices include:

(a) Plantations, both for industrial forestry and for export crops;
(b) Ranching schemes;
(c) Dam projects;
(d) Commercial logging;

(e) Colonization schemes; and
(f) Mining and industry;

The dispossession of peasants and indigenous peoples; Roads, Pollution and Tourism

5. Official solutions to the problem of deforestation have ignored or played down the fundamental causes of deforestation and have instead adopted policies that blame the victims of deforestation for their plight, while simultaneously pursuing solutions that can only result in the further degradation of forests and croplands through the promotion of industrialized forestry.

Specifically such policies include:

(a) The Tropical Forest Action Plan, as promoted by the World Bank, the UN Food and Agriculture Organization, the UN Development Programme and others;
(b) Sustained yield commercial logging, as promoted by the International Timber Trade Agreement;
(c) Policies to zone the forests;
(d) The commercialization and privatization of biological diversity, as promoted through the International Biodiversity Programme;
(e) Pollution control programmes that are directed towards managing specific pollutants rather than reducing the source of pollution.

6. Throughout the world, the victims of these policies are taking action to arrest deforestation and reverse the process of destruction. In Sarawak, Amazonians, the Himalayas, Thailand, the Philippines and elsewhere, people are standing up to protect the forests and their societies. Such peoples have proved that they are able to use the forests in the only way that is compatible with their preservation. It is not corporations, aid agencies and banks, which should

be entrusted with the design and implementation of the protection and regeneration of the forest wealth of the planet.

7. The victims of the development process, along with those concerned with their fate and the fate of the earth, therefore call upon the United Nations and national governments to take urgent steps:

(a) To restore ecological justice and integrity to humanity by returning to the millions of people both who live in the forest and who depend upon it, their right to sustainable livelihood
(b) To restore ecological justice and integrity to life on earth through ceasing further forest destruction and regenerating damaged forest lands through the guidance of indigenous peoples, peasants, and local communities, planting only their choice of trees and plants, with the aim of restoring ecological diversity and the survival of indigenous societies.
(c) To restrain the over consumption and wastage of resources by the world's privileged groups through making the necessary changes in lifestyle and consumption patterns consistent with the development of sustainable livelihoods throughout the globe, in order to satisfy the ecological, spiritual, social and aesthetic needs of people everywhere.

8. Specifically we call upon the United Nations and national governments:

(a)To empower forest peoples and those who depend upon the forests for their livelihood with the responsibility for safeguarding the forests and ensuring their regeneration by:

1. Achieving land security for rural peoples, both through revising land tenure legislation and through

land reform, as recommended in the Brundtland report;

2. Empowering local people with the right to a decisive voice in formulating policies for their areas;
3. Rejecting social and economic policies based on the assumed cultural superiority of non-forest peoples.

(b) To halt all those practices and projects which would contribute either directly or indirectly to further forest loss?

Such projects would include: Plantation schemes, Dams, ranching schemes, mining and industrial projects, commercial logging, the Tropical Forest Action Plan, the UN Biodiversity Programme, etc.

(c) To revise radically the policies of those agencies that currently finances the projects and practices causing deforestation. Funding for such projects should be ceased and instead directed towards projects that promote the protection and regeneration of forests. The agencies involved include: the multilateral aid agencies and banks, such as the World Bank, the Inter-American Development Bank and the Asian Development Bank; the UN Food and Agriculture Organization and the United Nations Development Programme; the overseas aid agencies of the developed countries; and major international corporations.

(d)To implement, through the agency of forest peoples and under their direction, a programme for regenerating degraded forestlands and reinvigorating local cultures;

(e)To take immediate steps to curb the wastage, misuse and over-consumption of timber products (f)To ban all imports of tropical timber from natural forests and tropical woods products.

(g)To take immediate steps to cut down the consumption of imported beef from tropical forest areas

(h)To restructure the present unequal world economic systemsnow the developed countries and their practices are favored in all economic systems. As a result, the poor countries of the Third World are the sufferers. This global system at present enables the developed countries to control and use an overwhelming and disproportionately high share of the world's natural resources. A fairer and more equitable economic system is therefore fundamental to any strategy for saving and regenerating the world's forests.

(i)To initiate a global shift towards developing sustainable livelihoods The basic goals of such a shift would be developing systems of production that are ecologically and socially sustainable. This will require:

1. Reducing the scale at which production is carried out and adopting practices which minimize the impact of production on the environment;
2. Maximizing local self-sufficiency;
3. Assuring that economic activities are subordinated to social and ecological ends.

Statement drafted by participants of the World Rainforest Movement Meeting in Penang, Malaysia on which included representatives from the following organizations on 14-17 April, 1989,

These institutions are:

(a) The Indonesian NGOs Network for Forest Conservation (SKEPHI) (INDONESIA)

(b) Sahabat Alam Malaysia (MALAYSIA)
(c) Haribon Foundation (THE PHILIPPINES)
(d) Project for Ecological Recovery (THAILAND)
(e) Research Foundation for Science and Ecology (INDIA)
(f) Japan Tropical Forest Action Network (JAPAN)
(g) Rainforest Information Center (AUSTRALIA)
(h) Probe International (CANADA)
(i) The Ecologist (UNITED KINGDOM)
(j) Survival International (UNITED KINGDOM)
(k) Forest Peoples' Support Group (UNITED KINGDOM)
(l) Bank Information Center (USA)
(m) Rainforest Action Network (USA)[60]

NEPAL
Biodiversity conservation in community forests of Nepal: Rhetoric and reality

Shrestha et al (2010) have analyzed the biodiversity conservation in community forests in Nepal. Nepal is exemplified as a biodiversity rich country that represents a significant share of global biodiversity, although it comprises 0.09 percent of global land area. It is situated on the central part of the world's top 20 hottest global biodiversity hotspots, the Himalayas. Six biomes and twelve out of 867 terrestrial eco-regions of the world are occurring in Nepal. Nepal’s biodiversity, thus, becomes a globally significant and locally important as biodiversity is the important source of livelihoods and income generation. Biodiversity conservation and sustainable utilization of biological resources have been mainstream agenda after rectification and enforcement of more about 20 international treaties and agreements related to biodiversity and environment conservation including Convention of Biological Diversity. Biodiversity conservation becomes a high priority in the forest sector policy of

[60]World Rain Forests Movement, Uruguay

Nepal. Government of Nepal aims *in situ* conservation of biodiversity by establishing new protected areas along with geographical expansion of current protected areas.

Although 22.5 percent of the total areas of Nepal are under legal protection, the current protected areas system is not fully representative of the major ecosystem, forest, and vegetation types. The Mid-hills has the greatest number of ecosystems (52 out of 118) and high species diversity but has poor representation in current protected areas system, contributing only 1.33 percent of the total protected areas. Nearly 32 percent of forests occur in the Mid-Hills and it also has the highest concentration of community forests in Nepal. Therefore, the issue of biodiversity conservation in community forests in the Mid-hills is critical. If not managed properly, could result significant loss of biodiversity.

Community forestry program is considered as one of the most successful natural resource management programs in Nepal in terms of restoring degraded land and habitats, conserving biodiversity, increasing supply of forest products, empowering of women, poor and the disadvantaged groups, generating rural income, and developing human resources. Although community forestry program has focused more on protection and production of forestry related needs for its user rather than conserving existing biodiversity, it is perceived that it has contributed to biodiversity conservation claimed that community forests have improved overall forest conditions including biodiversity. Pandey (2007) found comparatively higher tree species diversity on community-managed forest stands than the national parks and government managed forests. However, more rigorous studies are necessary to understand whether the current management practices in community forests have been ameliorating or aggravating or bringing no change in the forest biodiversity. We scrutinize the impact of community forest management practices, stakeholders' state of knowledge on biodiversity, and socioeconomic heterogeneity on forest biodiversity in community forests of Nepal.

Community forestry in Nepal

The community forestry program was initiated on 1978 on the ground of rapid decline of forests area and biodiversity. It is a partnership between local communities and the government for protection, management, and sustainable utilization of forest products and ecosystem services to meet the daily need of local community.

Master Plan for Forestry Sector fully recognized the need of peoples' participation, and Forest Act (1993) provided detailed guidelines and policy framework for community forestry. The main components of the program are: formation of community forest users' groups (CFUGs), the preparation of operational plan, approval of the operation plan by district forest office (DFO), and hand over of the forest to the community. In this legal and strategic framework, the CFUGs have been, managing, protecting, and utilizing forests for more than three decades. All people are involved in community forestry management program managing 25 percent of the total area of forests. In other words, 1.66 million households belonging to 14,431 Community forest users' groups have taken up the responsibility of 11.23 million ha of national forest.

Community forests management in Nepal has been exemplified as one of the most successful programs for participatory resource management. The success of community forestry is described in terms of restoring degraded land and habitats, conserving biodiversity, increasing supply of forest products, empowering women and disadvantaged groups, generating rural incomes, and developing human resources. However, the contribution of existing community forest management practices to biodiversity conservation in the form of enhancing species diversity and ecosystem functioning is questionable. We reviewed the role of community forest management practices to biodiversity conservation based on published materials and our own observations. Practices such as seedling plantation; controlling wildlife hunting, forest fire and grazing; regulating forest encroachment; protecting soil erosion prone area and water resource area assist biodiversity conservation, paradoxically other practices such as species selection; removal of unwanted species during silvicultural activities; leaf litter collection; elite dominance in decision making; and traditional knowledge depletion have detrimental impact on biological diversity and ecosystem function of community managed forest.

Despite of some positive steps towards the conservation, there are some serious negative impacts of current community forests management if not corrected, will pose serious threat to biodiversity. It is evident that anthropogenic, environmental, socio-economic, political, and knowledge factors play crucial role in conservation, maintenance, and degradation of forest biodiversity in community forests of Nepal. These factors solely or jointly affect structural, compositional, and functional aspects of forest ecosystem at different levels in different scale and intensity. By scrutinizing community forests management practices, it can be concluded that community forest user groups and policy makers have been giving less attention to the attributes of biodiversity, ecosystem functions, and services. Short-term economic motive, elite sanction, and knowledge gap are the major constraints for achieving the goal of biodiversity conservation in community forests.

Communities are not only unaware about maintaining biodiversity, forest health, and ecosystem services of the forest but also misinformed to set the goal of sustainable forest management. They are inclined toward increasing monoculture of high economic valuable species and greenery of the forest rather than the natural forest, which could be habitat of all types of living organisms from smaller lichens and fungi to larger plants and animals. Scientific knowledge about taxonomy, conservation status, methods of propagation, and utilization of species is necessary and that should be combined with the local or indigenous knowledge to design sustainable forest management goal.

Forests is not only the stocking of trees and sources of timber but also are is the store house of biodiversity and sources of many ecosystem services such as balancing environment, soil conservation, nutrient cycling, pest and disease control, drinking water, crop pollination, and climate regulation etc. Thus forest conservation should not be perceived only as increasing the number of economically important trees but should be perceived also as the conservation of ecosystem function and service of the forest. The maintenance of ecosystem function, every species, whether important economically or not, should be conserved and maintained in nature.

Community forestry has become an indispensable part of the rural livelihood and an important component of forestry sector of Nepal. There is no doubt that community forests have laid the foundation for biodiversity conservation by reversing the trend of deforestation and increasing regeneration. However, it is essential to change the current management practices that affect the composition, structure, and function of forest negatively.

Although little progress towards the policy amendment has been done, the practice has not been changed due to weak implementation institutions. Inclusion of biodiversity issues in community forestry plans and programs helps to maintain the resiliency of forest for a long run. We herewith call a policy imperative to incorporate biodiversity issues in community forestry in Nepal.[61]

Conservation of Forests in India

Conservation of forest is certainly a necessity that requires to be addressed as a priority. For the survival of human beings, a holistic approach is required to be adopted as regards protection of the plant kingdom as well as the wildlife with regard to the peaceful and mutually beneficial co-existence of all.

To prevent any kind of ecological imbalance a very pragmatic action plan has to be formulated. Towards achieving this many legislation have been enacted in India and elsewhere. At the international level also the world communities, being concerned with the deteriorating situation worldwide, have joined hands towards finding a lasting and sustainable solution by deliberating on the subject in various conventions like that in Rio-de Janeiro and the latest Doha round of talks. These are truly welcome moves taken by the world community.

Coming back to India, there are legislations galore to deal with the situation by way of wildlife protection, forest conservation, environment protection laws etc. No doubt, the aims and object of such legislations are in tune with the call of the hour. Forests are being

---

[61]Shrestha UB, et al (2010), "Biodiversity conservation in community forests of Nepal: Rhetoric and reality", International Journal of Biodiversity and Conservation Vol. 2 (5), pp. 98-104, May, 2010

denuded haphazardly. Deforestation in a rampant manner by various elements has depleted the forest areas forcing the wild life to lesser domains and as a result of this rampage of human habitat by wild pachyderms and other animals have become a regular phenomenon in certain areas.

People encroached forests who have been displaced from their original habitat for various reasons like construction of huge electricity generating dams, ethnic clashes, floods caused by breach of river embankments and dams etc. Being forced to the wall by making these people devoid of shelter, at a time when even the United Nations Organisation gives much priority to providing shelter to the homeless, they are compelled to establish their habitat by waging war with the nature by way of deforestation and environmental degradation.

The Union of India has passed the Forest (conservation) Act making it mandatory to obtain prior approval of the Union government for using forestland for non-forest purposes. Even for cultivation of tea, rubber, spices, and medicinal plants among others. In this regard, there is bar imposed in de-reservation of any reserved forests. For grant of any approval for such acts of using forest areas for non-forest purposes, an Advisory Committee is constituted under the statute. It thus connotes that with prior approval of the Central government; forest areas may be utilized for other purposes.

In Assam (India), in the not very remote past, the democratically established government demolished a great area of human habitation by engaging tuskers in the name of clearing reserved forestland from encroachment. Ironically enough, the area has been under human habitation for quite a long span of time of some decades.

Many multi- storied buildings, school buildings, community halls, prayer halls, libraries and many more established gardens etc. were razed to the ground causing loss of property worth several billions belonging to the citizens of the welfare state.

It is also a point to be noted that there was no forest as such for about half a century in the area. It was an act of high handedness on the part of the government for some hidden political agenda. However, after a huge furor that erupted after the incident, the eviction operation was stalled in the long run; but the damage was already done.

In referring to the incident, it needs to be asserted that laws are made for the greatest amount of happiness for the greatest number of people and therefore, human considerations must receive precedence over everything else. In the name of protecting the forest, human lives can never be sacrificed. It needs reiteration that laws are for benefit of man and not vice versa.

In a democratic country where welfare of the people is of paramount importance, the powers that be at the first instance must take recourse to explore the possibilities for providing protection to the people rather than giving primacy to preservation of forest over human beings. If human beings are sacrificed for protection of forest, only forests will remain and human beings will be extinct.[62]

This needs to be kept in mind by all the people at the helm of affairs, 'only when human beings exist they will be able to occupy the seats of power they are occupying now'.

Forest Policy

---

[62]Meri News – Power to People

Non-Legally Binding International Instrument for sustainable development of all types of forests has been agreed to as Global Forest Policy by all member countries of the United Nations and adopted by General Assembly. The Government of India has assigned the ownership of minor forest produce to the people living in and around forests for the purpose of collection, processing, trade and marketing through a national level legislation named as the Scheduled Tribes and Other Traditional Forest Dwellers (Recognition of Forest rights) Act, 2006. This will help the forest dependent people to improve their economy, and will also enhance contribution of forests towards achievement of Millennium Development Goals (MDGs).

National Forest Commission (NFC) is the first of its kind ever. Constituted earlier, it submitted its report on 28 March, 2006. The Commission took a view for long term betterment of Forests and wildlife in India as well as safeguarding the interest of forest dependent communities and also maintained the national commitment for ecological security of the country as mandated in National Forest Policy.

The report examined the current status of forests, review of forest policy, legal framework, institution and administrative structure of forestry sector. The goals and constraints of the forestry sector, approach to forests, wildlife and nature conservation, farm and agro-forestry, centre-state relations, forest and local communities have been considered in depth. The report also examined forest related international instruments, forestry research, relation between forestry and industry, forests and local communities in depth.[63]

---

[63]National Portal Content Management Team, Reviewed on: 12-07-2010

National Forest Policy, 1988

Government of India

The Government of India in the erstwhile Ministry of Food and Agriculture enunciated a Forest Policy[64] to be followed in the management of State Forests in the country. However, over the years, forests in the country have suffered serious depletion. This is attributable to relentless pressures arising from ever-increasing demand for fuel-wood, fodder and timber; inadequacy of protection measures; diversion of forestlands to no forest uses without ensuring compensatory afforestation and essential environmental safeguards; and the tendency to look upon forests as revenue earning resource. The need to review the situation and to evolve, for the future, a new strategy of forest conservation has become imperative. Conservation includes preservation, maintenance, sustainable utilization, restoration, and enhancement of the natural environment. It has thus become necessary to review and revise the National Forest Policy.

Basic Objectives:

The basic objectives that should govern the National Forest Policy - are the following:

(a) Maintenance of environmental stability through preservation and, where necessary, restoration of the ecological balance that has been adversely disturbed by serious depletion of the forests of the country

(b) Conserving the natural heritage of the country by preserving the remaining natural forests with the vast variety of flora and fauna, which represent the remarkable

---

[64]Resolution No. 13 /52/F, dated the 12th May 1952, National Forest Policy, 1988, Ministry of Environment and forests, Government of India, New Delhi

biological diversity and genetic resources of the country?

(c) Checking soil erosion and denudation in the catchments areas of rivers, lakes, reservoirs in the "interest of soil and water conservation, for mitigating floods and droughts and for the retardation of silt accumulation of reservoirs
(d) Checking the extension of sand dunes in the desert areas of Rajasthan and along the coastal tracts
(e) Increasing substantially the forest/tree cover in the country through massive forestation and social forestry programmes, especially on all denuded, degraded and unproductive lands.
(f) Meeting the requirements of fuel-wood, fodder, minor forest produce and small timber of the rural and tribal populations
(g) Increasing the productivity of forests to meet essential national needs
(h) Encouraging efficient utilization of forest produce and maximizing substitution of wood.
(i) Creating a massive people's movement with the involvement of women, for achieving these objectives and to minimize pressure on existing forests

The principal aim of Forest Policy must be to ensure environmental stability and maintenance of ecological balance including atmospheric equilibrium, which are vital for sustenance of all life forms, human, animal and plant. The derivation of direct economic benefit must be subordinated to this principal aim.

Essentials of Forest Management:

Existing forests and forestlands should be fully protected and -their productivity improved. Forest and vegetal cover should be increased rapidly on hill slopes, in catchments areas of rivers, lakes and reservoirs and ocean shores and, on semi-arid, and desert tracts.

Diversion of good and productive agricultural lands to forestry should be discouraged in view of the need for increased food production.

For the conservation of total biological diversity, the network of national parks, sanctuaries, biosphere reserves and other protected areas should be strengthened and extended adequately.

Provision of sufficient fodder, fuel and pasture, especially in areas adjoining forest, is necessary in order to prevent depletion of forests beyond the sustainable limit. Since fuel wood continues to be the predominant source of energy in rural areas, the programme of forestation should be intensified with special emphasis on augmenting fuel wood production to meet the requirement of the rural people.

Minor forest produce provides sustenance to tribal population and to other communities residing in and around the forests. Such produce should be protected, improved and their production enhanced with due regard to generation of employment and income.

Strategy:

Area under Forests: The national goal should be to have a minimum of one third of the total land area of the country under forest or tree cover. In the hills and in mountainous regions, the aim should be to maintain two third of the area under such cover in order to prevent erosion and land degradation and to ensure the stability of the fragile eco-system.

Forestation, Social Forestry and Farm Forestry:

A massive need based and time bound programme of forestation and tree planting, with particular emphasis on fuel wood and fodder development, on all degraded and denuded lands in the country, whether forest or no forest land, is a national imperative.

It is necessary to encourage the planting of trees alongside of roads, railway lines, rivers and streams and canals, an d on other unutilized lands under State/corporate, institutional_ or private ownership. Green belts should be raised in urban/industrial areas as well as in arid tracts. Such a programme will help to check erosion and desertification as well as improve the microclimate.

Village and community lands, including those on foreshores and environs of tanks, not required for other productive uses, should be taken up for the development of tree crops and fodder resources. The Government should provide technical assistance and other inputs necessary for initiating such programmes. The revenues generated through such programmes should belong to the panchayats where the lands are vested in them; in all other cases, such revenues should be shared with the local communities in order to provide an incentive to them. The vesting, in individuals, particularly from the weaker sections (such as landless labour, small and marginal farmers, scheduled castes, tribal, and women) of certain ownership rights over trees, could be considered, subject to appropriate regulations; beneficiaries would be entitled to usufruct and would in turn be responsible for their security and maintenance.

Land laws should be so modified wherever necessary so as to facilitate and motivate individuals and institutions to undertake tree farming and grow fodder plants, grasses and legumes on their own land.

Wherever degraded lands should be made available for this purpose either on lease or on the basis of a tree - patta scheme, it should be distributed to people. Such leasing of the land should be subject to the land grant rules and land ceiling laws. Steps necessary to encourage them to do so must be taken. Appropriate regulations should govern the felling of trees on private holding.

Management of State Forests:

Schemes and projects, which interfere with forests that clothe steep slopes, catchments of rivers, lakes, and reservoirs, geologically unstable terrain and such other ecologically sensitive areas should be severely restricted. Tropical rain/moist forests, particularly in areas like Arunachal Pradesh, Kerala, Andaman & Nicobar Islands, should be totally safeguarded.

The forests should be managed as per the National Forest Policy. The Central Government should issue necessary guidelines to the State Governments in this regard and monitor compliance.

In order to meet the growing needs for essential goods and services, which the forests provide; it is necessary to enhance forest cover and productivity of the forests through the application of scientific and technical inputs. Production forestry programmes, while aiming at enhancing the forest cover in the country, and meeting national needs, should also be oriented to narrowing, by the turn of the century, the increasing gap between demand and supply of fuel wood. No such program, however, should entail clear felling of adequately stocked natural forests. Nor should exotic species be introduced, through public or private sources, unless long-term scientific trials undertaken by specialists in ecology, forestry and agriculture have established that they are suitable and have no adverse impact on native vegetation and environment.

Rights and Concessions:

The rights and concessions, including grazing, should always remain related to the carrying capacity of forests. The capacity itself should be optimized by increased investment, silvicultural research and development of the area. Stall feeding of cattle should be encouraged'. The requirements of the community, which cannot be met by the rights and concessions so determined, should be met by development of social forestry outside the reserved forests.

The holders of customary rights and concessions in forest areas should be motivated to identify themselves with the protection and development of forests from which they derive benefits. The rights and concessions from forests should primarily be for the bona-fide use of the communities living within and around forest areas, specially the tribal. The life of tribal and other poor living within and near forests revolves around forests. The rights and concessions enjoyed by them should be fully protected. Their domestic requirements of fuel wood, fodder, and minor forest produce and construction timber should be the first charge on forest produce. These and substitute materials should be made available through conveniently located depots at reasonable prices.

Similar consideration should be given to scheduled castes and other poor living near forests. However, the area, which such consideration should cover, would be determined by the carrying capacity of the forests. Wood is in short supply. The long-term solution for meeting the existing gap lies in increasing the productivity of forests, but to relieve the existing pressure on forests for the demands of railway sleepers, construction industry (particularly in the public- sector), furniture and paneling, mine pit props, paper and paper board etc. substitution of wood needs to be taken recourse to. Similarly, on the front of domestic energy, fuel wood needs to be substituted as far as practicable with alternate sources like bio-gas, LPG and solar energy. Fuel-efficient Chulhas (hand-made oven) need to be popularized in rural areas as a measure of conservation of fuel wood.

Diversion of Forest Lands for No forest purposes:

Forest land or land with tree cover should not be -treated merely as a resource readily available to be utilized for various projects and programmes, but as a national asset which requires to be properly safeguarded for providing sustained benefits to the entire community. Diversion of forestland for any no forest purpose should be subject to the most careful examinations by specialists from the standpoint of social and environmental costs and benefits. Construction of dams and reservoirs, mining and industrial development and expansion of agriculture should be consistent with the needs for conservation of trees and forests. Projects, which involve such diversion, should at least provide in their investment budget, funds for regeneration/compensatory forestation.

Beneficiaries who are allowed mining and quarrying in forestland and in land covered by trees should' be required to repair and re- vegetate the area in accordance with established forestry practices. No mining lease should be granted to any party, private or public, without a proper mine management plan appraised from the environmental angle and enforced by adequate machinery.

Tribal People and Forests:

Having regard to the symbiotic relationship between the tribal people and forests, a primary task of all agencies responsible for forest management, including the forest development corporations should be to associate the tribal people closely in the protection, regeneration and development of forests as well as to provide gainful employment to people living in and around the forest. While safeguarding the customary rights and interests of such people, forestry programmes should pay special attention to the following:

One of the major causes for degradation of forest is illegal cutting and removal by contractors and their labour. In order to put, an end to this practice, institutions such as tribal cooperatives, labour cooperatives, government corporations, etc. should replace contractorsas early as possible. The benefits are as follows:

(a) Protection, regeneration and optimum collection of minor forest produce along with institutional arrangements for the marketing of such produce;
(b) Development of forest villages on par with revenue villages;
(c) Family oriented schemes for improving the status of the tribal beneficiaries; and
(d) Undertaking integrated are a development programmes to meet the needs of the tribal, economy in and around the forest areas, including the provision of alternative sources of domestic energy on a subsidized basis, to reduce pressure on the existing forest areas.

Damage to Forests:

The forests are mostly damaged through encroachments, fires and grazing.

Encroachment on forestlands has been on the increase. This trend has to be arrested and effective action taken to prevent its continuance. There, should be no regularization of existing encroachments.

The incidence of forest fires in the country is high. Standing trees and fodder are destroyed on a large scale and natural regeneration annihilated by such fires. Special precautions should be taken during the fire season. Improved and modern management practices should be adopted to deal with forest fires.

Grazing in forest areas should be regulated with the involvement of the community Special conservation areas; young plantations and regeneration areas should be fully protected. Grazing and browsing in forest areas need to be controlled. Adequate grazing fees should be levied to discourage people in forest areas from maintaining large herds of non-essential livestock.

Forest based Industries: The main considerations governing the establishment of forest based industries and supply of raw material to them should be as follows:

(a) As far as possible, a forest based industry should raise the raw material needed for meeting its own requirements, preferably by establishment of a direct relationship between the factory and the individuals who can grow the raw material by supporting the individuals with inputs including credit, constant technical advice and finally harvesting and transport services.

(b) No forest based enterprise, except that at the village or cottage level, should be permitted in the future unless it has been first cleared after a careful scrutiny with regard to assured availability of raw material. In any case, the fuel, fodder and timber requirements of the local population should not be sacrificed for this purpose.

(c.) Forest based industries must not only provide employment to local people on priority but also involve them fully in raising trees and raw material.

(d) Natural forests serve as a gene pool resource and help to maintain ecological balance. Such forests will not, therefore, be made available to industries for ' undertaking plantation and for any other activities.

(e) Farmers, particularly small and marginal farmers, would be encouraged to grow, on marginal/degraded lands available with them, wood species required for industries. These may also be grown along with fuel and fodder species on community lands not required for pasture purposes and by Forest department/corporations on degraded forests, not earmarked for natural regeneration.

(f) The practice of supply of forest produce to industry at reduction prices should cease. Industry should be encouraged to use alternative raw materials. Import of wood and wood products should be liberalized.

The above considerations will, however, be subject to the current policy relating to land ceiling and land laws.

Shifting Cultivations affect the environment and productivity of land adversely. Alternative avenues of income, suitably harmonized with the right land use practices, should be devised to discourage shifting cultivation. Efforts should be made to contain such cultivation within the area already affected, by propagating improved agricultural practices. Area already damaged by such cultivation should be rehabilitated through social forestry and energy plantations.

Wildlife Conservation: Forest Management should take special care of the needs of wildlife conservation, and forest management plans should include prescriptions for this purpose. It is especially essential to provide for "corridors" linking the protected areas in order to maintain genetic continuity between artificially separated sub-sections of migrant wildlife.

Forest Extension: Forest conservation program cannot succeed without the willing support and cooperation of the people. It is essential, therefore, to inculcate in the people, a direct interest in forests, their development and conservation, and to make them conscious of the value of trees, wildlife and nature in general. This can be achieved through the involvement of educational institutions, right from the primary stage. Farmers and interested people should be provided opportunities through institutions like Agricultural Science Centers (Krishi Vigyan Kendras), Trainers' Training Centers to learn agri-silvicultural and silvi-cultural techniques to ensure optimum use of their land and water resources. Short- term extension courses and lectures should be organized in order to educate farmers. For this purpose, it is essential that suitable programmes be propagated through mass media, audio-visual aids and the extension machinery.

Forestry Education: Forestry should be recognized both as a scientific discipline as well as a profession. Agriculture universities and institutions, dedicated to the development of forestry education should formulate curricula and courses for imparting academic education and promoting postgraduate research and professional excellence, keeping in view the manpower needs of the country. Academic and professional qualifications - in forestry should be kept in view for recruitment to the Indian Forest Service and the State Forest Service. Specialized and orientation courses far developing better management skills by in service training need to be encouraged, taking into account the latest development in forestry and related disciplines.

Forestry Research: With the increasing recognition of the importance of forests for environmental health, energy and employment, emphasis must be laid on scientific forestry research, necessitating adequate strengthening of the research base as well as new priorities for action. Some broad priority areas of research and development needing special attention are:

(a) Increasing the productivity of wood and other forest produce per unit of area per unit time by the application of modern scientific and technological methods.
(b) Re-vegetation of barren/marginal/waste/mined lands and watershed areas.
(c) Effective conservation and management of existing forest resources (mainly natural forest eco-systems).
(d) Research related to social forestry for rural/ tribal development.
(e) Development of substitutes to replace wood and wood products.
(f) Research related to wildlife and management of national parks and sanctuaries.

Personnel Management: Government policies in personnel management for professional foresters and forest scientists should aim at enhancing their professional competence and status and attracting and retaining qualified - and motivated personnel, keeping in view particularly -the Arduous nature of duties they have to perform, often in remote and inhospitable places.

Forest Survey and Data Base: Inadequacy of data regarding forest resources is a matter of concern because this creates a false sense of complacency. Priority needs to. be accorded to completing the survey of forest resources in the country on scientific lines and to updating information. For this purpose, periodical collection, collation and publication of reliable data on relevant aspects of forest management needs to be improved with recourse to modern technology and equipment.

Legal Support and Infrastructure Development: Appropriate legislation should be undertaken, supported by adequate infrastructure, at the Center and State levels in order to implement the Policy effectively.

Financial Support for Forestry: The objectives of this revised Policy cannot be achieved without the investment of financial and other resources on a substantial scale. Such investment is indeed fully justified considering the contribution of forests in maintaining essential ecological processes and life support systems and in preserving genetic diversity. Forests should not be looked upon as a source of revenue. Forests are a renewable natural resource. They are a national asset to be protected and enhanced for the welfare of the people and the Nation.

Protect the forests

Chandan Mitra[65] has advised that we have to save jungles and save the tigers. Without a holistic approach nothing can protect India's wildlife from human greed and bestiality. If we don't act now, the tiger, leopard, elephant, deer and even marine and avian species will face extinction.

Last Tuesday it was Gurgaon. On Wednesday, it happened on the outskirts of Bhubaneswar. On Thursday, it was near Guwahati. By the time January is out, the toll can only be anticipated to multiply. On

---

[65]Chandan Mitra (2011), "To save the tiger, save jungle', The Pioneer Sunday Magazine, January 16, 2011

average bloodthirsty villagers mercilessly beat three to four leopards to death every week in India. Some die in accidents such as the cub that got run over by a train in Assam. But mostly the big cats are mauled to death by gruesome methods. Having encircled and trapped the terrified creature that may have strayed into human habitation in search of food, villagers' pelt them with stones; beat them with iron rods and in a few instances are known to have even gouged their eyes out in an orgy of bestiality. Eyewitnesses say that a carnival atmosphere prevails while the hapless cat cries out in pain. People congregate with drums as if to celebrate victory in battle. Cunningly, the carcass is dragged outside village precincts, sprayed with kerosene and set alight to remove traces of the crime. By the time forest officials or the police arrive, if at all they do, the deed is done. If confronted, belligerent villagers dare the officers to act. Outnumbered, enforcers of the law beat a hasty retreat and file a report blaming unknown persons for the murder. Few are prosecuted; leave alone punished.

In recent years the supposed man-animal conflict has become a one-sided affair with a variety of wild creatures being regularly bludgeoned to death. A recent report said that enraged by the alleged depredations of a herd of elephants, villagers managed to catch hold of a two-year-old calf that got left behind and beat it to death the same way as they often do with leopards. Fearful of the tiger, people don't venture to kill them in frontal combat, but have increasingly started to use poison with which they lace bait and wait for the unwary beast to consume it to die a slow, painful death. This has been reported particularly from Rajasthan and eastern Uttar Pradesh where incidents of tigers straying from sanctuaries have risen markedly.

There are two worrisome facets to these developments. First, villagers unconvinced of the need to preserve the country's dwindling wildlife are defeating the Government's much-hyped conservation efforts at the grassroots. Second, steady encroachment of animal habitats is resulting in migration out of sanctuaries, enhancing the chances of more frequent confrontations between villagers and animals in desperate search of food. Even more than encroachment, the disappearance of animal corridors in Uttarakhand, Madhya Pradesh, Maharashtra and Rajasthan, the construction or expansion of highways running through Reserved Forests and the grant of mining leases in protected forest areas has led to the sharpening of the problem.

The tiger is to India's conservation efforts what cricket is to sport. While Government and private efforts at tiger conservation have heightened consciousness about the majestic creature, the bulk of attention and finances are routed to projects related to it. No doubt, the effort is most laudable and let us hope that the next tiger census (currently underway), conducted by the more scientific camera trap method, will show a rise in numbers beyond the paltry 1,141 that the last headcount revealed.

The tiger cannot be protected without a holistic policy towards environment and wildlife. For example, if streams in the jungle dry up because of rampant extraction of groundwater and bottling plants being set up at source, the tigers' prey too cannot survive. If deer are forced to migrate out of forests or die of thirst, tigers and other predators like leopards would be compelled to move towards human habitations in search of food and water. If forest-cover declines or degenerates, wildlife would find less and less greens to forage and over time their reproductive capacity too would be adversely affected.

An ecological balance involving forest cover, water sources, and prey base for big cats is essential for wildlife to prosper. It is not possible to ensure a significant rise in tiger numbers merely by pumping in funds or relocating some to reserves from which they were eliminated through poaching or inhospitable environs.

Leopards and elephants are at a huge risk in India because of human incursions close to their traditional habitats. The leopard, being a smaller cat compared to the tiger is endangered by the steady decline in its prey base in the jungles. Besides, by nature they live on the outskirts of forests rather than the deep interiors. On the periphery of Mumbai, for instance, leopard sightings were fairly common till recently, just as the Aravali highlands close to Delhi-Gurgaon was the leopards' terrain not before long. As townships and industrial complexes are built in these areas with mounting speed, the leopard is seriously threatened and compelled to abandon protective jungle cover to hunt for food. The accident last year in which two young leopards were run over by a speeding vehicle on the Delhi-Jaipur Highway (NH 8) is a telling example of the leopards' predicament.

Unfortunately, there is no quick- fix solution to this, except a long-term policy regarding the peripheries of reserved forests or shrub lands in the Aravalis that are the leopards' natural habitat. How much encroachment can be allowed to builders of housing colonies, shopping malls and entertainment parks in the neighbourhood of our burgeoning metros? The frenetic expansion of human settlement around Gurgaon, which began in the 1990s, never had any form of environmental clearance whatsoever. Instead of maximizing habitation within existing colonies, builders are in the business of promoting golf courses, artificial lakes, sprawling villas and other attractive features to draw high-end buyers to housing and farmhouse complexes being built on lands that were once traversed by a variety of wildlife.

The abuse of areas peripheral to National Parks is so rampant that it hardly bears recalling. With over 700 resorts in operation just outside the perimeter of Corbett National Park, the discomfort caused to and consequent dislocation of wildlife has assumed serious dimensions. The Environment Minister Jairam Ramesh's heart is in the right place, but he has failed miserably to curb human intrusion into tiger reserves. Has anybody thought of the disturbance caused to wildlife by the relentless foray of tourists on jeep safaris in Ranthambhore? As it is, the park is overcrowded, but unchecked movement of people inside the sanctuary must be among the reasons that forced tigress T 13 with her two hungry eight-month-old cubs to venture out of the park, risking death by poisoning or starvation.

Arguably, decades of neglect and unconcern cannot be reversed overnight. But in the absence of holistic thinking the tiger, leopard, elephant, deer and even marine and avian species will become critically endangered in the next few years. So, the cheetah can wait while something concrete is done on a war footing to save our existing, diverse wildlife heritage.

Conclusion

Both the governments and people destroy forests and are responsible for environment degradation and climate change. The United Nations must promulgate an international law, which would be binding on all member-countries to reserve one third of geographical area for forests to save the world.

All the industrialized countries contribute excessively to environmental pollution.

Now the developing countries are trying to reduce forest area and have accepted industrialization policy to increase state income. Loss of forest coverage affects climate, rainfall and invites natural hazards like cyclone.

Forest depletion is caused by timber mafias, state administration, mines' owners, industrialists, forest contractors, and politicians.

Destruction of forests is caused through cutting of wood, mines excavation and industrialization. In the twenty first century, forest is not a safe place even for elephants, tigers, bears and other animals.

Forest depletion is caused by corporate houses, forest contractors, industrialists, lease owners, bureaucrats, state police and governments. Conservation of forests is possible by strong judicial action.

The forest animals should be protected by law and practice. There should be elephant corridor, water reservoirs, provision for checking forest fire and provision for watching the forest check gates.

People residing in forest area should be partners in the management of forests.

(a) Tribal people residing in forest area should watch the forest;
(b) They should be allotted a portion of dividend in forest income; and
(c) Should not assist the forest contractors in looting the forests

It is alleged that political party–in-power destroys forests to garner more funds to bribe the voters to win elections. It is a fact that forest coverage is reduced in daytime with the knowledge of the government.

+++++

Chapter VI

ENVIRONMENTAL LAWS

Poverty is the cause of degradation of environment; but we emphatically say that the governments and politicians are the factors of degradation and mismanagement of natural wealth, forests, green canopy, air, water, rivers, sea, flora and fauna and are the causes of all disasters including environment.

Mrs. Indira Gandhi
Former Prime Minister of India

The world's biggest emerging economies are not only aware of the potentially devastating impacts of climate change, but have also increasingly recognized the economic opportunities and advantages of a low carbon pathway. Grouped as BASIC (Brazil, South Africa, India and China), these countries emerged as an increasingly influential coalition since they sidelined other leading blocs such as the European Union (EU) to work with the US to deliver the

Copenhagen Accord at the last year's summit.

The seriousness with which these key emerging economies are approaching emissions reductions and energy efficiency at home, clearly demonstrates their recognition of the opportunity that climate change presents and their determination to act without waiting for developed countries to reveal their cards.

India has committed to an economy-wide 20 per cent increase in energy efficiency by 2016-17, while expanding its renewable energy programme, already one of the largest in the world. It has an ambitious programme that aims to generate an additional 20000 MW of solar energy by 2022 and is geared up to meet the target of adding 10 per cent renewable energy power by 2012.

China has committed to reduce the energy intensity of its economy by 40-45 per cent from 2005 levels by year 2020. Its goal of a 20 per cent reduction in energy intensity by 2010 has seen a rigorous energy efficiency plan including massive investment in clean energy technology. It has set an aggressive target to produce 10 per cent of its primary energy through renewable sources by 2010 and 15 per cent by 2020 and is well underway to reforming the renewable energy law.

Environmental Law is a complex body of law made up of global, international, national, state and local statutes, treaties, conventions, regulations and policies which seek to protect the environment and natural resources affected, impacted or endangered by human activities.

In this chapter, Environmental Laws and Regulations in the United States of America, Japan and India are discussed. Most of the countries have promulgated environmental laws but these countries are not observing their laws strictly.

United States of America
Environmental Laws and Regulations

The United States Environmental Protection Agency administers the laws required to protect human health and to safeguard the natural environment - - air, water and land – - upon which life depends.

Although environmental laws are generally considered a 20th century phenomenon, attempts have been made to make laws for environmental controls throughout history. In 2,700 B.C., the middle-eastern civilization in Ur passed laws protecting the few remaining forests in the region. In 80 A.D., the Roman Senate passed a law to protect water stored for dry periods so it could be used for street and sewer cleaning. During American colonial times, Benjamin Franklin argued for "public rights" laws to protect the citizens of Philadelphia against industrial pollution produced by animal hide tanners.

Significant environmental action began at the beginning of the 20th century. In 1906, Congress passed the "Antiquities Act," which authorizes the president to protect areas of federal lands as national monuments. A few years later, Alice Hamilton pushed for government regulations concerning toxic industrial chemicals. She fought, unsuccessfully, to ban the use of lead in gasoline. She also supported the legal actions taken by women who were dying of cancer from their exposure to the radium then used in glow-in-the-dark watch dials. During the early 1960's, biologist Rachel Carson pointed out the need to regulate pesticides such as DDT to protect the health of wildlife and humans.

With the establishment of the Environmental Protection Agency (EPA) in 1970, environmental law became a field substantial enough to occupy lawyers on a full-time basis. Since then, federal and state governments have passed numerous laws and created a vast network of complicated rules and regulations regarding environmental issues. Moreover, international organizations and agencies including the United Nations, the World Bank, and the World Trade Organization have also contributed environmental rules and regulations.

Because of the legal and technical complexities of the subjects covered by environmental laws, persons dealing with such laws must be knowledgeable in the areas of law, science and public policy. Environmental laws today encompass a wide range of subjects such as air and water quality, hazardous wastes and biodiversity. The purpose of these environmental laws is to prevent, minimize, remedy and punish actions that threaten or damage the environment and those that live in it. However, some people believe that these laws unreasonably limit the freedom of people, organizations, corporations and government agencies by placing controls on their actions.

Federal Laws

Early attempts by Congress to enact laws affecting the environment included the Antiquities Act in 1906, the National Park Service Act in 1916, the Federal Insecticide, Fungicide and Rodenticide Act in 1947 and the Water Pollution Control Act in 1956. The Wilderness Act of 1964 could protect large areas of pristine federal lands from development. This ushered in the new age of environmental activism that began in the 1960's. However, it was the National Environmental Policy Act (NEPA) enacted in 1969 and the formation of the Environmental Protection Agency (EPA) in 1970 that started environmental legislation in earnest. The main objective of these two federal enactments was to assure that the environment would be protected from both public and private actions that failed to take into account the costs of damage inflicted on the environment.

Many consider NEPA to be the most far-reaching environmental legislation ever passed by Congress. The basic purpose of NEPA is to force governmental agencies to comprehensively consider the effects of their decisions on the environment. This is affected by requiring agencies to prepare detailed Environmental Impact Statements (EIS) for proposed projects. The EPA is the government's environmental watchdog. It is charged with monitoring and analyzing the state of the environment, conducting research, and working closely with state and local governments to devise pollution control policies. The EPA is also empowered to enforce those environmental policies. Unfortunately, the agency is sometimes caught up in conflicts between the public wanting more regulation for environmental reasons and businesses wanting less regulation for economic reasons. Consequently, the development of a new regulation can take many years.

Since 1970, Congress has enacted several important environmental laws, all of which include provisions to protect the environment and natural resources. Some of the more notable laws include:

The Federal Clean Air Act (1970, 1977 and 1990) established national standards for regulating the emission of pollutants from stationary and mobile sources.

The Federal Water Pollution Control Act (1972) amended by the Clean Water Act (1977, 1987), established water quality standards; provides for the regulation of the discharge of pollutants into navigable waters and for the protection of wetlands.

The Federal Safe Drinking Water Act (1974, 1977 and 1986) set drinking water standards for levels of pollutants; authorizing the regulation of the discharge of pollutants into underground drinking water sources.

The Toxic Substances Control Act (1976) provided for the regulation of chemical substances by the EPA and the safety testing of new chemicals.

The Resource Conservation and Recovery Act (1976) established cradle-to-grave regulations for the handling of hazardous wastes.

The Comprehensive Environmental Response, Compensation and Liability Act (1980), also known as the Superfund program, provided for the cleanup of the worst toxic waste sites.

The Food Security Act (1985, 1990) later amended by the Federal Agriculture Improvement and Reform Act (1996), discouraged cultivation of environmentally sensitive lands, especially wetlands, and authorized incentives for farmers to withdraw highly eroded lands from production.

The application, or enforcement, of an environmental law is not always straightforward, and problems can arise. Often, the biggest problem is that Congress fails to allocate the funds necessary for implementing or enforcing the laws. Administrative red tape may make it impossible to enforce a regulation in a timely manner. It also may be unclear as to which agency (or branch of an agency) is responsible for enforcing a particular regulation. Furthermore, agency personnel decline to enforce a regulation for political reasons.

State Laws

Most states, like California, have enacted their own environmental laws and established agencies to enforce them. California faced some of its first environmental challenges in the mid-1800's, with regard to debris from the hydraulic mining of gold. Water quality concerns, dangers of flooding, negative impact on agriculture and hazards to navigation prompted the state to act.[66]

Some of California's environmental regulations preceded similar federal laws. For example, California established the nation's first air quality program in the 1950s. Much of the federal Clean Air Act amendments of 1990 were based upon the California Clean Air Act of 1988. California also pioneered advances in vehicle emission controls, control of toxic air pollutants and control of stationary pollution sources before federal efforts in those areas. The Porter-Cologne Act of 1970, upon which the state's water quality program is based, also served as the model for the federal Clean Water Act.

California's state environmental regulations are sometimes more stringent than the federal laws (e.g., the California Clean Air Act and vehicle emissions standards). In other program areas, no comparable federal legislation exists. For example, the California Integrated Waste Management Act established a comprehensive, statewide system of permitting, inspections, enforcement and maintenance for solid waste facilities and sets minimum standards for solid waste handling and disposal to protect air, water and land from pollution.

Also, **Proposition 65 (Safe Drinking Water and Toxic Enforcement Act)** requires the Governor to publish a list of chemicals that are known to the State of California to cause cancer, birth defects or other reproductive harm.

Despite the state's leadership in environmental programs and laws, the creation of a cabinet-level environmental agency in California lagged more than two decades behind the establishment of the federal

---

[66]University of California, College Prep, University of California, US

EPA. Originally, organization of California's environmental quality programs was highly fragmented. Each separate program handled a specific environmental problem (e.g., the Air Resources Board), with enforcement responsibility falling to both state and local governments. It was not until 1991 that a California EPA was finally established and united the separate programs under one agency.

International Treaties and Conventions

Conventions, or treaties, generally set forth international environmental regulations. These conventions and treaties often result from efforts by international organizations such as the United Nations (UN) or the World Bank. However, it is often difficult, if not impossible, to enforce these regulations because of the sovereign rights of countries. In addition rules and regulations set forth in such agreements may be no more than non-binding recommendations, and often countries are exempted from regulations due to economic or cultural reasons. Despite these shortcomings, the international community has achieved some success via its environmental agreements. These include an international convention that placed a moratorium on whaling (1986) and a treaty that banned the ocean dumping of wastes (1991).

The UN often facilitates international environmental efforts. In 1991, the UN enacted an Antarctica Treaty, which prohibits mining of the region, limits pollution of the environment and protects its animal species. The United Nations Environment Program (UNEP) is a branch of the UN that specifically deals with worldwide environmental problems. It has helped with several key efforts at global environmental regulations:

The 1987 Montreal Protocol on Substances that Deplete the Ozone Layer: As a result of this global agreement, industrialized countries have ceased or reduced the production and consumption of ozone-depleting substances such as chlorofluorocarbons.

The Prior Informed Consent Procedure for Certain Hazardous Chemicals and Pesticides in International Trade: This agreement enhances the world's technical knowledge and expertise on hazardous chemicals management.

The Convention on International Trade in Endangered Species of Wild Fauna and Flora (CITES): This agreement protects over 30,000 of the world's endangered species.

In 1995 UNEP and the International Olympic Committee (IOC) signed a partnership agreement to develop environmental guidelines for sports federations and countries bidding to host the Olympic Games.

The Rotterdam Convention (1998) addressed the growing trade in hazardous pesticides and chemicals. Importing countries must now give explicit informed consent before hazardous chemicals can cross their borders.

The International Declaration on Cleaner Production (1998): The signatories commit their countries to implement cleaner industrial production and subsequent monitoring efforts.

In 1992, the UN member nations committed their resources to limiting greenhouse gas (e.g., carbon dioxide) emissions at or below 1990 levels, as put forth by the UN Framework Convention on Climate Change. Unfortunately, the agreement was non-binding and by the mid-1990's, it had had no effect on carbon emissions. The 1997 Kyoto Protocol was a binding resolution to reduce greenhouse gases. Although the United States initially supported the resolution, the Senate failed to ratify the treaty, and by 2001 the resolution was opposed by President Bush as threatening the United States economy.

JAPAN: **Environmental Protection in Japan**

Considering the absolutely horrendous record of Japan in ecology in the 1960s the 1970s with the Mina Mata disease, mercury poisoning, etc as Japan sacrificed all for economic growth, its present interest in the ecology is interesting. My first trip to Japan in the 1970s made me wonder about its international commitment in particular. Timber - exports to Japan from the US was already becoming a political issue in the US. Yet having seen many mountain areas in the USA where the trees had been harvested to supply Japan's factories, I was most surprised to see Japan's mountains where nary a mountain side had been scalped. I say harvested in the US, to contrast the situation in SE Asia in particular where corrupt elites were more than eager to supply Japan's factories even in the cost in lives of their own peoples as the tens of thousands died from floods caused by denuded mountain forests.

The Law

Digression: Anti-Neo- European Imperialism

Yet Japan does have today a strong interest in ecology. Look at the Kyoto Treaty, otherwise known as the Kyoto Protocol on Climate Change. I, being an opponent of Neo-European imperialism, being willing to see European, particularly French, Machiavellian manipulations under every rock, am highly suspicious that the Europeans added the name Kyoto to the treaty to obtain Japanese support, just as they bought Russian support, thereby turning the treaty into "law" when in reality they bought off the

Russians by promising support for Russian membership in the WTO. Having seen the recent tirade at an international environmental conference against America, by the president of Argentina, the leader of the country of which carried out the biggest bankruptcy, some would call "theft" in the history of the world, he has now became an icon of "international law" by his environmental attack on the US, to the cheers of the Europeans. Yes, "international law" and Neo-European imperialism is "law"

Science and Fantasy:

The Discovery Channel has acquired a reputation for credibility on science and history---it's educational. Yet in recent months I have seen amazing reports. Within the last 10,000 years there have been vibrant trade routes in western China and verdant fields in Egypt, now both barren desert regions. Tens of millions of years ago the North Pole and vast swaths of Canada were tropical hothouses. One story even had it that the last Ice Age, which had lasted for thousands of years, ended in a 20 year period. I think that all these could be called examples of "climate change." For the life of me, however, despite my fervent patriotism and great faith in American technological capability, I cannot fathom how the Americans did all this. I mean, ask any European, they will tell you with the deepest of candor that present climate change is the fault of the Americans. Considering that despite the most powerful of computers and satellites, weather forecasts of more than 3 days are no more accurate than a flip of the coin, I wonder how Europeans can reach such a conclusion. My simple mind thinks it leans more on a very heavy element of anti-Americanism than scientific evidence. But if they can prove to me how the Americans caused all the many, many previous examples of climate change I will gladly personally sign the Kyoto Treaty.

And I am a car hater. I am one of the few living American males who have a deep-seated hatred of automobiles. I grew up in Denver, which is rapidly turning into the new LA, but even decades ago you could see the sky turning black from what was clearly the effect of automobile pollution. I will certainly agree with that conclusion. Compounded with the tens of thousands of deaths year in, year out, from automobile accidents, more than killed in American wars, I am a fierce opponent of the automobile. Finally, I am convinced that America's addiction to oil will destroy it just as assuredly opium destroyed China. Imagine, financing the very peoples who are trying to kill you. But addicts are always the last to admit the truth. Still this does not prove the European case, nor disprove Neo-European imperialism. Even the Russians, once they approved the protocol said it was all about the deal on the WTO, as their scientists claimed there was not enough evidence to back European claims.

Back to Japan Law:

Of course, the Japanese passed legislation for the implementation of the Kyoto Protocol in June 2002. But even outside of that, modern day Japan has involved environmental law in affecting virtually every part of Japanese life. Japan is a densely populated nation, compounded with a geography that is mostly mountainous. This further pushes people to concentrate into limited areas and heavy population densities. For decades Japan has seen many court cases, in a normally non-litigious society, fighting over even sun light. Thus there is the practical aspect. A bad environment in Japan affects all Japanese, from the top to the bottom. But there is also the matter of face, a very important concept in Japan. Any scandal in Japan has an impact on a company's "face" in Japan, and environmental scandals are having that effect as well. Thus most responsible corporations give consideration to the environment from many aspects, from simple environmental pollution and waste disposal as well as giving consideration to the impact on the environment of procurement of raw materials and commercialization of products. Environmental consciousness is also having a business effect in consideration of the consumers' viewpoint. Environmentally sensitive products are increasingly in demand both from ordinary consumers as well as governmental procurement. To the contrary, corporations gaining reputations as polluters may suffer from the distaste of many consumers.

Varieties of Japanese Environmental Law

The keystone of Japanese environmental law, some even calling it the Constitution of Japanese environmental law is the Environment Basic Law. Although this law itself was enacted in 1993, it was an amalgam of the Environment Measures Basic Law of 1967 and the Natural Environment Protection Law of 1972. The Environment Basic Law has as its basic theme a society with a sustainable development capability such that a robust environment is enjoyed and secured for the future. This is for a society that can preserve the environment as well as develop the economy. As this law, as well as many other Japanese environmental laws, were enacted at a time of both rapid economic growth and when Japan was becoming a prosperous nation, it will be interesting to watch the future if Japan continues to face economic stagnation as well as an increasingly dangerous world confronting China and North Korea.

Another law is the 'Law promoting and forming the Environmental Society', which handles waste disposal and recycling. This law aims to achieve an efficient usage of resources. The law pushes many "R's" in Reduce pollution, Reuse resources, Recycle waste and Recapture energy.

There are also environmental laws targeted at specific industries, such as the Electric Utility Law and the Gas (as in the gaseous form, natural gas, etc) Utility Law. These laws seek to have the industries use these energies efficiently when they build their systems.

Then there is also the Environmental Impact Evaluation Law, which requires environmental impact statements for large projects before they are implemented.

Laws that regulate environmental pollution include the Air Pollution Prevention Law, the Water Quality Pollution Prevention Law and the Pollutant Release and Transfer Register (PRTR) Law. The Air Pollution Prevention Law sets standards for air pollutants and regulates them and seeks to prevent major air pollution prevention problems. Likewise the Water Quality Pollution Prevention Law sets standards for water pollutants and regulates them. Dangerous pollutants are to be prevented entering water bodies as well as the ground water. The Pollutant Release and Transfer Register Law requires companies which handle more than certain prescribed amounts of dangerous pollutant chemicals to file reports with the government. Over 300 such dangerous chemicals have been designated under the law.

There is also the Law for the Promotion of Measures against Global Warming, which is Japan's attempt to regulate waste gases and prevent global warming as part of the Kyoto Pact.

Another issue is environmental standards set out by the government, particularly the Environment Ministry. Some of these standards are for materials polluting the atmosphere; waters and land while other regulates noise and vibration pollution. Although the standards in and of them usually do not have a legal basis, there are some standards specifically set out by statute that are mandatory in effect and penalties often apply.

Local government units as well often have ordinances imposing even stricter environmental controls than national levels, as can be expected in the most densely populated regions where such pollution would have their most adverse impact.

Japan says that following the United Nations Conference for Environment and Development of 1992 (the "Earth Summit"), which called for sustainable development it has been striving to makes it legal framework incorporate such sustainable development.

Energy Conservation and Global Warming

Technological innovation advances on almost a daily basis and from the viewpoint of the environment, not to mention the dangers economically and geo-politically from depending on the unstable Middle East for the bulk of increasingly expensive oil resources, energy conservation has become a powerful force in the world. Save the environment! Save expensive energy! Cut off the funding of terrorists! What could be more logical? In this area the world has a big debt of gratitude to the Japanese who have lead the world. Not only have they led the world in energy saving appliances, they also came up with the first commercially available hybrid vehicles. Leave it to the American firms to follow up with hybrid sports utility vehicles. Now you know why dinosaurs go extinct -- and civilizations as well.

Japan, primarily due to the energy shocks of the 1970s and early 1980s, implemented a number of energy conservation promotion laws. At least they learned a lesson. Japanese legislation during that period pushed increasingly stringent energy conservation measures in appliances, vehicles, plants and offices. One measure was to put into a place a law requiring appliances to have energy efficiency rating labels. The most important legislation in this area was the Law Concerning the Rationalization of the Usage of Energy, otherwise known as the Energy Conservation Law. That law imposes requirements for energy conservation on products, and the places where they are made, factories or offices. Penalties can be imposed on violators. When setting out the guidelines or standards for the implementation of the law, the Japanese government tends to watch technological trends and push companies to meet the highest of technological capabilities.

Thus this law improves the efficiency of Japan's energy usage and conserves energy resources. The law is applied against both Japanese manufacturers and the importers of foreign goods. They are also required to label the product's energy efficiency. The law also requires factories and offices that consume more than certain levels of energy to meet energy conservation standards. Such operations are required to file reports with the government periodically on their energy usage situation. There has even been created a new position of "energy administrator" who must even pass a government licensing exam and who is responsible for filing such reports and prepare energy conservation plans. Of course energy-usage level depends on the type of industry. The violators can be fined. New buildings must implement energy conservation measures too.

Once the Kyoto Protocol is implemented, early in 2005 in all probability following Russia's bought approval, Japan will also be taking measures to reduce six types of waste gases such as carbon dioxide, and methane, etc. Theoretically by 2012 they are to reduce levels to 6% below those in effect in 1990. Businesses will be required to publicly announce their plans for reducing such gases and make public reports on the progress they are making on implementing such plans. Japan's Law for the Promotion of Measures against Global Warming, was meant for the implementation of the protocol.

Waste Disposal and Recycling

Japanese regulation on waste disposal, particularly industrial waste disposal is ramping up the pressure to greater and greater levels. In the 2000 amendment to the Law Concerning the Disposal and Cleaning of Waste Matter, more popularly known as the Waste Matter Disposal Law there was a further crackdown. Where the waste matter of a company is disposed of in an illegal manner, now not only is the party that was entrusted with the illegal disposal punished, but also now the waste making company as well is called to account.

The key point of this legislation is the concept of the recycling society, which is a terminology in fact found in legislation, to wit: "the Basic Law Promoting the Formation of a Recycling Society." This concept is defined in the legislation as "a society, which conserves on resources, and burdening the environment as little as possible, with the minimal production waste, the recycling of unused products as much as possible, and properly disposing of that which cannot be otherwise recycled."

The Basic Law Promoting the Formation of a Recycling Society was enacted in 2000. The law spells out basic principles and the roles of relevant parties. With respect to waste, the law seeks to reduce it, re-use it, recycle it, and recycle waste energy. The law also seeks to place responsibility on producers of waste, not just those handling the waste, and give greater responsibility to manufacturers for disposing of their products after they are no longer in use.

Other laws that deal with waste management and recycling are as follows:

(a) Green Purchasing Law (purchasing from environmentalist companies)
(b) Automobile Recycling Law
(c) Food Products Recycling Law
(d) Construction Recycling Law
(e) Household Appliances Recycling Law
(f) Containers & Packaging Recycling Law
(g) Waste Matter Disposal Law
(h) Amended Recycling Law

Disposition of Waste Matter:
The Liability of Waste Producers for Illegal Disposal

The 2000 amendment to the Waste Matter Disposal Law made the producers of waste products liable for illegal disposal of waste matter as well as those who illegally disposed of the waste matter. Most companies subcontract out the disposal of their waste to some kind of Garbage Company. Now, however, if the garbage company disposes of the waste in an illegal manner, the waste producing company can be made responsible for the expenses incurred in returning the damaged area to their original condition.

In the case of industrial waste, Japanese law basically takes the stance that the producer of the waste should dispose of it itself. If it subcontracts out the collection, transport or disposal of such waste, it must make a contract with a duly licensed waste disposal company. In the contract documents should be included the term of validity of the contract, the fee and the scope as well as the licensing details of the waste disposal company. When the company which produces the waste subcontracts the disposal of the waste to another company, not only must it be with a duly licensed waste disposal business, but the producing company must issue a waste disposal administration manifest at the time of handing over the waste and when the disposal is completed, get back the manifest and store it for 5 years.

The Waste Matter Disposal Law seeks to reduce the creation, appropriate classification, storage, collection, transport, reuse and disposal of waste matter. The law defines general waste and industrial waste. Industrial waste is waste product that is produced as a result of business activities and the law, together with pertinent cabinet order sets out nearly 20 types of industrial waste. The law puts the responsibility for the disposal of industrial waste on the shoulders of the producing company, strives to reduce the volume of waste via recycling and provides for businesses making it easy dispose of finished goods and containers.

Recycling

The Law Concerning the Promotion of the Effective Usage of Resources, popularly known as the Amended Recycling Law in Japan puts recycling responsibilities on the makers of products that most businesses in other countries can only have nightmares about. The law seeks to reduce the volume of waste products produced at factories or finished products that can no longer be used, as well as promoting effective usage of resources through recycling. Corporations are in many cases given the obligation to recycle their finished products that can no longer be used. Making classifications based on industry or product, the law promotes the policy to "reduce" through controlling the production of waste products by such measures as reducing materials used in products or increasing their useful life or "reuse" through reusing parts, etc. "recycle" through recycling as raw materials. These are:

(a) Industries where "reduce" policies are to be implemented include automobiles, personal computers, household furniture, and gas/oil appliances.

(b) Industries where "re-use" policies are to be implemented include automobiles, personal computers, and copy machines, etc.
(c) Industries where "recycle" policies are to be implemented include personal computers, etc.

The Amended Recycling Law of 2000 followed the old Recycling Law, officially called the Law Concerning the Promotion of the Usage of Reused Resources, enacted in 1991 in response to a society of consumption and increased business activity the amount of waste products increased at the same time that garbage dumps were filling to capacity. But that law was inadequate. Japan still was a society of mass production, mass consumption and mass wastage. So it was the 2000 amendment of the law.

Re-cycling of Household Appliances

The Household Appliances Recycling Law requires the recycling of television sets, air conditioners, washing machines and refrigerators, basically the larger of most household appliances. Many of the materials in those appliances, such as the metals and glass are to be recycled.

Manufacturers, Retailers and Consumers:

In addition to the Household Appliances Recycling Law other laws requiring recycling include the Automobile Recycling Law, the Food Products Recycling Law, the Construction Recycling Law and the Containers & Packaging Recycling Law.

The Household Appliances Recycling Law and the Automobile Recycling Law places different responsibilities on manufacturers, retailers and consumers. The consumer must return the used product to the retailer and pay the expenses for recycling it. The retailer returns the product to the manufacturer. The manufacturer is to recycle the product.

The reason that there are separate laws for recycling containers and packaging, construction waste, food waste and automobiles is due to the major impact on the environment the waste of such products cause. Thus particularly severe controls are imposed on those products and industries.

The Containers & Packaging Recycling Law (officially the "Law Concerning the Promotion, etc. of Separation, Collection of Containers & Packaging and their Re-Commercialization") seeks to require manufacturers to recycle container and packaging wastes. The public is to separate and take out the containers and packaging materials to be collected by local government authorities. It is hoped that third parties will then recycle and commercialize the waste.

The Construction Recycling Law (officially the "Law Concerning the Re-using Construction Materials"): The law seeks to promote the appropriate disposal of waste and the efficient usage of resources; construction materials are to be separated and recycled. The law applies to businesses engaged in the destruction of buildings above a certain size as well as the construction of new buildings above a certain size. The materials targeted by the law include primarily concrete, asphalt and wood.

There is also the Food Products Recycling Law (officially the "Law Concerning the Promotion of the Re-use of Food Product Resources"). The law seeks a reduction in and recycling of raw material byproducts from the manufacture of food products and food product wastes such as unsold food materials. Obligations are imposed on manufacturers and retailers.

Green Purchasing:

There are now laws in Japan requiring that the government, national or local, as well as government related corporations, give priority in procurements to environmentally friendly products. So corporations are getting the word. Environment friendly means more government business, unfriendly loses business. Popularly known as the Green Purchasing Law, it is formally called the Law Concerning the Procurement of Environmental Products by the Nation, etc." The law strives for the government, national and local, as well as government corporations, direct their massive purchasing power towards giving priority to purchases of products that use recycled materials, products designed for easy recycling and, that are useful in reducing waste as well as the burden on the environment. These government entities must publicly announce plans on procurement giving such priorities as well the results of procurement.

It is also hoped that such massive purchases of environmental friendly products will help to lower their prices as such recycled products are higher in price than ordinary products.

Pollution Dispute Resolution:

The most famous pollution case in Japan involved the Mina Mata Disease. This was certainly an environment-induced disease. Factories polluted the local seawaters with mercury products, which were ingested by fish and shellfish. Then the local people ingested those fish and shellfish. Severe neurological disorders followed. People had difficulty speaking, walking, palsy, many, many nasty side effects. Nearly 20,000 people claimed damage for which the government in the end recognized a little over 2000 as being damaged by the disease. The Japanese legal system proved a travesty for this legal problem. The pollution was officially recognized in 1956 but the final court case was not resolved until 1996, forty years to resolve. American lawyers, now demanding legal fees topping half a billion dollars for the Enron case could only salivate on this kind of case in the US. Despite that it would not have taken 40 years in the US.

But Japan did respond with legislation and there has not been such a massive environmental disaster since Mina Mata, as people's awareness of the environment was heightened. There are now laws covering almost every type of pollution--- air pollution, water pollution, sound pollution, vibration pollution, smell pollution, etc. The most recent of these laws has been aimed at dioxins, most commonly found involved in the incineration of waste, soil pollution, or the assassination of political rivals in some countries.

The Major Pollution Prevention Laws in Japan include the following:

(a) The Pollution Dispute Resolution Law
(b) The Law Concerning the Compensation of Pollution Health Victims
(c) The Dioxins Countermeasures Special Measures Law
(d) The Air Pollution Prevention Law
(e) The Water Pollution Prevention Law
(f) The Noise Regulation Law
(g) The Bad Smell Prevention Law
(h) The Vibration Regulation Law.
(i) The Soil Pollution Countermeasures Law

Most of Japan's environment legislation came out during the early 1970s following Japan's period of extremely rapid economic growth when all was basically sacrificed by both the government and businesses on alter of economic growth. As the pollution began to affect even people's daily health and prosperity spread, demand for the laws spread and 14 such laws were passed in 1970. In 1971 the Environment Agency, now upgraded to the Environment Ministry, was established. It will be interesting to see future reaction if Japan's economy continues to stagnate and government finances drown in red ink.

Factory Related Air and Water Pollution

Japanese legislation sets out standards for air pollutants from factories. Yet even if these standards are met, companies should work hard with local communities to prevent misunderstandings and convince them of the company's commitment to preventing pollution.

Legislation as well sets out standards for water pollutants from factories. In cases of pollution under this law based on negligence, not only the company, but also the individual employee(s) can be held responsible. Penalties of up to 300,000 yen and imprisonment of up to 3 months can be imposed.

Legislation related to air and water pollution designates polluting matters, and pollution standards for such matters. If these standards are exceeded, fines can be imposed. Compensatory damages may also be awarded for damages from such pollution. The air pollution legislation controls air pollutants from factories and automobiles. The water pollution legislation controls water pollutants going from factories into public water bodies as well as into the ground water. These laws permit compensatory damages for such pollution. Sounds like strict liability.

There are even criminal punishments for damaging people's lives or limbs. There also pollution volume restrictions, particularly for densely populated areas.

Ground Pollution:

Factory land can often get polluted with a variety of very nasty, even life-threatening chemicals. Thus Japanese legislation now requires testing of such land, particularly when such land is to be used for residential or public use such as for a park. One concern of course is that such chemicals can seep into the ground water and people will end up drinking it. As Japan increasingly moves much of it's manufacturing into SE Asia and China, there are increasing examples of factory land being converted into other applications.

The Land Pollution Countermeasures Law strives for measures to prevent damage to health from ground pollution and imposes an obligation on understanding ground pollution conditions. Thus when landowners convert their factory land to other uses such as residential or park use, a test for ground pollution must be carried out. When it is found that such land contains designated dangerous substances at levels exceeding designated standards, the prefecture governor can issue orders designating the area, publicizing it, and when believed dangerous to human health, order the land owner to remove the pollution, plow it up, restrict entry, seal or clean the land, etc. In most cases the land owner is liable in carrying out such orders, however if they can prove that a third party is responsible for such pollution they can collect their expenses from that polluter.

At the present time, the law requires only that the ground testing and countermeasures only apply when a factory is closed, not while it is still operating. However, when pollution can be seen to be exceeding levels set out by cabinet orders, the prefecture governor can order testing and reports.

Chemical Administration:

The world, being physical, is filled with chemicals, including about 100,000 that are made by man. Since some of those chemicals are dangerous to human health or to the environment, most governments impose some kind of regulations, as of course in the case of Japan.

Pollutant Release and Transfer Register (PRTR) Law imposes obligations on businesses handling more than certain levels of designated dangerous chemicals. The law requires such businesses to report to the government the volume of chemical air or water pollutants expelled, or the volume of products or waste moved.

The Japanese legislation related to the administration of chemicals is of two types. One group handles all chemicals, and the other group deals with specific chemicals. Specifically, Japanese laws related to the administration of chemicals include the following:

(a) The Chemicals Testing Law
(b) Pollutant Release and Transfer Register (PRTR) Law
(c) The Law Concerning the Regulation of the Testing and Manufacturing of Chemicals (the Chemicals Testing Law)
(d) The Law Concerning the Securing the Enforcement of the Collection and Destruction of chlorofluorocarbons (CFCs) (the CFC Collection & Destruction Law)
(e) The Law Concerning the Protection of the Ozone Layer by Regulation of Designated Substances (the Ozone Protection Law)

The Chemicals Testing Law strives to establish a system where a party seeks to manufacture or import new chemicals to test the characteristics of the chemicals in advance, in order to prevent environmental pollution by chemicals that are difficulties decomposing in the environment and that damage health.

The Ozone Protection Law passed in 1988 is a law, which seeks to regulate the manufacture and import of chlorofluorocarbons (CFCs) and hydro-chloro-fluorocarbons (HCFCs). Limits are imposed on the production, consumption and destruction of these substances. Manufacturers of these substances are required to obtain licenses from the government. Importers are required to obtain authorization based on the Foreign Exchange and Foreign Trade Control Law. In addition, parties using these substances are required to cooperate in the rationalization of the usage and restriction of their release.

The Ozone Protection Law was enacted as Japan's part in joining international controls on such damaging substances such as the Treaty of Vienna Convention for the Protection of the Ozone Layer of 1985 and the Montreal Protocol on Substances that Deplete the Ozone Layer of 1987.

The CFC Collection & Destruction Law, enacted in 2001, sets out the obligations of businesses in the collection and destruction of CFCs. It aims to control the release into the atmosphere of CFCs that are destroying the ozone layer and is one cause for global warming. The law requires the manufacturers of the regulated products, when the products have been used and are to be thrown out, to take measures necessary for the suitable and confirmed collection and destruction of the products.

The law targets specifically industrial air conditioners, industrial refrigeration units and automobile air conditioners. The party throwing out the used product hands it over to the party collecting the CFCs and is liable for the expenses for the collection and destruction. Japan has now stopped producing CFCs but as there are still many products around that still contain the stuff, controls are still necessary for their usage and disposal in order to restrict their release into the atmosphere.[67]

INDIA: **Environmental Regulations and Legal Framework**

Or Environment Protection: Indian Constitution Perspective

The State's responsibility with regard to environmental protection has been laid down under Article 48-A of our Constitution, which reads as follows:

(a)The State shall endeavour to protect and improve the environment and to safeguard the forests and wildlife of the country.

(b)Environmental protection is a fundamental duty of every citizen of this country under Article 51-A (g) of our Constitution, which reads as follows:

It shall be the duty of every citizen of India to protect and improve the natural environment including forests, lakes, rivers and wildlife and to have compassion for living creatures.

(c) Article 21 of the Constitution is a fundamental right, which reads as follows:

No person shall be deprived of his life or personal liberty except according to procedure established by law.

(d)Article 48-A of the Constitution comes under Directive Principles of State Policy & Article 51 A (g) of the Constitution comes under Fundamental Duties.

---

[67]Roderick See man's Japan Law info

(e) The State's responsibility with regard to raising the level of nutrition and the standard of living and to improve public health has been laid down under Article 47 of the Constitution which reads as follows:

The State shall regard the raising of the level of nutrition and the standard of living of its people and the improvement of public health as among its primary duties and, in particular, the State shall endeavour to bring about prohibition of the consumption except for medicinal purposes of intoxicating drinks and of drugs, which are injurious to health.

f) The 42nd amendment to the Constitution was brought about in the year 1974 makes it the responsibility of the State Government to protect and improve the environment and to safeguard the forests and wildlife of the country. The latter, under Fundamental Duties, makes it the fundamental duty of every citizen to protect and improve the natural environment including forests, lakes, rivers and wildlife and to have compassion for living creatures.

The subjects related to environment in the seventh schedule of the Constitution:

Central List (Entries)

(a) Article 52: Industries
(b) Article 53: Regulation and development of oil fields and mineral oil resources.
(c) Article 54: Regulation of mines and mineral development.
(d) Article 56: Regulation and development of inter-State rivers and river valleys.
(e) Article 57: Fishing and fisheries beyond territorial waters.

State List (Entries)

(a) Article 6: Public health and sanitation.
(b) Article 14: Agriculture, protection against pest and prevention of plant diseases.
(c) Article 18: Land, Colonization etc
(d) Article 21: Fisheries
(e) Article 23: Regulation of mines and mineral development subject to provisions of List-I.
(f) Article 24: Industries subject to the provisions of List - 1 of List-I.

Common or Concurrent List (Entries)

(a) Article 17 A: Forests
(b) Article 17 B: Protection of wild animals and birds
(c) Article 20: Economic and social planning.
(d) Article 20 A: Population control and family planning

As conferred by Article 246(1), while the Union is supreme to make any law over the subjects enumerated in List I, the States, under Article 246 (3), enjoy competence to legislate on the entries contained in List II, and both the Union and the States under Article 246(2) have concurrent jurisdiction on entries contained in List III. In the event of a clash, the Union enjoys a primacy over States in that its legislation in the Union and the Concurrent List prevails over State legislations. Also, the Parliament has residuary powers to legislate on any matter not covered in the three Lists (Art. 248).

Mandatory Requirements – Environment

The Electricity Act, 2003

This Act seeks to create a framework for the power sector development by measures conducive to the industry. Electricity Act does not explicitly deal with environmental implications of activities related to power transmission. The applicable legal provisions under this Act are as follows: Section 68(1) - sanction from the Ministry of Power (MOP) is a mandatory requirement for taking up any new project. The sanction authorizes SJVN to plan and coordinate activities to commission new projects.

The Forest (Conservation) Act, 1980

This Act provides for the conservation of forests and regulating diversion of forestlands for non-forestry purposes. When a project falls within forestlands, prior clearance is required from relevant authorities under the Forest (Conservation) Act, 1980. State governments cannot de-reserve any forestland or authorize its use for any non-forest purposes without approval from the Central government. (Annexure 1) The steps for forest clearance are briefly described below:

1. Identification of Forest Area involved (Location of Project)

By using tools such as the forest atlas and Survey of India maps, preliminary location of project is done. During route alignment, all possible efforts are made to avoid the forest area (like national park and sanctuaries) or to keep it to the barest minimum. Whenever it becomes unavoidable due to the geography of terrain or heavy cost involved in avoiding it, different alternative options are considered to minimize the requirement of forest area.

For selection of optimum proposal, the following criteria are taken into consideration:

(a) Any monument of cultural or historical importance is not affected by the project,

(b) The proposed alignment of the project line does not create any threat to the survival of any community with special reference to Tribal Community,
(c) The proposed alignment of the project does not affect any public utility services such as playgrounds, schools and other establishments,
(d) The alignment of the project does not pass through any sanctuaries, National Park, Biosphere reserves or eco-sensitive zones, and
(e) The alignment of the project does not infringe with area of natural resources.

To achieve this, selection of forest area involved is undertaken in close consultation with representatives from the State forest departments and the Department of Revenue. Minor alterations are made to avoid environmentally sensitive areas and settlements at execution stage.

Trees on such locations are felled but after stringing is complete and natural regeneration is allowed to specific heights and whenever required the tree plantation is taken.

2. Formulation of Forest Proposal

After finalization of forest area involved for project location SJVNL submits details in prescribed pro-forma to the respective DFO/ Nodal Officer (Forest) of concerned State Government. DFO/ Nodal Officer forward the details to the concerned Divisional Forest Officer (DFO) / Conservator of Forest for formulation of forest proposal for processing of clearance under the Forest (Conservation) Act, 1980. The DFO then surveys the relevant forest area required for the construction of project under the possible alternatives. Forest authorities conduct a cost-benefit analysis to assess the loss of forest produce, loss to environment vis-à-vis benefits of project.

Compensatory Afforestation (CA) scheme is prepared to compensate loss of vegetation and is the most important and integral part of the proposal. For CA, the forest authorities identify degraded forestland of twice the area of affected land. SJVNL provides undertaking/ certificate to meet the cost of compensatory Afforestation and the Net Present Value of forestland diverted. The NPV rate varies from 580 to 920 thousands of INR per hectare (as per Ministry of Environment and Forests (MoEF) Notification of dated. 23.04.04) and is payable to the "Compensatory Afforestation Fund Management and Planning Authority" (CAMPA). If the forest is rich in wildlife, then the Chief Wildlife Warden also gets a detailed assessment report prepared including measures to protect the wildlife, which is submitted with the proposal.

3. Approval of Proposal

The proposal is submitted to the state forest department and then forwarded to the principal chief conservator of forests in the state and finally to the state secretariat. The State Government recommends the proposal for further processing and approval to a) Concerned Regional Office of the MoEF if the area involved is 40 hectare or less b) MoEF, New Delhi if the area is more than 40 hectare. The approval process is illustrated in Appendix –II.

To facilitate speedy approval of forest proposal involving lesser area, Ministry of Environment & Forests had established Regional Offices in each region for processing and approving these proposals. The MoEF approves the proposal in two stages. In principle or first stage approval is accorded with certain conditions depending upon the case. Second stage or final approval is provided after the compliance report of the conditions stipulated in first Forest Proposal (FP) is received by MOEF -G O I from State Forest Department.

SJVNL follows all relevant guidelines including the directions of the Supreme Court in this regard from time to time.

Environmental (Protection) Act, 1986

The Environment (Protection) Act 1986 was introduced as an umbrella legislation that provides a holistic framework for the protection and improvement to the environment.

In terms of responsibilities, the Act and the associated Rules requires for obtaining environmental clearances for specific types of new / expansion projects (addressed under Environmental Impact Assessment Notification, 1994) and for submission of an environmental statement to the State Pollution Control Board annually. Environmental clearance is not applicable to hydro projects also.

SJVNL undertakes Environmental Impact Assessment for all projects as a standard management procedure as laid down in The Environment (Protection) Act, 1986 and also functions within permissible standards of ambient air quality and noise levels as prescribed by national laws and international regulations. The Environmental Clearance procedure is Appendix- III.

Other rules and regulations under the Environmental (Protection) Act, 1986 applicable to the operation of SJVNL are described below:

Air (Prevention and Control of Pollution) Act, 1981

The objective of this Act is to provide for the prevention, control and abatement of air pollution, for the establishment, with a view to carrying out the aforesaid purposes, of Boards, for conferring on and assigning to such Boards powers and functions relating thereto and for matters connected therewith. Decisions were taken at the United Nations

Conference on the Human Environment held in Stockholm in June 1972, in which India participated, to take appropriate steps for the preservation of the natural resources of the earth, which, among other things, includes the preservation of the quality of air and control of air pollution. Therefore it is considered necessary to implement the decisions foresaid in so far as they relate to the preservation of the quality of air and control of air pollution.

Water (Prevention and Control) Act 1974

The objectives of the Water (Prevention and Control of Pollution) Act are to provide for the Prevention and Control of Water Pollution and the maintenance or restoration of the wholesomeness of water for the establishment, with a view to carrying out the purposes aforesaid, of Boards for the prevention and control of water pollution, for conferring on and assigning to such Boards powers and functions relating thereto and for matters connected therewith.

Wildlife Protection Act, 1972

According to the Wildlife Protection Act, 1972 "wildlife" includes any animal, bees, butterflies, fish and moths; and aquatic or land vegetation, which form part of any habitat. In accordance with Wildlife (Protection) Amendment Act, 2002 "no alternation of boundaries / National Park / Sanctuary shall be made by the State Govt. except on recommendation of the National Board for Wildlife (NBWL)". Further, in terms of Supreme Court Order dated 13.11.2000 the State Governments seek prior permission of Supreme Court before submitting the proposal for diversion of forestland in National Park sanctuaries. Whenever, any part of Wildlife Sanctuary / National Park is getting affected by a hydro project the forest proposal in respect of such project is entertained by MoEF, GOI only after permission of de-reservation / de-notification of Wildlife Sanctuary /National Park has been accorded. After recommendation of Standing Committee of NBWL proposal for de-reservation / de-notification is ratified by Honourable Supreme Court.

The Biological Diversity Act, 2002

The Ministry of Environment and Forests has enacted the Biological Diversity Act, 2002 under the United Nations Convention on Biological Diversity signed at Rio de Janeiro on the 5th day of June 1992 of which India is also a party. This Act is to "provide for the conservation of biological diversity, sustainable use of its components, and fair and equitable sharing of the benefits arising out of the sued of biological resources, knowledge and for matters connected therewith or incidental thereto." As per the provision of act certain areas, which are rich in biodiversity and encompasses unique and representative ecosystems are identified and designated as biosphere reserve to facilitate its conservation. All restrictions applicable to protected areas like national park and Sanctuaries are also applicable to these reserves. SJVNL abides by the provision of act wherever applicable and try avoiding these biosphere reserves while finalizing the project infrastructure locations.

Hazardous Waste (Management and Handling) Amendment Rules, 2003

These Rules classify used mineral oil as hazardous waste under the Hazardous Waste (Management & Handling) Rules, 2003 that requires proper handling and disposal. Organisation will seek authorization for disposal of hazardous waste from concerned State Pollution Control Boards (SPCB) as and when required.

Ozone Depleting Substance (Regulation and Control) Rules, 2000

MoEF vide its notification dated. 17th July 2000 under the section of 6, 8 and 25 of the Environment (Protection) Act, 1986 has notified rules for regulation/ control of Ozone Depleting Substances (ODS) under Montreal Protocol. As per the notification certain control and regulation has been imposed on manufacturing, import, export, and use of these compounds.

Organisations as per provisions of notification shall is phase out all equipment, which uses these substances, and is aiming at CFC free organization in near future.

Other Environment – Related Laws

The Shore Nuisance (Bombay and Kolaba) Act, 1853: This is the earliest Act on the statute book concerning control of water pollution in India.

The Serais Act, 1867: The Act enjoined upon a keeper of Serai or an inn to keep a certain quality of water fit for consumption by "persons and animals use it" to the satisfaction of the District magistrate or his nominees. Failure for maintaining the standard entailed a liability of rupees twenty.

The North India Canal and Drainage Act, 1873: Certain offences have been listed under the Act contained in Section 70.

Obstruction in Fairways Act, 1881: Section 8 of the Act empowered the Central Government to make Rules to regulate or prohibit the throwing of rubbish in any fairway leading to a port causing or likely to give rise to a bank or shoal.

Indian Easements Act, 1882: Illustrations (f), (h) and (j) of Section 7 of the Act deal with pollution of waters.

The Indian Fisheries Act, 1897: The Indian Fisheries Act, 1897 contains seven sections. Section 5 of the Act prohibits destruction of fish by poisoning waters.

Indian Ports Act, 1908: the Indian Ports Act, 1908, has regulated Water pollution by oil.

The Indian Forest Act, 1927: Section 26(i) of the Act makes it punishable if any person, who, in contravention of the rules made by the State Government, poisons water of a forest area. The State Government has been empowered under Section 32(f) to make rules relating to poisoning of water in forests.

The Damodar Valley Corporation Act, 1948: The Act Government the Corporation to make regulations with the previous sanction of the Central Government for preventing "pollution of water".

The Factories Act, 1948: Factories Act 1948 is social welfare legislation intends to secure health, safety and welfare of the workers employed in factories. However' some of the provisions of this Act are concerned with prevention of water pollution.

The Mines Act, 1952: Chapter V of the Act deals with provisions regarding health and Safety of the employees. Section 19(i) Government upon arrangement for the quality of water for drinking purposes.

The River Boards Act, 1956: The Act provides for the creation of River Boards for regulation and development of interstate rivers and river valleys. One of the functions of the Board is to advise to the Government concerned on "prevention of pollution of the waters of the interstate rivers".

The Merchant Shipping Act, 1958: The International Convention for the Prevention of Pollution of the Sea by Oil, 1954 is the first treaty for the reduction of oil pollution of the sea. In order to give effect to this Convention, the Merchant Shipping Act regulates and controls the discharge of oil or oil mixture by an Indian tanker or ship within any of the prohibited zones or by a foreign tanker or other ship within the prohibited zone adjoining the territories of India. Further, there is a prohibition for discharging any oil anywhere at sea from an Indian ship.

Legal and Regulatory Framework for Hydro-projects:

The principal Environmental Regulatory Agency in India is the Ministry of Environment and Forests (MOEF). The Ministry formulates environmental policies and accords environmental clearance for the projects. The State Pollution Control Board (SPCB) accords 'No Objection Certificate' (NOC) and 'Consent for Establishment and Operation' for the projects.

The project features entail a Environmental Impact Assessment Study to be conducted which is a pre-requisite for obtaining environmental clearance from Ministry of Environment & Forests, Government of India.

Environmental Impact Assessment (EIA) is an important management tool for ensuring optimal use of natural resources for sustainable development, and was introduced in India initially for River Valley Projects in 1978-79. The scope of the EIA has been enhanced to cover other developmental sectors such as industries, mining schemes, energy, etc. To facilitate project proponents in collection of environmental data and formulation of environmental management plans, it is now mandatory under the Environment (Protection) Act, 1986, for different categories of developmental activities involving investment beyond certain thresholds. The notification was issued on 27th January 1994 and was amended on 4th May 1994. This, it is hoped would provide an opportunity both for the project proponents and Government to assess the impact of the concerned project on the environment before it actually comes into play.

The EIA study document fulfills the requirements for environmental clearance from various agencies at the state level. These include State Pollution Control Board and Committee of Experts working under the aegis of Department of Science & Technology, State Governments.

SJVN's Initiative: The regulatory framework and policy both at the central and state level for environmental and social issues applicable to the HYDRO Power Projects is also application to SJVN. In addition, SJVNL has also taken into consideration the requirements of multilateral funding agencies while finalizing the Environment Policy. SJVNL sees its responsibilities under the present legal framework as two fold as under: mandatory requirements under the law and the guidelines of funding agencies; and prescriptive requirements that influence management procedures addressing environmental and social issues.

SJVNL undertakes all its activities within mandatory requirements under the National law and the guidelines of funding agencies, and prescriptive requirements that determine the management procedures for addressing environmental and social issues. Mandatory environmental requirements for SJVNL at a national level include: Land Acquisition Procedures under Land Acquisition Act, 1894.

Forest clearances under the Forest (Conservation) Act, 1980; specifically environmental clearances under Environment (Protection) Act, 1986

During the operations of the projects regulations like Hazardous Wastes (Management and Handling) Amendment Rules, 2003 regarding disposal of used transformer oil and Ozone Depleting Substances (Regulation and Control) rules, 2000 putting restriction on use of ozone depleting substances come into force and require voluntary enforcement and funding agencies requirements some time. (The Forest & Environment Clearances procedure needs 3 documents). [68]

Nature Protection Legislation:

Birds and Habitats Directives

The SEA Directive is applicable to many sectors of activity that are significant within Integrated Coastal Zone Management (ICZM) context e.g. transport, town and country planning, industry, energy, waste management, and tourism. SEA not only looks at the physical environment, but also at the social and economic context. It supports development. There is considerable scope for synergy between the principals of ICZM and the SEA Directive relating to the decision making process, the information available, and the assessment tools employed (Mercadié, 1999). SEA will contribute to more transparent planning by involving the public and by integrating environmental considerations. This will help to achieve the goal of sustainable development.

Water Framework Directive (W F D)

Although a number of EU policies and Directives have an influence on coastal management, as indicated above, the Water Framework Directive is viewed as one of the most significant in facilitating ICZM. The EU Water Framework Directive (2000/60/EC) came into force in December 2000, establishing a new framework for Community action in the field of water

[68]Government of India – Law Ministry / publication division

policy. The WFD takes a holistic approach, addressing inland surface waters, estuarine and coastal waters and groundwater. A coordinated approach will therefore be required for the implementation of programmes and measures to achieve the objectives of the Directive. A 15-year period is allowed to each Member State, by which time the State must ensure compliance. Objectives of the Directive include:

(a) Protection and enhancement of the status of aquatic ecosystems (and terrestrial ecosystems and wetlands directly dependent on aquatic ecosystems);
(b) Provision for enhanced protection and improvement of the aquatic environment by reducing / phasing out of discharges, emissions and losses of priority substances;
(c) Protection of territorial and marine waters, and
(d) Establishment of a register of protected areas e.g. areas designated for protection of habitats or species

Integrating Marine Science in Europe

The position paper Integrating Marine Science in Europe (ESF, 2002) represents an initiative to establish a Europe wide summation of marine research, prioritize recommendations and to identify where future scientific challenges lie, while incorporating European societal needs. Key recommendations concerning Europe's coastal area emerging from the position paper are:

(a) Baseline interdisciplinary research is required to meet the challenge of progressing ICZM and governance;
(b) Within ICZM research, prioritization should be given to investigating the environmental impacts and the consequences on biodiversity of increasing tourism and leisure on the littoral zone, port developments, intense aquaculture

in inshore locations, selective fishing of top predators, and deep ocean disposal of domestic and industrial wastes;

(c) Systematic research on biogeochemical budgets of nutrients (carbon, nitrogen, phosphorous) and their ecological effects are required for contrasting estuaries and shelf systems;

(d) Europe should rapidly adapt new array-biotechnological chips to provide non-invasive, affordable, and high throughput systems for eco-toxicological screening of water quality;

(e) Natural and anthropogenic causes of ecosystem variability should be characterized and distinguished, particularly in the coastal seas;

(f) An integrated network of coastal monitoring stations is required to contribute to monitoring and forecasting the effects of global warming (e.g. coastal flooding, increased wave height, storm intensity);

(g) Understanding marine biodiversity is the blueprint for ecosystem regulation. Areas of high species and genetic biodiversity should be a focus for conservation and management efforts;

(h) A forum of marine scientists and policy makers should be convened to ensure effective communication and synergy between both parties for timely deliverance of relevant and sound scientific knowledge to policy makers.

The Eight Principles of Best Practice
(The EU DP on ICZM):

1. **Adopt a broad holistic perspective**: This principal advocates the need to take a 'systems' approach to ICZM due to the complexity of the physical, biological, cultural and socio-economic factors shaping coastal areas. The delineation of the coast according to administrative or jurisdictional

boundaries does not facilitate effective ICZM. Therefore, it is important to take a more wide-ranging perspective, which traces coastal influences to the extent of their natural and/or social boundaries.

2. **Local specificity:** In addition to taking a wide-ranging perspective, it is necessary to compliment the approach with a thorough understanding of specific issues in the coastal area of interest. The collection and analysis of data and information concerning local conditions is required to achieve this goal.

3. **Use adaptive management:** Using adaptive management means having the ability to respond to new information and conditions during a gradual process of developing and implementing ICZM programmes.

4. **Work with natural processes:** Working with natural processes is particularly relevant in the case of coastal engineering. In order to militate against negative impacts of hard engineering, alternative solutions, which work with natural processes, should be sought, including the use of soft engineering and/or 'setback and retreat' options where possible.

5. **Take a long-term view:** Taking a long-term view means planning ahead for the future to ensure that current management plans will have long-term benefits for the coast. Consideration should also be given to the lifespan of coastal management programmes to ensure the sustainability of coastal management initiatives.

6. **Use participatory planning:** Participatory planning involves the collaboration of all stakeholders in the formulation and implementation of ICZM plans. This inclusive process has many direct benefits and is essential if consensus is to be achieved.

7. **Ensure the support and involvement of all relevant bodies:** While participatory planning ensures the involvement of all stakeholders in the development and implementation of ICZM ('bottom up' approach), there is also a need to ensure equality of input to the process by responsible administrations. ICZM can only be effective if it is supported by all of the relevant administrative bodies ('horizontal integration' e.g. between government departments), and across all levels of government ('vertical integration' e.g. between local and central government).

8. **Use a combination of instruments:** Effective implementation of ICZM involves the utilization of multiple instruments including a mixture of legislative measures, policy programmes, economic incentives, technology solutions, research, voluntary agreements and education. The mix to be applied depends on the specific situation, which will differ according to: the geographic area, the nature of the issues to be addressed, the level of participation and cooperation among stakeholders, institutional structures, the legal basis of the initiative and the level of political and financial support available.[69]

Conclusion

There is no dearth of environmental laws in almost all countries. But these laws are not implemented for the purpose the laws are enacted. The governments permit forest land to railways, roads, hospitals, schools and colleges for benefits of people. But it allots forest lands to industrialists for industries, hotels and aerodromes through black deals.

---

[69]Cummins, V, Mahony, C and N. Connolly, "Review of Coastal Zone Management and Principles of Best Practices", Prepared for the Heritage Council by the Coastal and Marine Resources Centre, Environmental Research Institute, University College Cork, Ireland

The Environment and Forest Ministry is treated as a low-profile government department. There is dearth of financial support for this department. On the other hand governments try to exploit the natural resources and dispose these high-valued natural resources at throwaway prices to limited exporters or industrialists or foreign companies. The high value minerals, wood and free lands are easily transferred to them at very nominal prices or simply free. Smugglers, mafias and black marketers also exploit these resources. There occur kickbacks and under-cover transactions with knowledge of government officials and government.

The UN should take up an 'International Law for Protection of Environment' to protect the environment on earth. Violation of which should be treated as a criminal activity and the punishment should be at par with **'War Criminal Law'**. It should include one–third of geographical area under actual forest cover. The governments should prioritize green projects. Too much eagerness for mega industries is anti-poor, anti-national and is a cause of concern for environment.

The government must ensure clean drinking water to all. Vegetables, fruits, milk and all food items need to be examined by chemists to assess the purity of consumable items. It should study clean air possibilities in each locality and take necessary steps. There should be more number of buses and local trains to carry the passengers in all metropolitan cities. The movement of cars, scooters and two-wheelers should be banned after 7 PM. Use of bicycles should be popularized.

The policies and activities of governments in all developing countries lead to deforestation, urbanization, and industrialization. All countries must try to avoid war and protect the environment. And we can achieve WORLD PEACE.

Chapter - VIII

PRIORITY TASKS IN PROTECTING ENVIRONMENT

There was a bargain between BASIC countries (Brazil, South Africa, India and China), and the US at Copenhagen for availability of fast-track finance to developing countries. It was decided that about $30 billion would be available to help them during 2010-2012 to adapt to climate change and manage their own emission growths. In the long term, the developed countries committed to $100 billion public finance by 2020. In return, developing countries agreed to internationalize their domestic mitigation measures and make their actions more transparent. The evidence so far suggests that only a small portion of what is pledged is really new, and the major portion consists of recycled commitments, such as those that were made to meet the millennium development goals.

It is ironic that those very countries that supported the formalization of the Copenhagen Accord are not following the principles they themselves laid down in that document. More than ever before, this necessitates the need to restore the trust between developed and developing nations to enable any meaningful outcome.

Finance is just one part of the story. On the important issue of the second commitment period for Kyoto Protocol, the impressions are not encouraging either. It is almost a case where the countries are in a catch-22 with no clarity on the horizon in terms of clear commitments to the Protocol. In the initial days of the Cancun meeting, Japan has aggressively denied the Kyoto Protocol claiming that it "will not inscribe its target under the Protocol on any conditions or under any circumstances" — a wrecker for the negotiations.

Issues related to many aspects of transparency of actions by developing countries, under the heading of MRV, have become a central element of the climate negotiations. Despite the developed countries not keeping up to their part of the Copenhagen promise, India has taken the first step forward by developing a transparency and accountability instrument called the international consultation analysis (ICA or scrutiny over the funds that are given to developing countries to mitigate and adapt to climate change). The most outstanding element of the proposal is the differentiation of countries on the basis of their emissions, and an increased frequency of reporting for the high emitters.

The Global Canopy Program

A New Alliance for Investigating the Role of Forest Canopies in Maintaining a Stable Planet

Assessment and Monitoring:

The forest canopy is often popularly described as nature's last biological frontier. The amount of biodiversity contained there represents one of the greatest concentrations of life on earth. In addition, the canopy is where 'life meets the atmosphere'. The fluxes of gases, which occur at this interface, are increasingly thought to play a significant role in maintaining the earth's climate. A challenge for science here is that little is known of the structure/function relationships that occur in forest canopies. We do not even know the true extent of the biodiversity there. Further the precise mechanism and extent of the exchange of gasses across the leaf atmosphere boundary including the uptake of carbon in the canopy and its transfer to the soil, is also largely unknown.

Why is this important?

First, current human induced biodiversity loss is the 6th Earth extinction event which will dramatically alter future evolution on the planet.

Second, the extent of our ignorance about biodiversity in forest canopies is both an economic threat through lost commercial opportunity and governments therefore underestimate its value. The government cannot plan on an evolutionary time scale, and discount the value of biodiversity.

Third, our almost complete lack of understanding of structure-function relationships in forest canopies and their impact on maintaining global environmental conditions is a major threat to human welfare in many countries at the local and regional level.

Fourth, a lack of understanding at all levels of the role of forests in climate change, especially as sequesters of carbon, has led to a major breakdown in the implementation of the one treaty which is designed to fix the problem - namely the Kyoto protocol.

Why is our understanding so poor?

First we lack the scientific data on which to make sound predictions. Essentially this is because of the difficulty of access in forest canopies which has delayed the implementation of experiments other than those which ask: 'What is there?' as opposed to manipulative investigations asking 'how does it work?' or 'how will it change?'

Canopy science has now emerged from the pioneering days of 30 years ago using monkeys or climbing ropes to access the crowns of tall trees to the large scale operations of today using canopy cranes, dirigibles, towers and other techniques which enable repeatable access with ease but often at considerable expense.

Second, the natural sciences have not been able to corner the market in major funding for projects in its field in the way that the physical sciences have. Table 1 is a comparison between the recent funding priorities for the major physical projects and canopy science under consideration and by the European Science Foundation. Projects on forest canopies have not attracted the support of Governmental science funding bodies at a level commensurate with either the scale or urgency of the problem to be addressed. Part of the reason for this may be that no such program has been presented with international support which addresses the scientific questions at the right scale and that can dramatically capture the attention of the political aspects of the fundraising process which could benefit from the results and from the positive public attention the program could generate in terms of education and conservation.

Following the Tropical Rainforest Canopies:

Ecology and Management international conference at Oxford in 1998, a number of participants, including the author, convened a workshop under the auspices of the International Canopy Network (ICAN) and funded by European Science Foundation and the National Science Foundation, to address these issues. The outcome of that meeting was a Forest Canopy Planning Workshop Report (Nadkarni et al., 2000) at which 29 experts present from 9 countries agreed the following resolution:

We propose an integrated, coordinated study of canopies across major environmental and management gradients to investigate the role of forest canopies in maintaining global biodiversity, global environmental conditions, and the sustainability of forests.

A year later in November 2000, with funding from two UK foundations the Global Canopy Program (GCP) Secretariat Office, working in close partnership with ICAN was established in Oxford. Its mission is as follows:

(a) To seek to create the international framework for implementing the central research vision and goals of the Global Canopy Program as conceived at the Oxford canopy workshop,
(b) To determine the resources needed and to forge the international partnerships in research, education, training and conservation who wish to have a stake in the program
(c) To combine these groups into an alliance of organisations who support and expect to benefit from a proposal, which seeks funding at a level necessary for the task on a global scale, for submission to major national and international donors to implement the program.

This initiative will be formally launched at the 3rd International Canopy Conference in Cairns, Australia in June 2002. Since November an international

Steering Committee and Science Advisory Committee has been set up plus a network of in-country representatives. Research has been carried out into the scientific projects currently in progress around the world related to the issues above. Representatives of these groups have been contacted and all have expressed enthusiasm at the prospect of collaborating in a global program of research provided funding is available and a mechanism for such collaboration exists. Institutions and projects currently contacted have been divided into three potential networks:

(a) Canopy Biodiversity and Ecosystem Function Network
(b) Canopy Climate Change Network
(c) Canopy Conservation, Policy and Education Network

It is clear that those in the Climate change network are already quite well organized internationally often using standard protocols, shared data bases and an extensive network of towers to obtain measurements of gas fluxes in the canopy. These include such organizations as Flux net, and the Large Scale Biosphere-Atmosphere Experiment (LBA). Globally, funding for these programs is already at the $100 - $150 million level.

Those projects concerned with biodiversity and ecosystem studies are growing rapidly but are less well organized internationally as a network with few common protocols or shared databases. These include ten-canopy access jib cranes now situated in both temperate and tropical forests plus numerous towers, walkways, and other individual canopy access systems such as the Canopy Operation Permanent Access System (COPAS) under development and Operation Canopée.

Extensive forest related education and conservation organizations are in existence but few specifically focussed on forest canopies or the science being conducted within them. The flow of information at the policy level from canopy science has yet to be investigated but may benefit from better international co-ordination and it is the intention of GCP to enable this information to be easily accessed by scientists, the public, educators and decision makers and to support governments in their efforts to implement the Conventions on Biodiversity and on Climate Change.

One question now being tackled by the GCP is how to link these three areas together into one program and what benefits would arise to each group from such collaboration. We welcome input from interested collaborators on this question and also welcome contacts from researchers or institutions interested in linking existing projects or contributing new ones for potential funding within the framework of the proposed GCP. A 3- year grant from NSF in 2000 will enable ICAN to design the 'Big Canopy Database' which will provide a principal repository of shared information for the proposed GCP.[70]

There never has been a better time to scale up and co-ordinate forest canopy research activities into a much better organized and integrated research effort across the world to address the greatest scientific and conservation challenges facing humans over the next fifty years - namely the loss of genetic diversity and the impact of climate change.

FINLAND

Criteria and Indicators for Sustainable Forest Management in Finland

---

[70]Andrew W. Mitchell, "The Global Canopy Program", Director, ICAN-Global Canopy Program, Halifax House, University of Oxford, 6-8 South Parks Road, Oxford OX1 3UB, United Kingdom

A group of forest scientists of Finland have reported that sustainable forest management practices should be followed to safeguard the forests.[71]

Finland is located in Northern Europe between the 60th and 70th parallels of latitude and a quarter of the Finnish territory lies north of the Arctic Circle. The total surface area of Finland is 337,000 square km, and the land area is 305,000 Sq. km. 68 per cent of the total area is covered by forest, and the share of agricultural land is 8 per cent. Owing to the climatic conditions there is a lot of peat land in Finland, accounting for about 11 per cent of the total surface area. Finland lies in the boreal coniferous forest zone, whose four sub-zones, hemi-boreal as well as southern, central and northern boreal forest zones are determined mainly on the basis of the temperature sum and vegetation. There are altogether 24 tree species native to Finland, and the number of coniferous species is only four: Scots pine, Norway spruce and juniper as well as yew, which occur naturally on the Åland islands. Economically the most important tree species are Scots pine (45 per cent of the volume of the growing stock, Norway spruce (37 per cent) as well as downy and silver birch, altogether 15 per cent. The share of the other species is only 3 per cent. Certain deciduous species, such as aspen and goat willow are highly significant as they maintain a large number of species of living organisms.

In the Second Ministerial Conference on the Protection of Forests in Helsinki in 1993, the European countries and European Union made a commitment to promote the implementation of the principles of sustainable forest management established at the UN Conference on Environment and Development held in Rio in 1992, both nationally

---

[71]Jouni Suoheimo, Jaana Kaipainen, Heli Mikkela & Elina Nikkola, Ministry of Agriculture and Forestry, Finland

and internationally. The criteria for sustainable forest management and the quantitative and descriptive indicators for this were drawn up in the monitoring of the Helsinki Resolution, the so-called Helsinki process.

These criteria and indicators for sustainable forest management and the related principles on the level of praxis were approved at the Third Ministerial Conference in Lisbon in 1998. The signatory countries undertook to continue the application, revision and development of the criteria and indicators. In Finland national criteria and indicators have been applied since 1994, and the first comprehensive report on the state of sustainable forest management in Finland was completed in 1997. At this first stage of the application the pan-European criteria and indicators were adjusted to the Finnish conditions. In particular, the criteria were modified and complemented by including indicators for the biological diversity of forest ecosystems and socio-economic sustainability.

(a)Selection of criteria and indicators - the first round

The first criteria and indicators for sustainable forest management in Finland were established in 1995. The list of criteria covered all aspects of sustainable forest management: forest resources and their contribution to carbon cycles, vitality and health of forest ecosystems, wood products and other forest products, biological diversity and conservation of forest ecosystems, significance of forests in the protection of soil and waters, as well as the social, economic and cultural significance of forests. A number of qualitative and descriptive indicators were selected to show the realization of measures relating to each of the criteria.

(b)Assessment, Conservation and Sustainable Use of Forest Biodiversity

The criteria and indicators were tested in the research project concerning the implementation of the development strategy for sustainable development in forest management, the so-called Pirkanmaa project (Pirkanmaa is a region in Western Finland). The objective of the project was to establish the principles for a regional forest strategy and to design indicators and control methods for assessing the sustainability of forest management at the regional level. The project continued until the end of 1996. It became evident that the number of indicators chosen (160) should be reduced and they should be more concrete and easier to monitor in order to facilitate their application in practice. The measurability of the indicators and compilation of data could also be made more efficient through appropriate classification of the indicators.

(c) Development of the criteria and indicators

Owing to the changes in the operating environment of forestry, in 1998 it was noted that further development of the criteria and indicators was necessary, and a work group with broad representation from the various interest groups involved in the forest sector (ministries, forest research institutes, universities, and industry and nature conservation organisations) was appointed for this purpose. The task of the work group was to check all the national indicators for sustainable forest management, taking into account the national and international development and the most recent information. Another objective was to apply the criteria and indicators in the monitoring of Finland's National Forest Programme 2010 (published in 1999) and regional forest programmes. Further, the Finnish know-how and initiative in the international arena in the development of indicators and monitoring of sustainable forest management was to be maintained and reinforced.

The criteria and indicators were designed in the spirit of open cooperation and thus this work led to a national consensus on the content of sustainable forest management and factors through which the realization of sustainability can be measured and followed in practice. The revised list of indicators is based on research data, but it also includes a number of indicators for social values relating to forests and their management.

Organizing the compilation of data through criteria and indicators

The main objective has been to develop appropriate indicators for measuring the realization of sustainability in forest management and changes in forest ecosystems. A number of distinct indicators have been combined into larger wholes, and certain indicators for compiling basic data have been left out.

No objective or recommended levels for practicing sustainable forest management have been set in connection with the indicators, but such levels are defined e.g. in the implementation of the Finnish forest and environmental legislation, Finland's National Forest Program, regional forest programs, environmental programs and the national action program concerning biological diversity in Finland. The indicators show the realized development, but they do not necessarily describe the phenomenon as a whole or the causes for the development or changes. Indicators can be used to monitor and guide the implementation of the forest policy at all levels. The forest, environmental and biodiversity programs are implementation programs, and are measured by commonly accepted indicators.

One of the most challenging tasks relating to the indicators is the development of the compilation of data into a clear, continuous and efficient instrument, both nationally and regionally. The most important sources of data on the national level are the National Forest Inventory, forest statistics, statistics on the national economy, as well as statistics and databases on forest conservation and environmental issues in forest management. The Forest Research Institute, Forestry Development Centre Tapio, Finnish Environment Institute and the Regional Forestry and Environment Centers are responsible for compiling data on sustainable forest management.

Indicators for biological diversity

Indicators relating to the protection and management of biological diversity are divided into three hierarchical levels. Regional diversity covers the abundance and diversity of forest types, communities of organisms and ecosystems, i.e. their number and structural variety. Inter-species diversity refers to the abundance and diversity of species inhabiting the forests, i.e. variation in the number of species, their relative abundance and functional significance. Intra-species diversity is the genetic diversity within each species, i.e. the genetic variation of the species. In Finland the following indicators for the maintenance and protection of biodiversity are used:

Indicator 1: Instruments to regulate the maintenance, conservation and appropriate enhancement of biological diversity in forest ecosystems. The descriptive indicator contains data on the following instruments relating to forest management:

(a) International agreements and action programs,
(b) Finnish legislation, conservation programs and areas and their representatives,
(c) Economic instruments for protecting forests, monitoring and maintenance of sites of biological diversity in forests, producing information.

Indicator 2: Endangered and vulnerable species (estimated number of endangered species according to habitats based on survey)

Indicator 3: Protected forests and forests with harvesting restrictions (development in the total area of protected forests, ha)

Indicator 4: Valuable forest habitats and their protection (area of valuable habitats according to the National Forest Inventory in the territories of different Forestry Centers, percents)

Indicator 5: Tree species composition (dominance of different tree species in the total forest area, percents)

Indicator 6: Pure and mixed forest stands (whether the forest composed of one dominant species or a mixture of several species, share of each forest type of the total forest area, percents)

Indicator 7: Decayed and wildlife trees in commercial forests and conservation areas (m3/ha)

Indicator 8: Gene reserve forests (number and area (ha) of these)

Landscape – Ecological Approach to Conservation of Bio-diversity

Valeri Sergienko has described how landscape - ecological approach could be applied to conserve biodiversity in Karelian Isthmus (Russia).[72]

The problems of nature protection and use of natural resources under landscape-ecological planning of

---

[72]Valeri Sergienko,"Landscape - Ecological Approach to Conservation of Bio-diversity Karelian Isthmus", Forest Research Institute, St. Petersburg, Russia

forestry in the Karelian Isthmus in the Leningrad region are considered. A tendency to go to landscape principles of forest management is taken into account. Complex of aims, connected with "ecology" of forestry, includes theoretical elaboration of criteria and indicators of conservation, management and sustainable development of the regional forests with taking into account rational distribution of **specially protected natural areas** (SPNA) and working out effective measures on conservation of biodiversity ecosystem landscapes (plants, animal and micro-biota) Conservation of biodiversity, providing ecological safety and stability of the region are important conditions under landscape-ecological planning and forming the net of SPNA. The system of SPNA must be projected with taking into account all various types of protection-needing landscapes and natural complexes. This system must be a net of interdependent natural objects connected with each other by ecological corridors in the form of protective belts along rivers and lakes or as forests of the first group where forest exploitation is strictly limited. River net, watersheds in the form of bog systems and forest-protection zones are also such corridors.

The distribution of SPNA in the isthmus is irregular. Most of them are situated in the southern half. Few protected areas were established in districts that have boundaries with Finland, in the north, and in Priladozhsky district of the isthmus. On the whole, the area of SPNA in the isthmus occupies only 2.7 percent of the region area. The area of SPNA is 108000 ha, including forest protective plots, protection zones of reserves and water-protection territories. Forest protective plots include environment-protection categories of forests where harvest cutting is prohibited, border belts with full or partial prohibition of cutting, the water expanses of the Gulf of Finland, protection belts along roads, and others.

Realization of Russian-Finnish project on developing the stable tourism in the Karelian Isthmus will allow sanctuary Lindulovskaya Grove that was listed among the objects of the world heritage by UNESCO and other SPNA to become one of the objects of natural international tourism. European Union finances this direction within the TACIS project. Realization of the project will allow deciding a number of recreational questions in the Karelian Isthmus.

In the Karelian Isthmus the system of SPNA, in international meaning, is not developed enough. There are not any reserve and national natural park by classification of The World Conservation Union (IUCN) here. The status of protected objects here is lower than in IUCN system. However, there are a number of unique territories that should be given higher protection status (Sergienko 2000). Organizing SPNA of higher status is possible in the future.

At the present time, Nature Conservation Complex Scheme of Leningrad Region (KSOP) is being elaborated till 2005, including the Karelian Isthmus. Of 56 existing and 57 projected and proposed SPNA in the region, 19 SPNA exist, 9 SPNA are being projected and 6 proposed for including in the system of SPNA in the isthmus (Red Data Book, 1999).

SPNA existing in the Karelian Isthmus there are 10 regional sanctuaries, 8 natural monuments and 1 deontological park. Protection regime here prohibits or limits forest cuttings, melioration works and changing hydrological regime, building works, hunting as well as other forms of human activities damaging natural complexes.

Conservation and Sustainable Use (sustainable forest management)

The system of SPNA is based on including the set of landscapes, unique ecosystems and natural objects with rare and endangered plant and animal species, as full as possible. The aims of conservation of ecosystems and biota are:

1. Conservation of key (environmental) plots with stop-over sites, and White Sea-Baltic migration ways of birds;
2. Maintenance of reproduction of marketable animals and fishes;
3. Forming zones of regimented recreation in areas of traditional visit of people;
4. Conservation of environment around cultural and- historical objects and plots of river banks, as well as seaside and islands of the Gulf of Finland and Lake Ladozhskoye where biological productivity is high;
5. Protection of plots with rare and protected animal and plant species concentration.

Under quite difficult anthropogenic conditions in the Karelian Isthmus, a problem arises of establishing the optimal number of SPNA of small area (sanctuaries, natural monuments and mini-reserves on the basis of existing protected areas or other interesting objects). Pressure of economic activities on natural ecosystems of the Karelian Isthmus and its considerable dispersal on the territory does not allow establishing here large reserves (Sergienko, 1999).

About 1100 wild vascular plant species of 115 families in total have been registered in the isthmus (Illustrated key, 2000, Red Data Book, 2000). The flora was formed during the degradation of the last (Valdai) glacier in the post-glacial period. The flora has a distinctly migratory character and includes a number of very rare and protection needing species. Zone taiga plant species are predominant. Some of species are relict. Analyses of floras of SPNA and publications concerning protected areas showed out that 112 rare and protected vascular plant species (of 204 vascular plant species needing protection in

Leningrad region) have been revealed in the Karelian Isthmus (Red Data Book, 1993, 2000, Kotiranta *et al.* 1998). Red-listed plant species of the Karelian Isthmus are distributed as follows: extinct (or probably extinct) (5 species), endangered (11 species), vulnerable (38 species), and rare (58 species).

Among the rare and protected species of the isthmus of flora there are plants with a wide habitat range: forests, meadows, bogs, rocky outcrops, pebbles, seaside, typical and intra-zonal plant communities. Many of the rare species in the region needing protection are located outside, or on border of, their own natural.

Finding rare and protected plant in SPNA is the basis for monitoring and protecting rare, relict and endangered species in the region. At the same time, the aim to conservation rare plant communities of natural ecosystems unique by their importance and ecologically susceptible must be reached. Protection of such objects is necessary for conservation of historically formed biodiversity and for the balance of confound in nature.

Effective functioning of SPNA on the region, and managing them, depends on their importance for conservation of the most susceptible ecosystems against the anthropogenic influence. Integrating the net of SPNA of Russia in general European system of protected areas is need. It is for the considered region, which borders on the Baltic countries and Finland.

Siberian Tigers Disappearing

The Siberian tiger, also known as the Amur tiger, tops the list of animals on the verge of extinction, even though hunting these sub-species was outlawed in Russia back in 1947. Today there are only 500

Amur tigers left in the Khabarovsk and Primorye territories of Russia's Far East.

In the last 100 years, the global tiger population has decreased from about 1, 00,000 to 3,000 or 4,000 tigers. Three sub-species — the Persian (Turanian) tiger, the Bali tiger and the Javan tiger — have become extinct.

The number of tigers living in Russia has stabilized and the decline has slowed down in the last few years. "There should be about 600 tigers in Russia, which is as many as could live comfortably in their taiga habitat," said Mr. Vladimir Krever, WWF Russia biodiversity coordinator.

The Amur tigers are the most tolerant of human beings in the species. Unlike the bigger Bengal tiger, or the smaller but more aggressive Sumatran tiger, the Russian tigers are more peaceful and attack humans only in self-defense. The Amur tiger measures up to 220 cm from head to tail and weighs about 200 kg. It is second only to the Bengal tiger in size, but is much harder and can comfortably bear even the harsh Russian climate.

Between 50 and 80 tigers were shot annually in the far-east in the 1990s. Chinese pharmaceutical companies paid Russian poachers between $6,000 and $15,000 for the body of a large male tiger. In China, various parts of the tiger are believed to have strong medicinal properties. The border with China was completely porous back then, and customs officers had no experience stopping tiger derivatives smugglers, as this never happened during the Soviet era.

Logging is another threat endangering the Amur tiger. Its main feeding grounds are the cedar, oak and ash groves where their prey, wild boars, comes to feed. When cedars and oaks are felled, the boars leave, and the tigers go hungry. Hunting tigers is also much easier in sparsely wooded forest areas.

Everything is interdependent in nature. A decline in the number of tigers, who hunt old and diseased deer and boar, causes the number of hoofed animals to plummet due to epidemics. In addition, the tiger is replaced by the wolf, whose behavior is much more aggressive. A tiger kills only as many deer as it can eat, while wolves kill indiscriminately. The Global Tiger Summit, to be held in November in St Petersburg, will address the strategy for tiger conservation. The heads of Government of 13 countries would attend the summit, where tigers are found.

Mr. Krever said, "We expect the participating countries to adopt a joint declaration of the common goal: To double the number of wild tigers across their range by 2022,"

A Global Recovery Action Plan, which is being developed for the forum, should take into account both national tiger recovery programs and global elements, such as the illegal trade, storage and transportation of tiger pelts, international tiger protection programs, and efforts to promote awareness of the value of wild tigers to their respective ecosystems.

The first species strategy was approved in Russia in 1996 and was implemented the following year under the federal targeted program for the preservation of the Amur tiger. A network of state preserves, national parks and refuges was set up in the tiger's natural habitat and surrounded by buffer zones and protective forests.

But this is no longer enough to protect these tigers. The new Russian tiger recovery program involves a major extension of the protected territories.

Ecologists hope the Governments will approve the creation of a Russian-Chinese cross-border refuge on the Strelnikov Range in the Primorye Territory and the adjacent protected territory in China's Jilin Province. The refuge should include the Russian national park, Land of the Leopard, which consists of the Cedar Gully Preserve and the Leopard Reserve.

Prime Minister Vladimir Putin, who visited the Ussuri Preserve two years ago, promoted the idea of developing a new strategy. During his visit to the tiger preserve, he took part in the medical examination of a female tiger and then fitted her with a GPS tracking collar.

At a minimum, scientists would like to put GPS tracking collars on all tigers in the Ussuri and the Lazo preserves, two model conservation zones in the south of the Primorye Territory. Radio collars are no longer effective, as they can actually help poachers find the tigers.

Currently, there are just a few camera traps set up to identify tigers, but these devices are, without a doubt, the future of the tiger recovery effort. They are so effective because each tiger can be identified by its unique coat pattern. Photographs of the tigers are stored on a special flash card, which scientists use to compile data on each tiger living in the area.

Tigers do not trust humans in Russia and never let them approach too close. After centuries of merciless tiger hunting, fear of humans has become almost inbred, and no protection or conservation programmes can quickly undo this damage. But they can save many animals nonetheless.[73]

---

[73]Olga Sobolevskaya (2010), "As elsewhere, Siberian tigers disappearing fast", the Pioneer, Bhubaneswar, October, 2010

Fire in Mediterranean Forests
Past, Present and Future

Fire is a major ecological factor in many biomes of the world. In the Mediterranean ecosystems fire has acted as an integral part of their evolutionary history, by having shaped their adaptive traits. Fire has probably played an important role in the selection of many Mediterranean plants. The protective bark of the widespread cork oak and its remarkable capacity to survive after fire from aerial buds is difficult to be explained without the evolutionary intervention of fire. The specific regeneration behaviour of plants is closely related to their physiological traits and is strongly influenced by fire regime (fire season, intensity, and interval).

More specifically, plants of these ecological systems can regenerate through sprouting from intact buds situated at the base of the root crown or from other root rhizomes, or from underground organs such as the lignotubers or the bulbs. Other plants can preserve their reproductive units either in hard cones (e.g. Pines) remaining on the plant, forming thus a canopy seed bank, or by forming hard-coated persistent soil seed banks. Both seed banks are not destroyed by fire and they become available after its passage. Post-fire succession in the Mediterranean plant communities is an auto-succession that leads to the recovery of the pre-fire vegetation. This means that all species, which occurred in the site before fire, are present immediately after it, even in different numbers and relative cover. In this auto-succession, herbaceous plants are abundant in the early post-fire communities and within the herbaceous taxa, legumes are the dominant functional group. Pre-fire community structure is rapidly re-established. Woody plants dominate in the late post-fire communities, both in species numbers and in phyto -mass.

Fire frequency is an important parameter of fire regime. Very frequent fires may diminish plants that have either short life cycles, such as the rockroses or other long living plants, which require an adequate period before they can regenerate. Pines belong to the last category, as they require at least 6-8 years to produce cones and these cones require some period before they become mature. Although our knowledge on the factors that control species richness in post-fire Mediterranean environments is poor, available evidence indicated that species richness is more sensitive to fire severity and fire frequency than plant cover. The 'natural' window time between two consecutive fires is between 50 -60 years for the Mediterranean Basin.

Man and the Mediterranean Landscapes

Man early settled the Mediterranean Basin. Consequently, Mediterranean landscapes have long ago experienced the human impact. Indigenous agriculture and animal husbandry have been practiced here for more than 10000 years, in combination with deforestation practices and fire management. Plant community structure and diversity patterns have therefore being evolved under the influence of this interaction. These patterns were kept in a dynamic equilibrium at least until the Second World War. Since 1950 major changes have occurred to the economies, the livelihood and hence the landscapes of the Mediterranean countries.

A Study of Greece Forests[74]

There are two major forest species widely distributed around the Mediterranean, from sea level to relatively high altitudes and they alone account for about 25

---

[74] Note: Pinus halepensis Mill and Pinus brutia Ten are two measure forest species

percent of the forested area of the Mediterranean Basin.

These are both highly flammable seeding species, growing on virtually all kind of substrates, landforms and topography. Aleppo pine and East Mediterranean pine forests cover approximately 40 percent of the coniferous forests and approximately 9 percent of the total forested area in Greece. They develop at areas of low altitude at relatively dry Mediterranean conditions. Mediterranean forests of Greece host almost 10 percent of the plants, which are endemic in the fire-prone environments of the country.

Almost 1/5 of the fire events, which occurred in Greece during the last 30 years, have burst over Aleppo pine forests consuming four hundred thousand hectares of them. Aleppo pine ecosystems are resilient to fire provided that fire interval follows the 'norm'. This time window must not in any case be less than a minimum time required by Aleppo pine to accomplish its biological cycle that is to establish new seedlings and reach reproductive maturity. This period is not less than 25 years. Traditional use of Aleppo pine forests was primarily related to resin collection and secondarily to wood collection and grazing. During the last 30 years Aleppo pine forests attract other human activities, e.g. recreation and housing constructions. This shift is clearly reflected to the number of fire events starting at the wild land - urban interface.

Aleppo pine natural forests of Mountain Penteli in Attica are a typical example of such landscape changes and fire interactions, having experienced very frequent deliberate fires at quite short time intervals. Plant community structure and diversity are greatly affected. The short fire interval has stronger impact on the occurrence of the woody plant species than on the herbaceous.

In short, there has been an increasing interest in many terrestrial biomes on issues relating biological diversity and ecosystem function. Mediterranean ecosystems of the World have been proposed as critical in this scientific effort in the sense that they provide important models for searching new paradigms relating biodiversity with ecosystem stability and resilience. Given the fact that these ecosystems are under the threat of severe and progressing landscape changes, the need of full understanding the processes underlying these links is essential and becomes crucial under the foreseen climate change scenario.[75]

Malawi

Integrated Forest Resources Management

From time immemorial, Government of Malawi was the main producer of forest goods and services through Forestry Department. It became clear early in 1990's that Government was not able to produce sufficient forest goods and services single-handed. With the revision of Forestry Policy in 1996, emphasis has now been on creating conducive environment for the active participation of all stakeholders, including rural communities, in forest resources management.

Samuel Kainja[76] explains that local communities in Malawi are the major beneficially of forest goods and services. Forests goods and services are exploited often in unsustainable way for consumption and for sale. The majority of rural communities are poor and poverty contributes to environmental degradation through unsustainable wood fuel and charcoal production for sale and domestic consumption.

---

[75]Margarita Arianoutsou, Department of Ecology and Systematics, Faculty of Biology, School of Sciences, University of Athens, Greece

[76] Samuel Kainja, "Integrated Forest Resources Management And Utilization By Rural Communities in Malawi, Forestry Department, Malawi

Malawi is one of the Highly Indebted Poor Countries (HIPC). The key problem in dealing with this major stakeholder is how to provide tangible incentives in order to promote active and sustained participation in forest management and at the same time enable them to meet their needs. This calls for urgent community empowerment to manage and utilize forest resources in a sustainable way.

One of the successful initiatives aimed at promoting community participation in forest management started in 1996 in Mwanza District (Mkamanga, 2001). A total of five villages are involved in Sustainable Management of Indigenous Forest Project. This Project was developed as a joint exercise involving Forestry Department, as a Government institution, the Germany Government as a donor and Wildlife Society of Malawi, a Non-Governmental Organisation, as the implementing agency. With the support of Wildlife Society of Malawi, rural communities have established local institutions that are responsible for planning and implementing development activities that revolve around forest resources management. Rural communities are involved in commercial activities such as bee keeping, guinea fowl raring, tree planting and production of fruit juice from indigenous fruits of *Adansonia digitata and Tamarindus indica.* The Project has diverted the communities from sorely depending on roadside sale of charcoal and firewood, which was resulting in deforestation and degradation of the forest.

Financial gain from commercial activities has become a sustainable incentive for community participation in sustainable conservation of forests. Every month some of the financial gains are used for community development work while some cash is shared among the participants of the Project. As a result, of tree planting and forest management, the forests are now recovering from degradation and deforestation.

Waste Water Treatment

Waste water is simply water that has been used. It usually contains various pollutants, depending on what it was used for. It is classified into two major categories by source.

(a) Domestic or sanitary wastewater. This comes from residential sources including toilets, sinks, bathing, and laundry. It can contain body wastes containing intestinal disease organisms.

(b) Industrial wastewater. This is discharged by manufacturing processes and commercial enterprises. Process wastewater can contain rinse waters including such things as residual acids, plating metals, and toxic chemicals.

Wastewater is treated to remove pollutants (contaminants). Wastewater treatment is a process to improve and purify the water, removing some or all of the contaminants, making it fit for reuse or discharge back to the environment. Discharge may be to surface water, such as rivers or the ocean, or to groundwater that lies beneath the land surface of the earth. Properly treating wastewater assures that acceptable overall water quality is maintained.

In many parts of the world, including in the United States, health problems and diseases have often been caused by discharging untreated or inadequately treated wastewater. Such discharges are called water pollution, and result in the spreading of disease, fish kills, and destruction of other forms of aquatic life. The pollution of water has a serious impact on all living creatures, and can negatively affect the use of water for drinking, household needs, recreation, fishing, transportation, and commerce.

Objectives and Evolution of Wastewater Treatment:

We cannot allow wastewater to be disposed of in a manner dangerous to human health and lesser life forms or damaging to the natural environment. Our planet has the remarkable ability to heal itself, but there is a limit to what it can do, and we must make it our goal to always stay within safe bounds. That limit is not always clear to scientists, and we must always take the safe approach to avoid it.

Basic wastewater treatment facilities reduce organic and suspended solids to limit pollution to the environment. Advancement in needs and technology have necessitated the evolving of treatment processes that remove dissolved matter and toxic substances. Currently, the advancement of scientific knowledge and moral awareness has led to a reduction of discharges through pollution prevention and recycling, with the noble goal of zero discharge of pollutants.

Treatment technology includes physical, biological, and chemical methods. Residual substances removed or created by treatment processes must be dealt with and reused or disposed of in a safe way. The purified water is discharged to surface water or ground water. Residuals, called sludge or bio-solids, may be reused by carefully controlled composting or land application. Sometimes they are incinerated.

Since early in history, people have dumped sewage into waterways, relying on natural purification by dilution and by natural bacterial breakdown. Population increases resulted in greater volume of domestic and industrial wastewater, requiring that we give nature a helping hand. Some so-called advancement in cities such as Boston involved collecting sewage in tanks and releasing it to the ocean only on the outgoing tide. Sludge was barged out to sea so as to not cause complaint.

Until the early 1970s, in the United States, treatment mostly consisted of removal of suspended and floating material, treatment of biodegradable organics, and elimination of pathogenic organisms by disinfection. Standards were not uniformly applied throughout the country.

In the early 1970s until about 1980, aesthetic and environmental concerns were considered. Treatment was at a higher level, and nutrients such as nitrogen and phosphorus were removed in many localities.

Since 1980, focus on health concerns related to toxics has driven the development of new treatment technology. Water-quality standards were established by states and the federal government and had to be met as treatment objectives. Not just direct human health but aquatic-life parameters were considered in developing the standards.

Wastewater Treatment Types

Rural un-sewerage areas, for the most part, use septic systems. In these, a large tank, known as the septic tank, settles out and stores solids, which are partially decomposed by naturally occurring anaerobic bacteria. The solids have to be pumped out and hauled by tank truck to be disposed of separately. They often go to municipal wastewater treatment plants, or are reused as fertilizer in closely regulated land-application programs. Liquid wastes are dispersed through perforated pipes into soil fields around the septic tank.

Most urban areas with sewers first used a process called primary treatment, which was later upgraded to secondary treatment. Some areas, where needed, employ advanced or tertiary treatment. Common treatment schemes are presented in the following paragraphs.

Primary Treatment

(a) In primary treatment, floating and suspended solids are settled and removed from sewage.
(b) Flow from the sewers enters a screen/bar rack to remove large, floating material such as rags and sticks.
(c) It then flows through a grit chamber where heavier inorganic such as sand and small stones are removed.
(d) Grit removal is usually followed by a sedimentation tank/ clarifiers where inorganic and organic suspended solids are settled out.

To kill pathogenic bacteria, the final effluent from the treatment process is disinfected prior to discharge to receiving water. Chlorine, in the form of a sodium hypochlorite solution, is normally used for disinfection. Since more chlorine is needed to provide an adequate bacterium kills than would be safe for aquatic life in the stream, excess chlorine is removed by de-chlorination. Alternate disinfection methods, such as ozone or ultraviolet light, are utilized by some treatment plants.

Sludge that settles to the bottom of the clarifier is pumped out and dewatered for use as fertilizer, disposed of in a landfill, or incinerated. Sludge that is free of heavy metals and other toxic contaminants is called Bio-solids and can be safely and beneficially recycled as fertilizer, for example.

Secondary Treatment

Primary treatment provided a good start, but, with the exception of some ocean outfalls, it is inadequate to protect water quality as required by the Environmental Protection Agency (EPA).

With secondary treatment, the bacteria in sewage are used to further purify the sewage. Secondary treatment, a biological process, removes 85 percent or more of the organic matter in sewage compared with primary treatment, which removes about 50 percent.

The basic processes are variations of what is called the "activated sludge" process or "trickling filters," which provide a mechanism for bacteria, with air added for oxygen, to come in contact with the wastewater to purify it.

In the activated sludge process, flow from the sewer or primary clarifiers goes into an aeration tank, where compressed air is mixed with sludge that is recycled from secondary clarifiers which follow the aeration tanks. The recycled, or activated, sludge provides bacteria to consume the "food" provided by the new wastewater in the aeration tank, thus purifying it.

In a trickling filter the flow trickles over a bed of stones or synthetic media on which the purifying organisms grow and contact the wastewater, removing contaminants in the process. The flow, along with excess organisms that build up on the stones or media during the purification, then goes to a secondary clarifier. Air flows up through the media in the filters, to provide necessary oxygen for the bacteria organisms. Clarified effluent flows to the receiving water, typically a river or bog, after disinfection. Excess sludge is produced by the process and after collection from the bottom of the secondary clarifiers it is dewatered, sometimes after mixing with primary sludge, for use as fertilizer, disposed of in a landfill, or incinerated.

Advanced or Tertiary Treatment

As science advanced the knowledge of aquatic life mechanisms and human health effects, and the need for purer water was identified, technology developed to provide better treatment. Heavy metals, toxic chemicals and other pollutants can be removed from domestic and industrial wastewater to an increasing degree. Methods of advanced treatment include microfiltration, carbon adsorption, evaporation /distillation, and chemical precipitation.

Industrial Waste Treatment

Depending on the type of industry and the nature of its wastes, industries must utilize methods such as those used for advanced treatment of sewage to purify wastewater containing pollutants such as heavy metals and toxic chemicals before it can be discharged. Industries are permitted to discharge directly to receiving waters under the National Pollution Discharge Elimination System (NPDES) permit system or to municipal sewers under the Industrial Pretreatment Program. Pollution prevention programs are very effective in helping industries reduce discharged pollutants, by eliminating them at the source through recycling or through the substitution of safer materials. More and more industries are approaching or attaining zero discharge by cleaning and reusing their water over and over and over.

Combined Sewer Overflows

Combined sewer systems are sewers that are designed to collect rainwater runoff, domestic sewage, and industrial wastewater in the same pipe. Most of the time, combined sewer systems transport all of their wastewater to a sewage treatment plant, where it is treated and then discharged to a water body. During periods of heavy rainfall or snowmelt, however, the wastewater volume in a combined sewer system can exceed the capacity of the sewer system or treatment plant. For this reason, combined sewer systems are designed to overflow occasionally and discharge excess wastewater directly to nearby streams, rivers, or other water bodies. Some designs utilize an overflow at the treatment plant that diverts the excess flow to chlorination facilities for disinfection prior to discharge.

These overflows, called combined sewer overflows (CSOs), contain not only storm water but also untreated human and industrial waste, toxic materials, and debris. They are a major water pollution concern for the approximately 772 U.S. cities that have combined sewer systems.

CSO outfalls often result in violations of receiving stream-water quality standards and impairment to designated water uses. Violations can include aesthetics (including floatables, oil and grease, colors, and odor), solids, nutrients, harmful bacteria, metals, and reduced dissolved oxygen levels.

Historical and Regulatory Aspects

Environmental awareness and activism is not a present-day concept:

(a) In the mid-1700s Benjamin Franklin and others petitioned the Pennsylvania Assembly to stop dumping waste and attempted to regulate waste disposal and water pollution. European countries were correlating sickness with lead and mercury in the late 1700s. In 1855, Chicago became the first U.S. city with a comprehensive sewer plan, and all U.S. towns with populations over 4,000 had city sewers by 1905.

(b) In 1899 the Refuse Act prevented some obvious pollution of streams and placed the U.S. Army Corps of Engineers in charge of permits and regulation.

(c) In 1914 U.S. government agencies began pollution surveys of streams and harbors.

Reports filed by the early 1920s showed heavy damage from oil dumping, mine runoff, untreated sewage, and industrial wastes.

(d) In 1924 the Oil Pollution Control Act prohibited discharge from any vessel within the three-mile limit, except by accident.
(e) In 1948 the Federal Water Pollution Control Act and active House and Senate Public Works Committee in water pollution came about.
(f) In 1956 Congress passed the Water Pollution Control Act, in 1961 the Clean Water Act, and in 1965 the Water Quality Act, setting standards for states.
(g) In 1970 Congress and the president established the EPA.
(h) In 1972 Congress passed the Federal Water Pollution Control Act (the "Clean Water Act").
(i) In 1973 EPA issued the first NPDES permits.
(j) In 1974 Congress passed the Safe Drinking Water Act.

The Clean Water Act of 1972

The federal Clean Water Act of 1972 was prompted by growing national concern for the environment in the late 1960s, fueled by such concerns as the burning Cuyahoga River in Ohio, an unfishable, unswimmable Potomac River, and a nearly dead Lake Erie. It was the the most significant pieces of environmental regulations ever enacted.

National goals and objectives were established "to restore and maintain the chemical, physical, and biological integrity of the Nation's waters." There were two major goals:

(a) Eliminate the discharge of all pollutants into navigable waters of the United States; and
(b) Achieve an interim level of water quality that provides for the protection of fish, shellfish, and

wildlife and recreation (the "fishable, swimmable" goal).

To help do this, the following were established:

(a)A state grant program to support the construction of sewage treatment plants; the NPDES program, whose goal was to eliminate discharges to U.S. waters; and technological standards or discharge limits that had to be met, based on water-quality standards set by the states.

(b)A minimum required percent removal of pollutants was added in 1985.

(c)Secondary treatment was required, and limits were set for three major effluent parameters: biological oxygen demand, suspended solids, and pH.

The Water Quality Act of 1987 made several changes, addressing (1) excess toxic pollutants in some waters and (2) nonpoint source pollution. The construction grant program was phased out and replaced by financing projects with revolving fund, low-interest-rate loans. The amendments passed in 1987 also addressed storm-water controls and permits, regulation of toxics in sludge, and problems in estuaries. Penalties were added for permit violations. Also initiated were sludge-disposal regulations and funding for studies relative to nonpoint and toxic pollution sources.

The 1972 act has provided remarkable achievements, but there is still a long way to go. Forty percent of waters assessed by states still do not meet water-quality standards, mostly due to pollution from nonpoint sources. Other than from storm or combined storm sewer overflows, most of the remaining problem is not from pipes (point sources) but from sources such as farming and forestry runoff, construction sites, urban streets (storm water), automobiles, and atmospheric depositions, such as from power-plant air emissions (nonpoint sources). Current approaches to addressing nonpoint pollution include targeting and permitting by given watersheds and TMDL (total maximum daily load for a river stretch) assessments.

Many of the facilities funded by federal construction grants, which make up the wastewater collection and treatment infrastructure, are wearing out and are now undersized. Many, many dollars are needed to keep providing adequate treatment to maintain the status quo, let alone meet the needs of a growing populace.

Other Countries

Unfortunately, since the Industrial Revolution, most of Europe's rivers (not unlike in the United States) were utilized for transporting wastes to the sea, resulting in harm to human and aquatic health and causing coastal pollution. In earlier times, the rivers could handle the limited wastes discharged, through dilution and natural purification.

Significant progress has been made in treating the wastewater entering Europe's rivers, with measurable improvements in water quality. The agricultural sector (nonpoint pollution source) has not kept up, and nitrate levels are still high.

The fifteen-nation European Union's (EU) Urban Wastewater Treatment Directive has resulted in significant improvements in wastewater treatment capacity and methods. According to the European Environment Agency, increased treatment capacity has been realized in all EU countries except Sweden, Finland, and the Netherlands, where it is already efficient. The largest increase will be in southern Europe and Ireland. As a result, the EU's collection and treatment systems should be able to cope with all organic discharges from most member states by 2005. In Finland and Sweden most of the wastewater was being treated in tertiary plants in the 1980s.

Raymond Cushman and George Carlson

The liquid and solid material removed from domestic septic tanks is called sewerage (or Septage). Most sewerage is hauled to municipal sewerage treatment facilities and most sewerage haulers must be licensed.

Settling Pond

A settling pond, usually man-made, collects and slows water flow so that suspended solids (sediments) have time to precipitate or settle out of the water. Some applications of settling ponds include capturing runoff from farms (agricultural waste), construction projects (soil sediment) and mines (sediment and toxic waste). Settling ponds eventually fill and must be dredged to remain in operation. Polluted water from abandoned mines is diverted to settling ponds to remove solids such as iron oxide. When dredged, these sediments must be treated as contaminated waste. Pilot projects are underway to recapture iron oxide for use in paint pigments.

Constructed Wetlands

Constructed wetlands are wetlands that are specially built for the purpose of wastewater treatment and are utilized in place of naturally occurring wetlands. They provide a greater degree of wastewater treatment than natural wetlands, as their hydraulic loadings can be managed as required. Because these wetlands are constructed specifically for wastewater treatment, they should not be included in the jurisdictional group, which avoids the regulatory and environmental entanglement associated with natural wetlands. This is in accordance with Environmental

Protection Agency regulations. The treatment process can be either aerobic or anaerobic, depending on whether the wetlands are constructed with an exposed water surface or one with subsurface flow.

These wetlands can also be used to remove nitrogen, which is usually not removed during the standard wastewater treatment process. Nitrogen removal is accomplished by the growth of cattails and reeds, which utilize the highly nutrient wastewater and consequently remove nitrogen in the process. Sometimes the cattails and reeds must be harvested to complete the removal process.[77]

Air Pollution

Comes from many sources

Smog hanging over cities is the most familiar and obvious form of air pollution. But there are different kinds of pollution—some visible, some invisible—that contribute to global warming. Generally any substance that people introduce into the atmosphere that has damaging effects on living things and the environment is considered air pollution.

Carbon dioxide, a greenhouse gas, is the main pollutant that is warming Earth. Though living things emit carbon dioxide when they breathe, carbon dioxide is widely considered to be a pollutant when associated with cars, planes, power plants, and other human activities that involve the burning of fossil fuels such as gasoline and natural gas. In the past 150 years, such activities have pumped enough

---

[77]Waste Water Treatment, Pollution Issues, Pollution issues .com
(b) Ohio State University Extension, Food, Agricultural, and Biological Engineering "Wastewater Treatment Principles and Regulations" (c) Environmental Protection Agency, Office of Water (1993) "Constructed Wetlands for Wastewater Treatment and Wildlife Habitat
"

carbon dioxide into the atmosphere to raise its levels higher than they have been for hundreds of thousands of years.

Other greenhouse gases include methane—which comes from such sources as swamps and gas emitted by livestock—and chlorofluorocarbons (CFCs), which were used in refrigerants and aerosol propellants until they were banned because of their deteriorating effect on Earth's ozone layer.

Another pollutant associated with climate change is sulfur dioxide, a component of smog. Sulfur dioxide and closely related chemicals are known primarily as a cause of acid rain. But they also reflect light when released in the atmosphere, which keeps sunlight out and causes Earth to cool. Volcanic eruptions can spew massive amounts of sulfur dioxide into the atmosphere, sometimes causing cooling that lasts for years. In fact, volcanoes used to be the main source of atmospheric sulfur dioxide; today people are.

Industrialized countries have worked to reduce levels of sulfur dioxide, smog, and smoke in order to improve people's health. But a result, not predicted until recently, is that the lower sulfur dioxide levels may actually make global warming worse. Just as sulfur dioxide from volcanoes can cool the planet by blocking sunlight, cutting the amount of the compound in the atmosphere lets more sunlight through, warming the Earth. This effect is exaggerated when elevated levels of other greenhouse gases in the atmosphere trap the additional heat.

Most people agree that to curb global warming, a variety of measures need to be taken. On a personal level, driving and flying less, recycling, and conservation reduces a person's "carbon footprint"—the amount of carbon dioxide a person is responsible for putting into the atmosphere.

On a larger scale, governments are taking measures to limit emissions of carbon dioxide and other greenhouse gases. One way is through the Kyoto Protocol, an agreement between countries that they will cut back on carbon dioxide emissions. Another method is to put taxes on carbon emissions or higher taxes on gasoline, so that people and companies will have greater incentives to conserve energy and pollute less.[78]

Prevention and Disposal of Obsolete Pesticides

An inventory of obsolete pesticide stocks must identify not only the different types and amounts of pesticide formulations, but also the quantity of contaminated containers and equipment, contaminated soil and other materials that may need to be dealt with in order to deal with the problem as comprehensively as possible. In many cases, pesticide containers will have lost their labels. A basic chemical analysis of the products will need to be carried out in order to determine at least which chemical family the chemical belongs to. This is necessary in order to know how to package and label the chemical so that it can be safely transported to its place of final disposal or treatment.

Because the member companies represented by Crop Life International (CLI) have pledged to contribute to the costs of cleanup operations involving their products, the inventory must also make sure to note how much of the stocks come from CLI member companies or their precedents (i.e. companies that have merged or whose products have been taken over by other companies).

The inventory should also record the state of the containers and storage facilities for the pesticides. Are the pesticides safely contained? Where are they

---

[78]National Geographic – Air Pollution

located? It should not be located near water reservoirs, wells, near villages, near schools. If pesticides have leaked into the environment, the level of soil and water contamination also needs to be determined.

All of this information is needed to complete an environmental risk assessment for each site. These assessments allow authorities to set priorities for cleanup and disposal operations and to make an effective plan of action.

The environmental assessment process has been developed by FAO within the framework of a toolkit that allows countries to:

(a) Prioritize sites or regions for action on the basis of the risk they present to health and the environment;
(b) Identify safe storage sites for centralization of repackaged obsolete pesticides or future storage of pesticides;
(c) Plan the transportation of pesticides to minimize risk in the event of accident or spillage.

Taking an inventory of obsolete pesticide stocks and making environmental risk assessments are technically complex tasks. The people who are taking responsibility for cleaning up used pesticide stocks must be adequately trained, supervised and provided with the proper protective equipment as well as supplementary equipment such as digital cameras and GPS units.

The FAO Programme is committed to providing developing countries with the resources they need to assume complete responsibility for the taking the inventory of obsolete pesticide stocks. The Programme has published training manuals, guidelines and has developed the tools for taking stock of obsolete pesticide stockpiles and assessing soil and water contamination.FAO has also developed an Internet database tool for inventory taking. The database's on-line forms ensure that for each site the information is complete and presented it in standardized electronic and print formats. Once the data has been entered, the database can automatically generate an environmental risk assessment for each site and establish priorities for action.[79]

A number of lethal pesticides are banned in many advanced countries. These are:

(a) The pesticide Chlorpyrifos has been banned in the US, Sweden and Finland.
(b) Pesticide Lindane is banned in Denmark, Germany, Sweden, Finland, Indonesia, New Zealand and the Netherlands.
(c) DDT is banned in the US, Canada, Chile, South Korea, Singapore, Cuba, and most EU countries.
(d) Endosulfan is banned in Germany, Denmark, Indonesia, Bulgaria, Norway, Sweden, Colombia, Singapore and the Netherlands.
(e) Carbaryl is banned in austral, Germany and Sweden.
(f) Paraquat is banned in Denmark, Austria and Sweden.

But all these pesticides are not banned in most of the developing countries including India and China.

Debating Climate Funding

International cooperation on dealing with climate change faces challenges of increasing global imbalances, tensions over currency, fiscal constraints in developing countries and discord between the US

---

[79]FAO, UN

and China. Leveraging the private sector and making climate change finance a reality could be a step forward.

Last week, while climate policy watchers had their eyes on Tianjin — where the UNFCCC negotiators were making halting progress in their final meetings before the upcoming negotiations in Cancun — another debate on climate was being held in Washington. Ministers of Finance and Development, as well as representatives from the private sector, civil society and other development agencies, gathered for the annual meetings of the IMF and World Bank. World Bank President Robert Zoellick's opening speech set the tone by highlighting the increased impact on developing countries from climate-related natural disasters and other environmental and social stress factors. Mr. Zoellick also re-affirmed the World Bank's global priority on tackling climate change.

The backdrop to the meetings was not encouraging. There is a wide disparity between what science tells us, that global warming should not exceed 2 degree C (3.6 degree F), and the ambition of commitments under the Copenhagen Accord. Further, the gridlock in US legislation makes it difficult to reach our own commitments, weakening our ability to serve as a leader. There are challenges to international cooperation given the increase in global imbalances and tensions over currency, with tension between the US and China on these issues mirroring the tone in Tianjin. And there are fiscal constraints in the OECD countries that challenge the ability to finance the transition to a low-carbon and climate-resilient economy in the developing world.

But there was room for some optimism. The delegates were purposeful in their discussions, and pressed for continued action within, and in parallel to, the UNFCCC talks to keep up momentum to reach a positive outcome in Cancun.

How to address Climate Change Challenges

Katherine Sierra has assessed that the five key messages for addressing the climate change challenge emerged from the annual meetings:

Go for building blocks:

With UNFCCC officials clear that there are no prospects for a comprehensive global agreement in Cancun, the goal has shifted to Plan B: To reach agreement on a number of building blocks that were framed in the Copenhagen Accord that could ultimately shape an eventual global agreement. Likely candidates for agreement include: Mechanisms for supporting reductions in emissions from forestry (REDD+), building on the recent partnership forged by 58 countries at the Oslo Climate and Forest Conference; technology, including the setting up of regional innovation centers; a framework for adaptation, focusing on capacity building; and the principles of, and processes for designing, the Copenhagen Green Fund. But while convergence on these issues seems possible, the "building block" strategy may not advance due to the trickiest parts of the Copenhagen Accord-provisions for transparency about monitoring, reporting and verification of emission reduction targets and actions, and their linkages to the commitments on longer-term climate finance.

At the annual meetings, some participants were quietly discussing a "Plan C" — which no formal agreements on these building blocks will be created in Cancun, but there will be continued movement through bottom-up activities supported by coalitions of interested countries.

Make climate finance a reality:

The Copenhagen Accord included climate finance commitments of $30 billion in Fast Start financing to 2012, with long-term financing reaching $100 billion a year by 2020. Delegates acknowledged that meeting the Fast Start financing objective was critical to building trust, and countries are racing to demonstrate by Cancun that they are meeting these commitments. But the scope for the public sector to finance significant parts of the longer-term $100 billion commitment has finance officials worried. They will also be looking for the kind of leverage achieved by the Clean Technology Fund, with some $4 billion leveraging $40 billion in investment in clean technologies. And, while we wait for the report on possible sources of innovative finance from the UN's high-level group on climate finance due by the end October, the message is that we should not expect a recommendation on how to raise this level of finance but rather a menu of possibilities to inform the debate on economic and political tradeoffs.

Leveraging the private sector:

Climate negotiators are divided on the role that public versus private finance should play in meeting the Copenhagen Accord ambitions. But OECD delegates to the annual meetings were clear that achieving the $100 billion per year in longer-term finance would require significant private sector flows. There was a strong push for the continuation of carbon markets beyond 2012. So, extension of the Kyoto Protocol in Cancun will be critical. Even then, the Clean Development Mechanism needs substantial reform to reduce transaction costs, support investment at scale through programmatic schemes, and become more accessible to a broader range of countries, including the least-developed countries.

Other ideas included public-private partnerships with private capital; leveraging multilateral development bank risk mitigation capabilities; and using innovative public policy tools, like cross border feed-in tariffs, to support regional renewable investments.

Public sector climate finance:

In Tianjin, the focus was on the often-contentious intricacies in the design of the governance arrangements for the Copenhagen Green Fund and its links to other issues, like transparency. In Washington this past weekend, the message from contributing countries was that while the Copenhagen Green Fund will be important, there will be many channels for climate finance, including: Existing funds like the Global Environment Facility and the Adaptation Fund, leveraging of the MDBs, and bilateral support. The link to MDB and bilateral funds to the UNFCCC continues to be a debatable point, with developing countries asserting the primacy of the Copenhagen Green Fund as a key part of any financial mechanism, guided by and accountable to the UNFCCC. Also underscored during the annual meetings was the key element of transparency-to reassure developing countries that money is flowing and balanced across different constituencies, and to assure taxpayers that funds are achieving results.

Don't forget the most vulnerable. There was a call for structuring new funding to also reach least-developed countries. Capacity building to help these countries access the many funding channels will be critical. A focus on special constituencies with significant climate challenges (small island states, sub-Saharan Africa and mountain nations) was also on the agenda. Further, some emphasized the need to ensure that funds, whatever their source or delivery channel, adhere to strong social and environmental standards so that benefits reach the poorest, including indigenous peoples. The productive dialogue on opportunities for the most vulnerable, which has surfaced as part of the REDD+ partnership, may set the path for the broader climate finance architecture.

While global agreement on tackling climate change is not in the cards for Cancun, the Conference of Parties will have the opportunity to move forward on the building blocks to set action in motion. Climate financing will be at the top of the agenda including leveraging strategies for the private sector and debating the role and impact of public financing options. Ultimately, the least-developed countries, which have been, and will continue to be, hit hardest by climate-related natural disasters as President Zoellick emphasized at the annual meetings, need to see action, particularly financing, sooner rather than later.[80]

Conclusion

The government and government machinery must understand the severity of the problem of climate change. They should take the advices of environmentalists to make suitable and appropriate laws to save the environment. It is an irony that a corrupt government is more responsible for environmental loss than the innocent tribal people. The budget under Environment and Forest Ministry should be increased and all sanctioned posts should be filled up.

The idea of Global Canopy program for a stable planet is a positive action to save people and animals from ensuing disaster. This needs food security of all poor people and sustainable management, conservation and protection of forests all over the globe.

---

[80]Katherine Sierra, "Debating Climate Funding", The Pioneer Sunday Magazine, August 29, 2010

The ground water contains highly toxic poisons like arsenic and fluoride. It can be removed by the use of activated alumna, aluminum and sand filter, magnesium oxide, tri-calcium phosphate. Countries like the United States, Britain and France practicing these procedures and supply clean drinking water to their inhabitants. Most of the countries are unable to practice this, so people drink contaminated water and die through diarrhea and cholera. They drink water, which is even not suitable for domestic animals. It is a grave situation. People cover 10 to 20 kilometers to fetch water.

Industrialization causes air pollution and water pollution. The infected water and waste water must not be allowed to mix with river water or any source of flowing water as people use this water as drinking purposes in down-stream areas. Once the water resources are polluted, it is very difficult to clean them. The growth of cities and urban areas has posed serious water contamination process in all developing countries. The environment must look into it with seriousness.

Genetically Modified crop can be used in case of legumes, oilseeds and fodder. It can be used for draught and saline tolerance crops. But Genctically Modified crop should not be used for other crops and vegetables. If the GM crop is to be used, it must be evaluated case-by-case basis. Use of pesticides must be regulated.

An international Law must stop production and use of Endosulfan, Chlorpyrifos, lindane, DDT, Carbaryl and Paraquat in all countries to save the people from diseases and deaths. There are evidences that young boys and girls commit suicides because of failure in love and farmers commit suicides because agricultural prices of rice (un-husked rice) and wheat are less than production costs.

Tamarind and banyan trees should be popularized in different countries. Tamarind in food enhances urinary excretion of fluoride. Banyan tree provides clean air.

The developed countries and the World Bank should not emphasize on 'infrastructure development', which leads to corruption to the maximum in all debtor countries.

Climate funding is more important to save the world. If the United Nations could stop war or at least delay wars for years and restrict production and export of war equipment's and ammunitions, people all over the globe would avail clean air, clean water and better environment to live in peace.

But only politicians can save the environment because they are the real causes of destruction of nature. They convert agricultural land into industrial belts; they undertake projects and destroy forests; they cause classification of people and make majority of people nomads, labourers, peasants and hungry. They are the causes of wars, corruption, and growth of Terrorists, Naxalites and Maoists. They welcome natural hazards to remain in power and they avail golden opportunity to garner huge wealth for their family members. If they would desire to save the world, they can settle boundary disputes through mutual discussions and protect environment from destruction.

+++++

Chapter - IX

FIXING ACCOUNTABILITY
IN VIOLATION OF ENVIRONMENTAL LAWS

The world is suffocated with deterioration of environment. The abode of civilization has become a 'place of terror' as rich countries and rich people are constantly choking the rights of poor people and low-income countries. Their advices and monetary assistance have neither solved nor checked the sufferings of the poor. Human rights are continuously violated. Can the 'Thinkers' of the world search for a plan to solve their sufferings? We have to find out the causes of their sufferings and the paths to follow for peaceful solutions of their problems. We have to convert this world into a 'safe heaven' for all.

We have to follow the 'SWOT' (S+ W+ O+ T) analysis to solve all problems the world faces now. In order to draw a conclusion, we have to study S (Strength), W (Weakness), O (Opportunity) and T (Threats) of our planet. Each country, state, district or settlement can prepare its plans for solution of a problem. The government should not impose its decision without proper research studies. It is observed that the military rulers and autocrats exercise too much power for implementing their wishes.

Now, the corrupt governments are more worried to implement wrong policies with the help of police or military forces.

Even state policies and budgets are prepared without professional Economists.

The governments are simply guided by corporate houses, World Bank and developed countries. In turn the governments of developing countries appease them with thousands of acres of land, forests, mines and minerals, unlimited credit for non-profitable investments, foreign tours and fortunes. All developing countries are encouraging corruption and are involved in kickbacks. Foreign debt is the worst source for money laundering.

The public–private partnership (PPP) program adopted by the corrupt government is a new weapon to sell all buildings, roads, property and places to few individuals. Both politicians and bureaucrats are more prone to corruption as compared to earlier days.

Who creates pollution? Why the twenty-first century is facing climate change? Why the poor people or natives are made homeless? Who controls the political power – the politicians or conglomerates? Why black money is multiplying at geometrical proportions? The victims of pollution are fighting for their survival:

(a) First, victims are generally poor, hungry and innocent.

(b) Second, government officials feel that they are the government and they know the state very well.
(c) Third, the polluters benefit the politicians particularly the ruling party members.
(d) Fourth, the industrial houses purchase the head of the government such as President; Prime Minister or Chief Minister of a country or state, once they are interested to start a business.
(e) Fifth, the local courts cannot adjudicate independently because of interference from local governments. And finally, the voters have no power to call back the corrupt government. Moreover, the poor people are unable to raise voices against the government.

Achim Steiner, UN Under-Secretary General and Executive Director, UN Environment Programme (UNEP)[81] delivered a brilliant speech in Addis Ababa. The text is as follows:

Between 2000 and 2005, the annual forested area of Nepal increased by 1.3 per cent, soil quality and water supplies are better managed and local employment has risen. Uganda, a country where 85 per cent of the working population is employed in agriculture, has turned to organic production to boost exports and incomes. Farm-gate prices for organic vanilla ginger and pineapples are higher than for conventional produce. Since 2004 the number of certified organic farmers has grown from 45,000 to over 200,000 and the area of land under organic cultivation from 185,000 hectares to close to 300,000 hectares. The Green Economy work is also shedding light on the economic absurdities that in turn and in part are driving environmental degradation,

[81]Achim Steiner, UN Under-Secretary General and Executive Director, UN Environment Programme (UNEP), VII African Development Forum, Africa and the Green Economy, Addis Ababa, October 2010.

contributing to poverty and undermining sustainable development. Around US $27 billion of fisheries subsidizes, fueling over fishing and threatening the lives and livelihoods of one billion people who directly rely on fish as protein. Why are we investing in the means of capture? It is over captured. Why the governments fight against its countrymen, which are debarred from food and shelter?

Fossil fuel subsidizes totaling some US $500 billion a year which, according to research, rarely reaches the poor and benefits the middle classes, fuel companies and equipment makers. And which contribute to economic inefficiencies, greenhouse gas emissions and perpetuation of fossil fuel dependency. Or agricultural subsidies including fertilizer and pesticide ones that allied to food wastes represent one of the biggest market failures globally. Indeed if we could address food waste? Running on average worldwide at perhaps 40 per cent of all food produced and both a developed but also developing country challenge? There are some who reckon we could feed not just six billion but nine billion people now and today. Africa is well placed to be its leader and a Green Economy incubator, a Continent demonstrating to rest of the world that sustainability and development go hand-in-hand.

In this chapter we have cited only two examples: the Amazon forests and Rivers and Environmental problems in India. It would explain the environment situations on the globe. Let all politicians, administrators, scientists should find the solutions for a clean environment.

The Amazon Forests and Rivers

The facts and figures of Amazon would clearly speak the legitimacy and actual international laws that control the world. Who would be punished when the government tries to harm the people, destroy the environment, allows rather forces the poor people to perish without their faults.

(a) Privatizing the Amazon with safeguards

Friday, October 15th, 2010

Brazil will auction large swaths of the Amazon forest to be managed by private timber companies and cooperatives to help reduce demand for illegal logging. After years of legal battles and political opposition, the government is reviving concessions for private companies to log its national forests. The future of the Amazon forest is in danger. How can we combat deforestation and climate change? The private companies can digest the forests, oceans and even destroy the environment. How can we strengthen forest management without disturbing the natives?

The government will grant private companies logging concessions for nearly 1 million hectares (2.47 million) by year-end and, within 4 to 5 years, nearly 11 million hectares (27 million acres) and the size of the U.S. state of Virginia. Existing concessions total only 150,000 hectares (370,000 acres). Unlike the illegal slash and burn practice that has already destroyed nearly 20 percent of the world's largest rainforest, managed logging extracts only as many trees as the forest can naturally regenerate.

Antonio Carlos Hummel, head of Brazil's National Forestry Service further said at the Reuters Global Climate and Alternative Summit: When the government began preparing for concessions in 2003, it faced stiff opposition from conservative politicians who called it privatization of public assets. Back then we didn't explain the process well. Now, it's all cleared up. There hasn't been a questioning of privatization for over a year. Concessions actually helped establish more state control in the often-lawless Amazon region, where settlers and speculators often illegally occupied public lands, he added. While illegal logging usually produces wealth for only a few, forest concessions, at least on paper, generate lasting jobs and tax revenues for the government.

Aware of failed private timber concessions in Africa and parts of Asia, Brazilian lawmakers took certain safeguards. We included a series of community control mechanisms. He referred to non-government organizations that participate in public audits of concessions.

Deforestation rates in Brazil's Amazon, the world's largest rainforest, have fallen to their lowest in two decades after the government stepped up policing in recent years. Authorities have fined illegal cattle ranchers and loggers, confiscated their products, and cut off bank loans to them. But unless such tough controls are maintained, illegal logging could undermine demand for more expensive timber from managed forests. If next year controls ease off and the market is flooded with cheap wood, forestry concessions will suffer. The potential for forest management is huge with state governments and private entrepreneurs also beginning to jump on the bandwagon.

In addition, traditional forest dwellers have rights to about 19 million hectares (47 million acres) and resettled peasants hold 21 million hectares in the Amazon. Currently only two cooperatives of traditional forest dwellers have a federal license to log.[82]

---

[82] Raymond Colitt, "Privatizing the Amazon with safeguards", Brazil Amazon forest to be privately managed, Reuters, Oct. 11, 2010, International Environmental Law, News on Environment and Governance. We are grateful to www/ alphabetic / info for using their reports.

The biggest challenge for cooperatives is to obtain technology, training, and financing. There is red tape and a lack of environmental awareness at banks. Everything in this country is an incentive for deforestation, for developing destroyed forest. So we have to change the paradigm — finance standing forests. Privatization of Amazon forest is the only solution.

(b) The Oil Spills in the Peruvian Amazon

Thursday, June 24th, 2010

In the middle of the Peruvian Amazon, thousands of miles from the BP rig pouring oil into the Gulf of Mexico, oil spills have been a fact of life for more than 30 years. In villages like San Cristobal, the indigenous Achuar people believe their maladies are caused by exposure to oil. They suffer from fainting spells, vomiting, chronic diarrhea, headaches and skin infections.

For example, Isac Sandy a youth of 25 years of age is tall and shy, and got married in 2009. He suffers from frequent headaches, and he gets an injection to relieve the symptoms of an unknown skin condition in alternate days. If he avoids injection, his skin breaks out in a spotty white rash, and his entire body swells. There's a stream where we always go to fish, and we see a thin layer of oil on top of water. We catch fish there and eat them. The fish drink the water, and since we eat them, the oil must get into us that way. The river water is polluted.

A Peruvian government study published in 2006 found that most indigenous people living along this river — the Rio Corrientes — had unhealthy levels of lead in their blood. Lead and cadmium are associated with oil spills, which have been happening here for decades. It is reported that 95 percent of people have excess lead in their blood.

Whether the cause of these health problems is oil spills, other changes brought by outsiders, or a combination of the two, the Achuars' quality of life has worsened since oil companies arrived and little is being done to help them. In Peru, there are as many as 12, 500 of the Achuar people in this locality.

The bustling town of Trompeteros is the base of operations for Plus petrol, an Argentine oil and gas production company operating in the area. Trompeteros has electricity, running water, sewage systems, telephone service and even Internet. A few minutes downriver, next to Plus petrol's paved runway, the village of San Cristobal doesn't have electricity. The roof of the local school is literally caving in. Daniel Hualinga, the village elder, says: We have asked the company to help out and they tell us they have nothing — which the oil revenue is running low. The earth here is contaminated — and it will never be completely healthy again, never.

Wilson Sandy, who works for an indigenous monitoring program that tracks oil spills. About a dozen students sit on plywood benches in a house that serves as a makeshift school. Students study in Spanish and the indigenous Achuar language. During music class, they learn Achuar songs, which are traditionally sung for their gardens, animals and the forest. Like their parents, most of the kids suffer from the chronic stomachs, fainting, vomiting and fevers. Some people have more problems in health.

Peruvian oil industry analyst Aurelio Ochoa says that spills are an unavoidable part of the oil business. These are human projects, so there will always be a risk, as clean as the operation might be. Accidents happen, and they're going to keep on happening — here, in Alaska, in Louisiana, wherever.

The point is: who would be responsible for all sufferings of these people? It is the oil company or the government?

But the dense foliage and river labyrinths of the Amazon are a world away from the capital of Lima and Peru's legal system. The human-rights lawyer Miguel Jugo opines: Indigenous people have always suffered from inaction on the part of the state. Their rights are constantly violated. If the state starts to consult with indigenous people, the state will become responsible for meeting their requests, and the government doesn't want that.

Protests by indigenous peoples exploded across Peru's Amazon last June and confrontations with police left dozens dead.

According to the 2007 census, Peru is home to at least **60 indigenous ethnic groups**, most of them living in the Amazon River basin. The protests were sparked by government decrees meant to open up huge portions of the Amazon rain forest to development, but the government had failed to consult the indigenous people who live there. A year later, a new law has been created to require consultation with the indigenous people, but it still hasn't gone into effect. Meanwhile, more petroleum concessions are up for bidding — in all, three-quarters of the Peruvian Amazon is now open to private business.[83]

In response to an interview request, Environment Minister Antonio Barack released a statement saying oil drilling will not destroy the Amazon rain forest and that Peru must also worry about its energy security.

---

[83]Excerpts from, Toll of Oil Drilling Felt In Peru's Amazon Basin, NPR, June 23, 2010

He notes that Peru needs to improve the participation of local communities. In San Cristobal, relationships among the Achuar people, the oil company and the Peruvian state are only getting worse.

(c) Bio – Prospecting and Bureaucracy in Amazon

Thursday, November 26th, 2009

The task of harvesting the secrets of Brazil's vast Amazon rain forest could help in the battle against cancer. There are a number of clippers in the forest, out of which two clippers have been identified, which produces medicines for cancer.

About 70 percent of current cancer drugs are either natural products or derived from natural compounds, and the world's largest rain forest is a great cauldron of biodiversity that has already produced medicine for diseases such as malaria.

But finding the right material is no easy task in a forest that can have up to 400 species of trees and many more plants in one hectare area, and in a country where suspicion of outside involvement in the Amazon runs strong.

Dr. Drauzio Varella with a mix of enthusiasm and frustration says: If we had very clear rules, we could attract scientists from all over the world. We could transform a big part of the Amazon into an enormous laboratory. Now foreigners are barred to join the research team. The researchers from Sao Paulo's Paulista University are among a tiny handful of Brazilian groups licensed to study samples from the Amazon.

But a move by his team in the 1990s to partner with the U.S. National Cancer Institute produced a storm of accusations of "bio-piracy" and for years it has been blocked from the international cooperation and funding that could increase the chances of finding the Holy Grail of a cancer cure.

Their work has also been regularly delayed by bureaucratic demands, once stopping their collections for two years. In more than a decade of searching, the group has brought back 2,200 samples from this tributary of the mighty, tea-dark Rio Negro (Black River) to its laboratory in Sao Paulo, of which about 70 have shown some effect against tumors.

As well as the impact this could have on human health, it could bring resources for preservation and to improve the quality of life of people who live here. Robert Gallo, a U.S. researcher and leading AIDS expert who co-discovered the HIV virus, asked Varella during a trip to the Amazon in the early 1990s, which could undertake research for the medical potential of the forest.

Among the natural products being used to fight cancer today is Taxol, a chemotherapy drug that comes from the bark of the Pacific yew tree. David Newman, head of the Natural Products Branch of the U.S. National Cancer Institute, said several promising cancer drugs derived from natural sources as varied as deep-water sponges and microbes are currently going through clinical trials.

Out of an estimated 80,000 species of flower-bearing plants in the Amazon, only about a fifth have been identified. Newman said progress in Brazil has been greatly hampered by the inability of companies to patent a natural product under legislation passed in the 1990s, leaving no incentive to invest in research.

He cited the example of a Brazilian viper snake whose venom proved vital to the development of blood pressure drug captopril in the 1970s, a find that might not have happened under today's laws. Further analysis of the promising compounds found by

Varella's team has been held up while the university waits for access to a nuclear-magnetic resonance machine that can isolate the active elements.

We're still a long way from discovering an actual medicine that could cure a type of cancer but we have strong signs that some plants have substances that inhibit the growth of tumors. Their main hope is that growing concern over the environment and increasing government efforts to slow the destruction of the Amazon by ranchers and loggers will turn the tide in favor of sustainable forest industries, of which they say their work is a prime example.

Amazon is a dense forest where all types of trees, herbs, shrubs and clippers are available in plenty. Most of them are medicinal plants and should not be destroyed. We can find medicines and medicines for all diseases.[84]

(d) On Doing Something: The Amazon

Friday, October 9th, 2009

Four of the biggest companies involved in Brazilian cattle farming have joined forces to stop the purchase of cattle from newly deforested areas of the Amazon. Meat companies Marfrig, Bertin, JBS-Friboi and Minerva yesterday signed a formal moratorium in which they pledge better protection for the rainforest.

The move follows a three-year Green peace investigation, reported extensively in the Guardian in June, which exposed the link between forest destruction and the expansion of cattle ranching in the Amazon. The investigation prompted calls for action from key international companies, including food group Princes and footwear manufacturers Clarkes, Adidas, Nike, and Timberland, which

---

[84]Stuart Grudgings, In Amazon, a frustrated search for cancer cures, Reuters, November 17, 2009

threatened to cancel contracts unless their beef and leather products were guaranteed free from raw materials linked to Amazon destruction.

John Sauven, head of Green peace, said: "Today's announcement is a significant victory in the fight to protect the Amazon. Cattle ranching is the single biggest cause of deforestation globally, and the fact that these multibillion dollar companies have committed to cleaning up their supply chains will lead to real change in the Amazon." He added: "British companies have helped make this happen by getting tough with their suppliers, but this is not the end of the story. We now need to make sure that this agreement is properly enforced and extended to the entire cattle industry in Brazil."

Blairo Maggi, governor of the Brazilian state of Mato Grosso, which has the highest rate of deforestation in the Amazon and the largest cattle herd in Brazil, attended the signing in São Paulo. Maggi has announced the state will support efforts to protect the Amazon and will provide high-resolution satellite images to monitor the area.[85]

Clearing tropical forests for agriculture is estimated to produce 17 percent of the world's greenhouse gas emissions - more than the global transport system. The Green peace investigation compiled government records, company documents and trade data from Brazil, China, Europe, Vietnam and the US to piece together the global movement of meat, leather and cosmetics ingredients made from Brazilian cattle.

(e) Drilling the Amazon

Wednesday, July 8th, 2009

[85]Global brands refuse to endorse 'Slaughter of the Amazon', The Guardian, Oct. 5, 2009

"**Now the fish are going to disappear**," said Luis Umpunchi, an Awajún Indian, one of about 20 people gathered around a broken oil pipeline in the Jayais community, in the northern Peruvian province of Amazonas. Everyone was looking at the **oil spill** with concern. Some touched the black liquid, which had mixed with the mud resulting from a recent rainfall.

Another farmer remarked: That oil will reach the Marañón River, where our crops grow along the banks, who was harvesting plantains when he heard about the leak along the Norperuano pipeline. This pipeline belongs to the government-owned Petroperú Company, which has several pumping stations in Amazonas.

Station Number 6 in particular was taken over in May 2009 by indigenous groups near the town of Bagua as part of protests against decrees that opened up their land to mining, oil and logging companies.

When the police were sent in to break up a roadblock outside of Bagua on June 5, 2009, 24 police and at least 10 civilians were killed, although the protesters say the number of demonstrators shot in the crackdown was much higher. Two of the controversial decrees have since been overturned, as demanded by the native groups.

The populations most affected by the **oil spill** live in the Cenapa and Nieva river valleys. Indigenous communities, closer to towns like Bagua also fear that their rivers will be polluted, as occurred with the Achuar Indians. The Achuar live along the Corrientes River in the neighbouring province of Loreto, in the far northeast of the country, where the Argentine oil company Pluspetrol operates. Petroperú workers who arrived in Jayais to clean up the spill refused to talk about the cause of the break in the pipeline, which stretched across a ravine.

Native families in the Amazon jungle make their living from fishing, hunting, and growing plantains, maize and cocoa along the rivers and manioc in the hills.

Along the roads, merchants buy plantains from them, and sell the product in the market at four times of the farmer's price.

"We are not protesting because we are 'savages,' but because we need these resources to survive. The earth is our mother, and the forest is the pantry for feeding our families," said Umpunchi. Part of the spilled crude is likely to reach the Chiriaco River, subsequently ending up in the Marañón River, he said.

More than 70 percent of Peru's Amazon rainforest was divided into concessions for oil and natural gas investment between 2003 and 2008, according to a March report by the local non-governmental organisation Law, Environment and Natural Resources (known by its Spanish acronym DAR), which was based on official data. To promote private investment in the jungle areas, the administration of President Alan García passed a dozen decrees under the argument that they were needed to facilitate implementation of the free trade agreement with the United States, triggering indigenous protests in 2008, which have continued off and on until now.

The Awajún and Wampí peoples, in Amazonas province, feel threatened by the **mining and oil drilling activities**, which are going ahead in ecologically vulnerable protected areas, and have led to disputes between the companies and local residents over **water and land**. Julia Esamat, 53, a member of the Awajún community from the village of Wawas, in the Chiriaco district said:

This is my home. This is where my grandparents lived and I want my children to inherit it. We have moved forward ourselves, without the government. The authorities can't come now and take from us what is ours.

Nearly **60 petroleum concessions** were granted, 15 of which were approved in processes marred by irregularities, overlapping 12 protected areas in 10 of the country's provinces. Among them is the Santiago Comaina preserve in Amazonas, according to the DAR report.

The French firm Maurel and Prom holds a permit for exploration in lot 116 in Santiago Comaina. To gain access to the area, the company signed an agreement with the heads of the indigenous federations of Condorcanqui province. But because the native leaders did not consult the communities, they were removed from their posts, according to a May 2008 report in La República newspaper. Furthermore, gold and uranium exploration projects have been authorized in Amazonas, in the Cóndor mountain range, bordering Ecuador. But native groups in the Cenepa river valley say the concessions were transferred in an irregular manner from the Dorato Peru Company, a subsidiary of the Canada-based Dorato Resources.

In a November 2008 communiqué, Dorato Resources said it had acquired all shares of the Peruvian mining company Afrodita. According to Marco Huaco, a lawyer with Racimos de Ungurahui, a local NGO, and the transaction was carried out by means of front organisations. Huaco said the initiative **violates Article 71 of the constitution** because in order to authorize foreign investment in a border area, the executive branch has to issue a supreme decree declaring it a "public necessity" but it did not occur.

In addition, it violated International Labour Organisation (ILO) Convention 169, a 1989 agreement that requires prior consultation with local indigenous communities about economic activities that affect their land or means of livelihood. The Development Organisation of Cenepa Border Communities, one of the four indigenous associations in Amazonas province, filed three complaints in April about the case to the government Office on **Mining Concessions**.

The authorities replied that they were not aware of the Canadian company's participation, that the concessions were granted to Peruvian entities, and that they would investigate the claims. The group also brought the Cóndor mountains case before the United Nations special rapporteur on the rights and freedoms of indigenous peoples on June 18 2009.

The document presented to Anaya, to which this reporter had access, states that **the project affects 9,636 indigenous people in Cenepa** because it is situated at the head of the main tributaries to the Marañón River, and crosses the protected Ichigkat Muja National Park, which the government has recognized as "highly vulnerable" in ecological and human terms.

In several statements on rights to land title issued in favour of mining companies, the National Institute of Natural Resources says mining activities cannot be carried out in Awajún territory, according to the text presented to Anaya. If mining were carried out in that area, it would mean the partial extinction of this Amazonian native group.

The indigenous leaders will bring the case before the U.N. Committee on the Elimination of Racial Discrimination, the U.N. Special Adviser on the Prevention of Genocide and the Inter-American Commission on Human Rights.[86]

---

[86] Milagros Salazar, Peru: Petroleum Sullies the Amazon, Inter Press Service, July 3, 2009

(f) Think the Impossible:
Oil Can Wait - Just Save the Amazon
Tuesday, July 7th, 2009

Though half of Ecuador lies in the Amazon basin, its rainforest is shrinking faster than in neighbouring countries (by 1.67 percent a year).

It has been ravaged by logging, poachers and oil extraction. Settlers have streamed in to carve out a precarious life. Over the past decade they have been joined by thousands of refugees fleeing violence in Colombia, as well as guerrillas and drug traffickers who inflict it. Native tribes have been uprooted, forced deeper into the forest or have disappeared.

The government of President Rafael Correa now wants help to keep pristine one of Ecuador's most important remaining jungle areas, in the Yasuní national park. In a corner of the park known as ITT (after the Ishpingo, Tambococha and Tiputini rivers) lies (lays) an oilfield which preliminary seismic studies show holds almost 846 million barrels of oil, or around 20 percent of Ecuador's reserves.

The ITT area is unusually biodiversity. It is thought to be home to several hundred tribesmen who shun the modern world and whose way of life is protected under a new constitution promoted by Mr. Correa.

Oil companies, including Spain's Repsol and Chinese-owned Andes Petroleum, are already extracting **about 59,000 barrels a day** elsewhere in the Yasuní Park. Repsol tightly controls access to its field, keeping out would-be colonists. Further east, Petrocuador, the state oil company and the country's worst polluter, is developing a block adjacent to ITT.

In 2007 when Mr. Correa first mooted the idea that the world should pay Ecuador not to exploit the ITT oil this was widely dismissed as half-baked. Under the influence of a group of politicians from across the spectrum and environmentalists the idea is gaining flesh and credibility.

It now centers on issuing bonds for the value of the carbon emissions avoided by not burning the oil and by preserving the forest. These would be worth up to $5.2 billion at the current carbon price in the European emissions' market. The money would be lodged in a trust fund managed by international bodies such as the Inter-American Development Bank, and spent on alternative-energy projects in Ecuador. Bondholders would have a say in how the money is spent.

Last year Germany agreed to give €300,000 ($425,000) for feasibility studies, and last month reiterated its support. The scheme will go ahead once the first $350m is raised, says Roque Sevilla, a former mayor of Quito who is promoting it. The hope is that most of this money will come from European governments. If a future government in Ecuador opted to exploit the oil, it would have to repay the bondholders with interest, says Francisco Carrión, a former foreign minister who is another of the promoters.

He accepts that the main obstacle is Ecuador's poor reputation. In December the government defaulted on $3.2 billion in bonds-the third default in as many decades. As a result of Mr. Correa's expansionist fiscal policy, Ecuador risks running out of foreign-exchange reserves, increasing the temptation to tap the oil. Nevertheless, the Yasuní-ITT initiative, as it is called, is now worth a closer look.[87]

---

[87]Conservation in Ecuador: Trees or oil, Economist, July 2, 2009

(g) Forfeiting the Oil, Saving the Amazon: Is it a Net Deal? Monday, June 15th, 2009

Beneath the tropical jungles of northeastern Ecuador lies a vast pool of oil, representing one-fifth of the small Andean country's petroleum reserves and potentially billions of dollars in revenue.

Directly above that pool, the Yasuni National Park is home to a diversity of wildlife that is among the richest on the planet, Ecuadorian and U.S. biologists say.

Faced with these two treasures, Ecuador is pursuing an unusual plan to reap the oil profits without actually drilling for oil.

The idea envisions wealthy countries effectively paying Ecuador to leave its oil and the carbon dioxide that would result from using it in the ground. Environmentalists hail the proposal as a potentially precedent - setting approach to conservation in developing countries. Ecuador would sell certificates to governments or companies that would allow them to emit carbon dioxide in amounts corresponding to the carbon left underground in Yasuni. Proponents say the plan would help reduce overall levels of air pollution.

Matt Finer, a biologist with Washington-based Save America's Forests, who has studied Yasuni National Park emphasized: **From my perspective, this has got to work. This area is really of just supreme global conservation importance.**

Similar ideas have become increasingly popular across South America. Brazil has developed an Amazon Fund, which seeks to attract money to conserve the rain forest.

So far, Norway has pledged up to US $1 billion over the next several years. The Japanese government recently agreed to lend Peru US $ 120 million to protect 212,000 square miles of Amazonian rain forest over the next decade.

And Colombia is seeking funds from Norway to combat climate change by protecting forests.

But relying on other countries to send cash to save remote jungles has run into repeated obstacles, including a lack of clarity on what exactly they would be buying, how the money would be spent and, in the case of Ecuador, how the Yasuni certificates could be sold on carbon markets. Plus, the global economic crisis has made funding scarcer for environmental causes.

Roque Sevílla, a prominent Ecuadorian environmentalist who is on the committee in charge of the Yasuni initiative expressed: One of the issues that is difficult to handle in this financial crisis is to ask governments for taxpayers' money. So that's a huge problem. That's another reason we're trying to go to the carbon market.

Sevílla further said that focusing on carbon could save Yasuni. The 410 million tons of carbon dioxide that would avoid being emitted could raise $4 billion to $7 billion, Ecuador estimates. European countries could accept the Yasuni certificates as an equivalent to the carbon allowances traded on the European Energy Exchange in Leipzig, Germany. The exchange is a market for energy products such as electricity and natural gas, as well as carbon dioxide emissions rights. But such an arrangement is not allowed under the rules of the 1997 Kyoto Protocol, aimed at curbing greenhouse gas emissions — a treaty the United States rejected. Ecuadorians say they hope this type of pilot project could be embraced under climate change rules to be formulated at a meeting in Copenhagen in December.

The benefit to the planet is not that we leave the oil underground. That has no benefit. The benefit is the C02 that we keep underground. So the idea is: try to obtain compensation not for the oil but for the carbon. The money from selling carbon-emission certificates would go to a trust fund managed by international organizations. The interest would be spent on protecting national parks and funding alternative energy projects and other environmental initiatives.

Germany has expressed the most support for the Yasuni project. The German Parliament passed a resolution in June in favor of the project and has funded a study to outline how it might work. Ute Koczy, a lawmaker from the opposition Green Party, who traveled to Ecuador as part of a delegation studying the issue, said other countries, particularly the United States, should help find ways to support such a proposal.

The Ecuadorian proposal is still unique. There is no other proposal like it worldwide. That makes it kind of difficult to find support. Ecuador's president is getting very impatient and may give the whole area to (the Spanish oil and gas company) Repsol or to China or somebody else. He's under big pressure from the oil companies.

Lovejoy, who in the 1980s invented a policy tool known as debt-for-nature swaps said: Attacking climate change in this way could prove effective because it simultaneously addresses the two main drivers of greenhouse gas emissions — fossil fuels and deforestation. It really goes straight at the heart of the distortion of the global carbon cycle. I find it imaginative and encouraging that there is a government that would be even willing to consider foregoing using a natural resource like that. Ecuadorian officials said their country's history of oil-driven environmental degradation helped lay the political ground for such a measure.

Alberto Acosta, a former minister of mines and energy who helped develops the initial Yasuni proposal said: The petroleum activity in the northeastern Amazon has been the cause, directly or indirectly, of a vast process of devastation in the region. The worrisome thing is also that the Amazon provinces have more poverty and misery than the rest of the country. You have to do something so you don't repeat this situation.

Acosta's 2007 plan sought to attract international funding to equal the revenue the country would forgo by not drilling for oil, a simpler, if more vague, approach. Since then President Rafael Correa has vacillated over whether he supports the idea or favors drilling for oil. These ambiguities threaten the project.

Juan Fernando Terán, an environmental professor at the Simón Bolívar Andean University in Quito, Ecuador's capital, said the project's designers have failed to clearly explain the benefits of protecting the Amazon, its rich biodiversity and its role in regulating air and water currents far from this country. "If I knock on your door in California and tell you, 'Help me with a little money to improve the air in South America' — well, why? South America wouldn't matter to you. But Yasuni is much more than a museum."[88]

Others said Ecuador made it more difficult by proposing to save a national park, which, in theory, should already be protected. Joe Keenan, managing

---

[88]Joshua Part low, In Ecuador, an Unusual Carbon-Credit Plan to Leave Oil Untapped, Washington Post Foreign Service, May 26, 2009

director of the Latin America region for the Nature Conservancy remarked that kind of muddied the argument. My impression is it's a really innovative and daring idea, but I think it's probably ahead of its time."

(h) Not as They Please Anymore:
Defending Property Rights in Amazon
Monday, May 25th, 2009

Amazon Indians who have been blocking roads, waterways and a state oil pipeline since April are declaring an "insurgency" against Peru's government for refusing to repeal laws that the protesters say make it easier for foreign companies to take their lands, a national Indian representative said Friday. Peruvian officials warned that Indians participating in any uprising could be charged with sedition.

The Indians contend the laws – passed with special powers granted to President Alan Garcia to implement the Peru - US free trade pact that went into effect in February – open the door to privatization of their communal jungle lands and water resources for oil drilling, logging, mining and large-scale farming. Alberto Pizango, president of the Peruvian Jungle Inter-Ethnic Development Association, said the insurgency declaration means the Indians "refuse to recognize the authority" of the government. Instead, they will obey their ancestral laws and view any government security forces on their lands as an "external aggression."

The government "wants to take our lands and hand them over to giant multinationals for the oil, lumber, gold and other riches there that are coveted by the world's rich," said Pizango, who met with chief Cabinet Minister Yehude Simon on Wednesday in a failed effort to resolve the dispute. President Alan Garcia has prioritized foreign oil investment in the Amazon, where the government owns the rights to underground resources. Indians say his government does not consult them in good faith before signing contracts with oil companies.

A Duke University study published last year said contract blocks for oil and gas exploration cover approximately 72 percent of Peru's rainforest. Pizango said the Indians are willing to give their lives to defend the land and will radicalize protests that include at least 30,000 Indians across six provinces. Indians have clashed with police while blocking highways, waterways, airports and the flow of oil in a state pipeline. Garcia declared a state of emergency and suspended some constitutional rights in four jungle provinces May 9 a month after the Indians began their protests. Justice Minister Rosario Fernandez said Friday that Indians participating in the insurgency face five to 10 years in prison for sedition.

Human rights and environmental groups, Peru's ombudsman office and nine Roman Catholic bishops stationed in the Amazon side with the Indians, calling for the repeal of the laws. They say the government should respect an International Labor Organization accord protecting Indians' right to consultation on the use of their lands. Congress is set to debate the issue next week.[89]

(i) Making Social Policy in Courts:

Indigenous Rights, Farmers and the Amazon
Wednesday, April 8th, 2009

Campaigners fighting for the land rights of the Amazon rainforest's indigenous groups celebrated Friday their victory in Brazil's Supreme Court, saying it came as a "tremendous relief". The court upheld the integrity of a vast native reserve, paving the way for the eviction of white farmers who have resisted leaving, in a 30-year dispute over the rights of native

[89]Andrew Whalen, Amazon Indians declare `insurgency' against Peru, Associated Press, May 16, 2009

groups to lands in Brazil. In a 10-1 vote Thursday, the tribunal's judges reaffirmed the borders of the Raposa Serra do Sol reserve and ordered the rice farmers' expulsion. London-based Survival International, which has campaigned for more than twenty years for the reserve, said the ruling was a blow to state politicians who backed the rice farmers, and the Brazilian military. "This ruling will come as a tremendous relief not only to the 20,000 Indians who live in Raposa, but to the hundreds of thousands of others across the country," said Fiona Watson, Survival's campaigns coordinator, who has visited the reserve several times.

"At the heart of the case was a very simple principle — should Indians who have lived on the same land since time immemorial be able to continue living there peacefully, or should the farmers and landowners who are so powerful in South America be able to push them off in the name of development "Thankfully the court has come down decisively on the side of the Indians, and also rejected the army's shameful propaganda that Indian reservations somehow represent a threat to the country's sovereignty."

Christine Halvorson, programme director of the Rainforest Foundation, a British charity founded by musician Sting, told AFP the verdict marked a "tremendous victory" for the people of Raposa along with indigenous people across Brazil. But, she added: "The decision also brings with it 19 conditions that will have an impact on the future demarcation of indigenous areas and indigenous control and management of their land. "Those may spell a step backwards in terms of indigenous rights. There is a danger flag because of those conditions, but overall it's wonderful news." [90]

---

[90]Campaigners cheer Amazon victory, Agence France Press, Mar. 20, 2009

(j) Land Tenure and the Fate of the Amazon

Friday, March 6th, 2009

Grand plans to halt the destruction of the Amazon rainforest have come and gone over the years with scant success, so a degree of skepticism about Brazil's latest scheme seems justified. However, one positive sign is that, this time, the federal government seems to have recognized the importance of working with, rather than against, state governments in the region.

The new plan, discussed at a meeting of state governors and federal officials earlier this month, involve regularizing the titles to 80% of the private land holdings in Brazilian Amazonia over the coming three years. This, it is hoped, will encourage the occupants to stay and improve their land instead of abandoning it and moving on to clear the next patch of virgin forest.

A small-scale initiative under way near the village of São Luiz do Anauá in Roraima state provides an illustration of what the scheme hopes to achieve. The local soil is the colour of cement and almost as rich in nutrients. The area was deforested 15 years ago. Cattle ranchers came and went, and for the past few years the land has been unproductive. But now, neat rows of palms sit waiting to be planted, thanks to a bio-fuels company based in São Paulo.

Brazil lacks a central land register, suffers widespread forgery of title deeds and has a long history of squatters seizing land. A widely quoted study by Imazon, an NGO, reckoned that only 4 percent of private land in Amazonia is covered by secure title deeds. Much of the rest has been grabbed in the hope of establishing de facto ownership eventually.

The government's new scheme is, in principle, simple. Plots of up to 100 hectares (247 acres) will be given to the people farming them. Larger ones, of between 100 and 2,500 hectares, will be sold using various different pricing mechanisms. Plots of over 2,500 hectares will be reclaimed by the government, which is meant to own them anyway. Roberto Mangabeira Unger, the minister responsible for the new scheme, believes that solving the problem of insecure land title will "change the economic equation that has made pillage more attractive than either preservation or production in the Amazon."

In the past, however, similar initiatives have floundered, for a number of reasons. First, state and federal governments have disagreed over who should be responsible for what. The state governors particularly dislike INCRA, a federal agency charged with distributing small plots of land. Eduardo Braga, the governor of Amazonas, says, "INCRA abandoned the families it settled on land in the Amazon without electricity or infrastructure." The agency certainly has a poor record of preventing deforestation on the land it administers.

Second, the existing laws that govern what land can be used and what cannot are confusing and close to unenforceable. In the 1960s and 1970s, farmers were sometimes required to cut down trees as a condition for getting credit from the state. Some token efforts were made to change this regime in the 1980s, and then in 1996 a decree was issued requiring 80 percent of each plot of land to be preserved as forest, with only 20 percent to be cultivated or ranched. This law is widely ignored, and when the government has tried to enforce it, it has often met with strong resistance from the men with the chainsaws. Given this history of mutual antagonism, the process is unlikely to be smooth.

Still, some of these problems have been resolved in the new plan, which has the force of law via a presidential decree. On a federal level, the Ministry for Agrarian Development will handle some of the implementation, taking it away from INCRA, which could be described politely as troubled. Mr. Unger, a former Harvard law professor, seems to have succeeded in charming the governors of the states in the Amazon into a more co-operative mood. "We have Obama's teacher here," says José de Anchieta Júnior, the governor of Roraima, while addressing a public meeting in the state. "Things are looking up."

Nevertheless, there is a risk that the scheme, by making it easier to get secure title for dubious land claims, might somehow stimulate demand for virgin forest land, not damp it. And, as ever, enforcing the rules will be the difficult bit. President Luiz Inácio Lula da Silva's government has shown an indulgent attitude to violations of property rights elsewhere in the country by the Landless Movement, making it an unlikely guardian of them now. The new scheme is not bound to fail, but the skeptics will take a bit more convincing.[91]

INDIA

Status Report on Mining Leases in Orissa State

The Republic of India covers a land area of approximately 3,287,300 squares Kilometers and is topographically, geographically, environmentally, and culturally diverse. India is rich in mineral resources and has a long history of mining, mineral production, and mineral utilization. India is among the top ten mineral producing nations in the world. The Indian economy to a great extent depends on the value of the minerals produced, as these represent a major portion of the raw materials for the nation's industrial activities.

---

[91]The Brazilian Amazon: Preventing pillage in the rainforest, Economist, Feb. 26 2009

India is the third largest producer of coal in the world and one of the world's leading producers of bauxite (aluminum ore), iron ore, zinc, and limestone (approximately 122 Mt annually). The majority of aluminum, copper, leads and zinc ores mined in India are utilized domestically, as well as approximately 50 percent of the iron ore.

The Indian minerals industry produces more than 80 mineral commodities including mineral fuels, base and precious metals and industrial minerals. Approximately 4,000 to 5,000 mines (excluding artisan mines) operate throughout the country, the majority of which are small surface mines using manual mining methods and having relatively low annual production outputs. Of the total number of mines, approximately 500 are underground mining operations, most of which are small, having non-mechanized operations. Most of the more important mineral resources are mined and produced by Indian national or state corporations, which also operate some of the larger, more progressive and modern mechanized mines. The major non-coal mining sectors are: Bauxite (aluminum), Chromites (chromium), Copper, Hematite/ magnetite (iron), Lead/zinc, Manganese, Limestone, etc.

In the mineral map of India, Orissa occupied an important position both in terms of deposit and production. The mineral deposit of the state is not only vast but also equally diverse. It is one of the largest minerals bearing states in India, having 16.92 percent of the total reserves of the country.

Mining Lease

Emphasis has been given on grant of mining leases for mineral based industries for value addition so as to promote industrialization in the state. There are a total of 605 mining leases covering an area of 99,931.55 Ha in the state, which have been granted, with mining leases before 31st Dec 2005. Out of these 335 mining leases covering an area of 72,076.914 ha are working and in operation while 270 mining leases covering an area of 27,854.63 Ha are non – working.

The top 6 districts of Orissa where mining activities are being undertaken rampantly include Keonjhar (31.28 percent), Sundergarh (20.03 percent), Angul (10.24 percent) followed by Jharsuguda (8.87 percent), Koraput (6.3 percent) and Mayurbhanj (3.6 percent). The largest number of mining leases is in Sundergarh district, followed by Keonjhar (119), Bolangir (75), Kalahandi (72), Mayurbhanj (46) and Jharsuguda (26). Out of the 605 mining leases, maximum numbers of leases have been granted for Graphite ore mines (114), followed by Iron ore mines (75), and Quartz mines (72).

Iron ore mines (21,086 Ha), coal - mines (17,558 Ha) and Iron and Manganese mines (15,246 Ha) occupy the largest mining area in the state. Iron ore is abundantly available in the districts of Keonjhar (46 mining leases occupying 12,076 Ha of mining area), Sundergarh (18 mining leases occupying 5,650 Ha of mining area), Mayurbhanj (10 mining leases occupying 3,169 Ha of mining area) and Jajpur (1 mining lease occupying 190 Ha of mining area).

There are two major Coal bearing areas in the state – Talcher and Ib valley. Angul (12 mining leases occupying 9,590.15 Ha of mining area) is the major coal-bearing district followed by Jharsuguda (14 mining leases occupying 7,656.55 Ha of mining area), Sambalpur (1 mining lease occupying 170.305 Ha of mining area) and Sundergarh (1 mining lease occupying 140.84 Ha of mining area).

Iron and Manganese Ore Mines are mostly common in Keonjhar (38 mining leases occupying 13,870.9 Ha of mining area), Sundergarh (18 mining leases occupying 1,190.46 Ha of mining area) and Mayurbhanj districts (1 mining lease occupying 184.76 Ha of mining area).

Chromites is mostly available in Jajpur (16 mining leases occupying 4,320.93 Ha of mining area), Keonjhar (5 mining leases occupying 2,013.123 Ha of mining area) and Dhenkanal districts (3 mining leases occupying 960.8 Ha of mining area).

Koraput (2 mining leases occupying 4,647.177 Ha of mining area) is the major Bauxite bearing district in Orissa and produces 98.82 percent of the state's total production followed by Rayagada (1 mining lease occupying 1,388.7 ha of mining area) and Sundergarh (4 mining leases occupying 419.4 ha of mining area).

Dolomite is available in plenty only in the district of Sundergarh while Manganese ore is largely exploited in Sundergarh (20 mining leases occupying 2,940.44 ha of mining area), Keonjhar (15 mining leases occupying 2,306.28 Ha of mining area), Rayagada (5 mining leases occupying 580.07 ha of mining area) and Bolangir district (1 mining lease occupying 7.27 ha of mining area).

Out of the 605 mining leases granted, 38 leases covering an area of 19,420.295 Ha were held by M/S O. M. C Ltd out of which 17 leases are in operation covering an area of 14,568 Ha. Similarly, 30 leases covering an area of 17,556 Ha were held by M/S Mining Corporation Ltd out of which 29 leases are in operation covering an area of 17,447 Ha. M/S TISCO holds 10 mining leases in the state covering an area of 5,740 Ha while M/S SAIL holds 8 mining leases covering 6000 Ha in the state.[92]

---

[92] A. Aruna Murthy & Y. Giri Rao, "Status Paper on Mining Leases in Orissa", Vasundhara, 15, Sahid Nagar, Bhubaneswar, May 2006

Other significant mining lessees include M/s Rungta Mines having 12 mining leases (most of them for Iron and Manganese mining), M/s O M D C having 4 mining leases majority for Iron and Manganese mining and M/s NALCO has 2 mining leases for bauxite mining.

Economy of Orissa (India)

But Orissa state is the poorest state in the country as about 50 percent of people are poor. The government neglects agriculture and promotes industry. Agriculture is a loss bearing profession in the state. The government forcefully evicts their homestead land to handover land to industrialists. More than one million people, mostly the agricultural laborers have left for engagement elsewhere such as Surat industrial area of Gujarat.

It is a head reeling fact that more than 100 farmers committed suicides in the state in 2010 after crop-harvest failure due to untimely rainfall and yet, the government is a shy observer of the scenario. A number of farmers' organizations have roared in open seminars and conventions against the state government.

Forests are destroyed; climate change has become intolerable; people die in sunstroke; peasants sell their sons and daughters and there occurs starvation deaths. There are more than one hundred engineering colleges, one hundred management colleges and a number of medical colleges in the state and these are privately owned. This clearly speaks that few persons associated with administration are looting the state.

The government of Orissa sends its ministers to foreign countries to invite industrialists to start industries in the state. They are allowed both forest land, agricultural land and land earmarked for public utilities such as crematorium for funeral ceremony, grazing land, mines and minerals, electricity and water in single-window system at the terms dictated by the industrialists. The press, TV and Radio illustrate the richness of the state and how the state marches ahead with investment proposals of trillions of Indian rupees. This occurs when peasants commit suicides. Is it a sustainable development? Or, it is simply destruction of civil liberties.

The industrialists loot the minerals as they export the minerals to other countries at international prices. They destroy the purity of water and air. All the rivers are contaminated. This has changed the climate of the state. The Government of India under UPA and the state government under Biju Janata Dal are determined to invite industrialists at the cost of poor people of the state. Who would restrict them? It is also a fact that both the governments are killing young people declaring them as Maoists, Naxalites and Terrorists. They are put to jail without trials for many years.

All the forest areas vis-à-vis mining areas are now facing fierce battles between military and police forces of Government versus the Maoists. Is it the biggest democracy in the world? Can there be a war between the government and voters?

The mineral and forest wealth of the state has become a CURSE for the people. The governments are acting as the Emperors of the state / country and the hungry people are treated as beggars. How can we bring WORLD PEACE if elected representatives adopt corrupt practices in the governments?

The mining scams are noticed in as many as eight states in India. But no government has been dissolved yet. Till date, the Government of India has not engaged the Central Bureau of Investigation to enquire any deal of mining corruption. Why?

Bad Economics: The state's focus is on captive use and mineral processing. The policy stipulates:

(a) An application for allotment of mining lease will be considered after the applicant invests substantially in a value addition project within the state.
(b) The lease would be allotted only after the promoter has committed 50 percent of the proposed investment.

This is a wrong policy of the government. This incurs corruption before the start of the project. It is calculated that if a company gets 28,800 billion INR (Indian Rupees) from a bauxite industry, the government would get only 140 billion INR over a period of 20-22 years. In other words, the state government would get only US $1 when the industrialist would get US $206 from the project.

Violation of State Laws: The Orissa state de-reserves forests as a routine work for industries, or for any other projects including housing complex even. The government de-reserved 4 hectares of forestland in 1982 for one project and it de-reserved 4722 hectares in 1998-99 for 53 projects. It is a fact that 'Mines' control Indian politics. Indian governments make the peasants poor by allowing cheap prices to rice and wheat. The western advice for increasing agricultural production would make the country a desert within a decade.

The Real Violation: All the flaws deliberate or otherwise, pale before the following questions: what of tribal interests? How are these projects to be implemented in tribal; areas, in forests and lands constitutionally protected from exploitation by non-tribal entities? The government's answer is univocal: twist the law of the land, beyond recognition.

This is exactly what it did in Lanjigarh, inhabited primarily by the Kondhs, a scheduled tribe. The joint venture was formally signed on October 2004, violating the original memorandum of understanding OMC had signed with Sterlite Industries India Ltd, which was to set up both a refinery and operate a mine. Now, it looked as if two different companies were partners for the two different operations. In truth, Vendant was an offshoot of Sterlite.A year before the formal joint venture was signed; the Chief Minister had already laid the foundation for the refinery project. By that time, a reign of terror similar to that in Kashipur had descended upon villages such as Basantpada. Miraculously, the company had acquired land and begun on-site work.

The Central Empowered Committee found that the land was forcibly taken away from tribal people in Bandhagudha and Rengopali villages. Similarly, tribal people cultivating land in Jaganathpur were summarily evicted, and the land transferred to Vendant. Such actions flew in the face of state – level laws to protect tribal people, such as the Orissa Scheduled Areas Transfer of Immovable Property (by Scheduled Tribe Regulation) Act 1956 – it forbids transfer of land to non- tribal people. The atrocities committed clearly contravened Scheduled Caste and Scheduled Tribes (Prevention of Atrocities) Act, 1989. And in providing land to a private company, the state had also violated Scheduled v of the Constitution.

Views of Central Empowered Committee

1. Work on the refinery began without seeking clearance for 58.93 hectares of forestland that fell within the project site. This violated union ministry of environment and forests guidelines on seeking Central Clearance for such projects

2. The land acquisition notice issued by the district collector on June 6, 2002, clearly stated that 47.7

hectares of forest land had been included in the project site, a gross contravention of the Forest Conservation Act, 1980

3. The rehabilitation package violated Schedule v of the Constitution, for it had rendered tribal people landless

4. The Niyamgiri hill, which was to be mined for bauxite, was a biodiversity-rich area, and the state government had already planned to make it a part of a new elephant reserve.

5. Bauxite was also to be mined from nearby Karlaput, near to an existing sanctuary.

It is because the Chief Minister Naveen Patnaik emphatically says that " No One" can come in the way of Orissa' s dream to develop. This state is ready for war against its people.[93]

The state is now fighting against the Maoists, Naxalites and Terrorists in 18 out of 30 districts. All the newspapers are highlighting the deaths of the terrorists in front news with photographs. Even the state capital Bhubaneswar is not out of danger. In January 2011, all the political parties including the party-in-power stage demonstrations in front of the governor's office to mobilize public support. It has planned to enroll one member from all 800, 000 families in the state to strengthen the party. Politics has become an income generating profession in Orissa state.

The speech is like debate with arguments and counter arguments on "Development or Destruction". The party-in-power says industrialization, mining leases, reduction of forests are the signs of development.

[93]Down to Earth, April 15, 2004

The Opposition Party says:

- **(a) Destruction,**
- **(b) Loss of Peace**
- **(c) Rise of Naxalites, Maoists, Terrorists**
- **(d) Reduction of forest land,**
- **(e) Reduction of agricultural land**
- **(f) Unemployment**
- **(g) Farmer's Suicides and**
- **(h) Corruption**

India is at Cross Road

In an editorial, the Pioneer (January 17, 2011) has commented that the much pressure would be exerted to convince the Ministry of Environment and Forests to allow concessions to industrial houses because the country needs development. In other words, every political person in India has a value and can be purchased. Similarly, a strict minister could be dropped from the Ministry at the will of the political party.

Jairam Romesh has problems, but so does India. The Group of Ministers constituted to tackle the controversy arising out of the Environment and Forests Ministry's policy to prevent coal mining in forested areas will need to do a delicate balancing act between environmental protection and extraction of the fossil fuel that is crucial to meet the rising demand for electricity. The desire to find a middle ground became imperative after the Coal Ministry strongly objected to Environment and Forests Minister's no-go policy that prohibits coal mining in regions having 30 per cent gross forest cover or 10 per cent or more in weighted forest cover. Since this effectively bars mining in most areas rich in coal, it has caused outrage.

There is no argument with the fact that natural resources are an asset that needs to be tapped to power economic growth; conversely, not doing so is tantamount to criminal waste. The problem, however, has been that mining activities across the country have often flouted environmental guidelines and left the people of the area out of the development loop. All of these have led to rising opposition at the grassroots level that we now witness in mineral rich States.

He has been sincerely trying to enforce the rulebook — and create new rules to block backdoor manipulations. His activism has brought gravity and a sense of purpose to the Ministry he heads. So, it is not surprising that he has ruffled several feathers along the way. It is not just the Coal Minister who is upset with him; others like Surface Transport Minister Kamal Nath, Civil Aviation Minister Prafulla Patel and Steel Minister Virbhadra Singh or Beni Prasad Verma are also put off by what they believe does Mr. Jairam Ramesh raise obstacles in the execution of their schemes. The Group of Ministers will have to address this perception as well, because there cannot be progress on the environmental front if the Environment Ministry is seen as an obstructionist agency.

The good thing is that the ministerial panel will help foster better communication and understanding among the key players, leading to some kind of middle ground approach. Hopefully, it will also end the public, and often bitter, battle between Mr. Jairam Ramesh and his colleagues. Such tussles tend to divert attention from the core issues and degenerate into political point-scoring games. It is not that Mr. Jairam Ramesh has always been dogmatic; he has been flexible whenever it has been possible, such as on the new airport project for Mumbai or the Jaitapur nuclear power plant. Significantly, the first was cleared after the Prime Minister's intervention and the second keeping in mind the thrust that the Union Government seems to be giving to nuclear power generation as a clean energy source. But nuclear power generation of any significance is still some years away in the country, and there are niggling doubts on its economic efficacy. For the moment, we have to generate power with coal.

On July 31, 2011, the ministry of Environment and Forests allowed the POSCO (Company) of South Korea to start mega steal plant in **low-lying rice field** with 28 conditions and a port nearer to Paradeep port with 32 conditions as both UPA government of India and BJD government in Orissa state are worried to sanction the projects more than the south Korean government and company. But local people have started blocking the road of the proposed site.

Party of Pollution

Paul Krugman opines that Last month President Obama finally unveiled a serious economic stimulus plan — far short of what I'd like to see, but a step in the right direction. Republicans, predictably, have blocked it. But the new plan, combined with the Occupy Wall Street demonstrations, seems to have shifted the national conversation. We are, suddenly, focused on what we should have been talking about all along: jobs."

So what is the G.O.P. jobs plan? The answer, in large part, is to allow more pollution. So what you need to know is that weakening environmental regulations would do little to create jobs and would make us both poorer and sicker.

Now it would be wrong to say that all Republicans see increased pollution as the answer to unemployment. Herman Cain says that the unemployed are responsible for their own plight — a claim that, at

Tuesday's presidential debate, was met with wild applause.

Both Rick Perry and Mitt Romney have, however, put weakened environmental protection at the core of their economic proposals, as have Senate Republicans. Mr. Perry has put out a specific number — 1.2 million jobs — that appears to be based on a study released by the American Petroleum Institute, a trade association, claiming favorable employment effects from removing restrictions on oil and gas extraction. The same study lies behind the claims of Senate Republicans.

But does this oil-industry-backed study actually make a serious case for weaker environmental protection as a job-creation strategy? No.

Part of the problem is that the study relies heavily on an assumed "multiplier" effect, in which every new job in energy leads indirectly to the creation of 2.5 jobs elsewhere. Republicans, you may recall, were scornful of claims that government aid that helps avoid layoffs of schoolteachers also indirectly helps save jobs in the private sector. But I guess the laws of economics change when it's an oil company rather than a school district doing the hiring.

Moreover, even if you take the study's claims at face value, it offers little reason to believe that dirtier air and water can solve our current employment crisis. All the big numbers in the report are projections for late this decade. The report predicts fewer than 200,000 jobs next year, and fewer than 700,000 even by 2015.

You might want to compare these numbers with a couple of other numbers: the 14 million Americans currently unemployed, and the one million to two million jobs that independent estimates suggest the

Obama plan would create, not in the distant future, but in 2012.

More pollution, then, isn't the route to full employment. But is there a longer-term economic case for less environmental protection? No. Serious economic analysis actually says that we need more protection, not less. The important thing to understand is that the case for pollution control isn't based on some kind of aesthetic distaste for industrial society. Pollution does real, measurable damage, especially to human health.

And policy makers should take that damage into account. We need more politicians like the courageous governor who supported environmental controls on a coal-fired power plant, despite warnings that the plant might be closed, because "I will not create jobs or hold jobs that kill people."Actually, that was Mitt Romney, back in 2003 — the same politician who now demands that we use more coal.

How big are these damages? A new study by researchers at Yale and Middlebury College brings together data from a variety of sources to put a dollar value on the environmental damage various industries inflict. The estimates are far from comprehensive, since they only consider air pollution, and they make no effort to address longer-term issues such as climate change. Even so, the results are stunning.

For it turns out that there are a number of industries inflicting environmental damage that's worth more than the sum of the wages they pay and the profits they earn — which means, in effect, that they destroy value rather than create it. High on the list, by the way, is coal-fired electricity generation, which the Mitt Romney-that-was used to stand up to. As the study's authors say, finding that an industry inflicts large environmental damage compared with its apparent economic return doesn't necessarily mean that the industry should be shut down. What it means, instead, is that "the regulated levels of emissions from the industry are too high." That is, environmental regulations aren't strict enough.

Republicans, of course, have strong incentives to claim otherwise: the big value-destroying industries are concentrated in the energy and natural resources sector, which overwhelmingly donates to the G.O.P. But the reality is that more pollution wouldn't solve our jobs problem. All it would do is make us poorer and sicker.[94]

Conclusion

The government is the custodians of country. But the government comes to power through the assistance of industrialists, mafias, black- marketeers, contractors and cheats. So, clean administration is scarce in most of the countries. Now voters are also corrupt. This results in bad governance. Equity is not maintained among all sector of economy. Absolute power corrupts absolutely.

Governments are the principal enemies of environmental degradation and climate change. These high profile institutions destroy nature, pollute air and water, and reduce cultivable land, forest coverage and lease out mines in the guise of progress of the state. Governments also desire to lease out forests to save forests. There should be an 'International Law' to completely ban leasing out of mines and forests to industrialists and conglomerates of foreign countries to save natural forests, mines, islands, rivers, lagoons and large patches of land for all time to come.

---

[94]Paul Krugman (2011), "Party of pollution", The Opinion Page, The New York Times, October 20, 2011

Andrew Mitchell (2010) says: Then there's the immense potential of natural resources – sun, wind, rivers, tides - that developing countries often possess in abundance. By exploiting these resources, they can sell carbon credits and develop exciting new technologies. Imagine North African countries exporting solar power to Europe. Countries with significant hydropower from Nepal to Mozambique export to neighbouring countries such as India and South Africa.

Or take adaptation, where early action is not only cheaper but also opens up yet more opportunities. Let me give you a couple of examples. Vietnam saved over £4 million a year on maintaining its dykes simply by planting 12,000 hectares of mangrove forest. The cost is less than a £1 million. Some developing countries are currently replanting their mangroves to protect themselves from tsunamis – and in so doing are supporting biodiversity and fish nurseries. In Bangladesh, poor farmers are using "scuba rice" which can survive underwater for up to two weeks. In Sub-Saharan Africa, some countries are developing new agricultural techniques, including drip irrigation and low-till planting, to save water and reduce emissions.[95]

The Presidents, Prime Ministers or Military rulers leasing out mines, forests, islands or thousand acres of land to other governments or Corporate should be treated as **'Environment Criminal'** and that should be equivalent to **'War Criminal'** as practiced during World War II.

We have to protect the NATURE to usher in an era of WORLD PEACE. Let the world be in peace forever.

---

[95]Speech by Andrew Mitchell, International Development Secretary, at a Climate and Development Knowledge Network event at British Council on 18 November 2010

Chapter X

WORLD PEACE IS POSSIBLE

No nation, however large or small, wealthy or poor, can escape the impact of climate change. Rising sea levels threaten every coastline. More powerful storms and floods threaten every continent. More frequent drought and crop failures breed hunger and conflict in places where hunger and conflict already thrive. On shrinking islands, families are already being forced to flee their homes as climate refugees. The security and stability of each nation and all peoples – our prosperity, our health, and our safety – are in jeopardy. And the time we have to reverse this tide is running out.[96]

Barack Hussein Obama, President of USA

Volatile rainfall and temperature trends in many parts of the world have exerted significant pressure on available land, water and food resources leading to

[96]Barack Hussein Obama on Climate Change on Tuesday at the United Nations as released by the White House, New York Times on September 22, 2009

diminishing food stocks, inadequate water supply, mass migration and desertification. It is reported that rapidly changing variables in the atmosphere could expose an additional 250 million people to increased water stress in Africa by 2020, with yields from rain-fed agriculture dropping by 50 percent. The likelihood of flooding in Asia could rise from 10 to 40 percent, affecting lives and livelihood of millions. The loss of biodiversity in Latin America would have global ramifications and could precipitate mass displacement.

By 2050, water resources in Caribbean and Pacific Islands are expected to be insufficient to meet demand. Subsequently, millions will be pushed from subsistence to desperation and heightened competition for scarce resources would create flash points that could trigger violence. These developments have dire implications for peace and sustainable economic development. This panel will analyze recent trends in climate change, explore the climate-conflict nexus and consider recommendations to address potentially harmful effects and forestall potential violence.[97]

In this chapter, Environment for Peace: Securing the Future, Climate-related Disaster, Climate Change and the United Nations, UN sets Humanitarian Agenda, The Cost of Conflicts in Middle East, From Conflicts to Peace Building, International Community must Take Steps, Eco-tourism, Indian herbal medicines, Environment and World Peace, are discussed and suggestions and policy options are drawn for securing a better environment for world peace.

Environment for Peace: Securing the Future

The United Nations Environment Program (UNEP) and the United Nations Development Program (UNDP)

---

[97]Intergovernmental Panel on Climate Change

have joint poverty and environment projects in Kenya, Tanzania and Rwanda, and are also working together to help other countries to mainstream environmental considerations into their national MDG implementation plans. The UNEP and UNDP share concerns that the environment has not been taken as seriously as it should have been in MDG-related activities to date, a point that was strongly made by some ministerial delegations at the UNEP Governing Council meeting in February 2005.[98]

In response to findings from the Millennium Project, the Millennium Ecosystem Assessment and the UNDP 100-country study on the implementation of the MDGs, UNEP organized two workshops in July and October 2005 on mainstreaming the environment into the MDGs through the institutional frameworks and mandates of multilateral environmental agreements (MEAs). Based on the outcome of these consultations, a workshop organized in London in October 2005 explored the development of pro-poor markets for ecosystem services using the MEAs. These meetings have now resulted in the creation of UNEP-wide task force on conservation finance.

Environment for Cooperation

There is a growing understanding that environmental degradation, inequitable access to critical natural resources and the trans-boundary movement of hazardous materials all represent potential flashpoints for conflict. However, history has repeatedly shown that they are also catalysts for cooperation. Problems of shared resources regularly produce shared solutions. UNEP is working with the Organization for Security and Cooperation in Europe (OSCE), UNDP and NATO on the Environment and Security Initiative (ENVSEC) to help countries in

---

[98]United Nations Environment Program, Annual; Report 2005

Central Asia, the southern Caucasus and southeastern Europe to assess and address environment and security hot-spots that pose security risks to communities within and across national borders. An ENVSEC assessment in Eastern Europe (Belarus, Moldova, and Ukraine) started in late 2005.

In preparation for the 2005 World Summit, the UN Secretary-General constituted a High-Level Panel on Threats, Challenges and Change. The panel identified six clusters of threats to human security, including the economic and social threats posed by poverty, infectious disease and environmental degradation. Ninety per cent of current conflicts are found in the poorest 30 per cent of countries. The poorest countries have the greatest environmental challenges. Environmental degradation also intensifies poverty. This is why UNEP maintains that protecting and sustainably managing the environment and placing a true value on the planet's natural assets is the peace policy of the future.

According to the UN Millennium Project, "environmental sustainability is the foundation on which strategies for achieving all the other Millennium Development Goals (MDGs) must be built." The UNEP Poverty and Environment Project is designed to integrate environmental sustainability into national development processes and poverty reduction strategies so that economic and social development is not undermined by environmental degradation. Work plans are now being implemented in seven pilot countries— Mali, Mauritania, Kenya, Rwanda, Uganda, Tanzania and Mozambique—to demonstrate why the environment matters in terms of development and how environment can be included in national development processes.

Environment for the MDGs:

A key aspect of the Poverty and Environment Project is UNEP's cooperation with the UN Development Program (UNDP). The UNEP / UNDP Poverty and Environment Initiative were launched at the High Level Poverty and Environment Partnership 'Environment for the MDGs' event at the 2005 World Summit, in September in New York. The Initiative is a flagship for cooperation between the two UN agencies, and essentially means that UNDP and UNEP have combined their separate poverty and environment activities to demonstrate that an integrated approach should be taken to environment and development.

Environment for a secure future

Environment for peace UNEP-led ENVSEC assessments help to identify environmental threats, such as sources of cross border pollution, and necessary actions for their mitigation and elimination. They also serve to build confidence between countries and ethnic groups by facilitating dialogue on common environmental problems and offering possibilities for cooperation. The ENVSEC portfolio currently includes 40 projects prepared and implemented in cooperation with national governments, research institutions and non-governmental organizations (NGOs).

In May 2005, ENVSEC organized a sub-regional conference in Cluj-Napoca, Romania, in cooperation with Romania's Ministry of Environment and Water Management on Reducing Environment and Security Risks from Mining in South Eastern Europe and the Tisza River Basin. The conference adopted the Cluj-Declaration emphasizing the need for cooperation at all levels to assess and find solutions to environmental problems related to mining, many of which could become sources of regional conflict.

The publication '**Mining for Closure: Policies and Guidelines for Sustainable Mining Practice and Closure of Mines'** presents a basis for the development of corporate practice, regulatory frameworks, governance guidelines and financial and insurance markets suitable for the support of a modern mining industry in the region.

Central Asia's Ferghana Valley claimed global attention in early 2005 due to political developments in Kyrgyzstan and Uzbekistan. At the time, ENVSEC partners were finalizing a one-year process of identifying environmental threats to regional security and opportunities for cross-border dialogue in the area. The in-depth assessment for the Ferghana Valley was launched at the Meeting of the Parties to the Aarhus Convention in Almaty on May 27, 2005, and at the International Conference on Regional Cooperation in Trans-boundary Water Basins, in Dushanbe, in June 2005. Elsewhere, UNEP convened an expert group in March 2005 to help to define strategies for its Initiative on Environment and Conflict Prevention. UNEP started regional assessments in Latin America and the Caribbean and in the Asia-Pacific region in 2005. A similar assessment will be conducted in Africa in early 2006. The reports will be compiled and presented to the UNEP Governing Council in 2007 and will feed into the next Global Environment Outlook report, GEO-4, also scheduled for 2007.

Environment for Security

Nowhere is the importance of the environment as a foundation for development more obvious than in countries where the environment has been severely degraded. In Afghanistan, more than two decades of conflict, military activity, refugee movement and the collapse of national, provincial and local governance and institutional capacity have seen Afghanistan's natural environment severely degraded. In a country where more than 80 per cent of the population relies directly on the country's natural resource base for daily subsistence it is therefore crucial that peace building, environment and development go hand- in-hand.

In 2002, UNEP started work in Afghanistan by developing a Post-Conflict Environmental Assessment, which was published in January 2003. Based on identified environmental needs, UNEP was asked by the newly established Ministry of Irrigation, Water Resources and Environment to initiate a Capacity and Institution Building Program for Environmental Management. The purpose of the five-year program is to develop a stand-alone and self-sufficient environmental administration with the required technical capacity to implement newly developed environmental law and policy and re-establish sustainable resource management across the country.

Recognizing the importance of a strong environmental administration, UNEP has focused its assistance to the National Environmental Protection Agency (NEPA), the successor institution to the Ministry of Irrigation, Water Resources and the Environment. Sustainable management of environmental resources can only happen when national and local-level institutions have clear mandates, effective and coordinated structures, technically skilled staff and sufficient financial resources. To achieve these goals, UNEP provided technical support to NEPA for ongoing reform and reorganization. Concurrent with the development of the environmental institutions is the development of environmental policy and the establishment of a realistic environmental legal framework. In this regard, UNEP provided environmental legal support to NEPA during the drafting and review of key natural resource laws. The main focus was to support the development of the Environmental Act while ensuring

Afghan ownership and sufficient consultation between relevant ministries and stakeholders.

During the drafting of the act, UNEP also helped to ensure Afghanistan fulfilled its legal obligations under various multilateral environmental agreements. The new act, which came into force in late December 2005, is a fundamental step forward for environmental governance, and provides the legal backbone for NEPA to develop effective policies and regulations in 2006. Two priority areas include environmental impact assessment and pollution control. Moving away from Kabul into the provinces, UNEP and NEPA are seeking to reestablish community-based natural resources management structures and incentive programmes. In 2005, two pilot sites were identified near Herat where UNEP, in cooperation with UN-HABITAT, are supporting community-led reforestation efforts and restoration of local underground irrigation systems.

UNEP is also contributing technical expertise to the Green Afghanistan Initiative, which aims to coordinate activities, mobilize funds and provide technical expertise for UN, non-governmental and governmental projects aimed at 'Greening Afghanistan'. At the regional level, UNEP broke new ground by hosting a technical meeting between the Islamic Republics of Iran and Afghanistan on the shared Sistan Basin wetlands. The meeting helped to initiate a constructive dialogue on restoration and sustainable development strategies for the Sistan region between senior technical representatives.

The two delegations committed to establish national advisory committees as well as to develop a joint Global Environment Facility (GEF) project for the restoration of the Sistan wetlands. All of the above activities have included extensive technical and professional training to 25 national staff as well as the provision of equipment, including computers,

Internet connections and office furniture. In 2005, technical in-country training focused on environmental impact assessment, pollution control, multilateral environmental agreements and environmental law. Additionally, 10 staff members were sent to the Asian Institute of Technology in Bangkok for training in environmental management, geographic information systems, library management and report writing.

Support for Africa

The challenges facing Afghanistan are not unique to that country. A number of countries in Africa with severe conflict-related environmental challenges have requested UNEP's help. UNEP opened its field office to provide post-conflict environmental assistance to Liberia in April. Liberia is the first African country to receive post-conflict environmental assistance from the organization and UNEP has become the focal point for environmental issues within the UN Country Team and Common Country Assessment process.

The 14 years of conflict in Liberia displaced approximately 500,000 Liberians, either as Internally Displaced Persons or as refugees. UNEP is working to mitigate the current environmental impacts of displacement and also to provide environmental assistance for contingency planning undertaken by the UN Country Team to deal with possible future events. In the course of the year UNEP worked with UN agencies, the Government of Liberia and national and international NGOs to raise the profile of the environmental considerations of displacement in Liberia. This culminated in a two-week training workshop for 20 Liberians specialists to identify and address key environmental issues relating to the sitting and management of camps. In light of Liberia's history of timber-funded conflict, UNEP is also providing technical assistance to the Liberia Forest

Initiative, a body conducting forest sector reforms, to ensure the transparent management of forest resources.

In Sudan, the signing of a comprehensive new peace agreement on 9 January 2005 has brought renewed hope for political stability and development after a period of protracted armed conflict. Key issues to be addressed as Sudan moves towards reconstruction include food security and livelihoods, support of internally displaced persons and returnees, the rule of law and governance, education, mine clearance and infrastructure repair. UNEP has already successfully integrated $18.8 million for environmental capacity building in the Joint Needs Assessment. The prominence of the environment on the development agenda reflects the importance of natural resources in Sudan.

Following the Joint Needs Assessment, UNEP began a post-conflict assessment of the environment in Sudan in November 2005. A fact-finding mission was conducted in July, followed by a technical mission in September and October to hold discussions with key UN agencies and government stakeholders. UNEP has completed an environmental sector plan for Sudan and is providing technical environmental support to other UN agencies as needed. UNEP is currently working to establish field offices in both Khartoum in North Sudan and Juba in South Sudan. A full post-conflict environmental assessment is being planned for early 2006.

In October UNEP responded to a request from the UN country team in Sierra Leone to provide assistance to the government's plans on creating a new National Commission on Environment and Forestry. UNEP is also participating in a Joint Needs Assessment for Somalia, led by the World Bank. Somalia is one of the poorest and least developed countries in the world and as such presents unique challenges in terms of natural resource management. Due to the protracted civil war, up-to-date environmental data is United Nations Environment Program scarce. UNEP is the lead agency responsible for identifying key environmental issues in Somalia. In addition, UNEP is providing support to other agencies and is helping to identify crosscutting environmental issues relevant to other sectors.

A New Future for Iraq

UNEP has been working to support the rehabilitation of Iraq's environment and environmental management infrastructure since 2003. UNEP is part of the UN Country Team for Iraq. It screens all programs and projects for environmental impacts, and assists with mainstreaming environmental issues in the Iraq Trust Fund cluster system. During 2005, UNEP's work emphasized strengthening the capacity of the Ministry of Environment through a series of Ministerial consultations and training of Iraq's government officials. A variety of targeted workshops were organized on environmental topics such as MEAs, emergency response during oil spills, environmental site assessment, environmental law, biodiversity and natural resources management, remote sensing and environmental impact assessment.

UNEP has also helped the Ministry of Environment to identify training and other human resources needs. Progress has been made, in cooperation with the World Health Organization (WHO), towards the establishment of an Environmental Information Centre within the Ministry of Environment to provide a central depository for baseline data. In October 2005, UNEP trained four staff from the Ministry of Environment in library and information management at UNEP's headquarters in Nairobi.

Among the high-profilers environmental issues related to Iraq is the fate of the Iraqi Marshlands, the most extensive wetland system in the Middle East. By 2002 they were almost completely destroyed as an ecosystem as a consequence of massive drainage works and upstream damming in the 1980s and 1990s. Hundreds of thousands of Marsh Arabs were displaced, threatening a centuries-old culture. The impact on biodiversity was also catastrophic, with the possible extinction of a number of species. Since 2004, UNEP's Support for Environmental Management of the Iraqi Marshlands project has worked to help restore and manage the Marshlands environment, and to provide clean water and sanitation systems in an environmentally sustainable manner. This project is administered through the UNDG Iraq Trust Fund, with funding from the Government of Japan. In 2005, the project launched pilot projects in six communities, bringing immediate relief to 15,000 inhabitants by improving their basic living conditions. In addition, it has improved the capacity and knowledge of approximately 190 Iraqi decision-makers, technical experts, and community leaders in various elements of Marshland management. The project has also supported community-level initiatives, and trained community representatives on how to identify needs and put together proposals that reflect local priorities.

UNEP has also been improving dialogue and access to information and management tools, above all through the Marshland Information Network, which provides an Internet-based forum for data and information sharing. UNEP has also introduced the Iraq Marshlands Observation System for systematic monitoring of the re-flooding of the Marshlands. Such data analysis efforts have revealed that the total extension of wetland vegetation and surface area has reached approximately 50 per cent of the pre-drainage marshland extent.

Iraq also has an estimated several thousand contaminated sites from a combination of general industrial activity, military activity and post conflict damage and looting. During 2005, UNEP conducted a site assessment of five priority contaminated sites with the Iraqi Ministry of Environment. The assessment was managed remotely by UNEP's project office in Amman due to security constraints, with the on-the-ground work done by teams of Iraqi experts from the Ministry of Environment. The Assessment of Environmental Hot Spots in Iraq report, released in November 2005, identified the cyanide-contaminated Al Qadissiya site south of Baghdad, which is openly accessible to the public, as needing immediate risk reduction measures. In response to the report, a clean-up project at this hotspot site was formulated and funded by the Iraq Trust Fund as a 'quick impact project'. UNEP started the cleanup of the site in late 2005.

To address the large number of remaining contaminated sites, UNEP provided technical training to 300 Iraqi experts to support the development of an Iraqi-managed contaminated site assessment and remediation programme. In addition, 16 experts from the Iraq Ministry of Environment's Radiation Prevention Centre were trained in depleted uranium field measurement techniques, reconnaissance, sampling and site clean-up measures during two workshops organized in association with the International Atomic Energy Agency and WHO.

Occupied Palestinian Territories

In 2005, UNEP conducted a series of capacity building workshops on waste management and environmental impact assessment for Palestinian experts from the Environmental Quality Authority. UNEP also acted as the lead agency for the environment in the UN Common Country Assessment process for the Occupied Palestinian Territories. The major event in the region in 2005, however, was the disengagement by Israel from Gaza. It was agreed that UNEP would carry out an environmental assessment in Gaza following the disengagement.

The objective of the assessment was to identify areas of environmental interest and concern and use the results for interim corrective measures, if required, and long term resource planning. UNEP sent a team of eight UNEP staff members, plus external environmental experts experienced in asbestos, contaminated land, hazardous waste, marine and coastal environment, and water resources, to Gaza between 9 and 18 December 2005.

The fieldwork covered all 21 disengaged settlements and the Erez industrial site. Samples were taken and shipped to an independent laboratory in Europe. UNEP's partners were the Palestinian Environmental Quality Authority (EQA) and the Palestinian Water Authority (PWA) on the Palestinian side, and the Ministry of Environment on the Israeli side. Given that UNDP will be in charge of the work related to sorting, recycling and removal of rubble originating from demolished buildings, UNEP is also providing environmental expertise to UNDP on matters related to the disengaged areas in Gaza. The assessment report was published in 2006.

Climate-related Disaster

Dr. Pachauri emphasizes that melting Antarctic sheets and receding of Arctic caps are the most alarming climate story of this decade.

The first decade of the 21st century has clearly been a period when disasters of various kinds have not only caused enormous damage across the world, but concern on how these might increase in the future has grown dramatically. In 2003, there was a major heat wave in Europe, with Paris and surrounding areas being the worst affected, and resulting in approximately 35,000 deaths. The Fourth Assessment Report (AR4) of the IPCC has clearly brought out the increase that has taken place in heat waves, and that climate change is projected to increase the health risks due to heat waves and frequency of wild fires in Europe. More recently in 2010, Russia suffered from a severe heat wave, which led to forest fires on an unprecedented scale.

Several other disasters have also been witnessed in this past decade including the Asian tsunami, which hit a number of countries in Asia including India in 2004 and had an impact as far as the eastern shores of the African continent as well. Other occurrences, which caused large-scale devastation, were the recent earthquake in Haiti in 2010 and earlier earthquakes including the one that took place in Gujarat in January 2001, and the massive tremor in 2005 when a large part of Kashmir was devastated.

Several parts of the globe have also suffered from hurricanes during the decade, the worst of which were Hurricane Katrina during 2005 in the US and Cyclone Nargis, which took place in 2008 in Myanmar. The initial estimate of deaths due to the latter was around 100,000, but more authentic estimates raise this figure to 138,000 deaths. While earthquakes and tsunamis have no link with human induced climate change, certainly in the case of tsunamis sea level rise, which is the result of climate change, makes the impacts far more severe. The estimated increase in sea level rise on an average during the 20th century was 17 cm. Consequently, a tsunami of the type that Asia experienced on Boxing Day in 2004 would no doubt have caused much less damage a century earlier than was the case this decade. In general, climate change exacerbates stresses induced by other factors as in the case of water scarcity, which is becoming a serious problem in different parts of the world.

It was in 1992 that the United Nations Framework Convention on Climate Change (UNFCCC) was agreed on with high expectations that global action to reduce emissions of greenhouse gases (GHGs) would be taken in hand by different countries to meet the growing challenge of climate change, on which scientific consensus has strengthened over the years. To provide teeth to the UNFCCC, the global community agreed on the Kyoto Protocol in 1997, but it took eight years for this to be ratified by the requisite number of developed countries, collectively responsible for the specified level of emissions. And now there is serious questioning of this Protocol itself, which in any case was not ratified by the US and Australia.

The scientific basis for climate change has led to growing concerns among policymakers and the public at large across the globe, and several actions are being taken by countries on their own or collectively, which provide a concrete means for meeting this challenge. The European Union, for instance, has laid down ambitious targets for 20 percent reduction of emissions of GHGs by 2020 over 1990 levels. Other countries like Korea have also made some ambitious commitments which would not only result in the development of technologies and solutions for improving the efficiency of energy use overall but also a substantial shift away from carbon intensive forms of energy supply. On September 22, 2009, the UN Secretary General had convened a daylong meeting of world leaders to discuss the issue of climate change and this gathering attracted over a hundred world leaders from every corner of the globe. It is also worth noting that the Copenhagen Conference of the Parties, which took place in December 2009, attracted well over a hundred heads of States and heads of Governments.

It is, therefore, evident that the leadership of most countries in the world is now seized of the importance of taking action to deal with the growing challenge of climate change, but a binding global agreement as a result of the multilateral negotiations under UNFCCC has proved elusive. Yet, it would be difficult to ignore the fact that the first decade of this century in some sense marks a turning point on action to deal with climate change, because not only are schoolchildren across the globe seized of this problem but world leaders too. The IPCC and Mr. Al Gore shared the Nobel Peace Prize in 2007 and the citation for the award clearly stated "for their efforts to build up and disseminate greater knowledge about man-made climate change."

There is every reason to believe that if awareness on climate change spreads rapidly and people become conscious of the scientific basis for human induced climate change then action will follow in different countries and even down to sub-country and local levels, all of which will collectively help in addressing the problem. However, as the IPCC Fourth Assessment Report clearly specifies, "that neither adaptation nor mitigation alone can avoid all climate change impacts." It also states "adaptation is necessary both in the short term and longer term to address impacts resulting from warming that would occur even for the lowest stabilization scenarios assessed."

This refers essentially to scenarios defining the stabilization of the concentration of GHGs, because growing concentration levels would only lead to higher levels of climate change, which would be accompanied by impacts that would become progressively more frequent and more severe. Consequently, the AR4 states "adaptation and mitigation can complement each other and together significantly reduce the risks of climate change". The occurrence of a specific weather-related disaster cannot be ascribed to human induced climate change, but the trend in their increase is now clear. On the basis of observations, for instance, by the 2080s many millions more people than today are projected to experience floods every year due to sea level rise.

The number affected will be largest in the densely populated mega-deltas of Asia and Africa while small island States are particularly vulnerable.

It was also concluded by the AR4 that altered frequency and intensity of weather together with sea level rise are expected to have mostly adverse effects on natural and human systems. As these impacts become more prominent and more noticeable, action to reduce emissions of GHGs and to adapt to the impacts of climate change will naturally receive support from Governments and leaders of civil society. If that were to happen then clearly the first decade of this century would mark a turning point in our acknowledgement of the problem that we have contributed to since industrialization began and on which scientific evidence is now overwhelming and compelling.

Future generations may, for good reason, and then praise us for bringing about change in this decade which will have significant benefits to humanity and other living species for decades and centuries to come, and more importantly avoid climate-related disaster that would be caused by inaction.[99]

Climate Change and the United Nations

The Indian meteorological data chimes with US statistics, but the consensus signals the magnitude of a 21st century problem which the international

[99]Dr. R K Pachauri is the Chair of IPCC since 2002, Director General of TERI, Chancellor of TERI University and Head of Yale' s Climate and Energy Institute. He received the Nobel Peace Prize on behalf of IPCC along with Mr. Al Gore in 2007

system, devised in Europe and in the last century, is unable to manage.

The problem is global warming. Lest anyone doubt it or argue it ceased in 2005, here are the facts. In 2010, the earth's temperature was higher by 0.62 degrees Celsius on 20th century average making 2010, along with 2005, the hottest year since US records began in 1980. Last year was also the warmest in India since our records began in 1901. Nor was last year an aberration.

The year 2010 actually confirms global warming because it was the 34th consecutive year with temperature above the 20th century global average.

One effect is the diminishing of the Artic sea ice cover. It is at its third smallest since records began in 1979. Another effect is freak weather conditions across the globe.

Clearly, global warming is a clear and present danger. The effects are unfairly borne by the developing world because the problem originated in the industrialized north. The principle of common but differentiated responsibility, the corner stone of Kyoto Protocol, reflects historical reality. However, implementation of principle is near impossible in a world defined by states, which militate against a sense of global responsibility. India demonstrated a sense of it by changing policy on binding CO2 cuts in Cancun. But given the snail's pace and piecemeal nature of such expressions - China, for example, is unwilling to make similar concessions - what is needed is a reformulation of today's international political system so that countries do not merely serve the national interest at the expense of the collective, global interest.[100]

---

[100]Times of India –Editorial

Hence, the United Nations should convene conventions to discuss on global warming. It should promulgate special 'international laws' to reduce global warming. The world organization should also discuss on actions to be taken by the United Nations, if any country violates the 'Climate Laws' or 'Environmental Laws'. The action should be stringent and binding on all countries. If a country violates the Environmental Laws, the President / Prime Minister of those countries should be declared as Environment Criminal. This punishment should be declared as equivalent to War Criminal. The UN should take up this declaration in the Security Council and General Assembly to convince the world forum for arousing world debate on the urgency and intensity of the danger to the all-living beings of the world. A soft approach would not do justice for the greater interest of countries and people.

UN Sets Humanitarian Agenda for 2011:
Save more lives, more quickly

With climate change presaging natural mega-disasters, aid workers facing mounting attacks in conflict areas and the economic crisis crimping resources, the United Nations office coordinating the global humanitarian response announced its agenda for 2011 today: more lives saved, more rapidly, with fewer gaps and less duplication.

Ms. Amos Valerie Amos, who heads the UN Office for the Coordination of Humanitarian Affairs (OCHA) at UN Headquarters in New York, told Member States as follows:

In a changing world there can be no organizational status quo. In 2011, OCHA's structure, in the field and at headquarters, will be more adaptable to the evolving nature of crises, noting that 2010 had been an unprecedented year with more than **250 natural disasters**. By the end of 2011, OCHA will be a more focused organization. It will be better at managing its human resources and there will be greater clarity between the field and headquarters in terms of who does what in line with the Office's theme for '2011 responding in a Changing World'.

Established by the General Assembly in 1991 as the Department of Humanitarian Affairs to ensure a more effective and coherent response to emergencies by coordinating the actions of UN agencies and national and international organizations, OCHA has seen its caseload balloon over the past 20 years, culminating in the 2010 record. From the devastating earthquake in Haiti, which killed 220,000 people and made 1.5 million others homeless, to unprecedented flooding in Pakistan barreling down from the northern mountains to the flatter and agricultural south to affect over 20 million people, from Cook Islands in the Pacific, battered by tropical storms, to post-flood coordination in Albania, OCHA was on hand and on the ground.

Ms. Amos, who serves as Under-Secretary-General for Humanitarian Affairs and Emergency Relief Coordinator, stressed the need to learn the lessons of Haiti and Pakistan where delays, logistics and other issues prevented the initial operations from moving as effectively as desired, and she warned of the mounting complexities confronting humanitarian operations in the future, noting that climate change is playing its part.

Unpredictable and unprecedented weather patterns across Africa, Central America, and South and East Asia displaced tens of millions of people. As the frequency and intensity of natural disasters increase, mega-crises such as the flooding across Pakistan may well become the new normal, making us think again about the speed, scale and effectiveness of our response. Humanitarian work has also become more dangerous. The level of threats and the number of deliberate attacks on aid organizations - our people, equipment and facilities - have risen dramatically. Reaching populations in need to deliver essential services has become more difficult, noting that 63 humanitarian workers were killed in 2010.

And if negotiating these challenges was not enough, the humanitarian community is also dealing with increasing financial pressure. We are being urged to do more with less not only because of the global economic downturn, but also because countries that give us support must account to their populations for the way they have spent their money.

Ms. Amos listed an ambitious list of tasks for the coming year: to coordinate responses, mobilize resources through international appeals, manage quick-response funds, act as a voice for victims, negotiate access to those in need, and provide critical information and analysis as crises unfold. And she listed, too, the global challenges where OCHA will continue to improve its understanding. These are:

(a) Climate change,
(b) Food and energy price increases,
(c) Population growth and
(d) Urbanization.

OCHA, with over 350 aid agencies participated in joint planning exercises. 39 Member States fund this program and Ms. Amos has asked for US $208 million in voluntary contributions for 2011.[101]

The Cost of Conflict in the Middle East

The Strategic Foresight Group is a political think tank based in Mumbai, India. On its inception in 2000, SFG (Strategic Foresight Group) worked on issues

[101]UN Office for the Coordination of Humanitarian Affairs (OCHA) at UN Headquarters in New York, January 21, 2011

pertaining to the sub-continent but with time we have managed to branch out and gain credibility on a more global setting. We have released 3 reports so far on the 'Cost of Conflict' – focusing on conflict between India-Pakistan, Sri Lanka and now the Middle East.

These reports aim to measure the various costs incurred by nation states due to conflict. We measure these costs on several parameters – economic, military, socio-political and even environmental. These reports will help to highlight the detrimental effects of war and consequently push towards conflict resolution and a comprehensive peace process.

The Arab League suggested that SFG to work on a similar report that measures the cost of conflict in the Middle East.

The largest devastation caused to the environment in past Middle East conflicts has been during the Gulf War and the Iran-Iraq war. In the First Gulf War, 10 million barrels of oil were spilt at sea and almost 45 million in the desert. Kuwait suffered from severe landscape degradation with over 20 percent of tree cover lost. Perhaps the most shocking effect was the amount of carbon emissions released into the atmosphere from the burning oil fields. The First Gulf War led to an increase of 1.5 percent in worldwide carbon emissions. To put this number in perspective, in 2003, Saudi Arab constituted 1.17 percent of the world's carbon emissions! Egypt, Israel and Jordan constitute much less than this – between 0 .5 percent and 0.07 percent.

The Iraqi landscape has witnessed environmental devastation caused by countless wars. In Iraq the marshlands shrunk from 15,000 sq. km to a shocking 50 sq km, displacing 100, 000 -300,000 people who lived in the area. One can imagine the tremendous impact this had on the biodiversity in the region – including the extinction of certain sub-species of mammals and a threat to unique wetland bird species.

Other conflicts such as the 2003 Iraq war and the 2006 Lebanon war have caused immense damage through oil and water pollution. The costs are much greater than any benefits accrued from conflict – be it environmental, economic, sociopolitical or otherwise.

The Middle East is an extremely water scarce region and several countries such as Kuwait, Iraq, Israel and Egypt depend on other countries for a steady supply of freshwater.

Water sharing projects can make the peace process more feasible or vice versa. They include:

(a) The Sinai Underground Project;
(b) The 1987 Peace pipeline from Turkey to Gulf Countries, which if enacted would be the longest international water pipeline; and
(c) The much debated Red-Dead Sea Canal, which could be used in electricity generation and solar power.

Now granted the environmental aspects of water sharing projects like the peace canal are contested but they will also help to alleviate current environmental problems such as over-pumping of underground/fossil water resources as well as prevent disputes that may arise from the lack of something as essential as water.

Water will be one of the most prominent causes for disputes in the Middle East or one of the largest potentials for cooperation. Either way it will be a challenge.

The MENA (Middle East and North Africa) region is the water scarcest region in the world. Twelve of the world's 15 water-scarce countries are in MENA.

'Water-scarce' countries have an average of less than 1,000 cubic meters of renewable freshwater per person per year. A majority of the countries in the Middle East have freshwater resources that fall below 250 cubic meters! Moreover water does not have boundaries. It flows freely through countries and adequate allocation and distribution of this freshwater in an already politically tense region such as the Middle East is in many ways a challenge.

Environment Brief

The 'Cost of Conflict in the Middle East' highlights the environmental damage incurred by the region as a result of constant war. It is the first time in the last 60 years that a comprehensive assessment of costs of various conflicts in the region has been undertaken on 97 different parameters. The Governments of Norway and Switzerland, AK Party of Turkey and Qatar Foundation supported the project. Covering the different conflicts from Israel-Palestine, to Iraq and Lebanon, the report outlines the stress on water resources, arable land, forests, and other means of sustenance. Below are some of the key conclusions from the report:

In the First Gulf War, 10 million barrels of oil were spilt at sea and almost 45 million in the desert. In the future, if this amount doubles, it would mean 100-120 million barrels of oil would be wasted – which would equal one day's supply for the entire world.

In **Kuwait**, the First Gulf War caused severe landscape degradation as well, where an estimated 375,000 bunkers and trenches were hollowed into the ground and 20% of tree cover felled.

In **Iraq** the marshlands shrunk from 15,000 sq km to a shocking 50 sq km, displacing 100-300,000 people who lived in the area. There was also tremendous impact on the biodiversity in the region due to the

loss of the marshlands, the loss of agricultural land, extinction of certain sub-species of mammals and a threat to unique wetland bird species.
Between the First Gulf War and the Hezbollah war in 2006, a total of 1,000 miles of coastline and beaches in **Saudi Arabia**, **Kuwait**, **Lebanon**, and **Syria** have been destroyed due to oil slick, which has also polluted the coastlines of **Greece**, **Turkey** and **Cyprus**.

After the 2003 **Iraq** war over 300,000 tonnes of raw sewage are dumped into the Tigris every day. 80 percent of Iraqi's lack access to adequate sanitation, and today the majority of the population are facing rampant incidences of dysentery, cholera and typhoid.

The **Israel-Hezbollah** war of 2006 saw severe damage to the water networks where 45 main distribution units and 285 secondary units, 120 sewage disposal systems, 1 dam etc were destroyed. **South Lebanon** experienced the worst damage where agriculture constitutes 70 percent of all household income.

The report calculates that due to a large number of military bases the green cover in **Israel** has been reduced to a mere 13 percent. (Green Prophet would like to add that there is no other country over the last 100 years who has a net gain in the number of trees planted versus those harvested).

A future conflict in the Middle East could cause more carbon emissions than an industrialized country such as the UK currently produces in one year.The region has a scarcity of water and several countries such as **Saudi Arabia**, **Kuwait**, **Iraq**, **Syria**, **Egypt** and **Israel** have a dependency ration of above 50 percent and are highly dependent on their neighbors.

Climate Change Worrying

The report outlines the possible impact of climate change in the region, which could further exacerbate the water stress leading to conflict. The rise in temperatures and in sea levels could result in the displacement of 2-4 million people in **Egypt**; water shortage in **Syria** by 2020; further sharing of water systems – all of which could lead to a fight over natural resources if there is no cooperation and collaboration between neighbors.

The waterways in the region, such as the Euphrates River System, the Jordan River, the West Bank Aquifers, and the Shatt Al Arab Waterways feed more than one country, and any damage to one could have a cascading effect on several nations.

The report by Strategic Foresight Group argues that a comprehensive peace agreement will make several past projects feasible such as the Sinai Underground Project; the 1987 Peace pipeline from Turkey to Gulf Countries, which if enacted would be the longest international water pipeline; and the much debated Red-Dead Sea Canal, which could be used in electricity generation and solar power.[102]

From Conflicts to Peace Building

Conflicts associated with natural resources are twice as likely to relapse into conflict in the first five years, an imminent report suggests. Indeed the natural resource curse has been a primary determinant of intra-state conflict in terrible theatres of war such as the Democratic Republic of Congo and Liberia. Yet it

---

[102] Green Prophet, February 2, 2009: Green Prophet had the opportunity to interview Gitanjali Bakshi, Research Analyst at the Strategic Foresight Group. The group has produced a report on the environmental impact of conflicts in the Middle East, which was presented at the Palais de Nations in Geneva in February 2009.

extends far beyond the battle to acquire precious commodities. With climate change and population growth placing increasing demands on the environment, it is widely recognized that conflict over basic resources, such as water and arable land, will increase. This new report from the UN calls for environment and natural resource issues to be integrated into peace-building, decrying that less than a quarter of peace negotiations aiming to resolve conflicts linked to natural resources have addressed resource management mechanisms.

The suggestions are:

(a)Natural resources and the environment can be implicated in all phases of the conflict cycle, contributing to the outbreak and perpetuation of violence and undermining prospects for peace.

(b) The environment can itself fall victim to conflict, as direct and indirect environmental damage, coupled with the collapse of institutions, can lead to environmental risks that threaten health, livelihoods and security

(c) Natural resources and the environment can contribute to peace building through economic development, employment generation and sustainable livelihoods

They have offered recommendations as follows:

Further develop UN capacities for early warning and early action - include environmental and natural resource issues in international and regional conflict certification mechanisms to ensure that natural resources can be tracked more effectively

Address natural resources and the environment as part of the peacemaking and peacekeeping process - ensure that there are processes in place within peace agreements for the transparent, equitable and legitimate definition and realization of property rights and resource revenues and tenure

Integrate natural resource and environmental issues into post-conflict planning - systematically conduct post-conflict environmental assessments that identify environmental risks to human health, livelihoods and security and prioritize needs in the short and medium term. [103]

International Community Must

Save the Environment

Nick Mabey[104] as opined that conflict over natural resources, whether driven by need or greed, has always been a part of human society. There is also strong evidence that social tensions driven by past climatic change destroyed many advanced societies- such as the long-wave droughts, which drove the collapse of early civilizations in Mesopotamia and Peru.

The coming decades will see rising resource scarcity, greater environmental degradation and increasingly disruptive climatic change. In fact, in an increasingly uncertain world these trends are disturbingly predictable. The question is whether increasing environmental and resource pressures will reduce security and stability, or will our political, governance and security systems be able to manage them peacefully?

---

[103]Matthew, R, O. Brown and D. Jensen, "From conflict to peace building: the role of natural resources and the environment", United Nations Environment Program (2009), Eldis Org. Livelihood Connect reporter. June 30, 2009.

[104]Nick Mabey (2006), "Foreword – Inventory of Environment and Security Policies and Practices', Institute for Environmental Security', The Hague

The lack of focus on environmental security issues could suggest that security professionals in the major developed powers hold the more optimistic view. More disturbingly it could indicate that these new realities have yet to be integrated into security strategies and policy frameworks.

However, these issues are fast rising up the global political agenda. Geopolitical competition for fossil and mineral resources has become the main source of 19th century style "great power" tensions in today's interdependent world. By empowering autocratic rulers in Africa and Central Asia against their people, this competition is also setting the stage for violent internal crisis and the consequent disruption of energy supplies.

Security issues where resource and environmental factors play key roles are the stuff of day-to-day foreign policy: from land conflicts between pastoralists and agriculturalists in Darfur; to the role of oil in fuelling and sustaining of separatist conflict in the Niger Delta and Aceh. Many countries already face significant challenges in coping with existing climate variability; for example, the World Bank estimates that floods and drought in Kenya in the late 1990s resulted in direct economic costs of $4.8 billion, or 22 percent of GDP per annum

Though each particular crisis or conflict has its own unique dynamic based on local politics, economics and history; strong patterns are clear. The corrupting influence of point source revenues – whether from natural resources, drugs, pipelines or weapons - on elites is the most powerful source of underdevelopment and failing economies. The World Bank estimates that developing countries without major natural resources have grown 2-3 times faster than those with high resource endowment over the last 40 years. Politicized revenue allocation from natural resources based around ethnic, religious or regional lines has been a major driver of internal conflict.

Natural resource revenues are feeding corruption and organized crime, which destabilize governments; create extreme finance conflicts and provide a logistical infrastructure for international terrorism.

Politicized allocation of water and land is constantly driving low level conflict, which can spark into major violence when linked to ethnic, national and other divisions. Migration away from environmentally degraded regions causes confrontation across borders and inside countries, from Africa to Latin America.

There is no lack of tools and policy options to address these issues. A wealth of experience exists on managing environmental disputes, designing governance systems, anti-corruption measures, resource allocation mechanisms and participative resources management that could be used to reduce instability risks. There is also a wealth of international agreements– on forests, water, environmental democracy, desertification, and conflict resources – which could be strengthened as foreign policy tools.

However, despite a few high profile exceptions such as the action to control trade in "conflict diamonds", there has been a lack of concerted international effort to address the resource and environmental roots of instability. Cases, which have been addressed, have required extensive campaigning from non-governmental groups to secure action.

In a world of rising scarcity this reactive approach will not preserve security and stability. Strategists always caution against fighting the last war, and the need to explore future threats away from the biases of current priorities. However, despite a plethora of recent reports - from the Africa Commission, the UN

High Level Panel and even the Pentagon - identifying competition for oil and gas supply, resource scarcity and climate change as key drivers of political stress and conflict, the impact on practical action has been weak.

It is perhaps unsurprising that the identification of a new threat does not by itself result in an effective response. It takes time for countries to understand the strategic importance of new threats on their vital interests, and to reorder existing priorities. It takes even longer to develop effective instruments to respond. Security systems formed in the strategic certainties of the Cold War have struggled to respond to a new fluid strategic environment where the source of threats is constantly shifting. But this is changing.

The lessons of the past decade and in particular the Balkan Wars, Rwanda and 9/11 have radically transformed national security priorities. Across the major powers these now focus less on the strength of other countries, and more on the need to tackle instability and failing states; to achieve energy security; prevent the development of "ungoverned spaces" open to abuse by terrorists and organized criminals; and address the internal conflicts which can breed and support international terrorism.

Tackling these threats requires a very different type of security apparatus typified by three core approaches:

(a) **Preventive:** Greater emphases on effective governance, prevention of conflict, and stabilization of countries after conflict and crisis have emerged.

(b) **Integrated:** The need for "whole government approaches" is to combine military, diplomatic, developmental and justice system capabilities

(c) **Convergent:** ensuring the complementarities between different policy objectives and instruments are assessed when in setting priorities; for example, the economic, developmental and security benefits of tackling illegal logging.

These principles are also familiar as forming the core of "sustainable development" policy approaches, and in many ways security policy is becoming more like other areas of international policy. At the core of the challenge is how to motivate consistent investment of financial and political capital into long-term prevention of conflict and reduction of instability. This is a major task of strategic and public sector reform, and will take years to complete.

There is also a chance that the emergence of more traditional military threats could reverse this progress. Assuming this reversal does not happen, these trends will make it easier to incorporate environmental and resource issues into security policy, but only as one driver of future risks. Security strategies also need to better integrate other rising structural risks of instability driven by HIV/AIDs, religious fundamentalism, economic dislocation from trade shifts, rapid urbanization and drug trafficking and use.

Understanding how these different issues interlink and re-enforce vulnerability to crisis and conflict is at the core of defining effective responses. For example, how will commodity dependence, trade liberalization, organized crime, youth unemployment and climate changes evolve to impact the stability of the Caribbean? How this affect organized crime and the drug trade, and what will be done to lower the risk of crisis?

This survey shows that many countries are currently undertaking reforms to improve their conflict prevention and crisis response architectures. However, there is a need for much more radical and concerted change if security objectives are to be met.

Work carried out by UK Prime Minister's Strategy Unit showed that despite recent improvements, government systems have significant weaknesses in developing strategic approaches to reducing structural risks of instability and conflict in the medium to long term. These weaknesses are deeply rooted in all parts of government systems, and not confined to commonly discussed issues of deficient early warning and insufficient political will to act.

There is a critical opportunity to accelerate the process of systemic reform in the next few years. The political imperative for better systems to tackle crises is growing, not least in the European Union and its neighbourhood. The experience of DRC, Afghanistan and Iraq has further strengthened the cost-benefit case for investing in prevention. The increased emphasis on poverty reduction has liberated larger financial resources to be invested in fragile states, particularly in Africa - most of which are economically dependent on natural resources. Rising awareness of the future impacts of climate change is increasing attention on the environmental drivers of instability.

Experts on the environmental and resource aspects of security can help to drive these changes in governments along with actors from the health, conflict prevention communities and development. A joined-up approach outside governments will help drive joined-up action from governments.

This is probably best done through a focus on critical "problem clusters", rather than in a "grand theory" of system redesign, and there are many candid areas. Progress is already being made to strengthen international processes to prevent the use of natural resources to fund conflict, but more could be done to extend and deepen this approach.

More effort could be given to managing the negative cycle of natural resource is management, corruption, underdevelopment and instability, especially in energy exporting countries in Africa and Central Asia.

A much more detailed picture of the impact of climate change on stability, and the links between climate security and energy security, is needed to drive medium to long-term security and energy policy.

The growing impacts of climate change will multiply all these tensions, and the experience of the last decade is that climatic changes will happen faster than we currently expect. If effective systems for preventive action are not built the international community will face multiple re-enforcing crises, and be left trying to patch up societies with an expensive combination of humanitarian and military intervention, but there would be little chance of sustainable success.

We Must Save Antarctica

Diary of Amundsen, 1911

Erling Kagge explains that Antarctica must be saved, the way it is now.[105]

It was far better to ski toward the South Pole than to reach it. When I started out my journey in November 1992, everything was white all the way out to the horizon. As the weeks passed, I began to see more colours: variations of white, a bit of blue, green and yellow. By the time the strange-looking buildings of the Amundsen-Scott base appeared on the horizon 50 days later, I felt relief but also disappointment, and thought about skiing past it, back into the white nothingness.

---

[105]Erling Kagge (2011), "Keep Antarctica the way it is", The New York Times, December 16, 2011 (News from OSLO)

The South Pole was considered the last place on earth when a fellow Norwegian, Roald Amundsen, arrived with four companions, a few dozen dogs and four sledges **100 years ago on December 14.** He beat his famous rival, the British explorer Robert Falcon Scott, by a little more than a month. Scott never returned.

The world had been watching. Norway had just gained its independence. Britain was still a superpower but its empire was fading. Amundsen's expedition changed the way we thought about the world. It is a fact that Amundsen's feat touched Antarctica: **The whole world has now been discovered** (the New York Times dated March 8, 1912)**.**

We should use this anniversary to think about the future of this continent, the coldest, driest, windiest place on earth, where the ice is up to two miles thick in places. What Scott saw as a forsaken landscape — "Great God?

Amundsen wrote in his diary on November 13, 1911. "The country lay before us in the brilliant light. This is an awful place. Shining white, bright blue, utterly black illuminated by sunlight, the country looks like a fairy tale. Precipices, peaks on peaks, so cragged and so wild, it lies unseen and virgin-like. Amundsen found enthralling."

The terrain Amundsen saw was totally different from anything that he or anyone else had ever seen: an entire continent covered by ice and snow. Comparisons failed him. In his diary, he began by likening the landscape to Hardangervidda, the spare, treeless mountain range in western Norway where he had trained for his Antarctic expedition. But he realized that Antarctica's vastness resembles only itself.

I ventured into that vastness 81 years after Amundsen, skiing Nordic-style nearly 840 miles from the ocean ice to the South Pole. I was alone, without even a radio. For me, as for Amundsen, Antarctica was a land of dreams. It was an imagined land long before anyone had seen the continent. The Greek philosophers wrote of a terra australis incognita, the unknown land of the south.

Since the Age of Enlightenment, nature has been regarded first and foremost for its potential for exploitation. We Norwegians are petro-holics, for instance, and our oil has made us prosperous in a world of economic uncertainty. But the world should leave Antarctica as it is. I became convinced, as I wrote in my journal:

That the Polar Regions will have its greatest worth for mankind, not by being regulated and exploited, but by being left nearly untouched by man.

With all the challenges the world faces, we don't need to civilize another continent. In a world where people are living closer and closer and facing more rules and expectations, we still need a vast white nothingness — "something," as I wrote in my journey, "which is not fully explored and made ordinary... A continent may be a state of mind."

The land Amundsen explored and told the world about is still frozen in time. I hope this anniversary can be a reminder that Antarctica's value cannot be measured only in money and power, but also in emotion. There should exist in the world a place that is left almost untouched.

Environment and World Peace

Environment allows animal kingdom and plant kingdom to compete among them, but at the same time it allows them to live and grow in peace. Adequate availability of air, water, sunlight and space would keep the environment clean. When an individual is assured of engagement and food, when the nature follows a systematic climatic cycle, it would deem that all are safe and living in peace. Of course, world peace would be possible when the government undertakes policies and programs for the welfare of vulnerable people and there is no war among nations. It looks like a utopian thought, but it is possible.

The Twentieth century witnessed two great world wars (1914–1919 and 1939–1945). Each day 20 wars are being fought in the world even today. These wars are manmade; few individuals cause it because of whims of political leaders, boundary problems, and corruption and for assuming power. All these problems could be settled by international laws, strengthening the United Nations and through mutual discussions.

It could be possible if governments sincerely try to protect 'environment' in their countries by appropriate State laws and unbiased quick action.

It is possible by protecting forests, rivers, mountains, land and the tribal people. It is possible by restricting polluting industries and restricting vehicular traffic. It is possible by checking the growth of cities, towns and industrial houses.

It is desirable that we should not create problems; but it is possible that we can solve the existing problems amiably and amicably. The government should remember that 'the government is for the people, by the people and of the people.'

Excepting a number of countries, the peculiar geographical features and geographical locations control the habits and economic status of the people. The extensive range of hilly forests, several lofty peaks, long stretch of coalmines, excellent Rivera in system, brackish waters and coastal plains altogether have endows the state with a wide range of ecological habitats for a diverse and broad spectrum of vegetation. Many forests have a number of medicinal and economically important species, all of which need a scientific and sustainable management.

But degradation of forests would cause climate change, change in rainfall pattern, global warming, adding of CO2 in air and invites drought and flood. Forest supplies fire wood, forest fruits, edible roots, medicinal plants, and herbs for the use of tribal people. Forest grazing by goats, cows do not add costs to the peasants and tribal people. Forests supply log of wood, timber and bamboo for construction of houses in both rural and urban areas.

In other words, forest can sustain the environment and supply the living possibilities to a vast section of people, which are neglected by the governments. As long as forests survive to a minimum of 1/3rd or 1/4th of geographical areas, the climate would be conducive for the human population.

But the governments are constantly reducing forest area through infrastructure development process, such as railways, high ways, industries, irrigation dams or government offices. Moreover, unauthorized occupations by individuals have posed challenges to the governments and even courts. This has become a source of income to the corrupt officials. It is the corrupt governments and corrupt officials, which are responsible for loss of forest cover. But we can save the earth and its living animals and plants.

Seattle would be carbon neutral

Changing with the Climate

In Seattle, how changes in policy help prepare for changes in climate. **Seattle hopes to become the world's first climate-neutral city**. It's no small task: The City must account for, and reduce, the carbon footprint of everything from transportation to trash for hundreds of thousands of people. City Council President Richard Conlin expresses Seattle would be carbon neutral. The Cedar River Watershed - One-Way Seattle is adapting to a changing climate is by creating habitat management plans for the Cedar, Skagit, Pend Oreille, and Tolt Watersheds.

The climate is already changing and will keep changing —no matter how rapidly we are able to turn around greenhouse gas accumulation. So we will need a strategy for adapting to the expected impacts. Here is what Seattle is doing.

The outstanding example of the City's work to adapt to climate change is our program to manage the water supply that Seattle owns and operates, which serves not only the City, but also most of the surrounding King County suburbs. Seattle's water conservation strategy has reduced water consumption in our system to the levels of the 1960s, even though we serve more than 40 percent more people than we did then. We have developed a state of the art reservoir management and stream flow-forecasting model and implemented an asset management strategy that includes climate change as a risk factor. We can withstand the impacts of climate change and still guarantee the water supply for at least the next fifty years.

Seattle City Light has also long been a leader in energy conservation and developing carbon neutral resources, but as the climate changes, reduced snow pack and stream flows will impact our hydroelectric capacity. We will continue to mitigate climate impacts by relying on conservation and renewable resources for our future energy needs. In the next few years, we will have to figure out how to adapt our hydro system to changes in power availability.

The vulnerability of City infrastructure is a critical problem. We have adopted regulations and programs to ensure that buildings are as resilient as possible and to moderate expected issues such as increased storm water runoff. To address the impact of increased storm events on our drainage system and flooding problems, the City has adopted a Green Storm water Infrastructure program to employ natural, on-site drainage strategies to minimize the amount of storm water that flows into pipes and conveyance systems. Seattle's drainage system is designed for the "typical" Seattle rain event, a slow and steady rainfall. Sharp, sudden storms can overwhelm that. Rather than resize the entire storm sewer system, a hugely expensive and disruptive project, our best strategy is to reduce flow into it.

In transportation, we are expanding the options that people have to travel so they can manage in the event of infrastructure damage. We also have policies to ensure that new and rebuilt bridges and seawalls are able to withstand sea level rise, and to limit development in coastal areas.

Strategies to protect vulnerable populations from increasing numbers of extreme weather events are being incorporated into emergency management and public health planning. The City is developing improved assessments and mitigation programs for our urban watersheds and a campaign to expand and protect our tree cover. Seattle also has responsibility for four areas outside the City limits that we impact with our hydroelectric dams and water storage, and we have created habitat management plans for the Cedar, Skagit, Pend Oreille, and Tolt Watersheds.

Finally, we have adopted a race and social justice lens to analyze the impacts of budget, program, and policy proposals, and will use this to guide our work on climate adaptation.

Other specific steps currently underway include:

(a) Creating a methodology for analyzing sea level rise for City projects, which will be piloted with the Elliott Bay seawall replacement;
(b) Developing a planning tool for City staff to use to consider how climate change will impact new capital projects and existing buildings and incorporate adaptation options; and
(c) Including adaptation in the updates of the Climate Action Plan and the Comprehensive Plan.

Our next efforts will include preparing guidelines for climate change analysis for higher cost, longer lifespan projects with potentially high vulnerability and risk profiles, and developing a vulnerability and risk assessment methodology so that we can set priorities for investments in protecting City infrastructure.

All of these efforts are intended to use science-based assessments and implement strategies that will have measurable results. To the extent that we are successful, the people of Seattle will be protected from some of the unavoidable impacts of climate change, sometimes without even knowing what has been done and what the problems may have been that will be avoided. Will this cause people to be less worried about climate change—and less likely to support policies and changes that will prevent emissions in the future?

The evidence of change will be overwhelming. The people of Seattle and the political leadership have already clearly grasped the nature of the problem. Adapting to the impacts is the responsible public policy, and in no way should cause us to lessen our efforts to achieve carbon neutrality for the long run.

Strategies to protect vulnerable populations from increasing numbers of extreme weather events are being incorporated into emergency management and public health planning.[106]

Climate Protection Progress Report of Seattle

The City announced on December 8, 2010 that Seattle's greenhouse gas emissions in 2008 were 7 percent below 1990 levels, meeting the targets of the Kyoto Protocol. The reduction in climate pollution is even more remarkable considering Seattle's population grew 16 percent since 1990. The 2009 Climate Protection Initiative Progress Report details the city's myriad environmental and smart growth programs such as bicycle and pedestrian improvements; new transit options; electric car infrastructure; conservation efforts and green building programs. The Progress Report includes an inventory of 2008 greenhouse gas emissions produced by transportation, buildings and industry.

Goals of the Climate Protection Initiative

The City will reduce its climate pollution through broad-ranging strategies including investing in transportation choices, encouraging compact communities, promoting clean energy and conservation, leading by example, and inspiring others to take action.

In addition to reducing the City's contribution to global warming, the City will also prepare for climate

[106]Richard Conlin (2011), "Changing with the Climate", Feb 07, 2011

change by ensuring that Seattle's infrastructure, facilities, and services are ready to adapt to the projected impacts of climate change. The goal of the Seattle Climate Protection Initiative is to reduce greenhouse gases in Seattle by:

(a) 7 percent below 1990 levels by 2012
(b) 30 percent below 1990 levels by 2024
(c) 80 percent below 1990 levels by 2050

Strategies to Meet Our Goals

(1) Transportation Choices, Compact Communities: To reduce vehicle miles traveled, the City is currently working to expand transportation options, center growth in urban centers, and improve bike and pedestrian infrastructure to help bicyclists and walkers reach their destination safely.
(2) More Bus Service: In 2008, the City, in combination with King County Metro, purchased 20,000 hours of new bus service.
(3) More miles of bike lanes: Seattle Department of Transportation added 92 miles of new bike lanes and share- rows over the past three years, making it easier and safer for bicyclists to move about the City.
(4) Pedestrian Master Plan Complete: The first citywide action plan, which defines the steps needed to make Seattle a more walk able, livable, and healthy city and is a major step in improving options and safety for pedestrians. The Plan identifies areas of greatest need - where conditions are most difficult and where people need to be able to walk the most.
(5) Clean Vehicles, Clean Fuels: To reduce climate pollution from cars on the road, the City has developed a citywide fuel-reduction plan, individual departments are taking steps to incorporate hybrid and electric vehicles into their fleets, and the City is currently testing

Plug-in Hybrid Electric Vehicles and researching alternative fuels.

Some Current Accomplishments

Electric Vehicles (E V): Thanks to a major grant from the U.S. Department of Energy, the City of Seattle is on track to be "plug-in ready," or able to accommodate electric vehicles plugging into the grid, by the end of 2010. As part of the largest E V project in U.S. history, the U.S. DOE awarded Seattle $20 million of investment for EV infrastructure, which will support the development of approximately 2,500 charging stations and ensure that at least 1,000 Nissan LEAFs are sold to the area's residents. Seattle also received $500,000 for installation of electric vehicle charging stations at city-owned properties.

City Fleet Fuel Reduction: At the beginning of 2009, the City of Seattle set a goal of reducing fuel consumption in its fleets by 3 percent from 2008 levels, which translates to 80,000 gallons of fuel. In just the first half of 2009, the City reduced its overall fuel consumption by 2.7 percent, or 32,777 gallons, compared to the same period last year.

Evergreen Fleets Award: In 2009, the City earned a 4 star rating (out of 5 stars), a certification program that recognizes fleets for making smart, environmentally responsible choices. To receive the rating, the Seattle piloted new types of bio-diesel, upheld strict environmental standards when purchasing new vehicles, and implemented strategies to reduce fuel consumption, such as the "fuel duel."

Clean Energy, Efficient Buildings: To increase the number of buildings and infrastructure that use clean energy efficiently in Seattle, in addition to saving energy through Seattle City Light's conservation programs, the City is working to promote solar and other alternative energy sources and will provide homeowners and businesses with the tools to improve building efficiency, with the goal of increasing the efficiency of Seattle buildings by at least 20 percent by 2020.

Zero Net Emissions: In 2005, Seattle City Light became the first major utility in the nation to achieve a net zero greenhouse gas emission threshold, and has maintained its net zero emissions status since.

Energy Conservation: In 2008, City Light launched a five-year Conservation Action Plan that will save customers more than $310 million in energy bills over five years.

Home Energy Audits: To improve home energy efficiency, the City of Seattle will be providing 5,000 audits to Seattle City Light customers for $95 a piece over the next 18 months. This pilot program will be the largest of its kind in the United States. The homes will receive an Energy Performance Score (EPS), which indicates how well a home's energy use and carbon emissions compare to the Seattle's averages and goals. The City is working to make the EPS system an important factor in the real estate market and part of the standard information used to value a home.

New Buildings: In April 2009, the City of Seattle increased energy efficiency requirements for new buildings by 30 percent.

Community Engagement: To help Seattle residents lower their carbon footprint, the City is engaging businesses and residents through two innovative programs – Seattle Climate Action Now and the Seattle Climate Partnership.

Seattle Climate Partnership: The SCP has grown from 53 members in 2008 to over 160 members in

2009. New members include Microsoft, Xerox, and PCC Natural Markets.

Seattle Summer Streets: Over the 2009 summer, Climate Action Now and SDOT worked together to make streets something to celebrate. By closing down the streets to traffic and opening them to pedestrians and bicyclists, Summer Streets are a way to celebrate Seattle's unique neighborhoods, organize around a common goal, and enjoy shopping, cycling, strolling, and connecting with neighbors and community members.

Leadership, Leverage: To help create federal and state policies that advance local climate solutions, the City is currently active at the federal and state level and is encouraging cities throughout the United States to follow Seattle's lead by sharing resources and best practices, and by asking mayors to join the Mayors' Climate Protection Agreement.

Measuring Progress: Progress toward the Climate Protection Initiative is measured in three ways.

First, the Climate Protection Initiative Progress Report outlines some significant accomplishments made in the City's climate protection strategy areas.

Second, specific progress toward meeting the Climate Protection Initiative goals is measured through the community-wide carbon footprint, which is released every three years.

Third, to track progress on a yearly basis, the City has identified a collection of measures that give us early indications of progress. The City will use these measures as part of an ongoing evaluation of strategy areas and innovation.[107]

---

[107]Seattle Climate Action Plan, Seattle CAN. Org, Seattle. Gov.

Conclusion

Global warming would pose a serious problem in future within 2025. The international communities are meeting each year to derail global warming, but it increases. Similarly, Millennium Development Goals could not restrict the growth of poverty, hunger, disease or illiteracy.

The planet is warming so quickly that the world should expect abrupt and unpredictable consequences in a matter of years or a few decades. The sudden decline of Arctic sea ice as well as climbing extinction rates are the examples. The abrupt change of climate could lead to more loss of life, sufferings, environmental degradation and more costs.

A slight increase in sea level could overtop a levee during a storm, and a tiny rise in ocean acidity from carbon dioxide could make seawater inhospitable to coral. Fossil fuel emissions must be kept to half of present level. Global warming held to about 1.8 degrees to avert disastrous consequences including many feet of sea level rise and irreversible ecological harm.

The international organizations should attack the causes of global warming rather than the effects of global warming.

The Kyoto Protocol (1997) emphasized on mitigation, followed by adaptation, compensation and now with negotiations among member countries.

The governments of all countries must take steps to reduce carbon emission, industrialization, depletion of forests and number of vehicles.

The governments of all developing countries must differentiate between 'developments versus catastrophe'. A corrupt government thinks that devastation of forestland for industries is a developmental project and exhaustion of mines and minerals in forestland would assist the people of the state. But deforestation, pollution of air, water and soil lead to catastrophe. It further encourages climate change. We cannot exhaust minerals; disturb flora and fauna and should not challenge the nature. We must preserve forests, mines, minerals, and water resources for our future generations as we have borrowed them from our forefathers to hand over to our grandchildren.

The government is for the people, by the people and of the people. But most of the governments implement and execute new proposals on whims and the administrative officers and engineers immediately accept and support the proposal without ifs and buts because of their personal gain in the new schemes or proposals. They forget the fundamental ideology of democracy. In most of the governments, practitioner economists (research economists) are never recruited in the planning process. The administrative officers implement the proposals and make colossal loss to the people and the state.

Foreign funding in mega irrigation projects, village road concretization, integrated coastal zone management projects, urbanization projects or research projects would move the country into deplorable condition. The interest payment of foreign loan has surpassed the investment in health or education sectors in all developing countries.

The government should priorities pro-poor, pro-rural, and pro-agricultural policies to feed the people and award peace to all.

Terrorists, Naxalites and Maoists grow in many countries because of poverty, unemployment, hunger, income disparity, and poor governance. It spreads quickly when tribal youths fear that they would be evicted from parental land for industrialization through State police force. Corruption, inefficiency and sycophancy in administration ignite harassment to the sufferers. Police firing in forest areas challenges the youths and they become revengeful.

The forestland should not be diverted for any purpose; the river water should be clean and pollution free. Every person needs free air to breathe for healthier living but the corrupt governments plan for mega projects in forest areas without environmental clearance. All the developing countries rush for industrialization by the pressure of industrialists rather than voters of the country.

Environment cannot be protected as long as corrupt people rule the state.

There should be an 'International Law' to ban privatization of forests and complete ban on export-import of minerals for corporate benefits. The miscreants who cut and dig forestland for wood or minerals should be treated as 'Environment Criminals' at par with 'War Criminals' to save the World.

The United Nations Organization should be reorganized and should be empowered to promulgate 'international policies' to award peace to all humanity. The activities of the UN should be:

1. To award peace to all people: It is possible by encouraging 'Peace Forums' in all settlements, villages, towns, states and countries. The UN should institute 'Peace Prizes Fund' to award 100 peace prizes to dedicated peace workers, politicians, researchers, scientists, district magistrates and plant lovers of the world.

The UN peace Council must try to stop wars all over the world. There is no need to increase the size of territory by war.

2. To stop war between or among nations: It is possible to finalize geographical boundaries through a high-powered committee of ex-presidents and Nobel Laureates. A particular date should be fixed for finalization of country boundaries, for example, as on January 1, 2015 for all disputed countries.

3. To protect environment: Devastation of forests by the government or corporate or individual should be treated as 'Environment Criminal'. The UN should create Environment Council to safeguard the environment, forests, rivers and seas. To assist the people affected by natural disasters, the UN should organize 'relief work' with the help of member countries.

Creation and management of forests and reduction of industrial, vehicular or oil spill pollution could reduce the number of disasters. The mines and minerals should be reserved for future generations; it should not be exhausted within a couple of years. The governments should not utilize wealth of the countries (natural resources including minerals) for political and personal advantages.

We should not destroy nature; we must not fight against nature. Nature is more powerful to destroy the whole world including the people and all living beings. It is wise to have friendly relationship with nature.

Nature must be protected to allow every living being to live in peace. Let us live peacefully and allow others to live in peace. Let there be a green world. Let there be a peace environment in the whole world.

Unless we save forests and grow more trees, there would be no rain; if there were no rain, there would be 'no crop, no food and no safety,

There is vast increase in the amount of carbon dioxide reaching the atmosphere. The annual increase is three billion tonnes: and half the carbon emitted since the Industrial Revolution still remains in the atmosphere. At the same time as this is happening, we are seeing the destruction on a vast scale of tropical forests, which are uniquely able to remove carbon dioxide from the air. Every year an area of forest equal to the whole surface of the United Kingdom is destroyed. At present rates of clearance we shall, by the year 2000, have removed 65 per cent of forests in the humid tropical zones. The consequences of this become clearer when one remembers that tropical forests fix more than ten times as much carbon as do forests in the temperate zones. If we fail to act today then we will pay the price tomorrow not just in pounds and dollars but in human life. As in so many other areas of international development, the moral case is a clear, overwhelming and compelling one. We cannot have food-security, water-security, energy-security or any form of national security without climate security.

In Nepal, British aid is helping more than half a million households to make a living from the local forests. In just five years, this has contributed to an increase in the average household income of some 60 per cent as well as helping to save an estimated 1.2 million tonnes of carbon a year. There's the immense potential of natural resources – sun, wind, rivers, tides – that developing countries often possess in abundance. By exploiting these resources, they can sell carbon credits and develop exciting new technologies. Imagine North African countries exporting solar power to Europe. Those with significant hydropower from Nepal to Mozambique export to neighbouring countries such as India and South Africa.

Their future is no longer a choice between a growing economy and a cleaner planet, because their survival depends on both. It will do little good to alleviate poverty if you can no longer harvest your crops or find drinkable water.

The main threat to our environment is more and more people, and their activities: the land they cultivate more intensively; the forests they cut down and burn; the mountain sides they lay bare; the fossil fuels they burn; and the rivers and the seas they pollute. A recent study by our British Meteorological Office on the Amazon rainforest shows that large-scale deforestation may reduce rainfall and thus affect the climate directly. But the problem of global climate change is one that affects us all and action will only be effective if it is taken at the international level. There are one and a half billion people across the world that lack any means of accessing energy.

The corrupt governments are leasing mines and forests to industrialists and corporate house even today. This must be stopped by international laws.

We must try to achieve our common purpose: a world that is safer, cleaner, and healthier and a future that is worthy for our children. Each person must be assured of clean water, clean air and food security.

A hygienic and sustainable environment would strengthen WORLD PEACE movement. Let us try to make the environment clean, friendly and free of pollution.

THE END

Annexure 1

Greenhouse gases, Carbon dioxide (C02), Methane (CH4), Nitrous oxide (N20), Hydrofluorocarbons (HFCs), Perfluorocarbons (PFCs), Sulphur hexafluoride (SF6), Sectors/source categories, Energy, Fuel combustion Energy industries, Manufacturing industries and construction, Transport, Other sectors, Other Fugitive emissions from fuels, Solid fuels, Oil and natural gas, Other Industrial processes, Mineral products, Chemical industry, Metal production, Other production, Production of halocarbons and sulphur hexafluoride, Consumption of halocarbons and sulphur hexafluoride, Other Solvent and other product use, Agriculture, Enteric fermentation, Manure management, Rice cultivation, Agricultural soils, Prescribed burning of savannas, Field burning of agricultural residues, Other Waste, Solid waste disposal on land, Wastewater handling
Waste incineration, other

Annexure 2

Party Quantified emission limitation or reduction commitment, (percentage of base year or period), Australia 108, Austria 92, Belgium 92, Bulgaria* 92, Canada 94, Croatia* 95, Czech Republic* 92, Denmark 92, Estonia* 92
European Community 92, Finland 92, France 92, Germany 92, Greece 92, Hungary* 94, Iceland 110, Ireland 92, Italy 92, Japan 94, Latvia* 92, Liechtenstein 92, Lithuania* 92 Luxembourg 92, Monaco 92, Netherlands 92, New Zealand 100, Norway 101, Poland* 94, Portugal 92, Romania* 92 Russian Federation* 100, Slovakia* 92, Slovenia* 92, Spain 92, Sweden 92, Switzerland 92, Ukraine* 100, United Kingdom of Great, Britain and Northern Ireland 92, United States of America 93, * Countries that are undergoing the process of transition to a market economy

AUTHOR INDEX

+++++

SUBJECT INDEX

+++++

A MOVEMENT FOR A PEACEFUL WORLD

AUTHORS

Professor Suresh Chandra Mallick (b 1944) was a faculty member of the OUAT, Bhubaneswar (India) during 1968 - 2004. He is a researcher, writer, thinker and social worker. He is an Agricultural Economist with specialization in Agriculture, Poverty, Marketing, Policy and World Peace to motivate people's involvement in peace process. He held the post of Vice President, Indian Society of Agricultural Marketing during 2003 - 05. At present, he is the Chairperson of the Institute of Development Studies & Policy Research, Bhubaneswar.

Pritam Mallick (1975–2006) was extremely noble, friendly and knowledgeable and possessed extraordinary memory. He received B.A. (Honors) from Utkal University, M.A. from Central University, Hyderabad and M. Phil. Degree from Jawaharlal Nehru University and completed Ph. D. courses in JNU. He was a specialist in Monetary Economics and Econometrics. He remembered the Oxford Dictionary and Roget's Thesaurus to master English literature. He acquired deep knowledge in Astrology, Palmistry, Mathematics and Statistics. He contributed enormously for WORLD PEACE manuscripts as co-author. But his heavenly demise occurred on August 4, 2006.